THE WEST AND THE BIRTH OF BANGLADESH

THE WEST AND THE BIRTH OF BANGLADESH
Foreign Policy in the Face of Mass Atrocity

Richard Pilkington

© UBC Press 2021

All rights reserved. No part of this publication may be reproduced, stored in a retrieval system, or transmitted, in any form or by any means, without prior written permission of the publisher, or, in Canada, in the case of photocopying or other reprographic copying, a licence from Access Copyright, www.accesscopyright.ca.

30 29 28 27 26 25 24 23 22 21   5 4 3 2 1

Printed in Canada on FSC-certified ancient-forest-free paper (100% post-consumer recycled) that is processed chlorine- and acid-free.

Library and Archives Canada Cataloguing in Publication

Title: The West and the birth of Bangladesh : foreign policy in the face of mass atrocity / Richard Pilkington.
Names: Pilkington, Richard, author.
Description: Includes bibliographical references and index.
Identifiers: Canadiana (print) 20210153016 | Canadiana (ebook) 20210153245 | ISBN 9780774861977 (hardcover) | ISBN 9780774861984 (softcover) | ISBN 9780774861991 (PDF) | ISBN 9780774862004 (EPUB)
Subjects: LCSH: United States – Foreign relations – South Asia. | LCSH: South Asia – Foreign relations – United States. | LCSH: Canada – Foreign relations – South Asia. | LCSH: South Asia – Foreign relations – Canada. | LCSH: Great Britain – Foreign relations – South Asia. | LCSH: South Asia – Foreign relations – Great Britain. | LCSH: Bangladesh – History – Revolution, 1971 – Atrocities.
Classification: LCC DS341.3.U6 P55 2021 | DDC 327.73054 – dc23

Canadä

UBC Press gratefully acknowledges the financial support for our publishing program of the Government of Canada (through the Canada Book Fund), the Canada Council for the Arts, and the British Columbia Arts Council.

This book has been published with the help of a grant from the Canadian Federation for the Humanities and Social Sciences, through the Awards to Scholarly Publications Program, using funds provided by the Social Sciences and Humanities Research Council of Canada.

Printed and bound in Canada by Friesens
Set in Warnock Pro and Futura by Apex CoVantage, LLC
Copy editor: Frank Chow
Proofreader: Alison Strobel
Cartographer: Eric Leinberger
Cover designer: George Kirkpatrick

UBC Press
The University of British Columbia
2029 West Mall
Vancouver, BC V6T 1Z2
www.ubcpress.ca

To the victims

Contents

Acknowledgments / ix

List of Abbreviations / xi

Map of South Asia, 1971 / 2

Introduction / 3

Part 1: United States

1 Superpower / 19

2 Phase One Response / 42

3 Phase Two Response / 66

Part 2: Canada

4 Middle Power / 93

Part 3: United Kingdom

5 Former Great Power / 119

6 The Commons Debates and After / 146

Part 4: Cooperation?

7 Interplay between the Three Powers / 179

Conclusion / 199

Notes / 209

Bibliography / 263

Index / 273

Acknowledgments

The research for this monograph was generously funded, in part, by scholarships from the Social Sciences and Humanities Research Council of Canada and from the University of Toronto. Robert Bothwell and Ronald Pruessen deserve enormous credit for their insights, suggestions, constructive criticisms, and indefatigable good humour throughout the project. Their great generosity is truly appreciated. Randy Schmidt of UBC Press was a constant source of encouragement and support in bringing this undertaking to fruition. Of course, the usual caveats apply. Although I have benefited greatly from the guidance of others, any errors contained in this work are my own. I should particularly like to thank my family for all they have sacrificed to make this book possible. Their unwavering encouragement and support were essential, and only Sylvia, David, and Andrée know the full extent of my gratitude.

Chapter 4 of this book was previously published in substantially similar form as an article entitled "In the National Interest? Canada and the East Pakistan Crisis of 1971," *Journal of Genocide Research* 13, 4 (2011): 451–74. It is reproduced here with the permission of the publisher, Taylor & Francis, http://www.tandfonline.com.

Abbreviations

ABD	Action Bangla Desh
BDAC	Bangla Desh Action Committee for Great Britain
BSAC	Bengal Students Action Committee
CANDU	Canada Deuterium Uranium (nuclear reactor)
CIDA	Canadian International Development Agency
DHC	British deputy high commissioner in Dacca
DOP	Defence and Overseas Policy Committee
ECGD	Export Credits Guarantee Department
EEC	European Economic Community
FCO	Foreign and Commonwealth Office
FLQ	Front de liberation du Québec
FMS	Foreign Military Sales
IBRD	International Bank for Reconstruction and Development
IRA	Irish Republican Army
KANUPP	Karachi Nuclear Power Project
MOD	Ministry of Defence
NORAD	North American Air Defense Command
NSC	National Security Council
NSSM	National Security Study Memorandum
OMC	Office of Munitions Control
R2P	*The Responsibility to Protect*
SAD	South Asia Department

SEATO	Southeast Asia Treaty Organization
SRG	Senior Review Group
UNGC	United Nations Genocide Convention
UNHCR	United Nations High Commissioner for Refugees
UNSC	United Nations Security Council
WSAG	Washington Special Actions Group

THE WEST AND THE BIRTH OF BANGLADESH

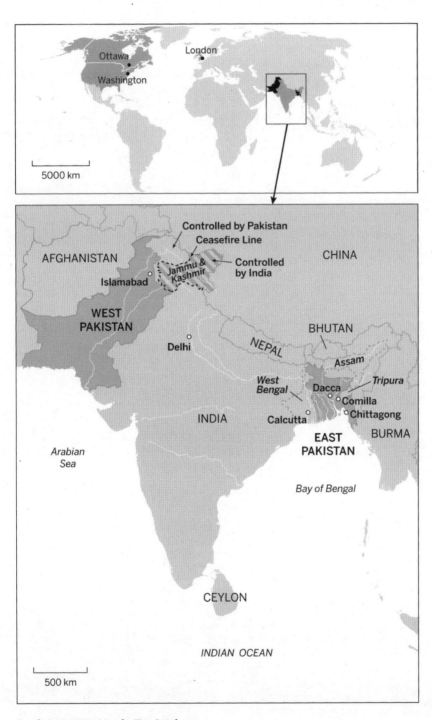

South Asia, 1971. *Map by Eric Leinberger*

Introduction

After the partition of the Indian subcontinent, Pakistan comprised two wings: West Pakistan (now referred to as Pakistan) and East Pakistan (now known as Bangladesh). On 25 March 1971, fearing the secession of the eastern wing, the military dictator, President Yahya Khan, unleashed his country's West Pakistani–dominated armed forces in a brutal campaign of massacre and repression in the East. During nine months of operations, the army butchered many thousands of civilians and some ten million refugees fled to India.[1] In December, the crisis was finally resolved, but only after a war between India and Pakistan during which Indian troops led Bengali guerrillas to victory in the East and after which East Pakistan achieved independence as Bangladesh.

This book investigates the formulation of and interplay between the American, Canadian, and British policies generated in response to the crisis in East Pakistan. It focuses primarily on the reactions of these three North Atlantic powers to the atrocities and other human rights abuses rather than on the subsequent issues of war on the subcontinent and the recognition of Bangladesh. It does not attempt to trace the development of each country's South Asian policy or each capital's responses to atrocity crimes over recent decades. Rather, it considers the decision-making processes in Washington, Ottawa, and London during the first few months after the clampdown, identifying the forces at play in determining policy and the nature, development, and resolution of debates over national interests and ethical concerns at a time of developing human rights awareness.

At the start of 1971, Britain, Canada, and the United States worked closely in a number of different areas, and relations between the capitals, while subject to minor irritants, were generally warm and certainly far from strained. All three were liberal, democratic, capitalist Cold War allies aligned against communism under the banner of NATO, a defensive alliance of which they were all founding members. Alongside Australia and New Zealand, they participated in the intimate world of signals intelligence sharing under the "Five Eyes" alliance. The allies, particularly Canada and the United States, had significant commercial and economic ties, and all three shared strong cultural connections through a common language.

The three North Atlantic powers cooperated in pairs on important projects. Canada and the United States combined to operate the North American Air Defense Command (NORAD) system, and London and Washington maintained a unique collaboration and exchange in the nuclear field. Although the so-called special relationship between London and Washington had diminished in terms of importance owing to changes in the international order, the tradition of close diplomatic cooperation and consultation continued. Strong bureaucratic ties were similarly maintained between London and Ottawa. Moreover, Richard Nixon, the US president, and Pierre Trudeau, the Canadian prime minister, enjoyed a satisfactory rapport, while Edward Heath, the British prime minister, maintained warm personal relationships with his counterparts in Canada and the United States.

Although close connections may arguably be considered sufficient grounds for focusing on the responses of these three international actors, there are further reasons to study their roles, for between them, the United States, Canada, and the United Kingdom had considerable potential leverage to exert on Islamabad. As powers on the world stage, they enjoyed significant diplomatic influence and each also supplied military materiel to Pakistan. Ottawa was a vital partner in a nuclear joint venture project in Karachi. Importantly, the United States, Canada, and the United Kingdom were three of the top four national providers of economic aid to Pakistan, donating some US$200 million annually around the time the clampdown commenced. This amount accounted for over one-third of the total external assistance received by Islamabad.

During the crisis, the decisions taken in Washington, Ottawa, and London were based on *perceptions* formed from information received in the three Western capitals and not necessarily, therefore, on what was *actually* happening on the ground in East Pakistan. Consequently, this book is based

Introduction 5

primarily on the archival records of the three North Atlantic powers and not on the limited amount of material currently available in South Asian repositories.

This study of the Western response seeks to inform our understanding of the embryonic development of Western human rights awareness, which proceeded to blossom further, indeed mushroom, in the years immediately after the crisis. As Samuel Moyn has observed: "Over the course of the 1970s, the moral world of Westerners shifted, opening a space for the sort of utopianism that coalesced in an international human rights movement that had never existed before."[2] Since the Second World War, and despite the adoption of the Universal Declaration of Human Rights in 1948, concern for such freedoms remained subsidiary to the pursuit of Cold War advantage. Even as late as 1968, which the United Nations declared the International Year for Human Rights, such matters remained only "peripheral."[3] Yet, in the 1970s, there developed a "genuine social movement around human rights ... transcending official government institutions."[4] US failure in Vietnam, the end of European empire overseas, and the Western embrace of Soviet bloc dissidents appeared to signal the "collapse of prior universalistic schemes," and the promotion of human rights provided a "persuasive alternative to them."[5] Interest and awareness swiftly snowballed across the West as ordinary people came to engage in the movement as never before. Nongovernmental organizations, such as Amnesty International in the United Kingdom, promoted large-scale grassroots advocacy, and politicians began to emphasize the importance of human rights concerns in the formulation of foreign policy.[6] In 1977, the new US president, Jimmy Carter, enthusiastically endorsed such values, and Amnesty International won the Nobel Peace Prize; human rights had rapidly acquired considerable "cultural prestige."[7]

Despite the growing public concern for human rights in the United States, Canada, and Britain, the majority of foreign service officers in these countries remained firmly focused on the promotion of national interests until at least the mid-1970s. Henry Kissinger was Nixon's national security advisor during the crisis and, later, secretary of state.[8] "A realist who firmly believed human rights had no place in foreign policy," he established the Bureau of Human Rights and Humanitarian Affairs of the Department of State in 1975 after intense pressure from Congress. Although he then manoeuvred for over two years to undermine its impact, he was, nevertheless, responsible for putting in place the institution and the operational procedures that would be used to encourage the subsequent consideration of human rights in US foreign policy formulation.[9] As Victoria Berry and

Allan McChesney have noted, by the mid-1970s human rights had become a more important political issue in Canada. In the Department of External Affairs, however, "there was no formal training in human rights for recruits prior to late 1986, and most officials ... [were] preoccupied with economic and security matters."[10] Thus, the crisis in South Asia unfolded at a time of considerable flux, when many in the West were initially starting to embrace the promotion of human rights but the institutional cultures in foreign service departments had yet to adapt to this change. The battles to sway and implement policies in response to the events of 1971, therefore, were fought on strangely unfamiliar terrains.

The parallel growth of interest in Holocaust studies in the 1970s reflected the rise to prominence of human rights concerns and, from that burgeoning academic field, the broader discipline of genocide studies duly emerged one decade later.[11] The most widely accepted definition of the concept at the heart of this new branch of study is that contained in the UN Convention on the Prevention and Punishment of the Crime of Genocide of 1948, which is often referred to less formally as the United Nations Genocide Convention (UNGC). Under Article II of the agreement, genocide is defined as the intentional destruction, "in whole or in part, [of] a national, ethnical, racial or religious group, as such." Political groups are not protected under the convention and, therefore, the large-scale massacre of suspected communists by the Indonesian military and its supporters (1965–66) was not considered genocide under this definition. Consequently, the East Pakistan case was arguably one of the first potential instances of genocide under the UNGC since the agreement entered into force.[12]

By early 1971, the United States had still to adopt the UNGC, and so the administration was under no legal commitment to respond even if it believed that the case of East Pakistan qualified as genocide as defined in that document. The Senate ratified the convention, with reservations, only in February 1986, some thirty-seven years after President Harry Truman had first submitted it to Congress.[13] This delay reflected concerns over the potentially wide scope of the convention and US sovereign rights rather than the fundamental purpose of the agreement. Given its promotion of liberal democratic values during the Cold War in particular, the United States had an apparent moral obligation to prevent a possible genocide. In contrast, both Canada and the United Kingdom had already made both ethical and legal commitments to uphold the UNGC before the crisis in East Pakistan unfolded, the former having adopted the convention on 3 September 1952, the latter on 30 January 1970.

Introduction 7

Under Article I of the UNGC, contracting parties commit to preventing genocide, but the convention does not stipulate what actions a signatory ought to pursue beyond calling on the United Nations to take appropriate measures (Article VIII).[14] It is important to note that the principle of non-interference in the domestic affairs of fellow nations is enshrined in the UN Charter (1945), Chapter I, Article 2.4: "All Members shall refrain in their international relations from the threat or use of force against the territorial integrity or political independence of any state, or in any other manner inconsistent with the Purposes of the United Nations." Except in cases of self-defence, only the United Nations Security Council (UNSC), under Chapter VII of the Charter, may authorize the use of military measures to restore order when faced with a threat to international peace.[15] Nevertheless, public condemnation and the possible imposition of, for example, economic or military supply sanctions remained lawful, so how would Washington, Ottawa, and London choose to respond to this early test case? At the time, did they believe the events in East Pakistan amounted to genocide, and, if so, how did they interpret their obligations under the UNGC? If they did not think the atrocities met the criteria of the UNGC, then what did they consider to be their moral responsibilities more broadly?

As previously noted, this book explores the perceptions held, and the formulation of policies by, the three North Atlantic powers, as recorded primarily in the national archives of those countries. It does not seek to investigate what happened on the ground using the records of Bangladesh, India, and Pakistan. No attempt, therefore, is made to determine whether or not the atrocities in East Pakistan amounted to genocide as defined by the UNGC, such an investigation lying beyond the scope of this research and the purpose of this book. Nevertheless, the Western response to the events in East Pakistan must be understood against a backdrop of domestic, regional, and global contexts, which provide lenses through which to better view and comprehend the emergency as it unfolded.

Systems of Forces

The domestic and regional settings in which the crisis unfolded were complex. Much fine material has been published on these subjects, a large part of it characterized by intricate and subtle discussion. In providing brief synopses for contextual purposes, it is recognized that some of the detail and nuance is inevitably sacrificed in the attempt to draw out the essential strands of the literature. Those seeking further illumination may wish to directly consult the sources on which these summaries are based.

Domestic Fission in Pakistan

After the partition of India in 1947, the Muslim-dominated nation of Pakistan comprised two geo-culturally distinct wings, one in the east and the other in the west of the subcontinent, separated by over one thousand miles (sixteen hundred kilometres) of Hindu-dominated Indian territory.[16] Geographic separation presented numerous communications challenges and encouraged orientation toward different markets and crop production. Moreover, at partition West Pakistan comprised 34 million people, speaking mainly Punjabi and Sindi, attached geographically to the Muslim world of the Middle East and the Arabian Sea. In contrast, the 42 million citizens of East Pakistan, sometimes referred to as East Bengal, spoke almost exclusively Bengali and looked outward to India and Southeast Asia. Importantly, many in the West considered the East to be populated by inferior converts not of the pure Muslim stock the former believed themselves to be but descended from Indian races and corrupted by Hindu culture. The majority of the vast peasant population of the East embraced non-mainstream Sufism, unlike their more orthodox Sunni co-religionists of the West. The next twenty-four years witnessed growing alienation between these distinct regions, as the central government, based in Islamabad,[17] failed in its nation-building project. Finally, in 1971, the East seceded to form the new state of Bangladesh.

At the birth of Pakistan, underlying geo-cultural differences between East and West were temporarily transcended as Muslims sought to unify against what many of them perceived to be the threat of Hindu domination. After independence, however, this concern receded, leaving a shared Islamic identity and the Muslim League, which had spearheaded the joint political battle for a separate Muslim nation, as the unifying forces between the two wings.

The bureaucrats and professionals of the Muslim-minority provinces of British India, who had worried most about any threat of Hindu dominance over an independent, but united, subcontinent, had always controlled the League's leadership and power base. At partition, these leaders and administrators of the Muhajir fled westward, where they joined with the elite of the Punjabi-dominated army and united executive, bureaucratic, and military authority in the West wing.[18] Consequently, the Bengalis of the East were grossly underrepresented in all institutions save those of the legislative arena, yet the legislators held little power. In the absence of a shared understanding of the Lahore and Pakistan Resolutions of the 1940s, which had sought to define the level of autonomy of each wing within a united

Introduction

Pakistan, the western Muhajir-Punjabi axis dominated the power structure of the new nation, causing resentment in the East.

Members of this bureaucratic-military elite were initially unwilling to allow the formation of democratic institutions, as they were unable to establish power bases in the East wing, where the majority of the population resided. They feared that a fully representative democracy would result in their loss of power to Bengalis, whom they generally considered ethnically and religiously inferior. The domestic political history of Pakistan until 1971 is the story of the West's continued attempts to cling to power while maintaining national unity. The East responded by resisting the introduction of Urdu as the sole national language and recording its displeasure with the centre by voting the Muslim League out of office, thus bringing the Bengali vernacular elite to regional legislative power in the 1954 provincial elections. In the absence of an effective nation-building program, the Muslim League and Islam had been the key uniting factors between East and West. Now the former stood utterly defeated.

During 1958, in light of the riots in the East Pakistan Provincial Assembly and mass demonstrations in the West, General Ayub Khan seized power and declared martial law in a military coup. His rule began an extended period of military control and witnessed a further centralization of power in favour of the West. Institutional under-representation and its apparently inevitable economic consequences exacerbated the underlying geo-cultural tensions between the two wings. During the 1960s, as Pakistan's economy grew as a whole, an increase in inter-wing economic disparity, driven by investment policies that continually favoured the West, served only to increase the frustrations of the Bengali vernacular elite. From 1949 to 1950, the gross domestic product per capita in the West was only 8 percent higher than that in the East; by 1968–69, the difference was 62 percent.[19] Moreover, the East's hard currency earnings from jute exports were consistently directed out of Bengal to support development of the West wing. The hopelessly inadequate protection afforded East Pakistan during the 1965 Indo-Pakistan War merely confirmed the region's vulnerability and its quite junior status compared with that of the West. In response, the Awami League, a major political party of the Bengali vernacular elite, published a six-point party manifesto in 1966. It focused on the need for political and economic regional autonomy in East and West, and demanded that the federal government be responsible only for defence and foreign affairs, yielding tax-gathering powers to the two federating units.

Meanwhile, throughout the 1960s, the political awareness of the Bengali population grew as the vernacular elite expanded, both university and college enrolment in the East increasing by over 100 percent between 1959–60 and 1965–66.[20] This growth in enrolment had two effects. First, it supplied a large base of politically active students. Second, students and former-student professionals provided a mechanism and a network for spreading Awami League support throughout the countryside. As discontent grew in the East, so did the ability to resist.

Violent anti-government protests in East and West forced Ayub to step down, in March 1969, to be replaced by General Yahya Khan, head of the Pakistani army. Although Yahya immediately declared martial law, dissolved the legislative assemblies, and abrogated the constitution, he kept a commitment made by Ayub and announced that fully democratic elections would be held in December 1970. Seats in the proposed new National Assembly, which was charged with the important task of drawing up a replacement constitution within 120 days, were to be apportioned to reflect to some extent the relative sizes of regional populations. Although the East, with its greater populace, could potentially gain a majority or otherwise control the new National Assembly, most observers believed that a varied mix of political parties would come to power, leaving neither wing, nor one particular grouping, in a position to dominate.[21] As Yahya explained when he visited Washington, DC, in October 1970, he anticipated a "multiplicity" of parties in both East and West, fighting against one another and leaving the president as the real power in the country.[22]

Yahya did not, however, foresee the consequences of one particular contingent event. On the night of 12 November 1970, a cyclone-induced tidal wave flooded East Bengal, claiming over 300,000 lives and wreaking devastation and havoc in coastal areas. Islamabad's relief effort was extremely poor and much criticized. As the election campaign entered its crucial final stages, Mujibur Rahman, leader of the Awami League, seized on and exploited the inadequacies in the response, portraying it as a timely and extreme illustration of West Pakistan's indifference to the East. On 26 November, he accused Islamabad of "almost cold-blooded murder."[23]

Resentment helped fuel an unexpected landslide victory for the autonomist Awami League, still promoting its Six-Point Program, in the December elections, in which it secured 167 of the 169 National Assembly seats assigned to the East. It neither won nor contested any seats in the West, yet it gained a clear overall majority in the 313-seat National Assembly as a

Introduction

whole. Pakistanis were about to see real power shift from West to East for the first time.

As the Awami League achieved political success, the ambitions of the Bengali vernacular elite increased still further. The Pakistan Peoples Party, which had secured a majority in the West, but with roughly only one-half of the number of seats gained by the Awami League, refused to cooperate in forming the new National Assembly, however. Zulfikar Ali Bhutto, its leader, feared the surrender of power to the East, which favoured better relations with India and a reduction in military expenditure, in direct contrast to his own policies and his talk of a "thousand-year war" against the Hindus. Consequently, two days before it was due to convene on 3 March 1971, Yahya postponed the first meeting of the National Assembly, severely disappointing Bengali aspirations at a time when the autonomist Awami League was able to supply the political vehicle, and the vernacular elite provide the mobilizing mechanism, for mass action in East Bengal and direct confrontation with Islamabad. Awami League leader Mujibur Rahman called a general strike in East Pakistan, bringing it to a grinding halt, and insisted on both a loosely federated Pakistan, under the Six-Point Program, and the immediate resumption of the democratic process. After weeks of apparently fruitless negotiations between East and West, Yahya sought to maintain the unity of Pakistan through the application of military might. On the evening of 25 March 1971, he unleashed his country's West Pakistani–dominated armed forces in a brutal campaign of massacre and oppression in the East.

The struggle against greater autonomy lasted until December 1971, when India successfully invaded East Pakistan, where it defeated the Pakistani army and supported the establishment of an Awami League government at the helm of a newly independent Bangladesh. During the intervening nine-month period, many thousands of civilian East Bengalis were killed, perhaps a quarter of a million girls and women systematically raped, and some ten million refugees fled to safety across the international frontier to India. The main motivation behind the atrocities appears to have been to terrorize the population of East Pakistan into submission, bringing the East once again firmly under the heel of Islamabad. In order to achieve this, the Pakistani army intentionally targeted specific groups with a view to eliminating organized resistance. Thus, politicians, intellectual leaders, student activists, and Bengali police and troops fell victim to numerous massacres. Importantly, West Pakistani authorities similarly targeted the Hindu population of East Bengal, which they perceived as subversive. As the atrocities continued, Bengali nationalists, trained in East Pakistan and India, resisted the clampdown by pursuing a campaign of guerrilla action against the West Pakistani authorities in the East.[24]

Regional Tension in South Asia

As the British left the subcontinent in 1947, Hindu India and Muslim Pakistan were born in blood. Before partition, the Indian National Congress spearheaded the push for independence from imperial rule for many years, but came to be perceived by many Muslims, particularly members of the Muslim League, as an organization run by Hindus for the benefit of Hindus.[25] Fearing the possibility of future oppression in a single independent country dominated by a Hindu majority, the League successfully pushed for the creation of Pakistan, a separate homeland for Muslims.[26] Thus, British India was divided into the two independent states of India and Pakistan at midnight on 15 August 1947. At this time, some twelve million people sought security in the lands of their own faiths and, as they fled, hundreds of thousands were massacred in intercommunal violence.[27] Yasmin Khan describes events as follows:

> Even by the standards of the violent twentieth century, the Partition of India is remembered for its carnage, both for its scale – which may have involved the deaths of half a million to one million men, women and children – and for its seemingly indiscriminate callousness. Individual killings, especially in the most ferociously contested province of Punjab, were frequently accompanied by disfiguration, dismemberment and the rape of women from one community by men from another. Muslims, Sikhs and Hindus suffered equally as victims and can equally be blamed for carrying out the murders and assaults.[28]

The consequent psychological scarring of the populations and mutual mistrust between the two governments was compounded in the eyes of many Pakistanis by calls from various Indian leaders for reunification of what the latter considered to be only a temporarily divided subcontinent. Pakistani suspicions of Indian intentions failed to dissipate over the following decades.[29] Indeed, both "Indian and Pakistani ideas of nationhood were carved out diametrically, in definition against each other, at this time,"[30] and the experiences of refugees and their families were "woven into the fabric of [each] national history."[31]

Even before the intercommunal violence had fully subsided, the contest for sovereignty over the territory of Jammu and Kashmir began. This

Introduction 13

former princely state of British India lay in a mountainous area on the border between the two new nations, and the Kashmir conflict, as it became known, fuelled ongoing Indo-Pakistani disharmony for decades to come.[32] At partition, Hari Singh, the Hindu ruler of the Muslim-majority state opted to join India. Pakistan, however, held his decision to be invalid, as he had already fled Kashmir and was no longer in control. The new Muslim nation argued that the residents of the territory should determine their own fate. India and Pakistan soon went to war, each seeking to control the disputed area. Hostilities formally ended only in 1949, and a ceasefire line was established that divided the contested land. Pakistan governed Azad Kashmir, in the west, and the Northern Areas, while India controlled the remainder of the territory.[33]

The dispute was never satisfactorily resolved and, in August 1965, inspired in part by India's poor performance in a 1962 war against China, Pakistan again tried to wrest greater control over Kashmir by striking a blow that would better position it in any future negotiated settlement governing the territory.[34] Pakistan infiltrated guerrilla units into the India-controlled part of Kashmir in an attempt to destabilize the region and stir Kashmiris into rebellion against New Delhi. The operation failed to spark a revolt, but responses and counter-responses by India and Pakistan soon escalated into a war of far greater intensity than that fought some two decades earlier.[35] The two sides engaged in a large-scale tank battle, and each suffered thousands of casualties. Over three weeks, India and Pakistan fought each other into a stalemate before agreeing to a UN-brokered ceasefire and returning to their original positions.[36] The Kashmir dispute persisted as a struggle not only over territory but also for national pride, and in 1971 the ceasefire line, originally intended as a temporary measure, still divided the two antagonists.[37]

Both India and Pakistan may be characterized as exhibiting considerable internal diversity, each home to a heterogeneous mix of peoples, languages, and political views. Yet the mass atrocities at partition, two recent wars over Kashmir, and regular clashes along the border generated profound mistrust between the political leadership of each country. As the East Pakistan crisis began, therefore, and in general contextual terms, Islamabad perceived India as the principal threat to its national existence. New Delhi viewed Pakistan as not only a military enemy but also a psychological menace, for a strong and successful Pakistan might attract the loyalties of the still-sizable population of Muslims to the south, thereby destabilizing India. Hence, in 1971, Hindu-dominated India had a vested interest in maintaining a weakened

Muslim-dominated neighbour.[38] The Indian reaction to the East Pakistan crisis, and especially the massive influx of refugees, may be fully understood only when considered in this context.

Global Stress in Brief

As the United States pursued a policy of Cold War containment, India remained officially non-aligned but in receipt of substantial Soviet military aid. By contrast, Pakistan became a key US ally in Asia and benefited from heavy US economic and military investment. When Pakistan used US weapons in the Indo-Pakistan War of 1965, however, Washington stopped military supply. In addition, it reduced its economic aid to Islamabad, although this remained significant. The curtailment of US military supplies caused Pakistan to seek support elsewhere, and it needed to look no further than neighbouring China, which shared a mutual dislike of India, with which it had itself warred in 1962. Islamabad and Peking became allied in Asia.[39] This global context of the crisis is inextricably entwined with the development of the US Cold War relationship with the subcontinent. As such, it is discussed in much greater depth in the following chapter, which considers the background to the US response (Chapter 1).

Framework of the Discussion

After this introduction, the book is divided into three main parts, spread across six chapters. These are followed by a further chapter, on the interplay between the United States, Canada, and the United Kingdom in determining their reactions, and the overall judgments in the Conclusion. Part 1 includes Chapters 1 to 3, which consider the formulation of US policy. Part 2, consisting of Chapter 4, investigates the Canadian response, and Part 3, comprising Chapters 5 and 6, discusses reaction in the United Kingdom. Each main part adopts the same general analytical framework, the varying lengths of the case studies being a reflection of the complexity of influences on the determination of the relevant power's response rather than any fundamental change in investigative approach. The US discussion is necessarily somewhat longer owing to the need to consider the response by Washington in the light of Nixon and Kissinger's contemporaneous secret initiative to pursue more harmonious relations with Peking. The basic structure for each part is built around discussion of the following: the specific context in which each power determined its response with regard to domestic, bilateral, and international influences; the available knowledge of atrocities and the motivations behind initial government reactions; the nature and extent

Introduction

of domestic bureaucratic and public dissent; the evolution of policy during the first few months after the clampdown; the availability of alternative options; and a brief consideration of the relevant aftermath.

The individual conclusions with regard to the US, Canadian, and British case studies may be found at the end of Chapters 3, 4, and 6, respectively. The US conclusion pays special attention to the personal influence on policy formulation exerted by Nixon and Kissinger. It goes on to discuss the wide-ranging and sometimes vociferous nature of dissent, even within the bureaucracy itself, and, importantly, the influence or otherwise on the determination of policy of the secret move to secure rapprochement with China. The Canadian conclusion considers particularly the motivations behind the development of Ottawa's four-strand response policy, paying close attention to the impact of Canada's own separatist issue in Quebec. The British conclusion considers the extent to which notably strong public sympathy for the victims of the clampdown influenced policy formulation and the development of London's response, which, though similar to that of Ottawa, bore crucial distinguishing characteristics.

Chapter 7 contemplates the levels of intimacy in the bilateral relations between each pair of the three North Atlantic powers, before tracing the onset of disharmonies later in 1971. It discusses the timing of discord with regard to its impact on South Asian policies and the nature of interplay between the powers in terms of collaborative opportunities both accepted and spurned.

The Conclusion to this study considers the potential options available to the administrations in Washington, Ottawa, and London through combination and coordination of their responses to the crisis in East Pakistan. It analyzes the techniques of obfuscation, diversion, and excuse employed by the three governments to manage adverse political reactions at home, and discusses the impact of government institutional culture based in part on the predilection to protect national interests narrowly defined. Finally, it contrasts the varied policies adopted in the three capitals before explaining the motives and influences that ultimately precipitated divergence and disagreement on South Asia between the United States and its North Atlantic allies.

In responding to the crisis, cooperation between the North Atlantic powers proved limited. In Washington, Nixon and Kissinger exerted great personal sway over the determination of policy and favoured a strategy of appeasement. Importantly, their secret initiative to secure rapprochement with China, which sprang into life only at the end of April, did not drive their thinking during the vital first month after the clampdown began as Kissinger has previously claimed. In Ottawa, the Canadian government developed a tentative response, unwilling to hazard bilateral ties with Islamabad or draw attention to its own separatist issue in Quebec. In the United Kingdom, considerable public sympathy for the plight of the East Pakistani victims influenced policy only to a limited extent. Nevertheless, London's response, though similar in form to that of Ottawa, in substance demonstrated a greater willingness to coerce Islamabad into ending its oppressive action.

PART 1

United States

1

Superpower

Part 1 of this book investigates how and why the United States formulated its policy in response to the crisis in East Pakistan. Though very much aware of the nature of the atrocities there, and despite vociferous public criticism at home, the US government not only refused to intervene militarily and economically but also failed to publicly condemn the actions of the authorities in Islamabad.

In his memoirs written some eight years later, Henry Kissinger argued that US inaction at the time of the slaughter was justified on the grounds that President Yahya Khan was acting as the main channel for secret communications aimed at securing rapprochement between the United States and China:

> We faced a dilemma. The United States could not condone a brutal military repression in which thousands of civilians were killed and from which millions fled to India for safety. There was no doubt about the strong-arm tactics of the Pakistani Military. But Pakistan was our sole channel to China; once it was closed off it would take months to make alternative arrangements.[1]

In the shared view of Kissinger and President Richard Nixon, failing to support Yahya risked not only losing their key intermediary but also offending Peking, as China and Pakistan were close allies in Asia. In their opinion, uninvited interference with regard to East Pakistan threatened to delay the strategic China initiative and imperilled the venture in the long term. Kissinger's memoirs, *White House Years*, published in 1979, clearly favoured the perspective of the US executive. In the absence until recently of much declassified material, the seventy-seven—page rationale contained therein provided the most widely accepted account of the reasons behind the US response.

Part 1 fills an important gap in the literature by providing a detailed, analytical account that closely examines not only the formulation of US policy in response to the atrocities during the critical first few months of the crisis but also the changing relevance of the China initiative during this time. It focuses, therefore, on the key response period – the three months between the start of the brutal clampdown on 25 March 1971 and the public announcement of Kissinger's visit to Peking on 15 July, during which the president and his national security advisor orchestrated the US reaction to the tragedy. After the key response period, no new substantial developments occurred in East Pakistan, with regard to either the ongoing human rights contraventions or humanitarian disaster, until the outbreak of the Indo-Pakistan War in December. By mid-July, Nixon's 1972 visit to Peking had already been agreed, and the world was aware of Sino-American rapprochement. The results of this investigation call into question Kissinger's justification for his and the president's initial reluctance to act.

The study of the US response is structured around three chapters. This chapter portrays the historical relationships between India, Pakistan, and the major powers, with particular focus on the US context, and the Sino-Soviet split of the 1960s that encouraged rapprochement between Washington and Peking. It discusses the apparatus used by Nixon and Kissinger to dominate and personalize foreign policy decision making in Washington before exploring their *realpolitik-* and national-interest-based world view, which largely excluded ethical idealism from their decision-making process. It then goes on to consider the president and his national security advisor's philosophy that held the reintroduction of China into world affairs to be a crucial Cold War initiative aimed at establishing an equilibrium between the major powers and therefore a sustainable world peace, before describing their sustained effort over several years to pursue Sino-American rapprochement.

Having established the environment in which the administrative battle over the US response to East Pakistan was fought, I examine in Chapter 2 phase one of the key response period, between the clampdown on 25 March and 27 April, the date on which the Pakistani channel to Peking unexpectedly sprang to life. Only immediately after this phase did Nixon and Kissinger attach great import to, and take significant steps to protect, their secret conduit to China. First, the chapter assesses the responses of the moral idealists. Archer Blood, the US consul general in Dacca at the start of the crisis, accused the government of Pakistan of "selective genocide," relayed reports of the atrocities to Washington, and joined members of his staff in formally dissenting from US official policy. Kenneth Keating, US ambassador to New Delhi, supported Blood, justifying his own stance on both moral grounds and US interests in South Asia as a whole. US public concern and condemnation is discussed in terms of the press, Congress, the responses of intellectuals, and the formation of US-based pro-Bangladesh associations. Second, the chapter analyzes the apathetic responses of Joseph Farland, US ambassador to Islamabad, the Department of State in Washington, and Nixon and Kissinger, who dominated the formulation of US policy. In securing US interests, State preferred the use of both carrot and stick. Farland, Nixon, and Kissinger, on the other hand, all favoured the exclusive use of the carrot if forced to act, but initially sought to do nothing. A close analysis of the documentary evidence suggests that the China initiative did not the drive the US response during phase one. The president and his national security advisor already had other reasons to promote inaction.

Finally, Chapter 3 examines phase two of the key response period, from 27 April until 15 July, before going on to analyze the policy options available to the White House. From May onward, East Pakistani refugees flooded into India, creating a humanitarian emergency and destabilizing the subcontinent to such an extent that the possibility of an Indo-Pakistan war loomed large on the horizon. Yet, as the pressures to act decisively in South Asia grew, Nixon and Kissinger continued their ever more fruitful negotiations with Peking and became steadily more dependent on Yahya as the designated conduit and acknowledged facilitator of Kissinger's clandestine mission. Consequently, during phase two, the president and his national security advisor considered good relations with Islamabad increasingly vital just when the mounting refugee crisis suggested the need for strong action. They chose to continue their policy of "quiet diplomacy," therefore, despite having several more potent options at their disposal.

South Asia and the Cold War

This section considers the global context in which the East Pakistan crisis unfolded, paying close attention to relations between Washington and the subcontinent. During the emergency of 1971, the United States and China allied with Pakistan, while the Soviet Union sided with India. A history of US relations with Islamabad sheds light on how the US-Pakistan alliance developed and on Washington's ability to influence President Yahya Khan at the time of the crisis. Similarly, an appreciation of the ties that bound Pakistan to China illuminates the relationship that permitted Islamabad to act as a conduit to Peking and made President Richard Nixon and National Security Advisor Henry Kissinger wary of offending China through any forceful action against its South Asian ally. Again, knowledge of Moscow's continuing close friendship with New Delhi, and its deteriorating relationship with Peking, is essential to understanding, respectively, Nixon and Kissinger's attitude to India throughout the crisis, and how the opportunity for Sino-American rapprochement developed.

British withdrawal from the subcontinent in 1947 created the opportunity for American involvement, as Washington pursued its anti-communist Cold War policy of containment.[2] In the years immediately after partition, the US attitude toward South Asia was marked by "casual concern bordering on indifference."[3] At that time, Washington considered the subcontinent to be of limited Cold War strategic concern and neither India nor Pakistan to be economic or military powers of potential consequence.[4] The outbreak of the Korean War (1950–53) triggered a substantial reassessment, however. Now convinced that the Soviet Union was "likely to exploit any weaknesses in the West's defense perimeter," the US sought allies to deter or inhibit a possible Soviet move, not into South Asia but into the Middle East.[5] Washington feared Moscow's aspirations with regard to the vast oil reserves and warm-water ports around the Persian Gulf and Arabian Sea.[6] When India maintained a policy of non-alignment, Pakistan became the obvious candidate for US support in South Asia.[7] Strategically positioned on or near the borders of both China and the Soviet Union, Pakistan appeared a useful obstacle to potential Soviet advance. It could also offer the United States a launching pad for spying operations over, and possible military incursions into, the sovereign territory of both communist powers.[8] Pakistan reciprocated the desire for an alliance. Fearing Indian intentions and its own continuing isolation, Islamabad was anxious to secure the support of a wealthy superpower.[9] In February 1954, President Dwight Eisenhower announced that Pakistan would receive US military aid, and the two countries signed a mutual defense agreement in May.[10] The United States would go on to establish a sizable electronic intelligence-gathering and spy-plane facility in Peshawar.[11]

Robert J. McMahon convincingly argues that the US-Pakistan alliance was a "monumental strategic blunder," built on a "grossly inflated fear of the Soviet threat to the Middle East and a series of illusory projections about Pakistan's likely contribution to Western defense efforts in that vital region."[12] The idea that Pakistan, in combination with neighbouring US allies, could somehow significantly hinder a Soviet push into the Middle East was "almost farcical," and the creation of a local anti-communist alliance was unlikely to deter anti-Western nationalism in the region.[13] The mutual security agreement bound the United States to an unstable state, proved a drain on American resources, and was greeted with fury in New Delhi, precipitating a rapid decline in Indo-US relations.[14] In addition, the provision of substantial US military aid to Pakistan created an imbalance on the subcontinent, encouraging India to seek closer ties with the Soviet Union to counter Pakistan's advantage, thereby increasing regional instability and effectively bringing the Cold War to South Asia.[15] During his second term, Eisenhower was already disenchanted with the arrangement, declaring it "perhaps the worst kind of plan and decision we could have made ... It was a terrible error, but we now seem hopelessly involved in it."[16] The president was unwilling to renege on the deal because of the probable diplomatic repercussions with Pakistan and the risk to US credibility on the world stage.[17]

As the United States provided military equipment with a view to containment, Pakistan happily increased its strength in the face of the perceived threat from India.[18] Between 1954 and 1965, Pakistan received over US$600 million in defence equipment and services from the United States, including M47 and M48 Patton tanks and B-57 light-attack jet-bombers, together with defence support assistance of approximately equal value.[19] The net result of the program was that, by the mid-1960s, US arms represented some 80 percent of Pakistan's arsenal of modern weapons.[20] By comparison, in the same period, India received only US$90 million of military assistance from the United States, less than 10 percent of that accepted by its Muslim neighbour.[21] In addition, between 1958 and 1968, the United States provided Pakistan with US$2.8 billion of economic aid. The annual commitment approached US$400 million in the early 1960s, representing 35 percent of Pakistan's development budget, 45 percent of its imports, or 55 percent of its total foreign economic assistance.[22] The support from Washington, in terms of grants and loans, exceeded by far that received from any other capital.[23] American support provided a vital lifeline to Pakistan, and military aid in particular profoundly affected Pakistani domestic politics, predictably strengthening the hand of the military.[24] The United States supplied military materiel on the understanding that it would never be used against India, but, as the Indo-Pakistan War of 1965 would prove, Washington could not control the use of arms once shipped.[25]

The year 1962 proved to be a watershed, as war between India and China triggered a realignment of major-power interests on the subcontinent. The Soviets had refused to take sides in a Sino-Indian border dispute that had continued for some time. In October, however, as the Cuban Missile Crisis brought the Americans and Soviets to the brink of war, Moscow decided to better secure its eastern borders by finally backing Peking's position. In response to this shift in fortunes, China promptly invaded the territory disputed with India, captured four thousand Indian prisoners, and called for negotiations with New Delhi. The United States replied by committing itself to supplying arms in support of India. The war ended in November 1962, following Chinese unilateral withdrawal.[26] Nevertheless, President John F. Kennedy sought to provide improved protection for India, the world's largest burgeoning democracy and a possible ally in containing China.[27] After the Chinese invasion, the United States provided India with equipment for six mountain divisions, machinery for several ammunition and arms factories, engineering supplies, and the nucleus of a modern air defence system. New Delhi even requested the supply of supersonic aircraft.[28] Islamabad became acutely distressed as its superpower backer commenced supplying arms to its perceived enemy. Consequently, President Ayub Khan sought to reduce Islamabad's dependence on Washington and to find allies among the major powers of Asia.[29]

Recalling the old Arab proverb "the enemy of my enemy is my friend," Pakistan considered China an obvious partner, and Islamabad actively sought to normalize relations with Peking. Pakistani objections encouraged the United States to deny the supply of sophisticated weapons systems to India. Nevertheless, this concession was not sufficient to discourage Sino-Pakistani rapprochement. Ironically, Washington's refusal to meet India's request for supersonic aircraft drove New Delhi ever closer to the Moscow, which proved only too ready to meet India's demands.[30]

The relationship between the United States and Pakistan continued to sour. When Ayub visited both Peking and Moscow in early 1965, and refused to offer the United States substantial backing over Vietnam, President Lyndon Johnson cancelled Ayub's trip to Washington, scheduled for April.[31] Worse was to come. In direct contravention of agreements with Washington, Pakistan used US-supplied arms against India during the Indo-Pakistan War that erupted on 6 September 1965. Two days later, Washington suspended all military and economic aid to both India and

Pakistan.[32] The embargo had three effects. First, it brought the war to an early halt, as Pakistan was heavily dependent on US supplies to maintain its armed forces, far more so than India. Second, it severely hurt Pakistan, both militarily and psychologically, sparking resentment and the collapse of US prestige in Islamabad. Third, it provided Washington with an opportunity to reshape its Cold War policy with regard to South Asia. The perceived communist threat to the Middle East had receded, and new satellite technology reduced the need for the US base in Peshawar. Pakistan was turning toward China, and India remained unhappy at the limited quantities and types of materiel it had received from the United States. Moreover, the United States did not wish to be seen as throwing fuel on the fire of Indo-Pakistani mutual resentment.[33]

In 1965, therefore, the warm relationship between the United States and Pakistan ended, never to be rekindled. The arms embargo was partially relaxed in March 1966, but only to allow the sale of non-lethal end-use items, such as medical, transportation, and communications equipment.[34] Although full US economic aid effectively resumed the following month, average annual flows amounted to only US$150 million, compared with US$400 million in the early 1960s.[35] In April 1967, Washington announced it would sell spares for previously supplied military equipment on a cash basis and resume grant-aid training on a small scale.[36] The embargo on lethal end-use items remained firmly in place, however, the gap in supply being largely filled by the Chinese.[37] Far from contented, Islamabad refused to extend the lease on the US facility in Peshawar, which was due to expire in 1969.[38]

As Nixon entered the White House,[39] Pakistan, once a close ally of the United States, had taken its own more neutral geopolitical course, and the special friendship between Islamabad and Washington no longer existed. The standoff over US military supply to India at the time of Kennedy's presidency had encouraged Pakistan to engage with China, a relationship cemented following the serious rupture in ties between Washington and Islamabad over the war of 1965. Economic aid from the United States, though still substantial, had decreased by more than half over the last decade, and full military supply had not been resumed. Pakistan had sought to develop relations with other powers in Asia in order to mitigate its reliance on the United States, but had failed to do so in a way that the United States understood and supported. Elsewhere, the relationship between Washington and New Delhi remained lukewarm at best. As the Nixon administration came to power, its policy on the subcontinent was merely to "avoid adding another complication to ... [its] agenda."[40]

In February 1971, the US embassy in Islamabad prepared a paper defining the US relationship with Pakistan. It noted that Pakistan preferred to maintain good relations with the United States to ensure the continued flow of economic aid and to avoid overdependence on China. As Peking had sought neither to promote revolution nor to interfere in Pakistan's domestic affairs, the report suggested that the Sino-Pakistani relationship was not "seriously inimical to our [US] interests." US political concern with regard to Pakistan was limited to its being the world's fifth most populous country and the resulting influence it might exert in western Asia and the Middle East. US economic interests were essentially developmental, as commercial opportunities remained limited, and Pakistan was not a source of essential raw materials for US manufacturers.[41]

Despite these minimal national interests, Nixon, a Republican, brought to the White House an unusually warm attitude toward Islamabad. "Nixon had been received [there] with respect when he was out of office; he never forgot this."[42] Nevertheless, owing to ongoing martial rule and its relatively small economic stature compared with that of its democratic neighbour to the south, Pakistan was not a favourite of American liberals. Kissinger believed that India, in contrast, "basked in Congressional warmth and was subject to Presidential indifference."[43] Initially, Nixon did not significantly change US policy toward Pakistan, save for one concession:[44] in October 1970, just before Yahya visited the White House and Nixon encouraged him to act as intermediary with Peking, the US president approved a one-time exception package of lethal military hardware for Pakistan, which included three hundred armoured personnel carriers and seventeen military aircraft.[45] Nixon's sympathy for Yahya and Islamabad had begun to show.

In early 1971, relations between Washington and New Delhi were particularly strained owing to US officials meeting with opposition leaders and being accused of interference in Indian domestic affairs, as well as protests over the one-time exception with regard to arms sales to Pakistan.[46] Yet, Washington and New Delhi had never enjoyed a particularly warm relationship. After partition, India had pursued a policy of non-alignment and consequently enjoyed a much closer association with the Soviets than the United States found comfortable.[47] Since the mid-1950s, Moscow had sought to reduce New Delhi's dependence on the West by exporting industrial machinery in an attempt to develop India's key industries.[48] Although Moscow had expeditiously sided with Peking in the 1962 Sino-Indian War, this proved only a small anomaly in its ongoing friendship with New Delhi. When the United States refused to deliver supersonic jets to India after the war of 1962, the Soviets provided MiG-21 fighters;[49] between 1965 and 1970, the Soviet bloc supplied India with US$730 million worth of military equipment.[50] In contrast, save for the limited supplies of arms between 1962 and 1965, US aid to India took a strictly economic form. Nevertheless, such financial assistance was substantial. New Delhi received US$4.2 billion between 1965 and 1971, including some US$1.5 billion while Nixon was in office.[51] In early 1971, therefore, New Delhi remained officially non-aligned and maintained beneficial relationships with both Moscow and Washington. It leaned, however, rather closer to the Soviet Union than to the United States.[52]

Whereas Sino-Indian relations remained strained after the war of 1962, the friendship between China and Pakistan flourished. Peking sought primarily to collude against India, but also to pre-empt any attempt by Moscow to exert its influence and to give Islamabad the opportunity to further reconsider its close relationship with Washington.[53] In 1963, Islamabad and Peking signed a trade agreement, the Chinese premier, Chou En-lai, visited Pakistan, and China announced a change in policy, supporting Pakistan's demands for a plebiscite in Kashmir. The following year, China extended a US$60 million interest-free loan, and in 1965 Chou visited Islamabad three times before the onset of the Indo-Pakistan War.[54] Peking supported Islamabad during the conflict, condemning India for its "aggression," and distracted India by placing Chinese troops on high alert along the Sino-Sikkim frontier.[55] Following the war, China replaced the United States as Pakistan's main weapons supplier, providing large quantities of hardware, including T-29 and T-54 tanks and MiG-19 fighters;[56] between 1965 and 1970, China supplied Pakistan with some US$135 million worth of military equipment.[57] As the next decade began, 25 percent of Islamabad's tanks and 90 percent of its modern fighter planes had been sourced from Peking.[58] In addition, in June 1966, the Chinese agreed to provide the equipment and technical expertise to establish a heavy machinery complex at Taxila.[59] The close relationship between China and Pakistan continued into the 1970s, thus placing Yahya in a strong position to act as a conduit to Peking on behalf of a friendly and sympathetic Nixon.

As the realignment in relations between the major powers and the subcontinent was occurring during the 1960s, another geopolitical event of great importance and direct relevance continued to develop: a deep fissure in the communist world in the form of the Sino-Soviet split. Ideological differences, including Peking's objection to Soviet de-Stalinization moves and Moscow's search for "peaceful coexistence" with the West,[60] and national rivalry led to the Soviet Union's withdrawal of all technical advisors and economic aid from China in 1959. Four years later, Peking took great offence as the Soviets signed the Partial Nuclear Test Ban Treaty with the United States and United Kingdom, accusing Moscow of joining the West in an anti-Chinese plot.[61]

The Sino-Soviet relationship soured still further in the mid-1960s, and border clashes occurred with growing frequency. Following the signing of a treaty with Ulan Bator, from 1966 onward the Soviets began establishing military bases in Mongolia and transferring combat units from Western Europe to its Far Eastern frontiers. As the Soviets rolled into Prague in the summer of 1968, Peking began to wonder which country would be next. In March 1969, a severe border clash occurred over disputed territory along the Ussuri River in Manchuria, leaving dozens of Soviets dead; 100,000 Soviet demonstrators reportedly attacked the Chinese embassy in Moscow in response, while Peking Radio claimed that over 400 million people had protested across China. Further military exchanges occurred throughout the spring and summer along the Amur River and the Sinkiang-Kazakhstan frontier. In 1964, the Soviet Union had only twelve divisions stationed along the four-thousand-mile Chinese border; in 1970, it had over forty, and a clear rift existed between Moscow and Peking.[62] An urgent meeting between Chou En-lai and the Soviet prime minister, Aleksei Kosygin, prevented further deterioration in the relationship.[63] Nevertheless, substantial Sino-Soviet tensions remained,[64] presenting Nixon with an opportunity to encourage rapprochement between China and the United States from his inauguration in 1969 onward.

Meanwhile, in China, the Cultural Revolution had erupted after 1965. Spurred on by Mao Tse-tung, Red Guards conducted purges of all those perceived to embrace bourgeois thoughts, intellectualism, or modernism. Universities closed, and China recalled nearly all its ambassadors from abroad, though often keeping the embassies open.[65] The revolution soured, leaving disruption in its wake.[66] The country was weakened at a time of perceived threat, and two main factions emerged in Chinese politics: Lin Piao insisted that China should combine with the Soviets to force the United States out of Southeast Asia; Chou En-lai argued that Vietnam had weakened the Americans and that China could now safely negotiate with Washington.[67]

In November 1968, Chou called for talks with the new Nixon administration, but the pro-Soviet faction blocked his attempts at rapprochement. Nevertheless, Sino-Soviet clashes over the coming months gave Chou's arguments greater force.[68] In early 1970, China and the United States reconvened

Superpower

stilted ambassadorial talks in Warsaw, but it was not until the fall of 1970 that Chou was finally able to convince Mao that the United States was not a threat to China but rather a valuable counterweight against Soviet pressure. After receiving Mao's backing, Chou won a clear victory in the internal feud with Lin Piao.[69] Thus, toward the end of 1970, China was ready and willing to engage in a process of rapprochement with the United States.

In summary, by early 1971, the once-close relationship between Washington and Islamabad had ended, but the United States continued to provide substantial economic aid, and Nixon exhibited a distinct personal sympathy for Yahya. Pakistan had developed a close association with its new arms supplier, China. Ironically, though Sino-Pakistani rapprochement had once soured relations between Islamabad and Washington, Nixon now considered such ties a considerable asset. India, though still officially non-aligned and receiving appreciable amounts of US financial aid, leaned more closely toward Moscow than Washington, while tension remained between New Delhi and Peking. Importantly, the Sino-Soviet split had developed, encouraging rapprochement between China and the United States.

Power and Strategy in Washington

Personalization of Foreign Policy

When President Richard Nixon entered office in 1969, he was determined to run foreign policy from the White House. He had visited over eighty countries while a congressman and then vice president and brought with him a passion for international affairs and a wealth of experience.[70] Indeed, Kissinger believed no American president had a greater knowledge of foreign issues.[71] Consequently, Nixon set about constructing the apparatus of power that would realize his wish. By early 1971, the president and his national security advisor dominated the State Department and other governmental agencies under a centralized system that facilitated the personalization of US foreign policy.

Robert Strong argues that Nixon wanted to act as his own secretary of state for three reasons: ideologically, the president believed State and the CIA to be "excessively liberal"; politically, he desired personal credit for his foreign policy initiatives; and psychologically, he wanted to avoid direct confrontation with dissenting officials.[72] Indeed, on recruiting Kissinger after his election victory, Nixon had expressed his views on the "untrustworthiness" of State and the "incompetence" of the CIA.[73] Kissinger generally concurred, believing the bureaucracy to be unimaginative and inclined to stifle presidential leadership.[74]

In what Roger Morris refers to as the "coup d'état at the Hotel Pierre," during the transition period after the elections Nixon and his new national security advisor "conceived and began what would become a seizure of power unprecedented in modern American foreign policy."[75] In a New York hotel, Morton Halperin, deputy assistant secretary of defence, proposed a new National Security Council (NSC) system in a paper endorsed by Kissinger and approved by Nixon on 28 December 1968.[76] The NSC had originally been established at the same time as the CIA under the National Security Act of 1947, with a view to integrating domestic, foreign, and military policies in matters of national security. Statutory members included the president, the vice president, the secretaries of state and defence, the director of Central Intelligence, and the chairman of the Joint Chiefs of Staff.[77] The NSC had faded into the background under Kennedy and Johnson, however, both of whom chose to use informal meetings to direct policy on key issues.[78] Using Halperin's blueprint, Nixon and Kissinger reinvigorated the NSC system under a new structure that usurped the power of State.

The formal NSC apparatus comprised interdepartmental committees, each normally chaired by the relevant assistant secretary of state. These reported to the Senior Review Group (SRG), chaired by Kissinger, which acted as the filter and conduit to the full NSC, chaired by Nixon. Importantly, the SRG replaced the Senior Interdepartmental Group, formed in 1967 to provide presidential advice on foreign policy issues, which was chaired and controlled by the under-secretary of state. The national security advisor, not State, therefore, would henceforth regulate the flow of information, advice, and decisions to and from the president. Nixon would issue National Security Study Memoranda (NSSM), which would be assigned to the appropriate interdepartmental committees for response. The president's decisions, in theory based on these studies, would be communicated by National Security Decision Memoranda.[79] The NSC system would have its own staff, recruited by Kissinger, and provide a focal point for coherent interagency long-range planning, a formal mechanism for monitoring the implementation of foreign policy directives, and a means of efficiently formulating timely advice. It would also provide Nixon and Kissinger with the formal vehicle by which to elaborate and impose their views on foreign policy.[80]

Nixon and Kissinger compounded the effects of their initial coup by four means. First, they rapidly expanded the NSC staff from twenty-eight in 1969 to fifty-two in 1971, thereby obviating the need to frequently employ State resources.[81] Second, Kissinger stopped top NSC personnel from meeting with Nixon to discuss matters in which they were expert. Only in exceptional cases did they attend meetings between the national security advisor and the president. Thus, Kissinger became the sole channel, the two-way valve, through which all information and decisions had to flow.[82] Third, in June 1969, Nixon ordered a substantial reduction in the number of meetings of the full NSC, instructing Kissinger to bring issues to him directly.[83] Consequently, full NSC meetings became a formality, during which the president and his national security advisor controlled the agenda and proceedings, and for which the NSC staff prepared Nixon's responses to anticipated questions concerning decisions already made privately and presented as *fait accompli*.[84] Fourth, Nixon appointed Kissinger, who already controlled the SRG, as chair of several other important committees, including the Washington Special Actions Group (WSAG), tasked with determining immediate US responses in times of international crisis.[85] As a result of these steps, Nixon and Kissinger's grasp on power continued to tighten.[86]

While strengthening the NSC, Nixon further weakened State by appointing William Rogers, an "adequate administrator," as secretary.[87] As the president's chief of staff noted: "The Secretary of State was a figurehead."[88] Although a "tug of war"[89] developed between Kissinger and Rogers, the secretary proved no match for the national security advisor, who nearly always received Nixon's support.[90] After all, as Kissinger observed, "in the final analysis the influence of ... [the] Presidential Assistant ... [derived] almost exclusively from the confidence of the President, not from administrative arrangements."[91]

Despite the power that they already exerted through the newly implemented NSC system, Nixon and Kissinger consolidated their position still further. Standard diplomacy demanded that all contact with foreign governments be made through State Department channels, thereby ensuring proper coordination between various agencies, each being given the opportunity to mould policy. On key initiatives, however, Nixon and Kissinger preferred to use back channels and secret diplomacy, which they believed offered greater flexibility. Thus, they worked around and beyond State and even the NSC system, as opposed to through them.[92] Indeed, Kissinger set up a back channel to the Soviets within the first few weeks of his assuming office in 1969.[93]

As Kissinger observed in his memoirs: "Eventually, though not for the first one and a half years, I became the principal adviser. Until the end of 1970 I was influential but not dominant. From then on, my role increased as Nixon sought to bypass the delays and sometimes opposition of departments."[94] "Once he had set a policy direction, he almost invariably left it to me to implement the strategy and manage the bureaucracy."[95] The NSC organization had usurped the power of a weak secretary of state and effectively placed foreign policy directly under the control of the president and his national security advisor. Moreover, Nixon and Kissinger often worked outside the bureaucratic system altogether, employing back channels and secret diplomacy. By early 1971, therefore, the apparatus of power had developed into "essentially [a] two-man system."[96] The personalization of US foreign policy had occurred.

Nixon-Kissinger World View

Nixon had originally been a staunch anti-communist, viewing the world through the lens of idealism. Nevertheless, by the time he became president, he had converted to the realist perspective already shared by his national security advisor.[97] On entering office, Nixon and Kissinger believed that a multipolar global system had replaced the post–Second World War bipolar arrangement; Western Europe and Japan had healed, the communist world had split between the Soviet Union and China, and newly powerful nations had emerged elsewhere. As the Soviets approached nuclear parity and budgetary concerns threatened America's ability to make international commitments, disenchantment over Vietnam provided a signal that a new approach to foreign policy was required.[98] "Nixon found himself in the position of having to guide America through the transition from dominance to leadership."[99] This realist awareness precipitated the announcement of the Nixon Doctrine in 1969 and the pursuit of Vietnamization in Southeast Asia.[100] Under the doctrine, the United States would honor its treaty obligations and provide a nuclear shield for its allies but, in cases of conventional external aggression, America would furnish only economic aid and materiel, the nation directly threatened being responsible for the manpower employed in its own defence. The United States would sanction direct military involvement in a foreign crisis only if an ally were attacked by a major power and aiding that ally in its defence were a vital US national interest.[101] Vietnamization sought to hand the prosecution of the Vietnam War to the South Vietnamese, while US troops withdrew from the arena. It was thus consistent with both the realist agenda and the Nixon Doctrine.

Realism further manifested itself in Nixon and Kissinger's search for a balance of power in the pursuit of national interests measured in terms of strength and security.[102] As Nixon explained in his first foreign policy report to Congress: "Our objective, in the first instance, is to support our interests over the long run with a sound foreign policy ... Our interests must shape our commitments, rather than the other way around."[103] The desire for a stable equilibrium was demonstrated in policies of détente with the Soviets and rapprochement with the Chinese.[104]

Realist philosophy left little space for moral ideals, however. Kissinger best explained his attitude toward this conundrum at a gathering of Nobel laureates in Paris, many years after the East Pakistan crisis. In the words of Walter Isaacson, his biographer, the former national security advisor observed:

> More than a dozen of his relatives had been killed in the holocaust, he said, so he knew something of the nature of genocide. It was easy for human rights crusaders and peace activists to insist on perfection in this world. But the policymaker who has to deal with reality learns to seek the best that can be achieved rather than the best that can be imagined. It would be wonderful to banish the role of military power from world affairs, but the world is not perfect, as he had learned as a child. Those with true responsibility for peace, unlike those on the sidelines, cannot afford pure idealism. They must have the courage to deal with ambiguities and accommodations, to realize that great goals can be achieved only in imperfect steps. No side has a monopoly on morality.[105]

As the East Pakistan crisis erupted, US foreign policy lay in the hands of two individuals who were intent on reducing direct US military commitments overseas, and who embraced the formation of a new global Cold War power equilibrium as the cornerstone of their world view. Importantly, to paraphrase Stalin, the US president's one-time archenemy, to make their omelette, Nixon and Kissinger were more than ready to break a few eggs along the way.

Reopening the Door to China

China's relationship with the United States had collapsed following the communist takeover in 1949 and the Korean War (1950–53). Save for a small group of sinologists who emphasized the need to heal the rift, the vast majority of informed Americans considered China an expansionist threat in need of containment. Improvements would not be possible until ideological change had occurred; instead, isolation would be the order of the day. Sovietologists supported this view, urging dialogue with Moscow while at the

34 · *United States*

same time discouraging the development of any links with Peking that might spoil such a strategy. The Nixon administration did not concur. "We were convinced that increasing America's foreign policy options would soften, not harden, Moscow's stance."[106]

By 1971, rapprochement with the Chinese had been on Nixon's mind for some time.[107] He first publicly raised his ideas on the subject in an article published in *Foreign Affairs* in October 1967:[108]

> Any American policy toward Asia must come urgently to grips with the reality of China ... Taking the long view, we simply cannot afford to leave China forever outside the family of nations, there to nurture its fantasies, cherish its hates and threaten its neighbors. There is no place on this small planet for a billion of its potentially most able people to live in angry isolation ... Only as the nations of non-communist Asia become so strong – economically, politically and militarily – that they no longer furnish tempting targets for Chinese aggression, will the leaders in Peking be persuaded to turn their energies inward rather than outward. And that will be the time when the dialogue with mainland China can begin. For the short run, then, this means a policy of firm restraint, of no reward, of a creative counterpressure [sic] designed to persuade Peking that its interests can be served only by accepting the basic rules of international civility. For the long run, it means pulling China back into the world community – but as a great and progressing nation, not as an epicenter of world revolution.[109]

During his years as an anti-communist idealist, Nixon had characterized China as a "dangerous, aggressive enemy."[110] Yet, the president's ever-increasing adoption of realist philosophy during the 1960s severely diluted this view. China, in isolation, was a threat to world peace; Peking must be included in a new balance of world powers.[111]

Clearly, the "short run" described in the 1967 article did not last many years in Nixon's opinion, as one of his first directives to NSC staff was an order to explore opportunities for Sino-American rapprochement.[112] This was the first of several NSSMs issued with a view to taking positive steps toward China. In Paris in March 1969, Nixon discussed the matter with French president Charles de Gaulle, who concurred with his view that the West ought to seek better relations with Peking.[113] By the end of the year, Kissinger had stated in a press briefing: "It seems to us impossible to build a peace, which we define as something other than just the avoidance of crisis, by simply ignoring these 800 million people."[114] Nixon believed, however,

Superpower 35

that his first "serious" public step toward better relations came in his first foreign policy report to Congress in February 1970,[115] in which he declared:

> We will continue to probe every available opening that offers a prospect for better East-West relations, for the resolution of problems large or small, for greater security for all ... This is also the spirit in which we have resumed formal talks in Warsaw with Communist China. No nation need be our permanent enemy.[116]

Nixon and Kissinger sent these two public signals to Peking in the full knowledge that the Sino-Soviet split might encourage a positive Chinese response.[117]

Although the president and his national security advisor sought to include China in the international system in order to eliminate the possibility of a rogue threat to world peace, they also had more specific aims. First, they intended to establish a new equilibrium of the three major powers – China, the Soviet Union, and the United States – through a system of triangular diplomacy. In his memoirs, Kissinger insisted that he and Nixon did not seek rapprochement with Peking simply to use a "China card" against the Soviets, thus forcing Moscow to seek better relations with Washington, for this was only part of the answer.[118] As he explained, quoting an October 1971 memorandum he sent to Nixon:

> We want our China policy to show Moscow that it cannot speak for all communist countries, that it is to their advantage to make agreements with us, that they must take into account possible US-PRC [China] cooperation – all this without overdoing the Soviet paranoia ... The Chinese want to relieve themselves of the threat of a two-front war, introduce new calculations in Moscow about attacking or leaning on the PRC [China], and perhaps make the USSR more pliable in its dealing with Peking. Specifically from us they want assurances against US-USSR collusion.[119]

Second, many believed that the solution to Vietnam lay in the capitals of the major communist powers. Without aid from either the Soviets or the Chinese, Hanoi would be unable to continue the war. Triangular diplomacy within a new power equilibrium would perhaps present the United States with an opportunity to disengage from Vietnam without leaving its policy in Southeast Asia in disarray.[120] Third, Kissinger felt that the "drama" of Sino-American rapprochement would give a boost to a US public demoralized over Vietnam – "a reminder of what America could accomplish as a world leader."[121] If they could succeed in ending the ongoing feud with China, Nixon and Kissinger believed, both the United States and the world had much to gain.

Courting Peking

There are three important reasons to consider Nixon and Kissinger's first practical steps toward better relations with Peking. Study reveals the amount of time and effort they had already invested in the initiative at the time of the East Pakistan crisis, the fragility of the rapprochement process, and the relative merits of the alternative conduits available to the president and his national security advisor.

The United States began to send public signals of its willingness to see a thaw in the frosty Sino-American relationship in 1969, when it loosened passport restrictions on its citizens travelling to China, allowed limited grain shipments, and suspended naval patrols in the Taiwan Strait.[122] Then, after his conciliatory statement toward China in his first foreign policy report to Congress, the president approved a partial relaxation of trade controls in April 1970. Nixon and Kissinger confirmed this signal later that year when both made further public statements for Chinese consumption.[123] The president granted an interview to *Time* magazine in October in which he claimed: "If there is anything I want to do before I die, it is to go to China."[124] Two months later, in another interview with correspondents from the same publication, Kissinger admitted: "Our China strategy has been both to develop a dialogue with them for its own sake and then to have a counterweight with the Soviets."[125] On 18 December 1970, China attempted to send a positive response. During an interview with journalist Edgar Snow, Mao Tse-tung said he would be happy to talk with Nixon in Peking. It is unclear when this news reached Washington, but this general invitation was published in *Life* magazine in April 1971.[126] Before this, on 25 February 1971, however, Nixon made a clear statement of his intentions in his second foreign policy report to Congress: "When the Government of the People's Republic of China is ready to engage in talks, it will find us receptive to agreements that further the legitimate national interests of China and its neighbors."[127] In early 1971, therefore, both Nixon and Mao had sent public signals concerning their general intent, but unfortunately nothing concrete had resulted; dates for any possible talks had not even been proffered, much less the participants and agenda considered and agreed. Although

Superpower 37

rapprochement appeared possible, the vital question remained of how to convert such indications into a tangible success. Meanwhile, Nixon and Kissinger had resorted to their preferred secret diplomacy in an attempt to finesse a breakthrough.

The president and his national security advisor sought to use back channels after missing an opportunity to re-engage with the Chinese in ambassadorial talks held in Warsaw in early 1970. A total of 134 such sterile, mid-level meetings had been held between the virtual isolation of the Chinese in the early 1950s and the end of 1968. Unfortunately, the conclusion of a minor repatriation accord had been their only concrete achievement.[128] In September 1969, Nixon and Kissinger instructed the US ambassador to Warsaw, Walter Stoessel Jr., to contact the Chinese with a view to restarting the talks, which had broken down the previous year. This approach occurred when Chou En-lai's faction was temporarily in the ascendancy in Peking, and so the Chinese agreed to meeting number 135, held on 20 January 1970.[129] Stoessel, as instructed, announced that the United States would be prepared to send a representative to Peking or receive a Chinese envoy in Washington. At the next meeting, on 20 February, the Chinese accepted the first option.[130]

By the summer of 1969, Nixon had already decided to concentrate on broader issues, rather than the specific grievances for so long painstakingly and pointlessly expounded in earlier Warsaw talks.[131] In his memoirs, Kissinger explained that to "overcome the preconceptions of two decades," talks had to take place not between blinkered "experts" set in their ways, but at the highest levels of government.[132] Even when the offer of high-level discussions had been received and accepted, however, Secretary of State Rogers insisted on setting preconditions and presenting long-standing grievances reflecting the entrenched attitudes in State.[133] Kissinger had not yet achieved his dominant status as Nixon's foreign policy confidant. Consequently, he and State reached an impasse that delayed further discussions. A meeting was finally scheduled for 20 May 1970, but the American incursion into Cambodia that spring led the Chinese to cancel the talks.[134] In his memoirs, Kissinger described this lost opportunity as "providential," as the US government was "simply not ready to speak with a single voice."[135] This experience reinforced Nixon and Kissinger's view that secret diplomacy through back channels, "unencumbered by vested bureaucratic interests and the traditional liturgy," would provide them with maximum flexibility should they ever be offered a second bite of the cherry.[136] They soon began an "intricate minuet" with Peking.[137]

38 United States

After the collapse of the Warsaw project, Nixon and Kissinger had "no idea how to approach the Chinese leaders."[138] Clutching at perhaps the largest available straw, in June 1970 they instructed General Vernon Walters, US military attaché in Paris, to attempt to contact his Chinese counterpart there with a view to establishing a back channel that bypassed the State Department and the need for any foreign go-between.[139] Walters tried twice, once during the summer and again in September 1970, but failed to elicit any response.[140] Unfortunately, during this time Chou En-lai's faction was still rebuilding its credibility following the Cambodian adventure.

In September 1970, Kissinger placed a second iron in the Parisian fire, encouraging his good friend Jean Sainteny, the former French delegate general in Hanoi and then director general of UNESCO, to convey to the Chinese ambassador to Paris the fact that the United States wished to establish direct contact.[141] On 18 January 1971, news reached Kissinger that Sainteny had finally succeeded in his mission the previous December, and that the Chinese ambassador had contacted Peking but was awaiting a response.[142] At the start of the East Pakistan crisis, therefore, no direct back channel through Paris had yet sprung to life. Meanwhile, however, Nixon and Kissinger had also attempted to bring two indirect, and therefore less convenient, conduits into operation, through Presidents Nicolae Ceaușescu of Romania and Yahya Khan of Pakistan.

In August 1969, Nixon became the first US president to pay a state visit to a communist country – Romania. He had been welcomed there while out of office in 1967, and considered a return trip a useful means of encouraging Eastern European countries to act more independently of Moscow.[143] Ceaușescu had a good relationship with Peking, and Nixon took the opportunity to ask him to make approaches to China at the highest level; Ceaușescu agreed.[144] On 17 December 1969, Chou En-lai used the Romanian channel to signal that China was interested in establishing "normal relations" with the West, but added little else.[145] It was not until 26 October 1970, when Ceaușescu visited the White House during a trip to the United States to mark the twenty-fifth anniversary of the United Nations, that the two presidents again broached the subject.[146] The next day, in a meeting with Kissinger, Ceaușescu confirmed he would again communicate US interest in establishing a secret channel of communication and make the White House aware of any Chinese response.[147]

On 11 January 1971, one month after the Pakistani conduit had awoken (see below), the Romanian channel once again bore fruit. Vice Premier

Gheorghe Rădulescu had visited Peking during November of the previous year and had received a message from Chou, whose faction had finally gained the upper hand.[148] The Romanian ambassador to Washington, Corneliu Bogdan, read the communication aloud in the White House Map Room. It was almost identical to that just received through the Pakistani channel and contained an invitation from the Chinese premier for the United States to send an envoy to Peking. Having already sent a response via Islamabad, Nixon scribbled the instruction: "I believe we may appear too eager. Let's cool it. Wait for them to respond to our [Pakistan] initiative."[149] Consequently, Kissinger did not issue an immediate reply, but chose to wait. Only some three weeks later, on 29 January, when Bogdan announced he would soon be visiting Bucharest, did the national security advisor respond. The reply was similar to that sent via Islamabad but, instead of being written, this time it was oral.[150]

In his memoirs, which deliberately sought to promote the importance of the Pakistani conduit, Kissinger asserted: "Contrary to our expectations, the Romanian channel turned out to be one-way."[151] He appears to have conveniently forgotten the above evidence to the contrary. Indeed, as Ceaușescu made a state visit to China in June 1971, when the Pakistani channel was fully operational, the White House consciously avoided bringing the Romanian channel back into play.[152] Although Kissinger did have legitimate concerns that "it would be difficult for Bucharest to avoid briefing Moscow,"[153] it appears that the Romanian conduit was both functional and two-way. Though the form and timing of the US response of January 1971 clearly indicated White House preference for the Pakistani channel, the Romanian option remained a possible alternative for communicating with the Chinese.[154]

By the time of the East Pakistan crisis, the conduit via Yahya and Islamabad had become not the exclusive but the preferred link between Washington and Peking. In 1969, during a short stopover in Pakistan, just a day before visiting Ceaușescu on the same world trip, Nixon had similarly implored Yahya to make overtures to China. Like his Romanian counterpart, the Pakistani president had agreed.[155] About this time, Kissinger also approached the Pakistani ambassador to Washington, Agha Hilaly, whose sister he had taught at Harvard, with a view to establishing a secure back channel.[156] On 19 December 1969, two days after the Romanian conduit had conveyed China's wish to establish "normal relations," the Pakistani channel confirmed the same news through Hilaly, and on 23 December the Pakistani ambassador relayed Chinese interest in resuming the Warsaw talks, which were subsequently reconvened, only to fall through in May the following year.[157]

On 25 October 1970, as the Pakistani president, like his Romanian counterpart, visited the United States to attend the UN anniversary celebrations, Nixon met with Yahya in the Oval Office.[158] Nixon explained: "It is essential that we open negotiations with China," and said that the United States would be prepared to "establish links secretly."[159] Yahya visited Peking in person that November,[160] but it was not until 9 December, two days after the Pakistani elections, that Hilaly dictated a message from Chou En-lai to Kissinger in Washington.[161] Declaring himself to be speaking not only for himself but also on behalf of Mao and Lin Piao, Chou explained:

> China has always been willing and has always tried to negotiate by peaceful means. Taiwan and the Straits of Taiwan are an inalienable part of China which have now been occupied by foreign troops of the United States for the last fifteen years. Negotiations and talks have been going on with no results whatsoever. In order to *discuss this subject of the vacation of Chinese territories called Taiwan,* a special envoy of President Nixon's will be most welcome in Peking ... We have had messages from the United States from different sources in the past but this is the first time that the proposal has come *from a Head, through a Head, to a Head. The United States knows that Pakistan is a great friend of China and therefore we attach importance to the message.*[162]

Nixon and Kissinger took this to be not only a positive response but also a clear indication of Chinese preference for the Pakistani conduit.[163] This was convenient for the United States because of Islamabad's geographical proximity to China and, in contrast to Bucharest, its lack of close ties to Moscow. There was nothing in Chou's memorandum, however, to suggest that use of the Pakistan conduit was a necessary condition of communication with the Chinese.

The White House appeared to be getting a second bite at the cherry just seven months after the collapse of the Warsaw talks. Nevertheless, Nixon and Kissinger were disappointed with Peking's focus on the Taiwan problem. In their written reply of 16 December, they insisted on discussion of a wider range of issues and suggested a meeting of envoys to prepare the way for higher-level talks in Peking.[164]

At the outbreak of the East Pakistan crisis, therefore, Nixon and Kissinger had invested two years of public and private efforts in trying to establish

Superpower

effective contact with the Chinese leadership. Enticingly, the arrangement of what the president and his national security advisor considered vital high-level talks with the Chinese communists did appear possible. Pakistan had been established as the preferred, though not the necessary, conduit. Nevertheless, nothing concrete, not even the scope of any agenda, had been agreed between the two capitals, and the fragility of the enterprise remained all too clear.

2

Phase One Response

Having established the context in which government officials battled to determine US policy, we now turn to phase one of the key response period and analye events between the clampdown on 25 March and 27 April, the date on which the back channel to Peking sprang to life.

Let's Do Something

Consulate in Dacca: "Selective Genocide"

Archer Blood, the US consul general in Dacca, was a respected and capable individual. A career diplomat, he received the US Foreign Service's Meritorious Honor Award for his work following the November 1970 cyclone in East Pakistan, and considered himself well apprised of the local situation. Yet, as President Yahya Khan unexpectedly unleashed his West Pakistani–dominated armed forces on the night of 25 March 1971, Blood was hosting a dinner for sixteen at his home in the city.[1] He had placed his faith in progress through negotiation, but suddenly found himself perched with his guests on the roof of his own home, "watching with horror the constant flash of tracer bullets across the dark sky and listening to the more ominous clatter of machine gun fire and the heavy clump of tank guns" in the distance.[2]

Surprised and ill-prepared, Blood soon became isolated. Dacca lay one thousand miles from the US embassy in Islamabad, and for some weeks no

Phase One Response 43

US officials were allowed to visit Dacca from the West. The army imposed a strict curfew, banned travel outside the city, and cut the inter-wing telephone service as well as that in East Pakistan; mail delivery became delayed and uncertain. Nevertheless, Blood determined to peer through the "fog of war" as best he could, using the undeclared wireless communication facility in the consulate to relay news of atrocities perpetrated in the East to the US embassy in Islamabad and the Department of State in Washington.[3]

On 28 March 1971, Blood sent a telegram titled "Selective Genocide."[4] He began: "Here in Dacca we are mute and horrified witnesses to a reign of terror by the Pak[5] military."[6] The West Pakistan authorities in the East had "marked for extinction" the Awami League hierarchy, student leaders, university faculty, and members of the National and Provincial Assemblies.[7] Blood continued: "Moreover, with the support of [the] Pak military, non-Bengali Muslims are systematically attacking poor people's quarters and murdering Bengalis and Hindus ... There is no rpt [repeat] no resistance being offered in Dacca to military ... We should be expressing our shock at least privately to GOP [the government of Pakistan]."[8]

The next day, he reported that American priests in Old Dacca had witnessed the army, without provocation, "set houses afire and then gun down people as they left their homes." Blood believed the casualty figures to be very high, and Hindus to be the "particular focus of [the] campaign." Troops were looting and standing by as non-Bengalis did the same. Early reports suggested that the Pakistani army had killed 1,800 policemen and, of the 1,000 soldiers of the East Pakistan Rifles, a Bengali regiment based in part at Peelkhana Camp, some 700 had been killed and 200 captured. The objectives of the army appeared to be to terrorize the population into submission and eliminate those elements of society it perceived as a threat to the Martial Law Administration.[9]

On 30 March, Blood transmitted the testimony of an American visiting Dacca University, who had been told that the students of Iqbal Hall had been shot down in their rooms or as they fled. The visitor had seen twenty-five bodies, the others having been rapidly disposed of by the army. At Rokeya Hall for girls, the troops had set the building ablaze and had mown down the occupants with machine-gun fire as they had sought to flee. Although possibly exaggerating, contacts had suggested that some one thousand students and faculty had been killed, some of the bodies rotting in two mass graves exposed by heavy rain.[10]

On the last day of March, Blood issued a situation report titled "Army Terror Campaign Continues in Dacca." By then, Hindus were "undeniably

[the] special focus of military brutality," large fires being observed in the predominantly Hindu areas of Dacca. A consular officer had observed truckloads of prisoners being driven into Peelkhana Camp, followed by steady firing of one shot per ten seconds for some thirty minutes. The firing had already started before the official arrived. Back at Dacca University, a non–Awami League businessman had visited Rokeya Hall, where he had observed six female bodies "apparently raped, shot and hung by heels from [ceiling] fans."[11] While admitting that "we are still hard put to estimate [the] number of casualties," Blood suggested that, besides the troops of the East Pakistan Rifles, the military had killed 600–800 policemen, 500–1,000 students and faculty, and 2,000–4,000 in the old area of the city.[12] Even after the army had established firm control over Dacca, it continued wanton acts of violence, paying special attention to the Hindu population.[13]

Under the circumstances, Blood had done well to gather so much detailed evidence of widespread atrocities, which he had then relayed back to his superiors in Islamabad and Washington. Yet, despite its knowledge, the US government maintained a "deafening silence." Yahya, having imposed strict press censorship and deported foreign journalists from the East, portrayed the wing as calm and the situation as under control. Despite having its own man on the spot in the person of Blood, Washington conveniently referred to such propaganda from Islamabad in describing accounts issuing from the East as conflicting, and so refused to condemn the clampdown.[14] Nevertheless, the *New York Times* reported on its front page that Senator Edward Kennedy (Democrat, MA) had accused the US government of deliberately suppressing reports of indiscriminate killing. Although the senator refused to reveal his sources, his aides confirmed that Blood's telegrams were circulating widely in the Washington bureaucracy.[15]

In the absence of what they believed to be an appropriate Washington response, consular officers approached Blood on 6 April with a prepared message, titled "Dissent from US Policy toward East Pakistan," to which they had attached twenty signatures. In January 1969, Secretary of State William Rogers had informed all posts that the airing of divergent views was welcomed and had established a dissent channel and a task force to encourage greater openness. The consul general duly forwarded the message to State in Washington and the US embassy in Islamabad. Indeed, he added his own thoughts, concurring with the view expressed. The message argued that then-current US policy served "neither our moral interests broadly defined nor our national interests narrowly defined." The US government was "bending over backwards to placate the West Pak dominated Government" and had "evidenced what many will consider *moral bankruptcy*." Although the "overworked term *genocide* ... [was] applicable," and despite the latest Pakistan policy document describing US interests in the region as humanitarian, not strategic, the US government had wrongly chosen not to intervene on the grounds that the clampdown was an internal matter of a sovereign state.[16] That same day, nine junior officers from State's Pakistan desk signed a memorandum in support of Blood's position.[17]

Blood's actions created a considerable stir in Washington, for he had not only dissented but also neglected to give the telegram a high security rating. Roger Morris quotes "White House sources" that claimed Assistant Secretary of State (Near Eastern and South Asian Affairs) Joseph Sisco, on hearing of the dissent, telephoned National Security Advisor Henry Kissinger saying: "My people seem to be leaving the reservation."[18] As Rogers explained to Kissinger on the day the "goddam message" was received: "It's miserable. They bitched about our policy and have given it lots of distribution so it will probably leak. It's inexcusable ... You know we are doing everything we can about it. Trying to get the telegrams back as many as we can."[19] Thus, the US bureaucracy engaged in a clampdown of its own.

Sisco promptly called a meeting in which he made it clear to the junior officers dissenting in Washington that condemnation was "premature" and that he was not "buying."[20] Joseph Farland, US ambassador to Islamabad, ordered the consuls general in Karachi, Peshawar, and Lahore, whom Blood had placed on the distribution list, to destroy all copies;[21] the day after its receipt, State reclassified the offending article as *Secret*.[22] Sisco drafted an immediate reply on behalf of State, castigating Blood for not using a higher security clearance and noting that, while State was "naturally concerned at the reported loss of life," it remained "impossible for us to establish at this time ... any reliable set of facts regarding the recent events in the area."[23]

As Washington sought to hide behind the fog of war, Blood fired a second salvo. On 10 April 1971, he followed up his dissent telegram with a more specific explanation of his position. The consul general again referred to the latest Pakistan policy document to justify his stance, and argued that the East Pakistan crisis was not a distinctly internal issue owing, in part, to an international obligation to condemn genocide.[24] It should be remembered, however, that in 1971 the United States had not ratified the UN Genocide Convention and so had no legal duty to act, though its ethical obligation appeared to remain.

It is unclear to what extent the Washington clampdown was carried out to block leaks or to prevent embarrassment internally. The actions subsequently taken against Blood, however, appear far from reasonable. When he visited Islamabad to receive the Meritorious Honor Award for his actions after the cyclone, embassy officers gave him the impression they believed he had "clearly gone off the deep end."[25] Indeed, when meeting Kissinger in May, Farland was happy to dismiss Dacca reporting as "grossly exaggerating the amount of killing and bloodshed there." Unfortunately, the ambassador did not trouble himself to offer any specific, first-hand evidence to support his claim.[26] Nixon went beyond simply discrediting Blood; the president ordered the consul general's removal from his post, which the latter vacated on 5 June 1971.[27]

Interestingly, Blood was not the only person to lose his position. In a conversation between Nixon, Kissinger, and Farland on 28 July 1971, Farland observed:

> And the head of USIS [United States Information Service] was just as tendentious in his reporting. Got rid of him. Shakespeare [head of USIS] got him out ... The one remaining, who is very critical of the situation, this fellow Eric Griffel, who is head of AID [in Dacca, Agency for International Development], he will be out in September. I wish he were out now. I don't think you could pull him out without ... repercussions on the Hill.[28]

Nixon offered, encouragingly: "Sick bastards. You just keep right on after it on this thing."[29] Thus, after the issue of the dissent telegram, Nixon and Farland engaged in a concerted and deliberate policy of removal. Again, although it remains unclear whether this was to block leaks or to prevent embarrassment internally, it should be noted that the latter could be conveniently achieved under the justification of the former.

Before his enforced exit, however, Blood continued to provide regular reports on atrocities throughout East Pakistan. US citizens in Chittagong witnessed "numerous incidents of cold-blooded murder of unarmed Bengalis by Pak military."[30] Even more disturbingly, in April and May, Blood and his colleagues became convinced that the army was engaged in a campaign of ethnic cleansing against Hindus. Although they did not agree that a deliberate policy to expel the Hindu population existed, even the normally skeptical officers of the US embassy in Islamabad conceded that Hindus were being singled out for harsh treatment, and they were concerned over Pakistani government propaganda that blamed Hindus for their role in the crisis.[31] On 14 May, Blood filed a situation report titled "Slaughter of Hindus," in which he spoke of numerous reliable eyewitness accounts of the

Phase One Response 47

army targeting Hindu villages and killing all the adult males. Although he could not quantify the scale of the slaughter exactly, he suggested that the cumulative toll was in the thousands.[32] Five days later, he itemized systematic army attacks on Hindu villages reported by reliable witnesses, including members of the consular staff. The villages concerned were now deserted save for army and non-Bengali looters, over ten thousand victims having been forced into flight. Prophetically, Blood suggested that India's refugee problems were only just beginning.[33]

Just before leaving Dacca, Blood summarized the situation for Hindus as follows:

> Evidence of a systematic persecution of the Hindu population is too detailed and too massive to be ignored. While the Western mind boggles at [the] enormity of a possible planned eviction of ten million people, the fact remains that the officers and men of the Pak Army are behaving as if they have been given carte blanche to rid Pakistan of "these subversives" and they have been both encouraging and acquiescing in the persecution of Hindus by Biharis[34] and Muslim Bengalis. That many Hindu homes and villages have not only been looted, but also occupied by non-Hindus suggests that the Army intends the dislocation of Hindus to be permanent.[35]

It is not the purpose of this study to construct a case for ethnic cleansing or genocide committed against the Hindu population of East Pakistan. Nevertheless, Blood's reporting of the sustained and systematic targeting of Hindus in terms of their slaughter and removal through terror, the theft of their possessions and occupation of their homes, and the defamatory propaganda campaign orchestrated against them, suggests a *prima facie* case worthy of detailed investigation.

Blood and his colleagues sought to penetrate the fog of war and supply Washington with the supporting evidence of atrocities it would have needed should it have chosen to adopt a moral stance against "selective genocide" in East Pakistan. The detailed information they forwarded on a timely basis gave the White House the justification and opportunity for stronger action, which it failed to accept. Even as Blood and his colleagues strongly dissented from what they considered to be the US government's "moral bankruptcy," unwittingly sparking a minor rebellion at State along the way, more powerful forces were at work, intent on adopting a conciliatory line with Islamabad. They conveniently dismissed Blood's reports as exaggerated and unreliable, though subsequent events would prove this was not the case. Despite the deaf ear turned by the White House and Foggy Bottom, others were prepared to listen.[36]

Embassy in New Delhi: "Time When Principles Make Best Politics"

Kenneth Keating, the US ambassador to New Delhi, was one of the first to respond to the shocking news relayed by Blood.[37] The consul general had included the US embassy in India on the distribution list of his "Selective Genocide" telegram, and Keating promptly added his weight to the call for action. On 29 March, Keating described himself as "deeply shocked at [the] massacre by Pakistani military" and concurred with Blood that the United States should "publicly and prominently deplore this brutality" and "privately lay it on the line with GOP [the government of Pakistan]." Indeed, he went further than Blood, demanding that Washington announce the "unilateral abrogation of [the] one-time exception military supply agreement" and suspend all military deliveries. For, Keating observed, "*this is time when principles make best politics*."[38]

Perhaps Keating's most insightful contribution to the US policy debate, however, came two weeks later in a telegram titled "South Asian Realities and United States Interests." He declared:

> Some home truths are apparent: Pakistan is probably finished as a unified state; India is clearly the predominant actual and potential power in this area of the world; Bangla Desh with limited potential and massive problems is probably emerging. There is much the United States can do to promote its interests in South Asia and beyond by timely accommodation to these new realities ... The longer the hostilities continue, the more United States interests will be adversely affected.[39]

He continued to argue that inaction risked the radicalization of East Pakistan, international criticism of US military and economic support of West Pakistan, destruction and waste of resources in Pakistan as a whole, increased humanitarian relief costs, and the danger of escalation. The current US policy would not change Islamabad's attitude or end the hostilities quickly. Consequently, the United States ought to immediately adopt a policy of public condemnation and terminate military supply and economic assistance:

> In sum, the United States has interests in India, West Pakistan, and "Bangla Desh" which probably cannot be equally well served. Where the necessity

Phase One Response 49

for choice arises we should be guided by the new power realities in South Asia which fortunately in the present case largely parallel the moral realities as well.[40]

Yet, the National Security Council (NSC) staff, Nixon, and Kissinger, men normally preoccupied with the larger picture, were surprisingly reluctant to consider the effects of the clampdown on the region of South Asia as a whole.

On 16 April, NSC staff prepared a report to Kissinger that outlined recommendations on US policy during the crisis and relayed the opinions of the embassies in Islamabad and New Delhi.[41] Unlike Keating, Farland based his findings primarily on the consideration of domestic politics in Pakistan rather than on the regional picture. Yet NSC staff took the trouble to both abstract and attach the US ambassador to Islamabad's reasoning and recommendations, while simply appending the US ambassador to New Delhi's telegram (see above) to the report, dismissively observing that it contained only his "familiar views on this subject."[42]

As the crisis progressed, Nixon and Kissinger's attitude toward Keating and India became ever clearer. In a private Oval Office conversation between the first two, Nixon observed: "Look, even apart from the Chinese thing, I wouldn't do that [take a strong stance against Yahya] to help the Indians, the Indians are no goddamn good."[43] In a White House meeting between the president, his national security advisor, and the US ambassador to New Delhi, Keating attempted to explain the Indian position and his regional concerns over the crisis. Yet, Nixon and Kissinger simply railroaded him, Nixon declaring: "Like all of our other Indian ambassadors, he's been brainwashed," and asking Keating: "Where are your sandals?"[44]

Keating, like Blood, continued to champion a strong US policy during the key response period. Nevertheless, Nixon and Kissinger conveniently ignored his views, believing him to have been "taken over by the Indians."[45] Before the end of July, they even discussed the possibility of his removal.[46] Yet, while Keating was certainly sympathetic to India's predicament, there is little evidence to suggest that his concerns were anything other than legitimate and objective. Indeed, Keating was one of the few to fully consider the regional implications of the crisis, and his assessment of 12 April proved remarkably prophetic.[47]

Public Sphere
As the clampdown in Dacca began, the West Pakistani authorities confined all foreign journalists to the Intercontinental Hotel before seizing their

notes and film and deporting them the following day.[48] Only Simon Dring of the *Daily Telegraph* (London) and Arnold Zeitlin of Associated Press eluded the initial roundup for several days, but they too were soon expelled.[49] Consequently, the opportunities to report on the crisis in the international press were somewhat limited. Nevertheless, the deportees, evacuees, and, in due course, refugees from East Pakistan provided sufficient information to support regular and prominent articles in American newspapers, along with frequent discussion of US policy in editorials.

On 28 March, Sydney Schanberg, recently expelled from Dacca, reported on the front page of the *New York Times:* "The Pakistani Army is using artillery and heavy machine guns against unarmed East Pakistani civilians."[50] Two days later, the *Washington Post* relayed Simon Dring's report in the London press: top Awami League members arrested; hundreds dead and a mass grave at Dacca University halls of residence; hundreds more killed in the devastation as the army started fires and shot civilians in the old section of Dacca.[51] Reports of atrocities continued to receive prominent coverage.[52] Perhaps Anthony Mascarenhas of the *Sunday Times* (London) provided the most vivid portrayal in an award-winning article relayed to newspapers across the globe. Mascarenhas spent ten days in East Pakistan at the end of April, six of those days travelling with army officers based at Comilla. He witnessed, first-hand, campaigns against Hindus in "village to village and door to door" army "kill and burn missions." Uncircumcised Hindu males were bludgeoned, shot, and loaded onto trucks for disposal, their villages razed to the ground. Mascarenhas declared: "This is *genocide* conducted with amazing casualness."[53]

A *New York Times* editorial on 31 March called on the US government to demand an end to the bloodshed, withhold all military supplies, and allow economic aid only if a major portion were allocated to relief in East Pakistan.[54] On 7 April, it declared: "On any basis, the United States would have a humanitarian duty to speak out against the bloodbath in Bengal."[55] Press condemnation of the US government's stance continued throughout the key response period and became particularly vocal in June, when the *New York Times* revealed that US military supplies were still being delivered to Pakistan, despite State Department assurances to the contrary.[56] Thus, despite Yahya's attempts to prevent independent press access to East Pakistan, and Islamabad's official propaganda, the American press still managed to make knowledge of the atrocities widely available to the American public and generally adopted editorial stances at variance with US government policy.

Phase One Response 51

Many American intellectuals joined the newspapers in support of the Bengali victims. Crisis committees were formed at several universities, the most energetic being at Harvard, Chicago, Berkeley, Washington, and New York, where activities included symposia, seminars, fundraising, and the writing of press articles and letters to Congress. In early April 1971, several groups of intellectuals spoke out on the atrocities. Members of the Bangladesh League of US Scholars, in Washington, demanded US action to halt what they called "genocide" and White House recognition of the Bangladeshi government-in-exile that had formed in India. The Association for Asian Studies urged the Pakistani government to end the destruction and the US government to provide humanitarian relief. In addition, a group of Harvard economists, including Edward S. Mason, Robert Dorfman, and Stephen Marglin, called on the US government to cease all military and economic aid to Pakistan until Islamabad withdrew its forces from the East. In due course, over two dozen American intellectuals combined to issue a statement condemning Islamabad's actions and urging a return to legitimate, responsible government.[57]

The month of April also saw the formation of Bangladesh associations at several US locations where concentrations of East Bengali students and expatriates could be found. These included the University of Indiana, Stanford, and Texas A&M campuses and the cities of Los Angeles, Boston, and Washington. By June 1971, such associations had been established in fourteen US cities. Of these, the Bangladesh Information Center, Washington, and the Friends of East Bengal, Philadelphia, were the two most prominent. Their activities were similar to those of the student crisis committees and included educational, publicity, and fundraising work, through news bulletins, public lectures, teach-in programs, and lobbying.[58]

Acutely aware of the reports of atrocities in the press and of Blood's telegrams circulating within State, members of Congress quickly moved to influence the US government's position.[59] On 1 April, Senator Kennedy called on the US government and Republican leadership to denounce the "indiscriminate killing,"[60] while Senator Fred R. Harris (Democrat, OK) demanded the immediate suspension of all US military and economic aid to Pakistan.[61] Two weeks later, Senators Walter Mondale (Democrat, MN) and Clifford Case (Republican, NJ) introduced a Senate resolution calling for the suspension of all military sales. On 4 May, Mondale joined nine other senators in writing to Rogers to demand that the latter ensure that the United States voted against providing foreign exchange assistance to Islamabad at Pakistan aid consortium talks,[62] unless Islamabad mounted an immediate and appropriate relief effort and Red Cross workers were allowed access to the East.[63]

Bipartisan congressional support for a stronger US stance continued throughout the key response period,[64] and Kennedy remained particularly vocal concerning the need for humanitarian relief.[65] After returning from a visit to the camps in India, on 10 June Representative Cornelius E. Gallagher (Democrat, NJ) announced the presence of some five million refugees and insisted that the United States immediately cease all military and economic aid to Pakistan.[66] On 15 June, he introduced House Resolution 9160 with a view to securing his demands.[67] This was a reflection of the Senate's proposed William B. Saxbe (Republican, OH)–Frank Church (Democrat, ID) amendment to the Foreign Assistance Act, which aimed to block all military and economic aid until the return to East Pakistan of the refugees in India. An NSC paper of 30 July noted that, in addition to those congressmen specifically mentioned above, Senator Edmund Muskie (Democrat, ME) and Representative John E. Moss (Democrat, CA) had been "particularly outspoken in their criticism of the Administration's policy."[68]

In the US public sphere, the press relayed news of the atrocities and generally demanded a firmer government stance. Intellectuals and rapidly formed Bangladesh associations called for official condemnation and, often, for further action in terms of the suspension of economic and military aid to Islamabad. In addition, both Republican and Democratic congressmen lent their voices in support of the victims in East Pakistan and the refugees in India. By the end of the key response period, several House and Senate resolutions had been tabled to restrict the powers of the US executive in determining its response. The public pressure on the White House was considerable. Yet, as with the protestations of Blood and Keating, Nixon and Kissinger again chose largely to ignore the furor.

Let's Not Bother

Embassy in Islamabad: Inertia
Throughout the key response period, and even during phase one, when Farland had no knowledge whatsoever of the China initiative, the US embassy in Islamabad proved reluctant to adopt either a moral or a forceful stance with regard to East Pakistan. Consequently, the formation of opinion there sheds light on how readily some US government officials and executives were able to justify a policy of inaction, even without being aware of an arguably more important global objective.

Phase One Response

US ambassador to Islamabad Joseph Farland was a Republican political appointee who had assumed his post in September 1969. He was a lawyer and former FBI agent, and had served previously as US ambassador to Panama and to Santo Domingo.[69] Although the last US policy paper on Pakistan had been prepared as far back as 1964, it took Farland until February 1971 to proffer a replacement.[70] Noting the lack of American political and economic interests in the country, he concluded merely: "Our primary objective is to maintain and, to the extent feasible, improve the ... relationship we have with Pakistan."[71] Like everyone else, Farland had failed to predict the Awami League success in the general election, and, on the evening of 25 March, he too was unaware of the impending clampdown in the East.[72]

Farland had received copies of Blood's atrocity reports, including "Selective Genocide." Yet on 31 March, in discussing his preliminary reaction to the crisis, he first displayed the moral apathy that he exhibited throughout the key response period. While admitting that "we can hold no brief" for what he conceded appeared to be a "brutal, ruthless and excessive use of force by Pak military," he declared:

> Since we are not only human beings but also government servants, however, righteous indignation is not of itself an adequate basis for our reaction to the events now occurring in East Pakistan ... The struggle is between Pakistani and Pakistani ... [and the] problems remain essentially internal to Pakistan ... *We believe firmly that we should keep our options open so as to be able to promote our interests as events continue to unfold.*[73]

He confirmed in a telegram six days later that the issue was "an internal affair of Pakistan and should remain so." In addition, he observed: "We have shared the disinclination, felt by many Americans today, over a USG [US government] involvement in a situation where US interests are not clearly and directly at stake." He went on to suggest that a statement of US sympathy with the people of Pakistan, combined with the private use of Nixon's "excellent" relationship with Yahya, was the appropriate way for the US response to proceed.[74] Adopting a realist attitude in the absence of any immediate threat to US interests, Farland helped lower the veil of Pakistani domestic sovereignty over East Pakistan in the hope of obscuring the ugliness of the crisis and any consequent need to act. Any mention in detail of the atrocities perpetrated or of the regional context was conspicuous by its absence from these and many subsequent reports from the US embassy in Islamabad.

On 13 April, a further telegram from Farland provided greater insight into his motivation for inaction. He revealed that a strong stance would "reduce to [a] minimum, if not eliminate entirely, our influence with GOP [government of Pakistan]."[75] Just over a week later, Farland again revealed his concerns that a more forceful policy would risk undermining US-Pakistan relations to the extent that "the duties of ... [his] post could well be turned over to a chargé d'affaires."[76] Again, on each occasion, he failed to discuss the atrocities in detail and viewed the crisis solely within its domestic context rather than the regional situation.[77]

Farland's reaction calls to mind Zygmunt Bauman's argument concerning the role of the modern bureaucrat in the Holocaust. Drawing on the work of Max Weber, who had identified the growing rule of reason as a central attribute of modernity, Bauman contended that modern, rational bureaucracy demanded efficiency, loyalty, compliance, and discipline under authority. The resulting substitution of technical for moral responsibility defused the conscience of the individual, leading to the social production of moral indifference toward victims. In addition, the hierarchical and functional divisions of labour combined with the dehumanizing quantification of victims as bureaucratic objects to create a distance between administrator and victim that removed the ethical inhibition of the former and rendered the latter morally invisible in the eyes of otherwise rational officials.[78]

Bauman used his contention to explain the moral apathy exhibited by German bureaucrats in perpetrating the Holocaust. Yet his argument concerning the substitution of technical for moral responsibility under the bureaucratic process appears to apply equally well to those engaged in determining third-party responses. It is not suggested that Farland had no legitimate reason to adopt a conciliatory approach toward the government of Pakistan. Nevertheless, the ambassador's blinkered focus on his own immediate technical responsibilities, as manifested in his concentration on maintaining working relations with the West Pakistanis, the fear of his post becoming trivial, and his domestic rather than regional outlook[79] combine with the frequent invisibility of East Pakistani victims in his reports to suggest that Farland in many ways behaved as a morally apathetic administrator, caught in the headlights of modern, rational bureaucracy.

One further motivation also came into play. During phase two, at a meeting in Palm Springs on 7 May, Kissinger informed Farland of the China initiative and charged the ambassador with arranging his secret trip. Farland voiced "mild complaints about living in Pakistan and expressed the hope that

Phase One Response 55

if the China meeting came off successfully, a new post could be offered."[80] Nixon appointed Farland US ambassador to Tehran in May 1972.[81]

Department of State: Carrots and Sticks
If Blood and Keating preferred to threaten Yahya, and Farland wished to entice him, then the State Department sought to offer both carrot and stick. On the one hand, as Christopher Van Hollen has argued,[82] State believed that the crisis would be resolved only if Yahya were encouraged through private diplomatic channels to offer genuine political concessions in the East.[83] On the other hand, however, State was prepared to support such encouragement through the application of pressure in limiting military and economic aid to the government of Pakistan.[84]

State's willingness to use its stick placed it at odds with the White House. Indeed, as Kissinger observed in his memoirs, "on no issue – except perhaps Cambodia – was the spilt between the White House and the departments so profound as on the India-Pakistan crisis in the summer of 1971."[85] The friction began almost immediately as State unilaterally banned the issuance and renewal of munitions supply licences to Pakistan as the crisis broke out.[86] Only pressure from Congress and the American public compelled Nixon to subsequently accept State's decision.[87] By July, Kissinger was so frustrated at State's continuing wish to see an end to the trickle of military supplies under licences issued before the ban that, in the middle of a Senior Review Group (SRG) meeting, he ranted: "The President always says to tilt toward Pakistan, but every proposal I get is in the opposite direction. Sometimes I think I am in a nut house."[88]

In his memoirs, Kissinger preferred to attribute the unauthorized ban on new and renewed licences to State's "traditional Indian bias."[89] In contrast, Van Hollen insists that the views at State were based on genuine concern over the risk to US relations with India and abhorrence that US weaponry was being used against the Bengalis.[90] Despite ongoing disagreements with Nixon and Kissinger's policy, however, State generally complied with White House demands. In addition, it collaborated in sweeping Blood's message of dissent under the carpet and colluded in the removal of the consul general from his post.

White House: Do Nothing
In his memoirs, Kissinger noted: "At the beginning of 1971 none of our senior policymakers expected the subcontinent to jump to the top of our agenda. It seemed to require no immediate decisions except annual aid

programs and relief efforts."[91] Indeed, only Joel Woldman, a South Asia specialist at the Pakistan desk of State's Bureau of Intelligence and Research, had suggested that a military clampdown was likely, but his report of December 1970 was duly ignored.[92]

Nevertheless, an awareness of the possibility of secession had been circulating in Washington since the announcement of the Pakistani election results becoming a matter of ever-greater concern as talks between Yahya, Zulfikar Ali Bhutto, and Mujibur Rahman continued to make little progress. On 16 February 1971, Kissinger issued National Security Study Memorandum (NSSM) 118, requesting an interagency study of US options should the East attempt to secede.[93] At an SRG meeting on 6 March, Kissinger described the subsequent reply, prepared under the chairmanship of Joseph Sisco, as a "very good paper."[94]

The report reaffirmed that, as an independent East Pakistan would be "more vulnerable to internal instability, economic stagnation and external subversion ... our consistent position has been that US interests are better served by a unified Pakistan." This was more so the case as the East also provided "a moderating influence over West Pakistani hostility toward India." Despite having "no realistic alternative" but to support unity if it wished to maintain satisfactory relations with Islamabad, the report noted that the United States "*should be able to adjust to the emergence of two separate states ... without serious damage to our interests*"; both new entities would wish to maintain ties with the United States in order to balance their relations with China and to continue receiving economic and military assistance. Consequently, while separation remained uncertain, the United States ought to maintain its ongoing position of expressing support for unity and continuing to suggest that the issue was an internal matter for Pakistan to resolve. If separation should appear imminent, however, then the United States ought to work closely with both East and West, letting the leaders of the former know that Washington would be prepared to recognize an independent East Pakistan. Importantly, given the size of Pakistani armed forces in the East relative to the vast local population, the report concluded that military intervention by West Pakistan was "very unlikely," and recommended: "*We should be willing to risk irritating the West Pakistanis in the face of such a rash act on their part, and the threat of stopping aid should give us considerable leverage.*"[95] Thus, the "very good paper," discussed less than three weeks before the clampdown occurred, observed that the United States was quite able to adjust to a divided Pakistan, without risk to its interests, and should act strongly to discourage any attempt by Islamabad to

Phase One Response 57

hold the country together by the use of force. Such advice, however, though apparently much appreciated at the time it was given, would be rapidly rejected at the time of its possible use.

Kissinger firmly believed, both before and during the crisis, that force would not hold Pakistan together, a view that reflected the position of the SRG.[96] Thus, on 26 March, when Kissinger informed Nixon that "the West Pakistani army has moved to repress the East Pakistan secession movement," he shared the same sense of shock experienced by Blood, Farland, State, and the international community in general at Yahya's imprudent course of action.[97] At the hastily convened Washington Special Actions Group (WSAG) meeting later that day, Kissinger explained: "I have no idea what caused the breakdown in talks. I was as much surprised as anyone else."[98]

On the day news of the crisis reached desks in Washington, Kissinger observed:

> I talked to the President briefly before lunch. His inclination is the same as everybody else's. He doesn't want to do anything. He doesn't want to be in the position where he can be accused of having encouraged the split-up of Pakistan. He does not favor a very active policy. This probably means that we would not undertake to warn Yahya against a civil war.[99]

Participants at the same WSAG meeting agreed – the US "should continue its policy of non-involvement."[100] Kissinger made his statement in front of officials before whom he could not mention the China initiative, yet even in private, he and Nixon adopted the same line. In a telephone conversation between the two only four days later, Nixon explained: "The main thing to do is to keep cool and not do anything. There's nothing in it for us either way." Neither mentioned the China initiative.[101] Consequently, the United States failed even to condemn the slaughter and, instead, limited its public statements to expressions of concern over the loss of life and calls for a peaceful resolution. Although it did protest over the expulsion of all foreign journalists from the East and privately expressed alarm that American weapons were being used on Bengali civilians, the United States also made a point of defeating Indian attempts to bring the crisis to the attention of the United Nations Security Council.[102] Nixon and Kissinger successfully avoided creating a rift between Washington and Islamabad, but their actions were consistent with neither the recommendations found in the response to NSSM 118 nor the position adopted by many in the US press and Congress.

The only area in which the United States proved quick to act was in the evacuation of its own citizens. At the WSAG emergency meeting on 26 March, State received instructions to make preparations for a mass exodus, should it become necessary.[103] Following Blood's recommendations, supported by Farland, the evacuation of all except essential officials began on 4 April 1971.[104] Even this action, however, was characterized as a "thin-out" so as not to offend Islamabad.[105]

As a largely unprepared White House considered its position, India led the ensuing barrage of international condemnation of Yahya's actions. On 31 March, Prime Minister Indira Gandhi expressed her "deep anguish and grave concern at recent developments" and alleged that a "massive attack by armed forces, despatched from West Pakistan, has been unleashed against the entire people of East Bengal with a view to suppressing their urges and aspirations."[106] Even the Soviets, not noted for their championing of human rights issues, backed their Indian ally, demanding an end to the bloodshed on 2 April.[107] One would have expected the United States, caught unprepared, to adopt the recommendations contained in the response to NSSM 118 and join with other governments in firing a further volley of condemnation in the direction of Islamabad. Instead, Nixon and Kissinger opted to lie low.[108]

An NSC paper for an SRG meeting on 19 April, which was discussed there in full knowledge of Blood's atrocity reports, reassessed US options with regard to the crisis. It concluded that "Pakistan as a unitary state cannot survive," and considered how, despite the United States' having "no vital security interest in South Asia as a whole," Washington might maintain "constructive" relations with Islamabad, work "cooperatively" with East Pakistan, and "support ... [its] relatively greater interest in India." Noting that the United States provided one-quarter of Pakistan's external aid, supplied military spares, and was processing the one-time exception arms package,[109] the report observed that the United States could *probably affect the course, direction, and pace of political negotiations.* This was especially the case as US leverage was at that time enhanced because of Pakistan's low foreign exchange reserves, which "could be exhausted within a few months unless international relief ... [was] forthcoming," the World Bank and International Monetary Fund being reluctant to provide further assistance.[110]

Without pressing a particular strategy, the paper outlined three options: "hands-off," "selective influence," and "all-out effort." The last of these had the advantages of encouraging better relations with East Pakistan and, importantly, India and reducing the likelihood of a protracted war.

Nevertheless, it risked rupture of ties with Islamabad, ran counter to US policy of non-interference in "internal affairs," and increased the opportunity for radical and Chinese influence in the West wing. Such an all-out effort would have involved: a strong letter to Yahya, indicating no discussion of political or military assistance until the bloodshed had ended and negotiations resumed; public criticism of Pakistani army actions; recognition of Bangladesh once the Bengalis had gained substantial control; cancellation of the one-time exception package and military supply of ammunition and spares for lethal end items; suspension of all "unobligated" economic assistance until negotiations were underway; provision of humanitarian relief; and denial of debt relief assistance.[111] Clearly, the United States had a wealth of options at its disposal, yet the SRG avoided making a recommendation. Instead, unwilling to commit to a decision, the participants agreed to seek Nixon's guidance.[112] Washington continued to drag its feet until the end of April, when, triggered by the resurgence of the China initiative, the White House finally formulated a clearer policy.

White House: Smoke, Mirrors, and Motives

A complex web of motives influenced the US president and his national security advisor during phase one of the US response, and various techniques were employed to avoid doing more than necessary. As discussed above, Archer Blood's inconvenient reports of atrocities were characterized as unreliable, and Keating was dismissed as having been "taken over by the Indians."[113] Thus, with the added assistance of propaganda from the government of Pakistan, which portrayed the rapid emergence of stability and calm, the United States sidestepped pressure to take a stronger official line by pointing to conflicting evidence swathed in the fog of war.

In addition, the administration was happy to draw down the veil of sovereignty over what it portrayed as a Pakistani domestic issue. Yahya did not conceal his appreciation, and he gushed in a letter to Nixon of 17 April: "I am deeply gratified that your Government has made it clear ... that the United States recognises the current events in East Pakistan as an internal affair."[114] As Samantha Power argues, the "UN charter had made noninterference in sovereign states a sacred principle,"[115] and this point had certainly not been lost on Kissinger. He contended in his memoirs: "For better or worse, the strategy of the Nixon administration on humanitarian questions was not to lay down a challenge to sovereignty that would surely be rejected, but to exert our influence without public confrontation."[116] While respect for domestic sovereignty as a pillar of international law was often strangely absent from Nixon and Kissinger's policy decisions in Cambodia, Laos, and Vietnam, among other countries, it provided a convenient justification for inertia in South Asia.

As discussed above, despite the recognition by both Keating and NSC staff of relatively greater US interests in India, Nixon and Kissinger focused on the domestic rather than regional aspect of the crisis during phase one. By failing to fully address the emergency in its more complex regional form, the president and his national security advisor again minimized the need to develop a more proactive policy. Thus, the fog of war, the veil of sovereignty, and the domestic focus, combined with the inertia inherent in large-scale government bureaucracies to facilitate the lethargic formulation of a much-limited US response.

Importantly, during phase one, the China initiative was not mentioned in Nixon and Kissinger's private correspondence or recorded private telephone calls that directly discussed US interests in Pakistan. During a face-to-face conversation in the Oval Office, on 13 April 1971, in the presence of White House Chief of Staff H.R. Haldeman, Nixon and Kissinger did discuss, in passing, the relationship between Islamabad and Peking. Nixon, apparently unaware of China's position, casually inquired: "Is China backing Yahya?" Kissinger replied: "That's why we mustn't go into it." The president agreed that Washington should remain uninvolved. More than two weeks after the onset of the clampdown in East Pakistan, Nixon was only just beginning to show a passing interest in its possible impact on the China initiative, which remained only a background concern until phase two of the key response period.[117] Given this, what were the real reasons underlying the Nixon-Kissinger response during phase one? A number of factors are apparent. The president and his national security advisor shared a world view based in realism, as opposed to moral idealism, and on avoiding direct US intervention in international affairs, except in the cause of preserving important American national interests.[118] As NSC papers made clear before and during April, no such interests existed in South Asia, so Nixon and Kissinger felt little urge to act. Kissinger described this position succinctly on 12 April: "There's nothing for us there to take sides in this."[119] In addition, several more specific reasons came into play.

Beyond occasional general references to the bloodshed, discussion of the atrocities and victims of the crisis remained conspicuously absent from the statements of Nixon and Kissinger throughout the key response period. Such moral apathy is particularly noticeable in several comments

Phase One Response 61

by Kissinger immediately following the clampdown. On 29 March, the day after Blood sent his "Selective Genocide" telegram, Nixon inquired during a private telephone conversation: "Got anything on the wires or anything of interest?" Kissinger replied indifferently: "There's nothing of any great consequence Mr. President. Apparently Yahya has got control of East Pakistan."[120] Two days later, at an SRG meeting, in response to a comment on the large number of people killed at Dacca University, Kissinger observed: "They didn't dominate 400 million Indians all those years by being gentle."[121] By the end of July, in a strange perversion of logic, a morally indifferent Nixon had even gone so far as to call those who dissented from official US policy the "sick bastards."[122]

When Nixon came to office, he inherited a comparable human rights crisis from his predecessor, Lyndon Johnson. On the campaign trail, Nixon had called for a determined relief effort to aid the victims of the Biafran emergency.[123] On reaching the White House, he immediately initiated a policy review of the US position, which embraced public neutrality and limited relief aid, Washington having already imposed an arms embargo on both sides. Yet, despite his concerns for the plight of the victims, the new president decided not to change course beyond increasing humanitarian assistance; US neutrality was maintained despite Nixon's sympathy for the Biafrans.[124] Thus, even in the face of moral concern, realism held sway. Given the president's relative indifference to the suffering of East Pakistani victims, he was never likely to take a firm ethical stance in the spring of 1971. Moreover, he had a profound liking for Yahya.

Despite their reputations as "hard-boiled" realists, Nixon and Kissinger "often permitted personal feelings about foreign leaders to color their national security decisions."[125] The president exhibited a fondness for Yahya and an empathy with Pakistan. In contrast, he disliked Indira Gandhi and had little time for India, a non-aligned country that attracted sympathy from rival Democrats. Nixon had visited Pakistan on no fewer than six occasions, including once as president,[126] and had been received with respect there while he was out of office. Kissinger claims that "he never forgot this."[127] Such warmth had manifested itself in the extension of the one-time exception arms deal in October 1970 and, as Kissinger reminded those attending an SRG meeting on 9 April, Nixon continued to maintain "a special feeling about Yahya."[128] In contrast, according to the national security advisor, India remained "subject to Presidential indifference," and Nixon's comments after meeting Indira Gandhi were "not always printable."[129] As the president himself put it somewhat more forcefully in a private conversation of 4 June: "I wouldn't do that [take a strong stance against Yahya] to help the Indians, the Indians are no goddamn good."[130]

The Nixon-Kissinger initial response, therefore, appears to have been based on moral apathy, wrapped in a fondness for Yahya and Pakistan, and covered in a thick skin of realist philosophy. Adding to these factors was the desire to buy time and a reluctance to act precipitately. Although the China initiative hovered in the background, it was not yet of major concern.

The China Initiative Springs to Life

In his memoirs, Kissinger groped for a simple, acceptable justification for White House indifference with regard to East Pakistan and found it in the convenient catch-all explanation of the China initiative – a strategic project in pursuit of a more stable, peaceful world. In trying to stretch this explanation to cover phase one of the crisis, however, Kissinger's argument became both confused and confusing. In the chapter dedicated to the China initiative itself, he noted that, in January 1971, of the *two* active conduits to Peking, the White House had only a "slight preference for the Pakistani channel."[131] Yet, 150 pages later, in a separate section dedicated to the discussion of East Pakistan, the former national security advisor identified one of his two major tasks throughout April as preserving the Pakistani conduit, the "*sole* channel" to Peking.[132] Given that nothing had been heard from the Chinese through either conduit since the January assessment, Kissinger had no obvious legitimate reason to promote the importance of the Islamabad connection to such an extent later in his memoirs. Yet, he did not offer any justification for this quite marked inconsistency and convenient change of emphasis. One feels compelled to ask, therefore, when the Pakistani channel became important.

Sino-American relations continued to improve in early 1971 when, in a gesture referred to as "Ping-Pong diplomacy," Peking invited members of the US table tennis team to visit China, where they were received by Chou En-lai on 14 April. In reply, that same day, the United States announced that it would be taking steps to ease the twenty-year embargo on trade with China, to expedite visas for Chinese visitors to the United States, and to relax currency controls.[133] Despite this public dance, however, the Chinese had not made use of the back channels since the start of the year. Peking had last employed the Romanian channel to deliver a message that arrived on 11 January, and Nixon and Kissinger had not heard anything via the Pakistani conduit since receipt of Chou's message on 9 December the previous year – a full four months earlier (Chapter 1). Kissinger was anxious at having received no response, and for good reason.[134] Beginning 8 February, the United States and South Vietnam had engaged in a joint offensive in Southern Laos, the former providing logistical, artillery, and air support for the latter's ground troops. Only the previous year, a similar American incursion into Cambodia had so antagonized the Chinese that they had cancelled scheduled Warsaw talks (Chapter 1). Fearing for the China initiative, on 27 April Kissinger sent urgent instructions to Jean Sainteny to approach the Chinese ambassador to Paris with a view to establishing an alternative means of secret communication.[135] Throughout phase one of the crisis, and for several months beforehand, therefore, far from operating as a crucial link to Peking, the Pakistani channel had been a disappointment, so much so that, toward the end of April, Kissinger had actively sought a substitute arrangement.

In addition, up to this point, there had been merely an invitation for a US envoy to discuss only Taiwan. China had not agreed to the broad agenda on which Nixon and Kissinger had insisted.[136] Indeed, on 11 January, when Kissinger received the message from Chou through the Romanian channel, the missive had served to emphasize China's sole focus on that matter: "The communication from the US President is not new. *There is only one outstanding issue between us – the US occupation of Taiwan.*"[137] To such determined realists, neither the China initiative itself nor the Pakistani channel were sufficiently well developed to be dominant factors in influencing the US response during phase one. At this stage, the China initiative had not been mentioned in Nixon and Kissinger's private correspondence or recorded private telephone conversations that directly discussed US interests in Pakistan. It is conspicuous by its absence.

Matters soon changed, however, after a watershed event on 27 April 1971. On the very same day that Kissinger sought to create a new conduit through Paris, Chou responded to Nixon's message of 16 December, dropping China's insistence on limiting talks to only Taiwan and inviting an envoy or even Nixon himself to Peking. Agha Hilaly, the Pakistani ambassador to Washington, delivered the Chinese reply to Kissinger personally. The arrangements for the proposed trip, Chou suggested, should be made through the president of Pakistan: "The Chinese Government reaffirms its willingness to receive publicly in Peking a special envoy of the President of the US ... or even the President of the US himself ... It is entirely possible for public arrangements to be made through the good offices of President Yahya Khan."[138] Nixon and Kissinger took this as clear confirmation of Chinese preference for the Pakistani channel and immediately stopped delivery of the message to Paris.[139] The game of smoke and mirrors had ended; the secret China initiative had suddenly sprung to life.[140] It was from this point forward that it played a prominent, and ever more dominant, role in the formulation of the US response to the East Pakistan crisis. The die was cast: the China initiative was alive and well, and Islamabad would now move to centre stage.

Nixon and Kissinger referred to the receipt of the Chinese missive in terms more usually associated with descriptions of religious ecstasy. In his memoirs, Kissinger portrays himself as having "experienced, amid the excitement, a moment of elation and inner peace," while Nixon was apparently "excited to the point of euphoria at the prospect before us."[141] Indeed, in a private conversation at the time, Kissinger admitted: "Mr. President, I have not said this before but I think if we get this thing working, we will end Vietnam this year."[142] Clearly, little would be allowed to stand in the way of this suddenly revitalized strategic initiative.

Before leaving on vacation the next day, Kissinger swung into action and accomplished three important things. First, he handed Hilaly an interim reply.[143] Second, he sent Nixon a memorandum outlining three packages of policy options on East Pakistan. He emphatically recommended, despite acknowledging the risk to future relations with India and East Pakistan, that the US continue economic aid, back the Pakistan aid consortium finance initiative, and provide food assistance. Moreover, he advised the continuation of military supplies but, "in order not to provoke the Congress to force cutting off all [military] aid," the withholding of shipments of "more controversial items." On 2 May, Nixon duly initialled his approval of Kissinger's recommendation and added the now famous handwritten comment: "*To all hands: Don't* squeeze Yahya at this time." The word "don't" was underlined three times.[144]

Whereas Nixon's "Squeeze" memorandum is well known, one important fact about it has generally remained hidden. For, as noted above, Kissinger took a third action before leaving on vacation. In the words of his deputy, Alexander Haig, in a memorandum to Nixon: "Henry has suggested, for reasons which you and he only are aware of, that *it would be most helpful if in approving this paper* [the 'Squeeze' memorandum] *you could include a note to the effect that you want no actions taken at this time which would squeeze West Pakistan.*"[145] This short extract not only ties "Squeeze" policy specifically to both Kissinger and Nixon but also directly links the China initiative to the first clear elaboration of East Pakistan policy, issued one month into the crisis but immediately after the receipt of Chou's message. During May

Phase One Response 65

and June, Nixon and Kissinger finally began to refer to the China initiative, sometimes obliquely, in private conversations on South Asian policy,[146] for only in phase two of the key response period did it come to dominate White House thinking.

Why did Kissinger, in his memoirs, contradict himself in describing the viability of the Romanian channel? Why did Nixon and Kissinger, when discussing East Pakistan in private telephone conversations before the watershed event, not also consider the impact of the clampdown on their China initiative? Why did Nixon, if concerned about the China initiative, not issue his "Squeeze" memorandum one month earlier, instead of waiting until immediately after Chou's reply of 27 April 1971? Why did Nixon and Kissinger not demonstrate a sense of euphoria on receipt of Chou's earlier missive in December 1970, instead of doing so more than four months later? Only by discounting Kissinger's attempt to use the China initiative as a catch-all justification and, instead, recognizing the two distinct phases of the key response period is it possible to satisfactorily answer these otherwise difficult questions and thus provide a comprehensive, more nuanced explanation of changing White House motivations in the formulation of US policy on East Pakistan during the spring of 1971.

3

Phase Two Response

Phase two of the key response period began on 27 April 1971, when President Nixon and Henry Kissinger received Chou En-lai's message, and lasted until 15 July, when the president announced the China initiative to the world. During this time, a wave of East Pakistani refugees flooded into India in pursuit of safety, pushing the subcontinent toward war. As the reasons for the United States to take a stronger line with Islamabad steadily mounted, however, so did Nixon and Kissinger's dependence on Pakistani president Yahya Khan for facilitating Kissinger's increasingly likely secret trip to Peking. As phase two progressed, the United States continued to place its China eggs into Yahya's welcoming basket.

Let's "Shake the World"

Refugees and Relief
Between the end of April and the middle of July 1971, around six million East Bengali refugees fled to safety in India, terrorized into escaping their homeland by the activities of the Pakistani army. Before the crisis was resolved in December, some ten million internationally displaced persons had inundated northern India in one of the greatest exoduses in modern history.[1] Table 3.1 summarizes the scale of the human catastrophe.

In early May, over 100,000 people per day swept across the Indo-Pakistan border, but the rate of flow only peaked a month later at 150,000, the

Table 3.1 East Pakistani refugees arriving in India, 1971

Date	Cumulative number (millions)	Net increase (millions)	Average daily increase (thousands)
17 April	0.1	0.1	4.5
1 May	0.9	0.8	57.1
15 May	2.4	1.5	107.1
29 May	3.7	1.3	92.9
12 June	5.8	2.1	150.0
26 June	6.3	0.5	35.7
10 July	6.7	0.4	28.6
28 August	8.3	1.6	32.7

Note: This table is constructed using statistics provided by the Indian Ministry of External Affairs.

Source: Bangla Desh Documents (New Delhi: Ministry of External Affairs, 1971), 446.

equivalent of over 6,000 people arriving every hour of the day and night.[2] US ambassador to New Delhi Kenneth Keating provided an analogy well suited to American minds: of the 5 million refugees in northern India in mid-June, some 3 million had descended on Calcutta, a city the size of New York.[3] The problem was vast.

The mixture of Hindu and Muslim refugees proved particularly revealing. At the start of the crisis, the total population of East Pakistan was some 75 million,[4] of which 85 percent were Muslim and 15 percent Hindu.[5] Consequently, one would have expected 3 Hindu refugees to have fled for every 17 Muslims. As the response to National Security Study Memorandum (NSSM) 133 of July noted, however, Hindus made up some 75 percent of the refugee population of 6 million[6] – not 3 but 51 Hindus had fled for every 17 Muslims, a ratio seventeen times higher than would normally have been anticipated. Some 4.5 million of the 11.3 million Hindus in East Pakistan had fled, representing 40 percent of the total Hindu population, compared with only 2 percent of East Pakistani Muslims. The initial flow of refugees had been in proportion to population mix,[7] yet by early June, 90 percent of those leaving were Hindu,[8] a ratio over fifty times higher than expected. While it is not suggested that the above figures are exact, they clearly lend weight to the evidence already discussed for *prima facie* cases of ethnic cleansing and possible genocide perpetrated against the Hindu population of East Bengal, as noted in Chapter 2.

Archer Blood highlighted the systematic persecution of Hindus in the atrocity reports he filed before leaving Dacca. In mid-May, even Joseph Farland, the US ambassador to Islamabad, observed that "Punjab is colored by an emotional anti-Hindu bias." Propaganda issued by the government of Pakistan stressed a perceived Hindu role in creating the crisis in the East, and the army was clearly "singling out Hindus for especially harsh treatment."[9] On 22 May, and again on 5 June, Farland confronted Yahya with evidence of "Hindu villages being attacked by the army."[10] The ambassador made it clear that, if true, such tactics "would make it difficult for the Nixon administration to continue to support Pakistan," but Yahya denied any such policy.[11] The US government duly swept this difficult issue under the carpet.

Unfortunately, even by mid-June, Nixon had not quite fully understood the scale of the refugee problem. Nor did he appear particularly sympathetic. A conversation on refugee numbers between Nixon, Kissinger, and Keating amply demonstrated both the president's ignorance and his callous attitude:

NIXON: "What is it, 300,000?"
KISSINGER: "No, it's about –"
KEATING: "Five million. And add that it's in a crowded part of India."
NIXON: "Sorry, it was 300,000 we were feeding."
KEATING: "That's right. That's correct. About five million, and of that about three of them –"
NIXON: "*Why don't they shoot them?*"[12]

There would appear little left to add.

Nevertheless, the United States did lend substantial support to the international relief effort that the United Nations organized, but which long remained subject to Indian and Pakistani insistence on exclusive control of key aspects of operations. At the end of April, when some 900,000 refugees had already arrived in India, Nixon approved the first tranche of US assistance – a US\$2.4 million package comprising US\$1.4 million worth of food and US\$1.0 million in other aid.[13] This amounted to US\$2.67 per refugee, but marked only the beginning of what became a substantial flow of American aid for humanitarian relief.

By 18 May, the United States had assumed responsibility for feeding 300,000 people but, owing to a surge in the exodus, this represented only

Phase Two Response 69

three days of newcomers.[14] At the end of the month, Nixon offered Indira Gandhi a further US$15 million worth of assistance, along with four C-130 transport planes to airlift refugees from overburdened Tripura to Assam.[15] Assuming an annual food allowance per person of US$32, the United States designated US$10 million of this new funding to meeting 50 percent of the food needs of 2.5 million people over the next three months, thus aiding in part approximately two-thirds of all East Pakistani refugees in India at that time.[16] Although by mid-June the US embassy in New Delhi had estimated that US relief aid should be not US$17.4 million but US$66–71 million, it should be noted that Washington had by this point donated more funds than any other capital, accounting for 35 percent of all contributions, the next largest donor being Moscow with 28 percent.[17] Moreover, on 24 June, State announced an extra US$70 million of refugee-related assistance to India.[18] In his memoirs, Kissinger estimated that over the course of the crisis, the United States provided US$240 million in relief aid, including some US$150 million to East Pakistan, on top of the US$87.4 million allocated to India.[19]

Van Hollen argues: "By expending large sums of money for the refugees in India, the White House hoped to reduce the barrage of criticism it was receiving from the media and the Congress."[20] Though the refugees undoubtedly benefited from America's generosity, Doctor Kissinger's offer of large quantities of humanitarian relief in the absence of a more forceful line on human rights issues would appear to have been addressing the symptoms of East Pakistan's malady rather than its underlying cause. Nevertheless, the soothing balm of relief provided Nixon and Kissinger with a potential salve for troubled American consciences at home.[21]

War and Worry
At the beginning of the crisis, Keating believed India wished to maintain a united Pakistan for three main reasons: first, an independent East Bengal could have destabilized neighbouring West Bengal, in India, which may even have sought to join it; second, secession could have exposed the new state to radical influence; and, third, East Pakistan acted as a restraining influence on the hawks in the West.[22] Nevertheless, New Delhi viewed Pakistan not only as a military enemy but also as a psychological menace, for a strong and successful Pakistan could have attracted the loyalties of Muslims to the south, thereby destabilizing India. Hence, in 1971, Hindu India had a vested interest in maintaining a weakened Muslim neighbour.[23] In addition, as the crisis unfolded, the flood of refugees into India created problems for

New Delhi on several levels. First, the Indian government had to organize and fund a massive relief effort. Second, the refugees entered some of the most overcrowded and politically sensitive areas of India, aggravating social tensions. Third, the systematic persecution of Hindus in East Pakistan risked sparking intercommunal conflict throughout the subcontinent.[24] These new issues added to Indian concerns over the intentions of the hawks in Islamabad and the destabilization of West Bengal, throwing fuel on the bonfire of resentment already smouldering in the region.

India clearly wished for an end to the crisis and the speedy return of the refugees, but how could this best be achieved? Both Washington and New Delhi were convinced that the disintegration of Pakistan was inevitable. Should India therefore seek to establish an independent Bangladesh through evolution or revolution? A focused discussion of the highly debatable nature of India's policy throughout the crisis lies beyond the scope of this work. One point, however, must be made clear. Although India had compelling and obvious reasons to ensure the return of refugees, it promoted guerrilla resistance in East Pakistan, thus discouraging a return to stability. The United States and the United Nations believed that New Delhi, despite its denials, was training and supplying the resistance fighters inside India and then sending them back over the border.[25] In addition, throughout the key response period, India refused international organizations permission to operate beyond New Delhi, reserving distribution outside the capital to its own "terribly over-worked" relief teams.[26] Linking these two policies, the United Nations High Commissioner for Refugees suggested that the "Indian refusal appeared [to] result from [the] GOI [government of India] desire [to] protect cross border infiltration from international view."[27] It appears that India did not do all in its power to rapidly conclude the crisis. Nevertheless, Islamabad, not New Delhi, continued to perpetrate the atrocities, while the Indian government found itself perched atop an increasingly volatile powder keg.

Kissinger was skeptical of Indira Gandhi's intentions throughout the crisis. As he noted in 1979: "I remain convinced to this day that Mrs. Gandhi was not motivated primarily by conditions in East Pakistan ... [but] to settle accounts with Pakistan once and for all and assert India's preeminence on the subcontinent."[28] It was not until the end of May, however, that Washington began to recognize the very real possibility that war, fuelled in large part by the developing refugee crisis, might break out in South Asia. On 23 May, in discussing with Nixon the massing of Indian troops on the East Pakistan border, Kissinger observed: "The last thing we can afford now [is] to have

Phase Two Response 71

the Pakistan government overthrown, given the other things we are doing."[29] This oblique reference to the China initiative provides clues not only to the importance of Yahya to the White House but also to the anxiety developing in Washington over Indo-Pakistani military confrontation. Two days later, in preparation for a Washington Special Actions Group (WSAG) meeting to consider the growing tensions, National Security Council (NSC) staffers presented a contingency study on future Indo-Pakistani hostilities with the intention of focusing "high level bureaucratic interest" on the possibility of a "blow-up in South Asia." After exchanges of small-arms fire and mortar barrages along the East Pakistan border over several weeks, Indira Gandhi had "reportedly" ordered her forces to prepare a plan for an "Israeli-type lightening [sic] thrust" beyond the eastern frontier.[30]

On 28 May, Nixon applied pressure in the hope of encouraging calm. In a letter to the Indian prime minister, he declared: "I am also deeply concerned that the present situation not develop into a more widespread conflict in South Asia, either as a result of the refugee flow or through actions which might escalate the insurgency which may be developing in East Pakistan."[31] That same day, he wrote to Yahya: "I would be less than candid if I did not express my deep concern over the possibility that the situation there might escalate to ... danger point."[32]

Two months into the crisis, refugees flowed into India in their millions, and Nixon believed the possibility of war on the subcontinent to be increasingly real.[33] Yet he still refused to take a strong line with Yahya, who by then was an increasingly important link in the vital chain bridge to Peking.

Eggs in One Basket

The China initiative presented Nixon and Kissinger with three problems in terms of how they handled Pakistan. First, Islamabad and Peking were closely allied, so offending the former risked upsetting the latter. This matter was of particular concern as, in early April, Chou En-lai wrote an open letter to Yahya expressing strong support for the latter's actions:

> The Chinese Government holds that what is happening in Pakistan at present is *purely an internal affair of Pakistan ... which brooks no foreign interference whatsoever.* Your Excellency may rest assured that should the Indian expansionists dare to launch aggression against Pakistan, the Chinese Government and people will, as always, firmly support the Pakistan Government and people in their just struggle to safeguard state sovereignty and national independence.[34]

The Chinese offered clear public support to Yahya, cautioned against foreign meddling, and issued an open warning to India. The only question such a strong statement seemed to leave was whether China would venture a conflict with India on behalf of Islamabad. Apparently, if the United States adopted a contrary stance on the East Pakistan issue, this would not be taken lightly in Peking.

Second, China was particularly sensitive to secessionist issues, given its strongly held belief in its own claims to Taiwan and Tibet; the former was already one of the most significant bones of contention between Peking and Washington, while the latter was the scene of China's own campaign of "internal" repression. Third, Nixon and Kissinger perceived Islamabad as Chou's chosen conduit for the next step toward rapprochement. It remained unclear whether an alternative channel would suffice, especially if, because of the first two points, breaking ties with Yahya would risk the China initiative in any case.

Nixon and Kissinger rapidly discounted the possibility of establishing another conduit, recalling the undelivered letter to Sainteny, of 27 April, on the very day Pakistani ambassador to Washington Agha Hilaly conveyed Chou's message. Over the coming weeks, the White House steadily became more dependent on Yahya, as he supervised and facilitated arrangements for Kissinger's secret trip to Peking. On 7 May, in response to a summons from Kissinger, Farland met secretly with the national security advisor, who was still on vacation in Palm Springs. Kissinger briefed the ambassador on the China initiative and Yahya's role before making him responsible for liaison with the president of Pakistan in arranging a proposed trip. This would comprise a covert return flight from Islamabad to Peking while Kissinger visited Pakistan as part of a declared world tour.[35] Some two weeks later, Farland informed the national security advisor that Yahya was "fully prepared to lay on [a] complete clandestine operation providing transport to [the] destination."[36] According to Kissinger, "Yahya was enthralled by the cops-and-robbers atmosphere of the enterprise."[37] He even lent his trusted personal pilot for the secret flight and created a cover story to explain Kissinger's temporary disappearance from public view.[38] As the problems on the subcontinent grew worse, Nixon's hands became ever more tightly bound.

On 10 May, the White House replied via Hilaly to Chou's message. Nixon accepted the Chinese invitation for him to visit Peking, but suggested secret, preliminary, high-level talks between Kissinger and Chou, on Chinese soil, preferably at a location conveniently accessible from Pakistan. The president

Phase Two Response 73

confirmed he would make all arrangements through Yahya. Importantly, he insisted: *"For secrecy, it is essential that no other channel be used. It is also understood that this first meeting between Dr. Kissinger and high officials of the People's Republic of China be strictly secret."*[39] In his message of 27 April, Chou had offered a public meeting. Yet, despite some later confusion over this issue,[40] a veil of secrecy was drawn at the insistence of Nixon and Kissinger, not the Chinese. In his response, received on 2 June, Chou accepted Nixon's proposals, agreeing to the preliminary talks, but suggested: "As it is difficult to keep Dr. Kissinger's trip strictly secret, he may well consider coming for the meeting in an open capacity."[41] Nixon and Kissinger, however, would continue to insist on the utmost confidentiality until the dramatic public announcement on 15 July.

Seymour Hersh and Walter Isaacson have suggested between them four reasons why Nixon and Kissinger were adamant with regard to secrecy. First, they wished to protect themselves from conservative attacks by the American right, for which Taiwan remained an emotional issue. Second, they wanted to avoid being paralyzed by public and congressional debate. Third, they sought to avoid dealing with what they perceived as the entrenched attitudes and inertia of the Department of State. Fourth, and on this Hersh and Isaacson concurred, they wished to "preserve the drama of the announcement."[42] Kissinger put it far more simply on his return: "We kept it secret so we would not have to negotiate with the *New York Times*. The speculation we got afterwards we would have gotten beforehand, and we would have been judged by whether we brought back what the *New York Times* demanded."[43] Indeed, the president and his national security advisor played their cards so close to their chests that even the secretary of state was informed of the trip only the day before Kissinger left Pakistan for China.[44]

Nixon and Kissinger's sense for the dramatic was captured in their reaction to Chou's acceptance on 2 June. They codenamed the trip "Polo," so associating the journey with the great achievement, high adventure, and everlasting fame of a celebrated Western explorer of China.[45] Kissinger declared of Chou's reply: "This is the most important communication that has come to an American president since the end of World War II,"[46] and that evening, Nixon toasted the success: "Let us drink to generations to come who may have a better chance to live in peace because of what we have done."[47] By mid-June, Kissinger and Chou had agreed on the exact dates of what they perceived to be a historic voyage: 9–11 July 1971.[48]

In the meantime, however, Romanian president Nicolae Ceaușescu made a state visit to China, arriving on 1 June. The Romanian ambassador to Washington, Corneliu Bogdan, took the trouble to visit the White House while the tour was underway, wondering whether Kissinger had anything to relay to the Chinese. Kissinger sent Alexander Haig, his deputy, to the meeting, with instructions to merely ask the Romanians to reiterate the message of January and thank them for their help. The Romanian channel, while still potentially active, had become a potential source of confusion in finalizing arrangements with Peking.[49]

On 1 July, Kissinger and a select group of assistants finally set out on the world tour or, as he later described it, "the most momentous journey of ... [their] lives."[50] Portrayed as a strategic initiative in pursuit of world peace, the clandestine mission also presented the White House with a more pragmatic opportunity. By October 1970, Nixon's popularity had fallen and, by the summer of 1971, with elections on the horizon the following year, the president's standing had dropped below 50 percent in the polls.[51] The dramatic announcement of Kissinger's trip and a future visit by the president himself to Peking offered a much-prized opportunity to revitalize Nixon's public appeal.[52] The China initiative remained as important as ever and grew enticingly more achievable at the very time White House dependence on Yahya's role was growing. Nixon and Kissinger, therefore, perceived a vast humanitarian crisis in South Asia and the risk of an Indo-Pakistan war as being insufficient grounds for endangering relations with Yahya and Sino-American rapprochement.

Let's Pamper Pakistan

On the Ground in South Asia

As Nixon and Kissinger obsessed about the China initiative, the atrocities in East Pakistan continued and desperate refugees continued to flood into India.[53] From mid-May onward, Archer Blood identified three trends: the beginning of ever-growing guerrilla resistance, the systematic persecution of Hindus, and the continuing deterioration of law and order.[54] In early May, the World Bank sent a mission to East Pakistan under the leadership of Peter Cargill, chairman of the Pakistan aid consortium.[55] The *New York Times* obtained a leaked copy of the subsequent report, which recommended the suspension of economic assistance. On 14 July, the day before the announcement of Kissinger's visit, it described the document as "damning," and again called for an end to US economic assistance to Islamabad.[56]

The report drew attention to the general destruction of property in the towns and villages of East Pakistan, severe damage to the transport and communications networks, substantial loss of vehicles and vessels, the continuation of punitive measures by the army, and ongoing insurgent activity. "People fear to venture forth and, as a result, commerce has virtually ceased and economic activity generally is at a very low ebb."[57] Despite Islamabad's propaganda to the contrary, East Pakistan lay a devastated and dangerous land.

Quiet Diplomacy or Appeasement?

Throughout phase two, the China initiative was the primary concern of the White House in determining its response to the crisis in East Pakistan. As Nixon obliquely put it on 15 June during a conversation with Kissinger and an uninitiated Keating: "Maybe there is going to be a Pakistan collapse, depends on what happens in the next 6 months. It may never be in our interest. But it certainly is not now for reasons we can't go into."[58] The White House, however, had to balance this strategic objective with its desire to defuse tensions in South Asia. Between 25 March and 15 July, Nixon and Kissinger limited US policy to four major components: public neutrality,[59] providing refugee relief funding, pressuring India and Pakistan for calm,[60] and encouraging Yahya to seek political accommodation in the East. The first three have been discussed above. We turn now to US attempts to encourage a negotiated settlement.

The White House recognized that East Pakistan would eventually become independent, but wished it to achieve autonomy through "evolution, not by a traumatic shock."[61] The problem was "how to bell the cat,"[62] and Nixon chose to do this through a campaign of "quiet diplomacy."[63] As the president tentatively explained in his letter to Yahya of 28 May: "It is only in a peaceful atmosphere that you and your administration can make effective progress toward the political accommodation you seek in East Pakistan."[64] Kissinger insists that while visiting Islamabad on the eve of his departure for Peking, he had several conversations with Yahya and his foreign secretary, Sultan Khan, encouraging them to "put forward a comprehensive proposal to encourage refugees to return home" and admit UN relief workers into the East.[65] These limited, friendly endeavours were far from compelling, however, as Nixon and Kissinger were at the same time taking great trouble to signal their support and appreciation for Yahya and insulate him from US condemnation and sanctions. Unwilling to take any risk with the China initiative, they made strident efforts to maintain military supply and to provide new economic aid.

On 28 June, Yahya announced plans for a conditional return to civilian government within four months. These, however, banned the Awami League and excluded from office all of its members accused of "secessionist activities." On his memorandum informing Secretary of State William Rogers, Sisco scribbled: "Banning Awami League makes political accommodation almost impossible."[66] Nearly one month later, on 23 July, Hilaly informed the White House that Pakistan would finally allow UN supervision of the resettlement of refugees in the East.[67] It is difficult to gauge from US records the extent of White House influence in the determination of these decisions, the first of which may hardly be considered a giant stride toward a solution to the crisis. Perhaps most telling were the comments in Kissinger's memoirs. During his visit to Islamabad in July, he concluded that most West Pakistani leaders were unable to conceive of dismemberment, and those who did so saw no way of surviving the political consequences.[68] "Quiet diplomacy," seeking the inevitable independence of East Pakistan by means only of evolution, clearly was not working. Nevertheless, Nixon and Kissinger continued their soft line with Islamabad. It is difficult, therefore, to distinguish between their policy of "quiet diplomacy" and one of outright appeasement.

A Self-Assessment

One need not rely exclusively on Kissinger's conclusions with regard to the success of the US reaction. On 10 July, NSC staffers issued a forty-page report discussing US policy on the subcontinent, in response to NSSM 133. In summarizing the document for Kissinger, Richard Kennedy and Harold Saunders of the NSC called it "by far the best paper so far produced on the situation in South Asia."[69] Yet, it exposed the severe present and future limitations of US policy.

In terms of humanitarian relief, the refugee problem was likely to worsen due to famine in the East, placing yet more pressure on India, which still had not allowed a UN presence in the camps. With regard to defusing regional tension, India continued to provide cross-border support for guerrillas and, although Pakistani army action against East Bengali Hindus was believed to be declining, it had not stopped, and intercommunal tension remained high. Moreover, political accommodation in Pakistan appeared "only a remote possibility." The report concluded: "The three major strands of our policy have met our immediate requirements but they have not provided the basis for a viable long-term resolution of the crisis."[70] Issued while Kissinger was actually in Peking, this was a somewhat disappointing "end-of-term" assessment.

White House Options

Public Stance

The opportunity to publicly condemn Yahya lay open to the US government from the start of the East Pakistan crisis. Especially if combined with a strong private letter to the Pakistani president, this option would have increased international pressure on Islamabad to desist and facilitated the adoption of a more morally upright US position. Yet throughout the key response period, and even during phase one, when the China initiative had not taken centre stage, the United States refrained from any public criticism of Yahya's actions. Instead, the White House limited public statements to expressions of concern over the loss of life and calls for a peaceful resolution of a domestic issue.[71]

This remained US policy despite the considerable weight of adverse public opinion. On 1 April, Senator Edward Kennedy demanded that the US government condemn the "indiscriminate killing,"[72] and the *New York Times* criticized the administration for failing to "speak out against the bloodbath" as even the Soviet Union had already done.[73] Such pressure would steadily increase over the key response period as the plight of the millions of refugees in India became ever more apparent.

In his memoirs, Blood explained that all he wanted was "some indication of disapproval ... a little morality injected into the *realpolitik* of Nixon and Kissinger."[74] Christopher Van Hollen, who was deputy assistant secretary of state in the Bureau of Near Eastern and South Asian Affairs between 1969 and 1972, concurred, believing "a more upright policy" was called for,[75] as opposed to mere offers of humanitarian relief. Moreover, Van Hollen argued that a "statement of US disapprobation" would probably not have caused Yahya to back out as intermediary, for he needed American goodwill and was honoured to have been chosen for the role.[76] Geoffrey Warner went even further, contending: "It would be extremely hard, for example, to sustain the argument that if the United States had not backed Yahya and his regime, the 'opening' with China would have failed. China's policy was no more primarily focused on South Asia than America's. What China wanted more than anything was reinsurance against the Soviet Union."[77] Indeed, one may readily add that China had reciprocated US interest in rapprochement despite pre-existing areas of great tension between Peking and Washington, such as their ongoing standoffs over Taiwan and Vietnam – China was still seeking accommodation in the face of these major difficulties. Would a Washington stance against Islamabad, if properly explained to Peking, have caused China to derail such important strategic talks? While Warner would appear to have made an important point, it is not the purpose of this analysis to speculate further on such hypotheses. Instead, it is to draw attention to the fact that, despite Nixon and Kissinger's insistence, it is far from clear that a public stance, or indeed perhaps even stronger action against Yahya, would have led to the collapse of the China initiative after it had finally sprung to life.

Armed Intervention

Although the United States enjoyed the elite status of being a military superpower, when Nixon took office in 1969 over 30,000 American personnel had died in Vietnam and 536,000 US troops remained stationed in Southeast Asia.[78] In early 1971, although the number of US personnel there had been significantly reduced, Vietnam remained Nixon's most intractable and important problem, and a key political issue. Gallup polls showed that 66 percent of Americans favoured the return of all US troops by the end of the year.[79] As morale deteriorated both in the military and on the home front, Nixon sought to withdraw US troops as quickly as reasonably possible while attempting to secure a negotiated settlement for the South Vietnamese.[80]

National discontent over US military commitments in Asia manifested itself on May Day 1971, when some 200,000 anti-war demonstrators descended on Washington and attempted to shut down the government. The mass arrest of 12,000 people over four days led to further protests against violations of civil liberties.[81] Between 1 April and 1 July 1971, during the key response period, there were seventeen congressional votes to restrict presidential authority over, or demand withdrawal from, Vietnam.[82] The Nixon administration was desperately seeking an "honourable" military retreat from Asia, and the American public was fatigued. The United States was not psychologically ready to commit to another armed intervention, especially when no important national interests were at stake.

Military Supply

Andrew Pierre has observed that, as well as potentially providing domestic economic benefits and security overseas, "it is clear that the provision of arms may provide influence and leverage."[83] Beyond the relationship of practical interdependency, military exports may give substance to treaty commitments, access to political and military elites, and symbolic indication of friendship toward and support of recipient regimes.[84] Kissinger was "especially inclined to use arms transfers as an instrument of foreign policy"[85] and, under his watch, US foreign military sales increased substantially between the late 1960s and mid-1970s, driven by the practical implications of the Nixon Doctrine and "spectacular" new deals with Iran and Saudi Arabia.[86] Both Nixon and Kissinger were apt to make personal commitments (e.g., to Israel and to Iran) without consulting the Pentagon or the Arms Control and Disarmament Agency, which was "regularly excluded from any participation in the decision-making process, in spite of its having statutory responsibilities."[87] Indeed, "except on routine decisions, the bureaucracy was often short-circuited," Nixon and Kissinger demonstrating "a strong tendency to use arms sales as a diplomatic instrument for immediate gain, with a rather laissez-faire or insouciant attitude toward the longer-term implications of the transfers for regional stability or the impact on the recipient nation."[88]

By the mid-1970s, the United States supplied some 39 percent of all world arms exports, the leading provider by far.[89] The increase, in terms of both the quantity and quality of weapons systems, became a source of "much unease" as the decade progressed,[90] and the supply of US arms to repressive regimes, especially those in Latin America, became an issue in Congress and a matter of deep embarrassment.[91] It was not until the introduction of the International Security Assistance and Arms Exports Control Act of 1976, however, that Congress was able to exert greater restraint on the White House. This measure prohibited the transfer of arms to any country engaged in "a constant pattern of gross violations of internationally recognized human rights, except in extraordinary circumstances." To assist Congress in making its judgments, the president had to provide annual human rights evaluations on a country-by-country basis.[92] All this, however, was too little too late for the victims in East Pakistan.

Between 1950 and 1970, defense expenditure accounted for 60–70 percent of Pakistan's total annual tax revenue,[93] and, as NSC staff noted, the stability of General Yahya's dictatorship was "heavily dependent on the continued strength and morale of the military." Arms purchases from the United States were of "paramount psychological and practical significance to the martial law regime."[94] In the mid-1960s, some 80 percent of Pakistan's modern weapons were US-made.[95] Washington, however, had suspended all military supply during the 1965 Indo-Pakistan War, and since then had modified the embargo only to the extent of allowing the sale of non-lethal end items (e.g., communications, medical, and transportation equipment), ammunition and spare parts for weaponry supplied before 1965, and the one-time exception package of three hundred armoured personnel carriers and at least seventeen aircraft.[96] It should be emphasized that, because the one-time exception package was held in abeyance (see below), the United States supplied no lethal end items to Pakistan during the key response period. Nevertheless, the issue of other military supplies remained of prime importance to Islamabad, not only for psychological reasons but also because so much of Pakistan's pre-1965 lethal equipment needed US-supplied spare parts to keep them operational. Many of these parts could be purchased on the international market, but direct sourcing from the United States presented Yahya with the simplest and most attractive option. The importance of spare parts had already been demonstrated in 1965, when the US embargo had helped foreshorten the Indo-Pakistan War.[97] Nixon and Kissinger, however, chose not to suspend the shipment of such items.

Pakistan was able to purchase munitions list items from the United States by two methods: from Department of Defense stocks or those of its subcontractors through the Foreign Military Sales (FMS) program, and commercially. In either case, it required licences issued by the Office of Munitions Control (OMC), which fell under the purview of the State Department. In "early April," State took the unilateral action of suspending the release of all items from FMS stocks and the issuance and renewal of new and old licences, respectively, by its own OMC.[98] Unfortunately, owing to what Van Hollen would later describe as a "textbook example of a bureaucratic snafu,"[99] these steps did not block supplies of commercial items under licences supplied beforehand, which remained valid for one year. Nor did they stop the shipment of FMS stocks already released into the pipeline but not yet shipped from the United States. Items supplied in these ways, therefore, remained unintentionally beyond the administration's control. Nixon effectively ratified State's actions in the "Squeeze" memorandum (see Chapter 2), approved on 2 May, when he advised the continuation of military supplies but, "in order not to provoke the Congress to force cutting off all [military] aid," the withholding of shipments of "more controversial items."[100] In the absence of any specific direction to the contrary, State continued its hold on issuing and renewing licences throughout the key response period. Furthermore, this ambiguous order was understood to forbid the supply of end items under the one-time exception package, none of which had been dispatched.[101]

On 17 May, NSC staffers identified US$44 million worth of military supplies on order from Pakistan.[102] Two months later, however, the value had decreased to only US$29 million. The May estimate had included US$18 million in "lethal" equipment, which almost certainly had related to the one-time exception package. As that particular deal was held in abeyance, its value was excluded from the July calculations. Of the US$29 million remaining in the pipeline on 13 July, US$4 million was still held in FMS stocks because of the ban on such releases. In addition, US$10 million related to sonar equipment no longer due for construction. Consequently, US$15 million remained eligible for shipment owing to State's "bureaucratic snafu."[103]

The *New York Times* exposed the loophole on 22 June, when it reported on its front page that a vessel was due to sail from New York to Karachi with military equipment on board, another already having recently departed for Pakistan with a similar cargo. The article noted that State was unable to explain why, despite having painted a picture of a full embargo, it was still allowing military supplies through.[104] The news sparked an array of complaints in the US press and Congress, and India made a formal protest to State.[105] In response, Rogers recommended the immediate suspension of all shipments of military equipment, but Kissinger disagreed,[106] arguing that the United States should "continue present policy rather than ... authorize even a temporary suspension on items beyond US [official] control."[107] This reflected his reluctance to withhold supplies, as already expressed in a Senior Review Group (SRG) meeting in April.[108] The national security advisor justified his position on the grounds that, despite receiving congressional and Indian criticism, the United States would "avoid [sending] the unfavorable political signal to Pakistan."[109] Nixon trusted the view of his favoured advisor, and US policy remained unchanged.

From the start of the crisis, representatives of the press and Congress had called for a complete embargo on military supplies.[110] As early as 15 April, Senators Walter Mondale (Democrat, MN) and Clifford Case (Republican, NJ) introduced a resolution calling for the suspension of all military sales.[111] By the end of July, John E. Moss (Democrat, CA) and Charles Mathias Jr. (Republican, MD) had introduced identical resolutions in the House and Senate, respectively, calling for a one-year suspension of all military supplies, including items under licences issued before early April but not yet shipped.[112] Yet despite such public pressure and the knowledge that even limited military supply was of great psychological and practical importance to Yahya, Nixon and Kissinger sought to continue the shipment of as many non-lethal items and spare parts as possible, taking full advantage of the loophole conveniently provided by State.[113] In early November, State revoked all the remaining licenes, representing US$4 million worth of military equipment, suggesting that US$11 million had been either cancelled or dispatched since 13 July, when US$15 million had remained eligible for shipment.[114] A General Accounting Office report of 4 February 1972, however, estimated that US$4 million of munitions list items had been exported during the crisis under valid licences.[115] This figure appears inconsistent with the unexplained reductions in orders from mid-July to early November. While it is possible that the government of Pakistan cancelled orders or simply allowed licences to expire, such actions would appear incompatible with its demand for the continuation of military supply. It is likely that the United States cancelled several orders no longer considered viable, but the anomaly would appear worthy of future investigation.

Economic Aid

Between 1958 and 1968, the United States committed US$2.8 billion in economic aid to Pakistan. Annual contributions approached some US$400 million in the early 1960s, representing 55 percent of Pakistan's total foreign assistance.[116] Washington had been by far the largest donor to Islamabad on the international stage.[117] Following the Indo-Pakistan War of 1965, annual aid levels fell on average to US$150 million.[118] Nevertheless, this still amounted to some 25 percent of all external economic assistance normally reaching Islamabad.[119] In addition, at the start of the crisis, Pakistan's foreign exchange reserves were at an unusually low level and due to be exhausted in a matter of months. These factors provided the United States with the opportunity, if it so desired, to use substantial economic leverage to influence the actions of the authorities in Islamabad.[120] Indeed, Kissinger noted that cutting economic aid would "infuriate the West Pakistanis."[121]

As the clampdown began, US commitments in the pipeline from previously agreed loans stood at US$120 million, a new US$70 million program loan was due for consideration, and a substantial portion of some US$87 million of PL-480 relief had yet to be shipped.[122] Not surprisingly, the potential impact of the suspension of non-relief economic aid did not go unnoticed by the US press and Congress. The *New York Times* led the way with an editorial of 31 March that called for the continuation of financial assistance only if a substantial proportion were allocated to relief in the East.[123] Fred R. Harris went one step further the next day, demanding on the floor of the Senate an end to all economic aid to Islamabad.[124] On 4 May, Walter Mondale and nine other senators wrote to Rogers calling for the United States to vote against further foreign exchange assistance for Islamabad at Pakistan aid consortium talks.[125]

Despite such public pressures, in approving the "Squeeze" memorandum on 2 May, Nixon chose to continue economic aid and back Pakistan

Phase Two Response 83

at consortium meetings.[126] Specifically, the president instructed that adjustments to US programs should be made only for developmental reasons and "not as a facade for application of political pressure."[127] Nevertheless, the White House deferred throughout the key response period the politically sensitive decision on the US$70 million program loan, originally scheduled to be made by mid-June.[128] Meanwhile, the US$120 million in the pipeline continued to flow.

At the start of the crisis, Pakistan declared a six-month moratorium on its repayment of foreign loans.[129] Despite this, Islamabad's foreign exchange reserves remained at uncomfortably low levels.[130] At his meeting with Farland on 7 May, Kissinger explained that the World Bank had concluded that Pakistan required US$250 million of "breathing room" over the next few months.[131] By June, the *Washington Daily News* estimated that the figure urgently required was closer to US$450 million;[132] China stepped in with a US$100 million interest-free loan to help relieve the stress.[133] Meanwhile, as Kissinger had promised Farland at their meeting, the United States continued to support Pakistan's case for assistance at consortium talks.[134] Despite American pressure, however, an informal gathering of consortium members in Paris, on 21 June, refused to extend aid or announce a date to reconvene. Of the eleven parties at the meeting, the United States was the only one that failed to recommend suspension.[135]

The substantial amount of economic assistance the United States provided Pakistan presented the White House with perhaps the most significant opportunity to adopt a more forceful line during the crisis. Under severe financial pressure, Yahya would undoubtedly have taken very seriously any threat to his economic lifeline from Washington. Yet, Nixon and Kissinger not only chose to continue crucial ongoing loan commitments but also placed the United States in the embarrassing position of being the only sizable Western economic power to row against the tide of developed-world dissatisfaction.

Aftermath

Kissinger set off on his world tour on 1 July, officially visiting South Vietnam, Thailand, India, Pakistan, and France before returning to the United States twelve days later. During his stopover in Islamabad, he undertook his covert mission to Peking between 9 and 11 July.[136] In a report Nixon later described as "a brilliant summing up,"[137] Kissinger could barely contain his thrill at having, in his own perception, created a gift to posterity: "We have laid the groundwork for you [Nixon] and Mao to turn a page of history ... The process we have now started will send enormous shock waves around the world ... Our dealings, both with the Chinese and others, will require reliability, precision, finesse. If we can master this process, we will have made a revolution."[138] No doubt equally dizzy with excitement, Nixon dramatically announced the successful trip to an unsuspecting world at 22:30 EDT on 15 July 1971. He revelled: "I have requested this television time tonight to announce a major development in our efforts to build a lasting peace in the world."[139] Though the reality of talks had not dulled in any way the enthusiasm of the president and his national security advisor for their strategic initiative, it had perhaps dulled the moral sensitivity of the latter, who, even as the human tragedy of East Pakistan continued, joked with White House staff that "Yahya hasn't had such fun since the last Hindu massacre!"[140]

Meeting in Peking, Kissinger and Chou had agreed that Paris would provide a more convenient channel than Islamabad for future communications. Vernon Walters, US military attaché in Paris, and the Chinese ambassador to Paris, Huang Chen, would act as point men for direct contact between the two powers. Nevertheless, Kissinger and Chou agreed to pass "non-substantive" information via the Islamabad conduit for, as the latter noted, Yahya "had been a good friend."[141] A message was successfully relayed via the new route on 19 July. Thus, within only four days of the announcement of Kissinger's visit to China, Paris had simply and effectively replaced Islamabad as the vital communications hub between Washington and Peking.[142]

This rapid and trouble-free change of conduits suggests that Yahya was a convenient but not a necessary facilitator of contacts between the two powers. Nixon and Kissinger, however, remained aware of the close alliance between China and Pakistan, which, along with their gratitude and loyalty to Islamabad versus their suspicion and dislike of New Delhi, continued to influence their formulation of a US policy tilted in favour of Pakistan until the crisis was resolved in December. On 16 July 1971, over three months after the clampdown began, the full NSC convened its first meeting to discuss the problems on the subcontinent. Nixon declared that, if it could possibly be avoided, he would not allow a war in South Asia until he had visited China. The president admitted he had "a bias" on the subject, but believed the Indians to be a "slippery and treacherous people," who "would like nothing better than to use this tragedy to destroy Pakistan."[143] Kissinger, whom Chou had left in no doubt of Peking's strong support for Islamabad,[144] backed Nixon; in the event of an Indo-Pakistan war, the national security advisor believed that China would intervene militarily and that, if this happened,

Phase Two Response

"everything we have done [with China] will go down the drain." Kissinger insisted that Yahya would not succeed in holding Pakistan together in the long term, disintegration was inevitable, and the US objective should therefore be to create an evolutionary change. Unfortunately, he did not believe this would be possible before an Indian attack, so Washington should have Yahya propose a comprehensive refugee repatriation package, allowing the United States to play for time.[145] While revelation of the China initiative had helped some in Washington better understand in hindsight Nixon and Kissinger's policy toward Pakistan during the key response period, observers now had to adjust to their insistence that India was intent on starting a regional war that would probably escalate to involve the Chinese.

As the United States continued to support Islamabad, Moscow and New Delhi signed a new accord. In his memoir, Kissinger insisted: "On August 9 came the bombshell of the Soviet-Indian Friendship Treaty."[146] With this agreement, he claimed, "Moscow threw a lighted match onto a powder keg."[147] The accord, he contended, eliminated Indian fears that the supply of Soviet weaponry might dry up during a war, and he admitted to being stunned by the "astonishingly sanguine" reaction of others in the government.[148] In constructing his portrayal of an aggressive India in his memoir, Kissinger conveniently overlooked his own understanding of the treaty at the time. In advising Nixon in 1971, he stated: "The treaty seems to *reduce* the danger that Indo-Pakistani hostilities will break out in the next several weeks, but not necessarily over the longer run," as the hawks may press Indira Gandhi, in the light of Soviet support, once the euphoria has worn off.[149]

As the major powers took sides, China and the United States supporting Pakistan and the Soviets aligning with India, there developed a real possibility of more serious escalation. By October, the number of refugees in India had swollen to some ten million, guerrilla resistance continued in the East, and troops faced each other across the borders between India and East and West Pakistan. When Pakistan launched an air strike against India on 3 December, war erupted, and Nixon and Kissinger, who had given up on securing the East, acted to preserve West Pakistan. The president ordered a tilt toward Islamabad and away from New Delhi in all US decisions. The next day, despite the Pakistani air strike, the United States accused India of aggression and proposed a UN Security Council resolution calling for a ceasefire and the withdrawal of Indian troops. The Soviets used their veto and laid the blame for the conflict firmly at the door of President Yahya Khan. As war raged, the United States suspended all economic aid to India and dispatched a carrier task force headed by USS *Enterprise* to the Bay of Bengal, where it was shadowed by a Soviet battle group. On 16 December, after less than two weeks of fighting, Pakistani troops surrendered in the East. India did not try to press for gains in the West, and the forces of the major powers stood down. East Pakistan subsequently gained independence as Bangladesh. China did not intervene militarily given the speed of the campaign, winter snows in the Himalayas, the risks of escalation, and internal problems resulting from a suspected coup attempt by Lin Piao, Mao Tse-tung's designated successor, who had died in a mysterious plane crash in September, probably while attempting to flee to the safety of Moscow.[150] Kissinger made a second trip to Peking in October 1971,[151] and Nixon finally made his long-desired state visit to China in February 1972. At the end of his trip, the president proposed a toast: "We have been here a week. This was the week that changed the world."[152]

Nixon never forgot Yahya's role in helping bring about rapprochement with the Chinese. As he put it, somewhat ironically, in a handwritten letter thanking the man who had ordered the brutal clampdown in the East: "Those who want a more peaceful world in the generations to come will forever be in your debt."[153]

The US response to the East Pakistan crisis must be considered against three layers of context – domestic, regional, and global. The government of Pakistan's brutal clampdown in East Bengal violated human rights on a massive scale at a domestic level. The systematic persecution of Hindus and the massive flood of refugees into India fuelled ongoing tensions between Islamabad and New Delhi to such an extent as to create the real possibility of a regional war on the subcontinent. Importantly, all of these actions played out against a global backdrop of Cold War alignments and Nixon and Kissinger's prized initiative in search of Sino-American rapprochement.

The watershed event during the crisis occurred on 27 April, when Chou En-lai replied to Nixon's message of the previous December, thus bringing the China initiative to life and establishing Pakistan as the chosen conduit between Washington and Peking. From this point forward, the China *démarche* became the dominant factor determining US policy in South Asia. Before this turning point, however, the desire for rapprochement did not drive the US response.

On the surprise receipt of Chou's missive via the Pakistani channel, Kissinger was able to cancel his recent attempt to establish an alternative conduit

Phase Two Response 87

through Paris. Moreover, already one month into the crisis, but immediately after the communication from Peking, Nixon issued the "Squeeze" memorandum, which for the first time clarified the US government policy of "quiet diplomacy" with regard to East Pakistan. Because of this China breakthrough, Nixon made it clear: "*To all hands: Don't* squeeze Yahya at this time."[154] Only from this point forward did the president and his national security advisor begin to refer in a substantive way to the secret China initiative in the declassified records of their private communications that discussed developments in South Asia.

In his memoirs, Kissinger clumsily and confusingly attempted to use the convenient catch-all explanation of the China initiative as a simple, acceptable justification for White House indifference with regard to East Pakistan throughout the crisis. He even directly contradicted himself in two separate sections of his work. Yet, the search for evidence to substantiate his contention is fruitless. Indeed, new archival documentation and a close reading of that previously available further contradict his claim. Before 27 April, substantive discussion of the China initiative was conspicuously absent from the declassified records of Nixon and Kissinger's private exchanges on the East Pakistan crisis. The China initiative remained fragile, Peking not having replied to Nixon's demand, made in December of the previous year, that the agenda for any talks include issues beyond just Taiwan. The White House had not heard from Peking through either the Romanian or the Pakistani conduit for months. Indeed, Kissinger was so convinced the Chinese were unhappy with these intermediaries that he was urgently trying to establish a new link via Paris on the very day that Chou's message was received. There is no evidence to suggest that Islamabad's role in the China initiative was anything other than a background consideration in determining US South Asia policy during phase one. Consequently, one has little choice but to contradict Kissinger's account and adopt a revisionist posture.

Between 25 March and 27 April, White House policy was characterized by inertia: in the absence of any concrete opportunity for rapprochement with China, let alone one established through the Pakistani channel, Nixon and Kissinger did not adopt a forthright stance but instead chose to do nothing. Archer Blood, the US consul general in Dacca, sought to see through the fog of war, providing detailed reports of "selective genocide" and the systematic persecution of Hindus in Dacca, and so gave the White House the opportunity to take a firm moral line against Islamabad, despite the latter's creative propaganda. Nixon and Kissinger ignored his accounts, however. As a frustrated Blood dissented against the "moral bankruptcy" of US policy, sparking a minor rebellion at State, the blinkered and bureaucratic ambassador to Islamabad, Joseph Farland dismissed his reports as exaggerated, and Nixon ordered Blood's removal from office. Kenneth Keating, the ambassador to New Delhi, linked the need for a firm US position on moral grounds to US interests in the region as a whole, but the White House considered him to have been taken in by the Indians. The press, intellectuals, and members of Congress called for condemnation of Yahya and the introduction of sanctions, and Bangladesh associations sprang up across the United States, yet the White House refused to respond to public and private pressure.

The US government employed several techniques to promote inaction. First, it hid in the fog of war, referring to conflicting reports from East Pakistan in spite of the detailed evidence provided by its own man on the spot. Second, it drew down the veil of sovereignty, describing the clampdown as a domestic issue in an attempt to absolve itself of any duty to act. Third, Nixon and Kissinger focused on the domestic aspect of the crisis rather than the regional context, thus avoiding the need to consider in detail a comprehensive response. Consequently, during phase one, the US government did little more than issue public statements of concern at the loss of life, call for a peaceful resolution, evacuate large numbers of its own citizens, block Indian attempts to bring the issue to the attention of the United Nations, and crush the rebellion in State.

The motives that precipitated the phase one response are manifold. In general terms, Nixon and Kissinger, who had come to personalize and dominate the determination of US foreign policy, embraced a realist philosophy in which moral ideals came a distant second to the advancement and protection of US national interests, of which there were few in South Asia. This combined with moral apathy, exhibited in their reluctance to specifically discuss the atrocities and in their general indifference to the human suffering, to provide little incentive to overcome the standard bureaucratic penchant for considered and cautious action. More specifically, however, Nixon's warm relationship with Yahya and sympathy for Pakistan versus his dislike of Indira Gandhi and indifference to, if not suspicion and distrust of, India played an important role in the formulation of the US response in these early stages.

During phase two, now driven by the China initiative, the United States adopted a policy in South Asia that comprised four components: public neutrality, the funding of refugee relief, efforts to defuse regional tension, and "quiet diplomacy" in pursuit of political accommodation between

Phase Two Response 89

Islamabad and the East. Unwilling to condemn Islamabad, the United States became the leading international contributor to refugee aid, going on to donate US$90 million to India and US$150 million to Pakistan by the end of the crisis. Conveniently, the balm of relief helped soothe American consciences and assisted Nixon and Kissinger in dealing with criticism at home. Nixon wrote to both Yahya and Indira Gandhi to discourage regional conflict, but admitted his own bias against, and remained highly distrustful of, India. Although the US government held back the shipment of controversial items of military supply so that Congress would not demand a full embargo, and deferred a decision on a US$70 million developmental loan, the White House was unwilling to apply firm pressure on Yahya, either publicly or privately. Under the policy-strand of "quiet diplomacy," Nixon and Kissinger refused to condemn the atrocities in the East, continued to provide US$120 million in economic aid already in the pipeline, and stood alone in imploring other members of the Pakistan aid consortium not to suspend financial assistance to Islamabad. In addition, they did all they could to maintain the limited supply of military spare parts, which were of great psychological importance and practical convenience to the martial law authorities in Pakistan. Nixon and Kissinger took this last step despite State's attempts to suspend military supplies in order to pressure Yahya into political accommodation in the East. Even as it became clear that such accommodation remained only a remote possibility and that evolutionary change toward what Kissinger considered the inevitable independence of East Pakistan was highly unlikely, the White House maintained its profoundly sympathetic stance toward Islamabad.

In phase two, the systematic persecution of Hindus in East Bengal created one of the greatest exoduses of refugees in modern history. By mid-July, some seven million displaced people had flooded into the sensitive areas of northern India and beyond in pursuit of safety. Despite the fact that Hindus represented only 15 percent of the population of East Pakistan, they formed the clear majority in the camps. Concerns over the specific targeting of Hindus fuelled communal tensions within India. Combined with ongoing Indo-Pakistani mutual resentment, these new pressures pushed the subcontinent toward the real possibility of regional war. Nevertheless, US policy remained unchanged as the China initiative grew to offset such concerns.

Nixon and Kissinger had invested some two years of effort in encouraging Sino-American rapprochement. This major geopolitical initiative sought to end Chinese isolation and secure world peace by establishing a new equilibrium of major powers in what the president and his national security advisor considered a multipolar world. As the White House gradually finalized agreement with Peking on Kissinger's initial visit, the possibility of rapprochement became more concrete. In addition, the White House placed more and more of its eggs into Yahya's welcoming basket, as the Pakistani president played an increasingly important role in arranging the trip. Not only was Islamabad the chosen conduit but China was also a close ally of Pakistan. Peking remained sensitive to secessionist issues owing to its own concerns over Taiwan and Tibet. Although Van Hollen and Warner raise grave doubts about White House reasoning, Nixon and Kissinger believed that offending Yahya would have seriously jeopardized their strategic China initiative. Even if an alternative conduit could have been found, and especially if the step of replacement were combined with condemnation of or sanctions against Pakistan, the Chinese could have taken such measures as an affront. Consequently, throughout phase two, the president and his national security advisor sought in large part to further appease Islamabad.

Nixon and Kissinger's actions during the key response period call to mind the story of King Canute attempting to hold back the tide. The waves washed in on the subcontinent as the disintegration of Pakistan became inevitable, refugees poured into India, and the possibility of war grew steadily. The waters surged at home as Congress introduced resolutions to restrict White House action. The surf lapped ever more closely as the US military supply pipeline to Islamabad and Pakistani funding began to run out. Unlike Canute, however, who sat before the tide to demonstrate to his subjects that he was not omnipotent, Nixon and Kissinger refused to yield to the inevitable. Instead, they fought in vain, and without due concern for his victims, to preserve a warm relationship with a general who brought to the subcontinent one of the bloodiest episodes in its recent history.

PART 2

Canada

4 Middle Power

This chapter investigates how and why Canada, a middle power with important ties to Pakistan through the provision of development aid and collaboration on Islamabad's nuclear power program, formulated its policy in response to the crisis in East Pakistan. It considers the main influences on Canadian foreign policy at the start of 1971, particularly Ottawa's relationship with the subcontinent; the construction of the Canadian response within a contested environment, as the high commissioners to Islamabad and New Delhi battled each other in their attempts to sway policy in Ottawa; the development of the Canadian position over a difficult summer and the aftermath as India and Pakistan moved toward war; and the impact of the lingering issue of Quebec separatism on the formulation of Canada's East Pakistan response.

Canada and the World

National Interests Overseas

South Asia remained firmly on the periphery of Canadian foreign policy until after the Second World War.[1] Over the following decades, Ottawa developed closer ties to the subcontinent as Canadian policy makers, proud of their nation's success and prosperity, sought to promote an "orderly and gradual path to independence within the Commonwealth as a model for others."[2] They encouraged economic development in the style of Western capitalism and strove for continuing cordial ties between the new states and their former British masters. Canadian development aid flowed as part of a wider Western exercise to prevent, where possible, the advance of communism (Chapter 1) and improve opportunities for current and future trade and investment.[3] During these years, as a result of participation in United Nations peacekeeping missions and playing the role of mediator in international disputes such as the Suez Crisis, Canadians came to perceive themselves as conciliatory "umpires" on the world stage.[4]

The Liberal prime minister, Pierre Trudeau, came to power in Canada in April 1968. A bilingual francophone lawyer from Montreal, he had travelled widely but had received no formal foreign policy training. Nevertheless, he believed strongly that Canada should distance itself from its self-perceived historical role as mediator and peacekeeper as he discerned a tendency for the nation to "sacrifice its [own] interests for the greater good."[5] Consequently, he ordered a comprehensive review of Canada's role on the international stage, which resulted in the publication of *Foreign Policy for Canadians* in June 1970. Comprising six pamphlets, this study concluded that previous policy had been too reactive, failing to fully develop Canadian influence abroad. Indeed, the review "explicitly criticized the rhetoric of liberal-moderate peacekeeping and peace-promoting policies."[6] Instead of playing the "helpful fixer," Canada would in future strive in its foreign relations to act in its national interest, emphasizing the promotion of economic growth.[7] As political scientist Douglas Ross explains: "Calculation of the national interest, narrowly construed, would be the hallmark of the first Trudeau ministry."[8]

Trudeau also embraced the concepts of federalism and national unity in the face of demands for secession from powerful separatist political forces in the province of Quebec. The clampdown in East Pakistan began only five months after the October Crisis of 1970, during which Trudeau had invoked the War Measures Act and sent the Canadian army into Quebec at the request of Premier Robert Bourassa. Bourassa called for this action to confront an apprehended insurrection led by the Front de liberation du Québec (FLQ), which had kidnapped both the Quebec minister of labour and a British diplomat. After numerous arrests, the perceived insurrection rapidly subsided. Nevertheless, the threat of secession by more peaceful means remained. Seeking to avoid unwanted foreign interference in what it perceived as a domestic issue, when confronted with separatist movements elsewhere in the world, Canada adopted a position of neutrality, asking that other states take no position on its own internal problem in return.

Throughout the Biafran emergency in 1967–70, the Trudeau government duly applied this policy. During the Nigerian civil war, the Ibo minority failed to secede and establish its own country. In suppressing the rebellion, the Nigerian federal government imposed a blockade on rebel-held areas, resulting in considerable hardship and starvation. Ibo sympathizers accused the Nigerian federal government of genocide. Reluctant to take a position on Biafra given its own sensitivities to Quebec, the Trudeau government maintained a neutral stance, despite pressure from the more liberal-minded members of the Canadian public. In addition, it encouraged a negotiated political settlement.[9] When confronted with moves toward secession overseas, Trudeau had not only the incentive to maintain, but also a track record of maintaining, Canadian neutrality, even in the face of reported human rights abuses.

As the Vietnam War continued in Southeast Asia, Canada remained "aloof."[10] Although Trudeau supported the idea of containment, he rejected what he perceived as counterproductive measures employed by the United States, such as the air war against the North Vietnamese.[11] Public opposition to the war was considerable and, while certainly not neutral, Canada remained a non-belligerent primarily interested in the restoration of peace. Lessons learned from observing American difficulties in Vietnam, as well as a new focus on the promotion of limited national interests and an ongoing reluctance to take non-neutral positions on issues of foreign separatism, provide the broad context within which the Canadian government formulated its policy on the East Pakistan crisis.

Engagement with South Asia

In early 1971, Canadian relations with Pakistan were generally "harmonious," except for two "irritants."[12] Behind the United States, Canada was the second-largest contributor of aid to Pakistan, Cdn$340 million[13] having been allocated to Islamabad up to March 1971, and Trudeau had just visited a Canada Deuterium Uranium (CANDU) nuclear reactor during a trip to South Asia in January.[14] The Karachi Nuclear Power Project (KANUPP) reactor was being built under a Canada-Pakistan joint venture initiated in 1965 and would be inaugurated in November 1972.[15]

Pakistan was highly dependent on Canada for completion of this nuclear initiative, which was expected to provide one-third of the electricity for the developing metropolis of Karachi. Islamabad had not ensured sufficient involvement and training of its own personnel, nor had it undertaken a sister project to become self-sufficient in the provision of reactor fuel. Under this "short-sighted" policy, as Munir Ahmad Khan, chairman of the Pakistan Atomic Energy Commission from 1972 to 1991, explained, Pakistan had committed to a "turn-key plant to be operated with continuing Canadian help and inputs of fuel, materials and spare parts. This made Pakistan most vulnerable."[16]

The project had continued satisfactorily after Islamabad signed a nuclear safeguard agreement in October 1969, following assurances from Ottawa that it would arrange matching safeguards for similar projects in India. The continued absence of an Indian agreement and Canada's impartial stance over Kashmir, however, remained ongoing causes of friction in an otherwise cordial relationship. In the absence of significant Canadian exports to Pakistan or large numbers of Pakistani immigrants to Canada, Ottawa's relationship with Islamabad focused on economic development aid to what it recognized as a country with a sizable population situated in a strategically important location.[17] Canada supplied only military spare parts and approved non-offensive equipment after partially relaxing a full embargo imposed during the Indo-Pakistan War of 1965.[18]

Until 1971, Canadian policy had been to "pursue, *mutatis mutandis,* parallel policies toward India and Pakistan."[19] Canada maintained a program of nuclear power cooperation with India that had begun during the 1950s. Ottawa agreed to supply a research reactor in 1955, and New Delhi negotiated a deal for a power reactor in the 1960s. Unfortunately, India refused to be bound by non-proliferation safeguards and, to the utter dismay of Canada, would eventually use plutonium generated from the research reactor to explode a nuclear device in 1974. The continued failure to negotiate a safeguard agreement was an irritant in the Indo-Canadian relationship at the beginning of 1971 and, as noted above, of considerable concern to Pakistan.[20]

Despite such difficulties, however, Ottawa maintained its nuclear cooperation with India and provided New Delhi with more economic development aid than it did any other country.[21] Indeed, Canada had invested over Cdn$1.3 billion and, at the start of 1971, was India's fourth-largest donor.[22] Despite some friction, the two governments remained on good terms, and James George, the high commissioner to New Delhi, even wished to see Canada develop its relationship with India much further, believing India to be no longer peripheral but a pole of strength in Asia against the emerging communist giant of China. Although there were occasional, limited signs that Ottawa was beginning to consider George's views by 1971, Canada's relationship with India, in parallel to that with Pakistan, remained focused

Middle Power 97

on providing economic development aid to the largest democracy in the world.[23]

The clampdown in East Pakistan came as a surprise to Canada and to the international community as a whole. Although Canada maintained no permanent representation in the East, John Small, the high commissioner to Islamabad, made regular visits to oversee development initiatives.[24] In mid-March 1971, he paid such a call and reported to Ottawa that, owing to "overwhelmingly autonomist sentiment" and the severe limitations on the West Pakistani–dominated army's ability to impose national unity, he "doubt[ed] any agreed solution [could] be found," and believed the most likely outcome to be the independence of the East.[25] Nevertheless, talks held between President Yahya Khan and Mujibur Rahman, head of the Awami League political party and democratically elected leader of both the East and the country as a whole, soon appeared to be leading to some form of agreement. Thus, as he left to return to Islamabad on 20 March, in common with many observers around the world, Small was optimistic that, despite the odds, a solution was indeed imminent.[26] Such widely shared confidence proved misplaced, however, as Islamabad ordered the commencement of a campaign of military oppression against sections of the civilian population in the East, commencing on 25 March.

Contesting and Moulding the Response

Initial reports from Dacca were unclear. In the absence of any permanent Canadian representation and of foreign reporters, whom the army had quickly rounded up and shipped to Karachi, the "fog of war" descended.[27] As the Awami League described the "cold blooded army killing of unarmed civilians," Islamabad insisted that the military was simply restoring order and that the situation was very much in hand.[28] Indeed, on 31 March, Yahya wrote to Trudeau explaining that any difficulties in East Pakistan were "well under control" and accounts to the contrary were misleading.[29] Small observed, however, that censorship made reports in West Pakistani newspapers "worthless" and that official releases were highly questionable. Despite the deliberate interruption of telex and telephone communications with the East, eyewitnesses began relaying reports of the use of tanks, machine guns, and flame-throwers in Dacca, and of attacks on the Awami League offices, the old city, university residences, and Hindu shrines. The small East Pakistani military and police forces had been "disarmed, dispersed or rounded up," with many killed and wounded. Bodies lay in the streets.[30]

In the absence of concrete information and not wishing to act precipitately, the Canadian government prevaricated. In response to questions in the House of Commons on 2 April, Secretary of State for External Affairs Mitchell Sharp stated: "We do not yet have facts." He continued by noting that the situation was unclear, that intervention might not help, and that Canada was ready to assist in humanitarian efforts.[31] Initially highly justifiable, given the need to establish what was really happening in East Pakistan and to formulate a response based on proper consideration rather than knee-jerk reaction, Sharp's first public statement already loosely embraced two threads of what would ultimately evolve into a four-strand Canadian policy. One was that of public neutrality during the crisis, another, the application of the balm of humanitarian relief.

As events unfolded, reports of atrocities continued to flow and a battle to influence Canadian policy developed between the high commissioners to Islamabad and New Delhi, with Small's views ultimately holding the greatest sway. In the absence of representation in Dacca, Ottawa and Small turned to the British for further information.[32] The United Kingdom confirmed to the Canadian High Commission in London that "Awami League supporters generally seem to have been hunted down" and "the Hindus, in particular, have apparently been slaughtered in large numbers." Although the army itself had almost stopped shooting people in Dacca, non-Bengalis were "on the rampage, with the army turning a blind eye."[33] In addition, the British high commissioner to Islamabad informed Small that the army had exterminated members of the small East Pakistani military and police forces in Dacca, burying the latter in a municipal dump. West Pakistani troops had "laid [the] university waste," many bodies there having been bulldozed into a mass grave.[34]

Despite the ongoing influx of atrocity reports,[35] Sharp maintained the developing Canadian position of neutrality, exhibiting impressive skill in obfuscation in the House of Commons. On 7 April, five days after receiving the telegrams referred to above, in response to a question as to whether the government had received any news about mass killings in East Pakistan, Sharp insisted: "I have no information *directly* from any representative of the Canadian government."[36] Having employed this deft sidestep, he continued by admitting that there was undoubtedly a good deal of bloodshed and denounced "violence on *both* sides."[37] He concluded: "I do not think pious declarations against violence are going to achieve anything. We are searching for some means by which we can be constructive, by supplying relief or something of that kind."[38]

Middle Power

As Sharp remained evasive in public, the formulation of Canadian policy continued behind the scenes. In his very first communication after the clampdown, Small had made it clear that he now believed there was "no hope of reconciliation."[39] As he had explained further on 6 April, given the inadequate size of the army in the East and its consequent inability to control the vast rural population beyond the main urban centres,[40] "I cannot visualize discovery of any Bengalis of stature or with sufficient following who could now be found to bear the odium of dealing with their oppressors. The Pak[istan] of ... Jinnah is dead."[41] In the absence of viable military or political solutions, Small believed that independence, in time, was inevitable. Noting the adverse reaction in Islamabad to early condemnation of its actions by Moscow and New Delhi, on 8 April Small argued that to remain on good terms with Islamabad and "aloof" from recriminations and quarrels between India and Pakistan, Canada should adopt an approach that was noncommittal or neutral. He contended that Canada should consider the clampdown an internal matter for Pakistan to address and should express humanitarian concern over the effect of events on the Pakistani economy, Canadian aid programs, and any hardships endured by all those in the East.[42]

Small's opinion was of particular importance as, more than his counterpart in New Delhi, he had the ears of the key actors in Ottawa. On 29 March, Under-Secretary of State for External Affairs Edgar Ritchie had written a personal letter to the Canadian high commissioner to Islamabad offering congratulations on the latter's "excellent reporting," which had been noted by Trudeau himself.[43] Less than a month later, Small's analytical abilities were again praised in a memorandum to the prime minister from his close foreign policy advisor Ivan Head.[44] Small's opinions were not shared by George in New Delhi, however, which became apparent as Ottawa attempted to formulate policy before replying to Yahya's letter of 31 March.

George believed the soft policy proposed by Small to be lacking in moral fibre and "much too gentle."[45] Without suggesting specific steps, he countered: "Are we going to gloss over [the] fact that [the] majority (75 million) is being suppressed by [the] minority (55 million)?[46] Are [the] issues only legal and constitutional or also political and moral?"[47] Nevertheless, and somewhat contradicting his questions above, George admitted that Canada should temporarily maintain "a low profile" until it was able to "see more clearly." Meanwhile, it should occupy the safe ground of expressing "humanitarian concern [and] plea[s] for restraint and peaceful (i.e. political) settlement."[48]

Small hit back strongly in response to George's criticism. He maintained that Canada should "distinguish between rumours and emotions ... on the one hand and facts and genuine [Canadian] interests on the other." For the high commissioner to Islamabad, such national interests centred less on the overt promotion of Canadian values abroad[49] and more on Canada's realist "primary interest" of maintaining good relations through an ongoing program of Pakistani development assistance. In addressing George's point about ethical principle, Small twice labelled the former's response as emotional,[50] while continuing to present his own judgment as based on the firm foundation of reason. Questioning the propaganda of the Awami League and New Delhi, as well as that of Islamabad, he observed that, "while much blood has tragically flowed, loose talk of genocide must be discounted."[51] Six days after Small delivered this riposte, Head wrote to Trudeau, attaching sections of Small's telegram and stating: "It is one of a continuing series of reports of a remarkably high caliber which he [Small] has been filing in the past two months on the subject of Pakistan's internal difficulties."[52] Head did not go to the trouble of attaching George's telegram, nor did he fail to note Small's comments about the high commissioner to New Delhi, observing that George had argued "somewhat emotionally."[53] Conveniently, whether by chance or design, Small had recommended a course of action that fit neatly with the more general foreign policy goals of the Canadian government: a focus on the promotion of national interest, narrowly interpreted, and adherence to neutrality in the face of separatist issues overseas.[54]

On 22 April, in a telegram consistent with that in which he countered George, Small argued for the continuation of Canadian development aid to Pakistan. While recognizing that funds for East Pakistan should be held in abeyance until the situation could be normalized, he maintained that funds to the West should be continued, along with ongoing cooperation on KANUPP, thereby protecting Canadian investments made to date and the future of Canada's national interest in Pakistan: ongoing influence supported by development ties and aid.[55]

Small's recommendations as to how Ottawa should respond soon became manifest in the policies adopted by Canada both privately and publicly. At the beginning of May, just over a month after the crisis began, Sharp summarized Canadian policy considerations and recommendations for Trudeau. The minister observed that the Pakistani army controlled the urban areas in the East, but not the vast population of the countryside, where guerrilla resistance was ongoing. Given the limited size of the army compared with the populace of East Bengal, it appeared that the military would not be

Middle Power 101

able to achieve a victory. Leaders in Islamabad faced a dilemma: they could not win in East Pakistan, but neither could they withdraw for fear of the domestic political consequences. The crisis, therefore, was likely to worsen. Noting that elements of public opinion in Canada demanded action to alleviate the suffering, he advised the following policy, consistent with Small's recommendations:

> Humanitarian objectives in Pakistan will best be served by declining to adopt a public position against the military government ... Canada can best exert an influence by maintaining contact with the military government and, without threatening to cut off aid or assigning blame, nevertheless [use] our position to help them [Islamabad] realize the futility of trying to apply a military rather than a political solution.[56]

Canada should funnel relief aid through international agencies and maintain development assistance in the West to avert administrative collapse, but any possible future commitments of economic aid should be tailored to encourage a political solution and assessed in terms of not only economic but also political cost.[57]

The following day, Trudeau sent his reply to Yahya's letter of 31 March. The prime minister did not apportion blame in expressing his distress at "reports of heavy casualties and destruction of property in East Pakistan." Instead, he recognized that the "search for a political solution to [the] current problems is the responsibility of the government and people of Pakistan and not that of Canada." Trudeau continued that Canada would join with other members of the international community in providing emergency relief assistance, if so requested.[58] Into its evolving four-strand policy, Ottawa had firmly incorporated three threads, suggested by Small and recommended by Sharp: first, the adoption of a neutral public position; second, the use of soft private influence in encouraging Islamabad to seek a domestic political solution; and, third, the provision of humanitarian relief to the East Pakistani victims.

As Trudeau's letter of 5 May made its way to Islamabad, Small was just returning from a ten-day tour of East Pakistan. Reporting back to Ottawa, he confirmed that the main towns were under the control of the Pakistani military and admitted there was "just a chance" that the army might succeed in its mission to force the wing into submission. He noted, however, that there remained "a large reservoir of hatred, bitterness, resentment, and revolt among intellectuals," the countryside remained susceptible to the resistance campaign, and the martial law regime appeared unlikely to facilitate an acceptable form of reconciliation. The high commissioner contended prophetically that, with Indian help, "within three months a serious guerrilla movement will be operating ... [and the] military forces [will be] fighting for their lives." Doubtless, he argued, there would then soon develop a major refugee problem and increased tension between Pakistan and India. He affirmed his belief that the final outcome would be the independence of East Pakistan. In addition, Small recorded the "brutality" of the army and its "policy of hunting down and exterminating upper class Hindus and persons labelled as miscreants and anti-social elements." On receipt of the telegram at the Department of External Affairs, an officer underlined many of the points Small had made. He did not, however, highlight the plight of the victims.[59]

As Small toured East Pakistan, his counterpart in New Delhi visited the refugee camps beginning to appear near Calcutta. In response to George's drawing of attention to the subject, Ottawa thanked him for his information but suggested that he avoid visiting the camps in person in the future and send a junior instead. In the opinion of the Division of Pacific and South Asian Affairs, the risk of "political exploitation" of the refugee problem by India demanded that the high commissioner maintain a low profile.[60]

In an attempt to resolve their differences of opinion on the crisis, George and Small met in New Delhi at the end of May. After what Small describes as "some effort,"[61] they agreed "what CDN [Canadian] interests [were] involved in this situation and what [the] CDN [Canadian] govt [government] might do." In a joint telegram, they concurred that India, if it had not already done so, would start arming and training the guerrillas if international pressure alone did not cause Yahya to soon find a political solution to the East Pakistan problem. The high commissioners believed, however, that direct military intervention by India at the time was very unlikely, especially as New Delhi was concerned about Peking's support of Islamabad. In conclusion, they called on Ottawa to encourage restraint between India and Pakistan, no longer be guided by a "rigid parallelism" in its treatment of the two nations, and, above all, provide substantial humanitarian aid through international organizations. In a thinly veiled message, they noted that "the silence of lesser powers can be misinterpreted by both India and Pakistan."[62] Despite this temporary collaborative effort, George and Small continued to see matters, at least in part, from the perspective of the country to which each had been posted.

Middle Power 103

On 1 June, feeling that his views were still not being heard at the appropriate level in Ottawa, George took the unusual step of writing directly to Trudeau, attaching the joint telegram recently prepared. Under the impression that he held the confidence of the prime minister after they had enjoyed some personal time together during Trudeau's visit to South Asia in January, he was very direct in imparting his views: the "situation in Asia is crying for attention and not getting it ... Whom have we got near the top in External Affairs that knows Asia?"[63] Unfortunately for George, Head became aware of the letter and was barely able to contain his indignation. While on summer leave, George visited Ottawa and, as he had requested, lunched with Trudeau on 28 July. In a handwritten memorandum to the prime minister, issued on the morning of the appointment, Head tersely questioned the "propriety" of George's letter. Insisting that he and Sharp had informed Trudeau about whatever they considered appropriate, Head demanded to know "what evidence does he [George] have ... that External [Affairs] has no one who 'knows Asia' in top positions?" Claiming to have a letter from George with "far out" claims that only Trudeau and Indira Gandhi appreciated him, Head implored Trudeau: "Do not give George the impression that he can name his own next post."[64]

There is no record on file of what transpired at the Trudeau-George luncheon. On 23 May 1972, however, a few months after the East Pakistan crisis ended, George was demoted to Canadian ambassador to Tehran. In contrast, Small's career took an upward trajectory: he was appointed Canadian ambassador to Peking on 8 June 1972.

Beginning in May, the crisis had already taken an even more serious turn, as Small had predicted. Over 100,000 refugees per day had swept across the border into India. The rate of flow only peaked a month later, however, when this figure reached 150,000. By mid-June, 6 million refugees had sought sanctuary in India, the figure rising to over 8 million by the end of August.[65] The outflow of human suffering exacerbated regional tensions and transformed the crisis into one with an ever greater international flavour.

In early June, with the situation deteriorating, Ottawa determined to establish the interdepartmental India-Pakistan Task Force. Arthur Andrew, the director-general of the Bureau of Asian and Pacific Affairs, chaired the preliminary meeting on 30 June, explaining that, subject to an outbreak of hostilities between India and Pakistan, the panel would remain not an operational but an "essentially informative" body with the goal of coordinating activities between government agencies with respect to humanitarian aid, political considerations, and any future peacekeeping activities. As well as the Department of External Affairs, the Canadian International Development Agency (CIDA) and the Department of National Defence were represented.[66] George attended the first full meeting on 21 July, shortly before his ill-fated lunch with Trudeau, and expressed his concerns over the probable future escalation of the crisis and consequent possible military conflict between India and Pakistan.[67] His views were duly noted and the flow of information coordinated in accordance with the task force's brief. As Andrew had anticipated, however, until war broke out on the subcontinent in December the task force did not undertake an operational role.

Public Sphere

In his memorandum to Trudeau in early May, Sharp had referred to Canadian public opinion, elements of which he believed demanded action to alleviate suffering. Although it is notoriously difficult to measure public sentiment, it is perhaps useful to briefly consider the nature of the exchanges in Parliament and the press headlines in Canada at the time of the crisis. Reaction to the mass atrocities and possible genocide in East Pakistan was somewhat restrained in the House of Commons. As early as 2 April, one Member of Parliament, Heath MacQuarrie (Progressive Conservative, Hillsborough) used the term "genocide" somewhat indirectly, when he asked about the government's position on "widespread reports in respectable and responsible journals concerning the alleged bloodshed in East Pakistan which is said to have reached the proportions of genocide." As expected, Sharp sidestepped MacQuarrie's question by suggesting that the government did not have reliable information.[68] His dissembling was successful, and there were no heated exchanges or other references to "genocide" during April and May, with most MPs using terms such as "cruel war" to refer to events on the subcontinent; difficult questions were few and far between. On 4 May, Pierre de Bané (Liberal, Matane) asked Sharp whether Ottawa had censured Islamabad over the "atrocities." This time, Sharp sidestepped the question by stating that official Canadian policy was to favour a political settlement.[69] From early May until the summer recess in July, discussions in the Commons focused primarily on the developing refugee crisis in India and the provision of humanitarian aid.[70] Given the restrained nature and the brevity of the debates, it is reasonable to infer that, in general terms, the crisis did not spark a passionate response from MPs' constituents.[71]

Coverage of the East Pakistan emergency by the major national English-language newspaper, the *Globe and Mail*, included a number of front-page articles, however. At the beginning of the crisis, under the

Middle Power

headline "Civil war in East Pakistan," the paper relayed reports from the Press Trust of India that "at least 10,000 civilians were killed in the bitter fighting throughout East Pakistan as troops used tanks and artillery."[72] In mid-May, it highlighted the plight of over two million refugees who had been forced from East Pakistan by Islamabad.[73] Less than a week later, under the headline "Widespread terror and bloodshed in East Pakistan reported by Bengali refugees," it observed that "the army is shooting Bengalis on sight" and that Bengalis and non-Bengalis were killing each other. Moreover, in order to clear communications routes and pockets of Bengali resistance in urban areas, "the West Pakistani Army [had] embarked on a scorched earth policy."[74] Importantly, on 14 June, the *Globe and Mail* broke the news of Anthony Mascarenhas's exposé in the *Sunday Times* (London) under the headline "West Pakistani charges army with genocide." Correspondent Robert Duffy noted that, according to Mascarenhas, "the Pakistani Army is carrying out a Government policy of systematically murdering and terrorizing the Hindu population of East Pakistan, as well as exterminating secessionist elements in the Moslem Bengali population. Five million people, mostly Hindu, have already fled to India from this terror."[75] In an editorial of 7 July, the newspaper expounded its own position on how Ottawa should be responding to the East Pakistan situation. Chastising Sharp for his "tawdry way of approaching" the crisis, it implored the Trudeau administration to call for "the duly elected to govern East Pakistan," cut off aid to West Pakistan, and increase assistance for the refugees.[76] Although news and views concerning the atrocities and the crisis were readily available to Canadian citizens, the force of public opinion as a whole remains difficult to identify with precision beyond observing that the debates in the House of Commons in Ottawa did not rival in scale or passion those of its sister parliament in London (Chapter 6).

A Difficult Summer

Soon after the clampdown, as High Commissioner George noted, India supported the goal of maintaining a united Pakistan. New Delhi wished to avoid instability on its northeastern frontier that could spill over into its already sensitive tribal areas, and it remained concerned about the possible development of pan-Bengali nationalism. Quite rapidly, however, India perceived that a united Pakistan was no longer "possible or desirable," and so set about creating conditions that would eventually encourage East Pakistan's independence.[77] Not long after the crisis began, India seized "a golden opportunity"[78] to weaken its neighbour by supplying arms, training, and safe havens for East Bengali guerrillas moving across the frontier. The Indians, in George's opinion, did not want war, but support of the guerrillas ensured that New Delhi could surreptitiously encourage eventual independence by ensuring that the Pakistani army could not control the rural areas in the East. India sought to exploit Pakistan's problems to its own advantage without being held internationally accountable.[79] As the situation in South Asia deteriorated, Ottawa added the fourth and final strand to its policy: it would call on both Islamabad and New Delhi to do whatever possible to relieve tension in the region. Before Trudeau could send letters to Yahya and Indira Gandhi, however, Ottawa needed to deal with the issues of humanitarian relief, Pakistan aid consortium funding, and the ongoing supply of military spare parts and non-lethal end items.

Sharp announced the first major allocation of federal aid in the House of Commons on 28 May. Ottawa would provide Cdn$2 million of relief in the form of food, medical supplies, and other funding.[80] Including Cdn$18 million announced later, in November, a further Cdn$2 million in private donations, and other contributions, Canada had allocated almost Cdn$25 million for victim relief by the end of the year.[81] While this was an impressive amount, placing Canada among the world's most generous donors, Edgar Ritchie observed in late September that India required some Cdn$400–600 million to offset the refugee costs it would incur between the clampdown and the end of the year. At the time of his writing, Canada had donated only Cdn$6 million and the international community had committed only Cdn$214 million.[82] For six months, besides enduring political pressures, India had clearly also been bearing the lion's share of the economic cost of the refugee crisis.

Pakistan faced a "serious economic situation" with regard to its depleted foreign exchange reserves. It had unsuccessfully approached the World Bank with a view to obtaining an agreed three-month debt moratorium.[83] In mid-April, Islamabad had unilaterally declared a suspension of payments and was seeking Canada's backing in rapidly convening a Pakistan aid consortium meeting on the issue and in supporting payment relief for a full six months.[84] After their New Delhi meeting at the end of May, High Commissioners George and Small had reached a consensus that, in no longer observing a "rigid policy of parallelism" in dealing with India and Pakistan, the next meeting of the consortium would be the best place to start to apply some pressure on the latter.[85] Consequently, when the delegates met in Paris on 21 June, Canada voted to suspend aid to Pakistan, despite requests to the contrary from Islamabad. The Pakistani leadership was far from delighted,

Middle Power 107

but this was a collective action by several countries from which only the United States dissented.[86] As Washington did not have sufficient voting power to prevent the suspension of aid, Ottawa was able to help apply more pressure on Yahya without adversely affecting its relationship with Islamabad to a significant extent.

In terms of military supply, Canada had provided no lethal end items to Pakistan since the onset of the Indo-Pakistan War of 1965, but had begun selling both spare parts and non-lethal end items in the intervening years. On 6 April, just after the clampdown began, External Affairs placed Pakistan on a list of countries to which licences for the sale of military supplies would no longer be granted. Nevertheless, officials released Cdn$2.5 million worth of communications equipment for an ongoing project. John Harrington, director of External Affairs' Division of Pacific and South Asian Affairs, observed that this could rather handily be used as an example to show the Pakistanis that not all military equipment had been embargoed.[87] This less than transparent situation was brought to light in a House of Commons debate on 30 June, when Sharp admitted under questioning that, despite the apparent embargo, some previously issued licences had not been revoked. The secretary of state for external affairs went on to explain that he had undertaken a thorough review over the previous few days and that all licences in the pipeline had now been suspended, including those for maritime aircraft equipment that sat at a Montreal dock ready to be loaded onto the *Padma*.[88] This full embargo "substantially lowered Canada's popularity in Pakistan in both official and other circles."[89] The impetus for such questions was a telegram from the Bangla Desh Association of Canada, which suspected a possible shipment. It remains unclear whether this debate ultimately stemmed from the disclosure toward the end of June that the United States had been supplying arms to Pakistan through similar loopholes.[90]

The cessation of all military supply added to an embarrassment some two weeks earlier over Sharp's statement in the House of Commons, in which he observed: "The preferred settlement, of course, would be one in which those individuals who have been elected pursuant to the recent election in Pakistan should be given the responsibility of governing Pakistan, particularly East Pakistan."[91] The press read more into the minister's statement than was really there. The *Globe and Mail* featured the headline "Sharp supports separatist rule to halt East Pakistan conflict."[92] This forced the minister to clarify his position the following day, when he stated that "Canada is *not* supporting any movement for the separation of East Pakistan from Pakistan," and claimed, quite rightly, that his remarks had been "misconstrued."[93]

108   *Canada*

Although Sharp's original statement did not endear him to the authorities in Islamabad, his clumsiness and the embargo did not undermine ties with Pakistan for long. The general level of cordiality soon returned, even if, inevitably, relations were conducted in an atmosphere of tension.[94]

Three Canadian parliamentarians undertook a private study tour of India and Pakistan in early July at the invitations of New Delhi and Islamabad. Having met senior officials and visited the refugee camps, they returned demanding greater Canadian humanitarian aid and international pressure on Pakistan to pursue a political solution to the crisis that granted East Bengalis the right to autonomous government. As might be expected, the Canadian government refused to condemn Islamabad or to raise the East Pakistan issue politically at the United Nations.[95]

Canada pursued two of the important threads of its policy in providing relief aid and adopting a neutral stance both publicly and privately. The remaining two strands, privately encouraging a political solution and a reduction of tension on the subcontinent, were addressed through letters from Trudeau to Indira Gandhi[96] and Yahya that were delivered in early August. In the former, Trudeau recognized the strains placed on India but insisted that military action, which had become a concern as tensions rose in South Asia, would not provide a solution. He noted that the return of the refugees was the crux of the current problem, and "it is widely understood that this will not come about ... without a *realistic* political settlement in East Pakistan." Although Indira Gandhi had recently rejected the possible deployment of UN High Commissioner for Refugees (UNHCR) observers in northern India, Trudeau encouraged her to consider alternative formulations of such a presence. In addition, he shared the fact he was also writing to Yahya, urging both a *realistic* political solution and restraint.[97]

To Yahya, Trudeau reiterated his belief that war on the subcontinent would lead to instability and would not solve the current problems. He confirmed that he had urged Indira Gandhi to exercise restraint. In a somewhat frank manner given the normal diplomatic form of such exchanges, however, Trudeau insisted that the current trend in refugee outflows had to be arrested in order to fundamentally reduce tension, and that "ways must be found to achieve a *realistic* political settlement." The prime minister emphasized that political measures to restore confidence are "in my view essential."[98]

Trudeau did not presume to advise Yahya how such a realistic solution could be achieved, nor did he explain exactly what he meant by the term. After all, the Awami League had won 167 of 169 East Pakistani seats in the

Middle Power

proposed 313-seat National Assembly, giving it an overall majority across Pakistan, and there remained no viable alternative East Pakistani leadership, as Small had already noted. Given Sharp's recently "misconstrued" comment in the House of Commons, it is apparent that "realistic" entailed some kind of acceptable accommodation with Mujibur Rahman and the League.

The letters to Yahya and Indira Gandhi were delivered around the time Islamabad announced the military trial of Mujibur Rahman for crimes against the state. The trial was to take place in secret, commencing 11 August. Recognizing that this was a serious, if not fatal, obstacle to the pursuit of political accommodation, Trudeau immediately wrote to Yahya. Noting that Mujibur Rahman was regarded in many places as the elected spokesman of East Pakistanis, Trudeau made it clear that his trial would be seen as a political rather than a judicial act. In diplomatic language that was both careful and suggestive, Trudeau recommended that Yahya consider the significance of "a humane and magnanimous decision" for the future of Pakistan.[99] Even as any remote prospect of a viable political solution faded, however, Canada failed to change its strategy.[100]

Also in August, Moscow and New Delhi signed the Indo-Soviet Treaty of Peace, Friendship, and Cooperation. With both China and the United States already aligned with Pakistan, this development added a further complication to the crisis. Observers disagreed as to whether it increased or decreased tensions in South Asia. Small, in conversation with Yahya almost a month after the agreement was signed, asked "how he [Yahya] saw [the] USSR-India treaty and whether he thought the Russian [government] would exert restraining influence on India? ... [The] President replied he hoped so and on balance thought so."[101] The reason for such optimism was that the diplomatic victory achieved by Indira Gandhi was seen by some as relieving any pressure on her from hawks in the Indian cabinet. Nevertheless, Small argues in his memoir that, in practice, with the treaty, India "gained both the material and the psychological support required for a move from covert aid to the Bangladeshi guerrillas to all-out war in the form of an invading army."[102] In any case, the treaty certainly reaffirmed the alignment of the major powers.

The United Nations reacted timidly to the crisis from the outset, with Secretary-General U Thant initially adopting the attitude that the issue was an internal problem of a member state.[103] Later, as three major powers, each possessing the ability to veto any Security Council proposals, lined up on either side of the dispute, it became apparent that the United Nations would be unlikely to find a viable political solution.[104] Its actions were effectively limited to the deployment of UNHCR observers to monitor the refugees and the limited coordination of some of the relief efforts. Ottawa briefly considered a Canadian-led initiative in August, but the outline for a UN military observer mission in South Asia did not even reach Sharp's desk. As Arthur Andrew explained: "We would not propose to put the matter to the Minister at this time" owing to the "monumental technical and political difficulties, both domestically and internationally."[105] The inability of Canada or other powers to find a solution to the East Pakistan crisis caused Sharp to voice his frustration in the UN General Assembly in September, expressing his "serious concern" that the international community had no means to stop the growing tragedy.[106]

On 5 October, Sharp faced questions from the House of Commons Standing Committee on External Affairs and Defence about Canada's policy during the crisis. Ritchie's briefing notes for his minister provide a useful insight into official thinking at the time. In Ritchie's opinion, there were some grounds for "moderate hope," as Yahya had made some concessions. Someone more moderate had replaced the hardline military governor of East Pakistan. Pakistan, unlike India, had accepted UNHCR observers.[107] Islamabad had declared a general amnesty for those in East Pakistan alleged to have committed offences, and new elections were scheduled for December. *Prima facie*, this was encouraging news in the search for a realistic political settlement.[108]

Unfortunately, one needed only a glimpse beneath the surface to soon realize that a viable political solution remained very far away, if achievable at all. The general amnesty did not apply to Mujibur Rahman or other leading figures in the Awami League, and the elections were being held to replace seventy-eight Awami League incumbents owing to their "activities in the secessionist movement." In essence, the democratically elected Awami League leadership, with its overwhelming majority in East Pakistan, was effectively excluded from the new political process. The restoration of representative democratic government under civilian rule in East Pakistan was essential to stem or reverse the flow of refugees into India. In providing relief, as Ritchie admitted, "in a sense ... Canada and the other members of the international community [were] only treating the symptoms of the problem and not its cause."[109] The same month that the Standing Committee met, Ottawa sent a six-man task force headed by the CIDA president to assess the situation in the refugee camps. This visit led to the recommendation of the Cdn$18 million of extra relief funding made in November.[110]

Middle Power

Aftermath

As end of the year approached, the risk of war on the subcontinent grew substantially. No realistic political solution lay on the horizon and some ten million refugees remained in India, imposing a severe economic burden and, especially given the fact that the majority of such refugees were Hindu, aggravating intercommunal tensions. In addition, a possible Indian military intervention was favoured by the weather: as the monsoon receded, winter snows arrived in the Himalayas, inhibiting the ability of the Chinese to engage in sabre rattling or, indeed, more direct intervention. Guerrilla activity in East Pakistan, sometimes supported by Indian regular forces, increased and the Pakistani army in East Bengal was placed under severe pressure.[111] As Small noted, mid-November estimates placed the number of guerrillas in East Pakistan at some seventy to eighty thousand, exceeding the number of West Pakistani troops. Given that conventional wisdom, in such circumstances, called for a 10:1 ratio of regular to irregular troops for the former to maintain the upper hand, Islamabad faced inevitable defeat if the guerrillas and India maintained their ongoing policy. "Barring a miracle," Small observed in November, "talk of Mujib [Mujibur Rahman] and a political settlement through his auspices is daily becoming more and more irrelevant." Moreover, the possibility that India might seize the opportunity to bring a quick and decisive end to the crisis loomed large.[112]

As border clashes in the East between Indian and Pakistani troops became ever more regular and severe, Canada tried unsuccessfully to defuse the situation. By this time, External Affairs believed New Delhi had "settled upon a policy of escalating Indian Army activities."[113] On 17 November, Sharp announced the Cdn$18 million of extra relief funding for the refugees, and later in the same month Ottawa instructed the Canadian ambassador to Moscow to call on the Soviets to urge restraint on India. Canadian efforts were to no avail, however, as Pakistan launched an air strike against Indian targets in the West on 3 December and war broke out in the subcontinent.

As George wrote at the time, India "hoped until [the] last moment [that] war could be avoided."[114] Reflecting on events over thirty years later, he observed that Indira Gandhi dominated the Indian executive and soon determined to create for Yahya more problems than he could solve, thereby opportunistically ensuring the independence of East Pakistan, possibly with the added encouragement of international pressure. George concluded that India finally went to war to achieve a quick end to the crisis, making the most of the ideal weather conditions and the fact that the guerrillas had gained

112   *Canada*

the upper hand. Despite US concerns to the contrary, India did not wish to destroy West Pakistan, where it fought merely a holding action. According to George, Indira Gandhi had no wish to create instability simultaneously on both her northwestern and northeastern frontiers, and ultimately had a "genuine distaste for military solutions."[115] After the Pakistani army surrendered in the East on 16 December, and New Delhi immediately offered a unilateral ceasefire in the West that Islamabad accepted, India emerged the clearly dominant power on the subcontinent in any case. Canada recognized the newly independent nation of Bangladesh on 14 February 1972.[116]

Secession Overseas and the Issue of Quebec

The discussion of East Pakistan is a discussion of provincial autonomy and independence, of cultural difference, and of perceived exploitation. Accordingly, it is important to address the influence of Ottawa's sensitivity to Quebec separatism on the determination of the Canadian response to the East Pakistan crisis. This matter was very rarely raised in the official documents but, as George argued, the issue hung over the formulation of policy.[117] The clampdown in East Pakistan began only five months after the October Crisis of 1970. It would appear unlikely, therefore, that Trudeau and other policy makers in Ottawa were insensitive to any implications for Quebec policy in the formulation of their response to the East Pakistan crisis, even if only at a subconscious level.

The issue of Quebec separatism arose again in June 1971 at the Victoria Constitutional Conference. Trudeau wished to obtain agreement with the provinces on amendments to the Canadian Constitution in the hope of finally negotiating the patriation of important legislative powers that remained with the United Kingdom. Quebec wanted provincial priority in social affairs. Premier Robert Bourassa was unable to negotiate acceptable terms, and the Quebec cabinet subsequently rejected the final proposal, temporarily ending Trudeau's ambitions. This failure served as a reminder of the deep-felt autonomist, indeed sometimes separatist, urges in Quebec. Ottawa, however, was quick to deny that its policy with respect to East Pakistan was in any way formulated with such considerations in mind. In response to a *Globe and Mail* editorial of 7 July, which had linked the two issues, suggesting that "obsession" with the issue of Quebec separatism was preventing firmer Canadian support for the democratically elected but secessionist representatives of East Pakistan,[118] Sharp wrote a firm letter of rebuke. If there was "an obsession with our own separatists" at work, then that would be "an obsession of the *Globe and Mail*, not the Government of

Canada."[119] Some six weeks later, John Harrington prepared a memorandum titled "Comparison of Situation in East Pakistan to Quebec," in which he concluded that there was not a general tendency in the press, apart from the Quebec-based newspaper *Le Devoir,* to compare the two situations.[120]

Intriguingly, George insisted that the matter of Quebec loomed over the crisis, and the force of Sharp's rebuke of the *Globe and Mail* suggests an acute sensitivity to the issue of separatism. Moreover, the Biafra precedent, in which Trudeau maintained Canadian neutrality despite reported human rights abuses and public pressure, provides evidence of a previous instance of reluctance to sacrifice impartiality. Yet, the documents so far released contain no further substantial information beyond that discussed that links the formulation of policy on East Pakistan with sensitivity to the issue of Quebec. Nevertheless, the incentive to avoid supporting a foreign separatist cause was apparent, and there are occasional tantalizing suggestions that ministers and officials were both consciously and subconsciously aware of the dilemma. Although the development of a foreign policy that did not directly encourage separatism in East Pakistan could be and was justified for some by other Canadian national interests, it was nevertheless convenient for the federal government not to have associated itself directly with support for a secessionist movement overseas.[121]

Canadian policy during the crisis comprised four strands: first, the maintenance of public impartiality with regard to the respective positions of East and West Pakistan and those of Islamabad and New Delhi; second, the encouragement, through soft private influence, of Islamabad in seeking a domestic political solution; third, the urging of restraint on both India and Pakistan; and, fourth, the provision of humanitarian relief to the East Pakistani victims. In refusing to condemn Islamabad's action publicly and privately and in maintaining the ongoing development aid program, Canada sought to maintain its sway in Pakistan in the longer term and to facilitate the second policy strand, that of being able to exert soft influence on the West Pakistani leaders. The third strand aimed to encourage a reduction in tension on the subcontinent to provide time for a viable political solution to be found. The last sought to reduce the suffering of the victims, but addressed the symptoms of the problem rather than the underlying cause. By hiding in the fog of war and drawing down the veil of sovereignty over what it portrayed as a domestic issue, Ottawa was better able to protect itself from demands for firmer action. This combination of initiatives was publicly presented to portray Canada as taking a caring and responsible, if pragmatic and realistic, approach to a serious international problem. Conveniently, this stance also protected Ottawa's ongoing and future relationship with Islamabad, deemed desirable in terms of national interest narrowly construed, and maintained Canadian neutrality with regard to a foreign secessionist issue that might have stirred unwelcome comparisons with its own debate over Quebec separatism. In these respects, the policy was largely successful.

Nevertheless, there were two disadvantages to this approach. First, in failing to discontinue development aid, or at the very least to publicly or privately condemn Islamabad, Ottawa adopted the moral low ground in a situation where a military dictatorship was attempting to maintain power by denying democratically elected representatives their right to govern and by perpetrating systematic atrocities and gross human rights abuses. Second, with regard to encouraging a peaceful settlement in South Asia, the policy was inherently flawed from the outset, a fact that became increasingly apparent as the Awami League leadership was excluded by Islamabad from any political solution. If, as Sharp admitted early in the crisis, Islamabad would be able to achieve neither a military victory nor a politically viable withdrawal without first attaining its goals, and if, as Small insisted at the same time, no political leader in East Pakistan could negotiate anything other than extreme autonomy, if not independence, of the East, then a soft policy of influencing Islamabad behind the scenes was extremely unlikely to succeed.

Although Canada preferred to use the carrot in its dealings with Islamabad, it nevertheless had two potential sticks in its armoury. Ottawa was Pakistan's second-largest source of development aid and a vital partner in the vulnerable KANUPP initiative. However, although a soft policy had little chance of success, a harder policy would also appear unlikely to have succeeded, especially given the ongoing support for Pakistan from two key players on the international stage: China and the United States. Each of these major powers continued to back Pakistan throughout the crisis. China, because Pakistan was an ally in Asia, maintained political support as well as a US$200 million line of credit to purchase arms.[122] The United States, in part because of Washington's attempts to achieve rapprochement with Peking, like Canada, refused to condemn Islamabad either publicly or privately and continued its substantial program of development aid.

Consequently, while it is very difficult to condone Ottawa's position on moral grounds, it is also difficult to see how Canada alone could have pressured Pakistan into a successful political solution without risking serious

Middle Power

damage to the two countries' relationship, and to no immediate practical avail. Seen in this light, Ottawa's soft policy toward Islamabad, balanced with the need not to unnecessarily sour relations with India, could appear a justifiable option in very difficult circumstances. Nevertheless, it is certainly possible to argue that Canada's broader global interests in the longer term, through the promotion of its democratic and human rights values, would have been better served had Ottawa risked sacrificing its relationship with Islamabad and promoting its relationship with New Delhi, even if this almost certainly would not have led to a viable political solution in East Pakistan.

Canada made continued efforts to encourage a political settlement and maintain the peace. After some initial hesitation, it placed a full embargo on military supplies to Pakistan; in a collective action with others, it voted for the suspension of consortium aid to Islamabad; and it provided humanitarian relief. Trudeau sent several letters to Yahya and Indira Gandhi urging both of them to act with restraint and the former to implement a realistic political solution. As war loomed in South Asia, in the absence of a viable UN initiative, Ottawa instructed the Canadian ambassador to Moscow to call on the Soviets to urge moderation on New Delhi. From the outset, however, without necessarily knowing that China and the United States would turn out to be such strong supporters of East Pakistan, the dialogue in External Affairs revolved around maintaining Canadian economic and political influence in Islamabad in the short, medium, and long term. Discussion of moral issues remained disturbingly absent. The only dissenting voice was that of James George, the high commissioner to New Delhi, who, in raising the matter of ethical considerations, was labelled "emotional." As the East Pakistan crisis developed, even Ritchie was forced to admit that the only successful strands of Canadian policy – remaining neutral and providing relief aid – combined to treat the symptoms and not the underlying cause. Although it was extremely unlikely that firmer Canadian action would have led to the resolution of the crisis or averted the war, there was in Ottawa's policy, and in the government's failure to adjust that policy when it clearly was not working, an unfortunate lack of principle and an uncomfortable air of appeasement.

PART 3

United Kingdom

5

Former Great Power

By 1971, Britain was no longer a great power, nor was it the hub of a vast empire. Nevertheless, it maintained ties to the Indian subcontinent through the provision of substantial economic aid and lingering connections that had survived in less influential form into the post-imperial age. Chapters 5 and 6 explore how and why a weakened United Kingdom developed its response to the crisis in East Pakistan. Chapter 5 establishes the context and analyzes events from the clampdown through early May. It sets the post-imperial stage, discussing Britain's traumatic decline after the Second World War and the deterioration of London's relations with Islamabad and New Delhi in the postwar period up to the early 1970s. It then considers the forces influencing the Conservative government that had come to power in 1970 and the consequences of a visit to South Asia made by Prime Minister Edward Heath just over two months before the East Pakistan emergency began. Finally, it considers diplomatic concerns in the buildup to and commencement of the clampdown, identifying the reasons behind the introduction of key components of the initial British reaction.

Chapter 6 investigates the forces at work in the elaboration of the British response from early May until the parliamentary recess in August, a period after which the attention of policy makers turned to the potential outbreak of war on the subcontinent and focus moved away from the initial issue of human rights, the policy with respect to this having already been defined. It considers influences in the public domain, including two important parliamentary debates, the British media reaction, and the response of the sizable South Asian immigrant community in the United Kingdom. It then analyzes policy development during the early summer, the impact of Pakistani president Yahya Khan's potentially game-changing announcement at the end of June, and the subsequent repercussions until the adjournment of the House of Commons. Finally, it considers the thematic issues of the British supply of arms, economic aid, and humanitarian relief to the Pakistani government.

Post-Imperial Stage

Trauma and Eclipse

After the Second World War, Britain faced an acute dilemma that had been building over decades only to be severely aggravated by the onset of global conflict and the consequent economic drain on the treasury. The country was confronted with a choice between seeking economic stability and growth or maintaining its former peacetime commitments to military spending and influence overseas. It could not reasonably expect to do both, and, in choosing the former, it reluctantly relinquished its previous role as a great power and pursued a path that, in the postwar years "implied Britain's demotion to the status of second-rank nation."[1]

The country was already strategically overcommitted before 1939, and the war proved disastrous from a financial standpoint. To compound matters, the postwar economic recovery was weak.[2] Britain's relative military strength declined substantially, to the point that it could no longer hold its own against the developing US and Soviet superpowers (Chapter 1), both of which considerably outpaced the United Kingdom in economic and military terms.[3] By 1967, Britain's defence expenditure amounted to just US$7 billion annually leaving it only sixth in the world rankings, behind the People's Republic of China, West Germany, and France, and far behind the new superpowers (Soviet Union, US$50 billion; United States, US$76 billion).[4] Imperial retreat – the withdrawal from its colonial empire – became the "political and diplomatic corollary of this strategic contraction,"[5] a withdrawal encouraged by centrifugal forces in the colonies themselves.

In British India, the war served only to strengthen the desire for independence. Humiliations in Southeast Asia, such as the rapid fall of Singapore in 1942, had psychological and political consequences in the form of severe blows to British prestige. Unrest encouraged by the Indian National

Former Great Power 121

Congress, the British promise to withdraw after the war, and international demands, particularly from the United States, to pursue accommodation with the nationalists all exacerbated the pressures on London at a time of economic weakness. Policy with regard to the Raj became a matter of negotiating a rapid retreat. Britain withdrew from the subcontinent in 1947, leaving behind a region partitioned into the embryonic entities of independent, post-colonial India and Pakistan.[6]

This first wave of imperial retreat did not trigger immediate decolonization across the empire. Between 1947 and 1960, only three further colonies beyond South Asia – the Sudan, the Gold Coast, and Malaya – followed the Indian lead.[7] Britain hung on to former glory until it experienced a further shock to national prestige during the Suez Crisis of 1956, after which it became clear both at home and abroad that London could no longer act independently on the international stage.[8] A second wave of decolonization occurred in the early 1960s. Rebellions and small wars had erupted in several colonies during the latter part of the previous decade, often reflecting domestic responses to British weakness and the changing international setting. France established the precedent of facilitating the path to independence of many of its African colonies, offering an example both to other imperialists and to African nationalists. The Soviet Union took advantage of the Cold War propaganda opportunity to charge Western European governments with oppression.[9] Again reluctantly, and from a position of relative economic weakness, London accepted the seemingly inevitable. Between 1960 and 1964, seventeen of its colonies, many of them in Africa, gained their independence.[10] As Secretary of State Dean Acheson observed somewhat acerbically at the end of 1962: "Britain has lost an empire and has not yet found a role."[11]

Acheson's comments struck a raw nerve in London, where government policy shifted hopefully in the direction of maintaining influence east of Suez. Some 25 percent of British exports were sent to regions beyond the canal, and fully 50 percent of Britain's supply of oil came from Kuwait.[12] Could the country still project sufficient power to play a useful role in Asia? The answer, much to the regret of many in power, was no. By 1967, the Labour prime minister, Harold Wilson, found himself no longer able to reconcile growing domestic demands for economic regeneration and the costs of commitments overseas. As Paul Kennedy remarked: "Eventually, untidily and not a little reluctantly, Whitehall[13] accepted that its military aims and capabilities could no longer be global in scope."[14] In January 1968, the government agreed to a withdrawal from east of Suez within four years, finally relinquishing old dreams of imperium and reorienting Britain toward a reviving Europe.[15]

In the face of a shrinking empire, Britain turned to its immediate neighbours in search for economic advancement and a new international role. Membership in the European Community,[16] an organization built on cooperation between several highly developed Western European nations, offered a solution that reflected the reality of geography and the decline in Britain's trade with its colonies and former colonies.[17] Imports from these dropped significantly from 42 percent of total external purchases in 1950 to only 26 percent in 1970. Moreover, exports, on a similar basis, were cut in half, from 48 to 24 percent.[18] David Reynolds believes this shift to have been "perhaps the most profound revolution in British foreign policy in the twentieth century."[19]

Over the preceding decades, many of the former British colonies had elected to join the Commonwealth, a voluntary association of independent states, including the United Kingdom, which was established by the London Declaration of 1949. Under the symbolic leadership of the British sovereign, the organization was developed to acknowledge shared cultural ties between free and equal member states and to promote democracy and the rule of law. The growth of the Commonwealth from eight members in 1955 to twenty-eight in 1967 reflected the swell of former colonies achieving independence during this twelve-year period.[20] Britain's application for membership in the European Community, and its likely subsequent trade reorientation, remained a considerable concern for Commonwealth members, including both Pakistan and India, as Wilson's Labour government gave way to the Conservatives in the election of June 1970.[21]

Between 1945 and 1970, Britain experienced a traumatic decline in its status on the world stage. Nevertheless, it still possessed a sizable economy, even in global terms. In addition, it remained a nuclear power and an important member of NATO in the West's Cold War standoff with the Soviet-led Eastern Bloc. It also wielded veto power as a permanent member of the UN Security Council. London's influence had diminished significantly, but it was far from disappearing altogether.

Fading Influence on the Subcontinent

By the time Britain beat a hasty retreat from the Indian subcontinent in 1947, it had ruled over the Raj for over a century, a region considered the jewel in the crown of empire. Despite the growing resentment felt by the majority of future Indians and Pakistanis before independence, the onset of

Former Great Power

communal violence at partition, and the rapid decline in Britain's international status during the Cold War, London nevertheless remained the "preponderant external influence" in South Asia until the mid-1960s.[22] In the cases of both India and Pakistan, Britain maintained this status through a combination of political, economic, and cultural ties. In addition, the Indian military maintained close links with the armed forces of the United Kingdom. This influence survived friction with India over what New Delhi perceived as London's latter-day imperialistic adventure in Suez in 1956 and India's furious reaction to Britain's support of a Security Council resolution demanding a plebiscite over Indian-controlled Kashmir the following year.[23]

Many of the first generation of post-colonial leaders in India and Pakistan were products of the British system and retained a certain affinity for the former imperial power. Jawaharlal Nehru, prime minister of India from independence until 1964, had been educated at Harrow and Cambridge before studying law at the Inner Temple, passing his bar examinations in 1912. Ayub Khan, leader of Pakistan from 1958 to 1969, received his army officer training at the Royal Military College, Sandhurst. The next generation, however, lacking similar connections, displayed less interest in and liking for things British, and adopted a less nostalgic, more pragmatic view of bilateral ties. Thus, Nehru's death in 1964 marked something of a turning point in terms of London's dealings with the subcontinent.[24] In addition, since the mid-1950s, the United States had pursued an increasingly "assertive" regional policy in South Asia, effectively extending the Cold War to the subcontinent. As America came to supply most of Pakistan's weaponry, Washington's influence grew in Islamabad as London's waned. By the mid-1960s, the United States had clearly taken over from Britain as the main external influence on Pakistani affairs.[25]

The Indo-Pakistan War of 1965 proved to be a watershed for British ties to South Asia. As the belligerent armies engaged, Britain called for both sides to act with restraint, but was particularly critical of India's advance into the Punjab. The force of the Indian backlash took most British observers by surprise. New Delhi perceived London to have expressed preference for Pakistan and the damage to relations could not readily be reversed.[26] This injury was compounded when Britain halted all military supplies and assistance to both sides. As Pakistan had become dependent almost exclusively on US arms, London's decision had little impact in Islamabad. By contrast, India was more reliant on British materiel, some GB£11 million of which was in the pipeline when the flow was cut off.[27] Indian preference for British supply resulted in greater inconvenience to New Delhi.[28] As Paul

McGarr has noted, by the end of 1965, British influence in India, already in decline, had "all but evaporated."[29] The Soviet Union's brokerage of the Tashkent Declaration, which ended the war, served to underline this point.[30]

In the aftermath of the 1965 war, Britain explored the possibility of adjusting its policy in South Asia, but resolved to continue its antebellum approach, maintaining even-handedness in dealing with India and Pakistan.[31] As London contended with how best to restore good relations with New Delhi, it confronted another challenge. In January 1966, Indira Gandhi became prime minister of India. Unlike her father, Nehru, she had no great affinity for Britain. Worse still, for British observers, she appeared not just indifferent toward them but seemed to have a large "chip on the shoulder."[32] The British were unsure as to why, but staff of the high commissioner to New Delhi speculated that this might have been a result of her academic failure at Oxford, which she left without completing her degree after struggling with the Latin requirement. In addition, she was favourably disposed to approaches from the Soviet Union and was inclined to view bilateral ties through a lens not of soft nostalgia but of hard pragmatism.[33] By 1970, the once close relationships between Britain and, respectively, India and Pakistan had become rather distant, each independent state asserting its right to resist external pressure from its former colonial master. China and the Cold War superpowers were now the main competitors for influence, and Britain had become something of a "bit player" on the regional stage.[34]

Challenges Closer to Home

Andrew Marr describes Edward Heath as a "genuinely compassionate and unusually brave politician" whose reputation has suffered unfairly owing to comparisons with Margaret Thatcher and Britain's subsequent economic renaissance under the favourable global conditions of the 1980s.[35] Heath's compassion was perhaps best demonstrated when he arranged the rescue and resettlement in Britain of some 28,000 Ugandan South Asians who were expelled by Idi Amin in 1972.[36]

When the new prime minister and his Conservative government took power in the summer of 1970, they were confronted with a number of urgent challenges either happily adopted or reluctantly inherited from Wilson. Domestically, the economy continued to struggle along as it had for many years. Symbolic of the general malaise was the need, in February 1971, for the government to take over the flagship British company, Rolls-Royce, to save it from imminent bankruptcy and collapse. In addition, Heath faced a contest with the powerful trades union movement. This would result in

Former Great Power

a crippling standoff with the miners in early 1972, but by the end of 1970 employees of the power companies were already working to rule and the electorate was suffering the consequent blackouts. The postal workers would very soon begin to strike.

Heath's major foreign policy initiative, "the cause that excited him more than any other," was his plan to reorient Britain and secure membership in the European Community.[37] He entrusted the role of secretary of state for foreign and Commonwealth affairs[38] to Alec Douglas-Home, a former prime minister and a man who, Heath believed, had the necessary talent to help him broker Britain's entry to Europe.[39] This substantial project would occupy much of their time throughout the East Pakistan crisis of 1971, Heath negotiating with the French leader, Georges Pompidou, in Paris in May and the government issuing a white paper on the terms of entry in July.

As East Pakistan sought provincial autonomy or secession after years of exploitation, Britain was confronted with its own dilemma concerning the future of Northern Ireland.[40] Throughout the 1950s and most of the 1960s, the situation there had not loomed large on the radar screens of Westminster. Northern Ireland had a devolved government at Stormont and its own distinct system of political parties that sent representatives both to Stormont and to Westminster. This facade of representative government, however, hid the discrimination experienced by many in the Catholic community at the hands of the Protestant majority, particularly in the fields of employment and housing. Inspired by a sense of injustice, the US civil rights movement, and protests against apartheid in South Africa, the Catholic "ghettos" reached "simmering point" and demonstrations began in 1968.[41] In the summer of 1969, violence erupted and Prime Minister Wilson sent troops to the province in August. The military faced a thankless task and soon found itself condemned by Catholics and Protestants alike.[42] Moreover, in November 1969, the Irish Republican Army (IRA) split, leading to the formation of the Provisional IRA, which was prepared to use force and terror in the Catholic cause and demanded British withdrawal and the reunification of Ireland.[43]

Heath inherited this poisoned chalice on assuming power the next year. He believed Catholics should be given a stake in running the province by representation on a power-sharing executive, and pursued policies to that end. The situation in Northern Ireland deteriorated to such an extent, however, that in August 1971, as the East Pakistan crisis continued, the Conservative government approved the mass internment, or imprisonment without trial, of over three hundred Catholics in Operation Demetrius. Heath would impose direct rule the next year. London's difficulties in Northern Ireland would not be lost on certain sympathizers of West Pakistan.

As Heath took on a domestic intercommunal problem from Wilson, he also inherited a lesson from the experiences of the Labour government in formulating its response to an overseas secessionist issue during the Nigerian civil war (1967–70). Whereas Canada remained neutral and encouraged a negotiated political settlement, Britain took sides in the conflict, supporting the federal government in Lagos. Wilson sought a "One Nigeria" solution, a policy justified publicly as necessary to prevent the breakup of the country along tribal lines and the message such a fragmentation might send to other African nations, many of which had been delimited by Europeans after the nineteenth-century scramble for Africa without regard for the desires of the indigenous communities. Privately, however, London also wished to protect its supply of Nigerian oil, which represented some 10 percent of British oil imports, at a time when the repercussions of the Six-Day War of 1967 were still disrupting supplies from the Middle East. Wilson believed that backing the Nigerian federal government was the "safest bet."[44]

In pursuit of the "One Nigeria" solution, London maintained its supply of arms to Lagos, justifying this as merely a continuation of previous policy. The suffering of the Ibo secessionists of eastern Nigeria was exposed by journalists, humanitarian campaigners, and British charities, however. During the summer of 1968, images of the victims of the famine, which was caused by the Nigerian government's blockade of eastern Nigeria, began to make newspaper and television headlines around the world. Wilson's government found itself in the acutely embarrassing and politically undesirable situation of backing the Nigerian government in the face of vociferous public sympathy for the plight of the Ibo, as portrayed in shocking images of eastern Nigeria's starving children. When Heath confronted the crisis in East Pakistan, it was clear that the last time a British government had taken sides in a post-colonial secessionist dispute, its fingers had been painfully burned.

On Tour in South Asia
En route to the Commonwealth heads of government meeting in Singapore in January 1971, Heath took the opportunity to tour several Asian countries. Both Pakistan and India featured on the prime minister's itinerary. His first port of call in South Asia was the former, where he enjoyed a two-day stopover on 8 and 9 January. His briefing book for the tour highlights the key recent developments in Anglo-Pakistani bilateral relations.

Former Great Power 127

Heath's visit was the first by a British prime minister since 1958. Its aim, in light of recent developments in Islamabad's relations with Moscow and particularly Peking, was to emphasize to Yahya the advantages afforded Pakistan by its historical ties with Britain, the Commonwealth, and the West. Among specific topics of discussion, cyclone relief, economic aid, bilateral trade and investment, arms supply, and Britain's neutrality in Indo-Pakistani affairs were of particular relevance in the crisis that began some three months later.

In response to the suffering in East Pakistan when a cyclone struck on 12–13 November 1970, the British government had contributed on a timely basis GB£1 million of humanitarian relief and made available four naval vessels to help in the distribution of supplies to the local area. A consortium of five British charities made a joint public appeal to raise a further GB£1 million, and the Royal National Lifeboat Institution dispatched twenty inshore lifeboats to assist in the rescue operations. Whereas Yahya had warmly welcomed the scale and speed of British assistance, criticism in the British press of Islamabad's inefficient response had not been appreciated in West Pakistan.[45] During his visit, Heath planned to announce a further GB£2 million British government donation to the East Pakistan reconstruction effort.[46]

Britain was a member of the Pakistan aid consortium, a body formed in 1960 under the leadership of the International Bank for Reconstruction and Development (IBRD) to provide a program of economic aid for the emergent country.[47] London had already provided aid loans before the formation of the consortium, contributing GB£113 million since 1951, with its gross aid disbursement for 1969–70 amounting to some GB£12 million. Consequently, Pakistan received more British aid than any other country save India, contributions that it valued highly, given its severely ailing economy.[48] Indeed, the value of development aid was expected to increase in the near future, as Britain aimed to raise contributions to its worldwide overseas aid program by over 50 percent by 1974–75.[49]

In addition to providing substantial aid, Britain remained, behind the United States, Pakistan's second-largest trading partner, exporting around GB£50 million worth of goods per year, including machinery and transport equipment, and importing some GB£30–40 million worth of Pakistani products, 40 percent of which comprised jute and jute manufactures. British private investment in Pakistan amounted to some GB£100 million, much of which predated partition. This figure represented over a third of assets invested privately from overseas.[50]

During the Indo-Pakistan War of 1965, Britain banned supplies of lethal equipment to both sides. "Lethal" was defined to include, among more obvious items, small arms, bombs, and ammunition. This policy was adjusted in March 1966 to allow British manufacturers to sell arms on strictly commercial terms to both Pakistan and India. Consequently, although no military aid flowed from London to either Islamabad or New Delhi, arms supplies did. Britain sought to avoid actively promoting arms sales, despite their being in its commercial interest, in order to avoid the risk of creating or exacerbating a military imbalance on the subcontinent or, somewhat patronizingly, to discourage the diversion of South Asian monies London deemed better spent on development. Britain's purpose in restoring supply had been, beyond economic advantage, to maintain traditional links between the armed forces and to reduce the tendency for South Asians to seek arms elsewhere, particularly from Britain's Cold War adversaries such as China and the Soviet Union. Arms sales from Britain to India exceeded those to Pakistan, but only because New Delhi had shown more interest in purchases. Nevertheless, this imbalance did chafe a little in Islamabad.[51]

The value of British arms supplies to Pakistan was not substantial. The Pakistani navy, however, had recently expressed interest in the very large purchase of five Type 21 frigates, worth some GB£60 million. Inconveniently, Islamabad had reached it Export Credits Guarantee Department (ECGD) limit. As a result, London faced a choice between several options: making the sale on a cash basis, significantly increasing the limit, funding the frigates through military aid, or refusing supply. The matter would be up for discussion during the January talks.[52]

Mistrust and hostility continued to characterize the relationship between Pakistan and India. Britain, therefore, was careful to tread a fine line with regard to its position on the dispute over Kashmir. Its policy, which reflected its decision to adopt a neutral position on the subcontinent after the 1965 war, was to avoid taking sides on the issue. Instead, London maintained that the dispute ought to be resolved by the two countries immediately concerned. Britain was prepared, however, to play the role of facilitator in negotiations, if so invited. Islamabad accepted this policy, although it continued to encourage greater support for its own position.[53]

Pakistan would have preferred a less vociferous British press, fewer British arms going to India, and the support of London in the Kashmir dispute. Nevertheless, despite these minor irritants, at the start of 1971 Anglo-Pakistani relations "remained cordial,"[54] and Heath believed Yahya to be genuine and determined in his aim to restore civilian rule to Pakistan.[55]

Former Great Power 129

On 9 January 1971, the prime minister and the president held private talks during which they developed a personal rapport. The exchange overran its allotted schedule, and the visit to Pakistan as a whole was deemed "highly successful."[56] Heath promised to "see how Britain could help" the Pakistani navy secure its frigates.[57]

Later on the same day that Heath and Yahya met, the former left for India, where he would tour until 12 January. Heath expected a chilly reception. Anglo-Indian relations had not yet recovered from the setbacks over British policies during the 1965 war, when London had been accused of partiality toward Pakistan. Indira Gandhi's lack of affinity for the British did not help. Britain, on the other hand, remained concerned at her "leftward lurch" and India's closer association with the Soviet Union. Yet India remained the world's largest democracy and a country in which Britain maintained significant interests. Heath, as he had in Pakistan, hoped to emphasize the importance of Indian ties with Britain, the Commonwealth, and the West. He wished to establish a better modus vivendi between London and New Delhi.[58]

Britain provided India with more economic aid than it did any other country. On the eve of Heath's visit, London was sending New Delhi GB£45 million per year for development.[59] That was approximately quadruple the amount it was making available to Islamabad, but this was simply a reflection of the fact that India's population was some four times larger.[60] London was second to Washington in generosity, with Washington contributing almost three times as much. Since partition, Britain's total development aid to India had amounted to GB£428 million.[61] Exports to India were valued at some GB£60 million annually, GB£10 million more than to Pakistan, but this flow was beginning to decline. Imports from India were also going down, but still amounted to some GB£100 million per year, more than double the value of imports from Pakistan.[62] Like Pakistan, India purchased British arms under commercial terms. Thus, the economic ties between Britain and India were significant.

In the personality notes given to Heath before his visit, he was warned that Indira Gandhi was "wilful, petulant, hereditarily imperious," and maintained "an ingrained suspicion of British and American policies."[63] Despite these ominous signs, the British prime minister's visit proved a success in personal terms. He and Indira Gandhi appeared to get along well both in private talks and in public, with Morrice James, the British high commissioner to New Delhi, remarking that the visit yielded "a potential benefit upon which ... we can hope to build."[64] Nevertheless, he described Indira

130 United Kingdom

Gandhi as "Janus-faced," and warned London to be cautious in its assessments.[65] Stanley Tomlinson, deputy permanent under-secretary of state at the Foreign and Commonwealth Office (FCO), observed: "The visit was an immense success, but is unlikely to have effected any real long-term change of heart in Mrs. Gandhi."[66] At the start of 1971, therefore, relations between London and New Delhi were a little less strained. Moreover, Heath had established good rapport with Indira Gandhi, as he recently had done with Yahya. He would attempt to call on this personal chemistry in writing to both South Asian leaders during the East Pakistan crisis.

Action and Reaction

Buildup to Crisis

Heath had been enthusiastic about supplying the five frigates to Pakistan, as he had concerns over possible future Soviet expansion into the Indian Ocean. Supporting the Pakistani navy in this way would aid British shipbuilding, boost bilateral relations with Pakistan, and help counterbalance any future Soviet intentions. The United Kingdom had already supplied frigates to India, and so Heath believed that, even though a commercial deal with Islamabad would be unpopular in New Delhi, it could be satisfactorily explained away. By the end of February, however, no solution had been found to the financing problem. The secretary of state for trade and industry believed that it would be too risky to extend commercial credit and raise the ECGD limit, as Pakistan's economy continued to decline and a request for rescheduling of existing debt liabilities appeared imminent. Douglas-Home was firmly of the opinion that the frigates must be sold on commercial terms, as a departure from this policy would be equivalent to providing Pakistan with military aid and would therefore be "bitterly resented" in India. With these two options dismissed, the remaining choice was between Pakistan's somehow paying on a cash basis, despite its economic woes, or a refusal to supply, with its consequent effect on London-Islamabad relations. On 24 February, Douglas-Home wrote to Heath, explaining the situation and suggesting that the ball be tossed into Pakistan's court, placing the onus on Islamabad to devise a way of paying without an extension of commercial credit.[67] There it would remain, only to be returned to Britain several months into the increasingly tense East Pakistan crisis.

On 1 March, Yahya postponed indefinitely the first meeting of the Constituent Assembly. In response, Mujibur Rahman, the leader of the Awami League, called for non-cooperation and non-violent demonstrations in the

East wing. The South Asia Department of the FCO (unfortunately abbreviated as SAD) believed that although this increased the possibility of a split between the two wings, Yahya appeared determined to prevent this. In addition, SAD head Iain Sutherland doubted whether the army could prevent the East from seceding if it elected to do so, and "certainly not without serious and widespread clashes with the civilian population."[68]

Despite Mujibur Rahman's demand for non-violent confrontation, the East was soon seized by what Frank Sargeant, the British deputy high commissioner in Dacca (DHC) described on 4 March as "hooliganism, looting, arson, and mob violence in a framework of general strike, road blocks, and stoppage of all traffic." Sargeant worried that the situation could rapidly degenerate into one of "anarchy, breakdown of essential services, and widespread bloodshed," especially if Mujibur Rahman should call for independence in a major statement announced for 7 March. Accordingly, he sought permission from London to pursue further a pre-arranged four-stage evacuation plan should the situation deteriorate. His office in Dacca remained open, manned by a skeleton staff, but was not accepting telephone calls, as it had been "threatened with attack unless closed."[69] The DHC had already warned British nationals to purchase supplies and remain at home. In response, the FCO confirmed that the DHC already had permission to implement further stages of the evacuation plan at his discretion, and established a Pakistan Emergency Unit the following day, tasked with responding to the situation and coordinating an extraction if necessary.[70]

On confirmation of his authority, Sargeant implemented the second stage of the evacuation plan on 5 March, calling on British nationals to leave by commercial means. He believed that "women and children at least would then be best away from East Pakistan." He did not, however, expect to make a decision on implementing the two remaining stages until 7 March.[71] Douglas-Home offered reassurance: "I am grateful for your careful and comprehensive reports. You are in the best position to assess the situation and I have full confidence in your judgment. Best wishes to you all."[72]

Sargeant replied to Douglas-Home on 6 March: "This is very encouraging to us all." In the same telegram, he took the opportunity to demand "maximum co-operation from available sources of help," and complained vigorously about the lack of assistance he had received from a British airline in arranging the evacuations. The DHC's stress and irritability did not go unnoticed in London. John Graham, private secretary to Douglas-Home, made the handwritten observation: "This tel. shows, I fear, that Mr. Sargeant is not unnaturally inclined to be out of patience with distant authority!"[73]

132 *United Kingdom*

Although Mujibur Rahman did not call for independence the following day, the situation in East Pakistan remained tense. On 11 March, Sargeant complained again, this time about being "hopelessly overloaded."[74]

Four days later, however, the situation changed for the better. Yahya flew to Dacca on 15 March to engage in talks with Mujibur Rahman in the hope of finding a solution to the political impasse. The following day, the FCO's Pakistan Emergency Unit was stood down. With its help and that of Sargeant and his staff, about 250 people, the majority of them women and children of the British community, were evacuated on special commercial flights arranged by the FCO on 9 and 14 March.[75] Without providing specific information, SAD noted that attacks by Bengalis on the Bihari (non-Bengali) communities since the start of March had been on a scale greater than it had initially thought.[76]

Sargeant continued to show signs of stress under pressure. On 16 March, he wired the FCO, complaining that the BBC had broadcast inaccurate information to evacuees just over a week earlier, thereby creating problems for him and his staff. He received a reply not from SAD but directly from Tomlinson, the deputy permanent under-secretary of state, who remarked: "I am distressed that these broadcasts should have caused so much concern." He continued: "Greetings to you and Joan and all your staff. You have had a tough time since you arrived in Dacca and I have much admired the way you have coped."[77]

Meanwhile, the talks between Yahya and Mujibur Rahman appeared to be making good progress, and Sargeant recognized that the "president [was] in a conciliatory mood."[78] On 22 March, in a note for Douglas-Home, Sutherland agreed that "there now seems a chance of the President's achieving his object."[79] On 24 March, the very day before the clampdown began, Sargeant wired the FCO that "it appears increasingly as if there will be an interim central government."[80]

Thus, on the eve of the crisis, Sargeant and the FCO foresaw a settlement. They did not see the clampdown coming, nor did they expect such an action to necessarily succeed, and certainly not without substantial civilian bloodshed. In addition, Britain's chief representative in Dacca had already exhibited signs of stress under pressure, a fact that had not gone unnoticed in Whitehall.

The Clampdown Begins
Before discussing the clampdown and London's response, it is useful to consider the main British players at the start of the crisis. The Conservative

politicians most directly involved were Alec Douglas-Home (foreign secretary) and Richard Wood (minister for overseas development, a more junior position).[81] The diplomats at the FCO in London were led by Denis Greenhill (permanent under-secretary of state, the senior civil servant at the FCO).[82] Greenhill was assisted by, in descending order of seniority, Stanley Tomlinson (deputy under-secretary of state, with responsibility for South Asia), Kenneth Wilford (assistant under-secretary of state, with responsibility for South Asia), Iain Sutherland (head of the South Asia Department), and Hugh Byatt (Sutherland's chief assistant).

Britain was represented in Pakistan by Cyril Pickard (high commissioner to Islamabad), Reginald Burrows (deputy high commissioner in Islamabad and Pickard's second-in-command), and Frank Sargeant (deputy high commissioner in Dacca). In India, Morrice James (high commissioner to New Delhi) and Peter Male (James's deputy in New Delhi) looked after British diplomatic concerns. Along with Prime Minister Heath, it is these thirteen British actors on the foreign affairs stage who would feature most prominently in the race to formulate the government's response.

Contrary to British expectations, Yahya unleashed his West Pakistani–dominated army on the evening of 25 March, cutting communications within and from East Pakistan, including the diplomatic wire services. Sargeant, taken unawares, used a secret emergency transmitter in his residence to report directly to the FCO the next day. In an urgent flash he observed: "Heavy fighting during night. All safe."[83] Meanwhile, in West Pakistan, Joseph Farland, the US ambassador to Islamabad, informed Pickard that the "army [had] moved in" and was "apparently taking up positions on rooftops [in Dacca] and firing to clear [the] streets."[84] The same day, following Yahya's address to the nation and before more detailed reports of atrocities began to appear, Pickard expressed his fear of "bloodshed on a large scale." He contended that "our first consideration must be [the] safety of our own nationals," and that preparations should be finalized for an emergency evacuation if required.[85]

Following Pickard's lead, the focus in London centred on the extraction of British citizens. Burke Trend, the cabinet secretary and head of the civil service, immediately demanded an update on the current contingency plans for such an event. Following the exodus of the 250 people in mid-March, over 700 Britons still remained in East Pakistan, 400 of whom resided in the vicinity of Dacca, 200 around Chittagong, and 100 elsewhere.[86] Yet Sargeant did not call for an emergency airlift, as he had no means of communicating with his charges, the streets were dangerous, and the airport was closed.[87] The burden of responsibility for a further 300 foreign nationals also rested on his weakened shoulders, Britain having accepted responsibility for non–South Asian Commonwealth citizens as well as the nationals of Denmark, Finland, Iceland, Ireland, the Netherlands, Norway, Sweden, and Switzerland.

On 27 March, more detailed and specific reports of atrocities began to filter through to London. Major Cox, Sargeant's assistant military advisor in Dacca, reported that gunfire and explosions appeared to be concentrated around the police headquarters, the East Pakistan Rifles barracks, the university, and the residential area around Mujibur Rahman's home. From a hotel rooftop near the high commission building, he had personally seen troops firing "in a most callous manner at anyone who moved on the streets."[88] Anticipating that news of the atrocities would reach the British press, and given the Pakistani government's recent resentment of media criticism over its handling of the cyclone response, Pickard expected the "rapid deterioration of our relations with [the] Pakistan government." Moreover, he feared a public backlash in West Pakistan, where the British community would then be "exposed to mob violence." Consequently, he was considering curtailing the local distribution of British newspapers.[89]

In its attempt to prevent news of its activities from leaking out of East Pakistan, the army had not only severed, to the best of its ability, all means of electronic communication but also rounded up and deported the foreign press corps after confiscating films, tapes, and notes.[90] Two journalists escaped the dragnet, among them Simon Dring of the *Daily Telegraph*. Before flying out on 28 March, Dring had toured the city, surveying the destruction, including the "shambles at Iqbal University students hostel, where 200 students [were] believed to have died." Sargeant had no doubt that when Dring reported his findings, Anglo-Pakistani relations would "take a plunge for the worse."[91]

Shortly after expressing his concerns, the DHC wired London, noting that, by implementing "a reign of terror," the Pakistani military "appear[ed] to be firmly in control of the Dacca area." They had achieved this result at great cost, however. In the old town, "huts and small shops have been deliberately fired and the owners machine gunned," and similar operations were continuing elsewhere. The police force had been "largely shot down" and the East Pakistan Rifles attacked. Sargeant estimated the casualties at around five thousand, and the bodies of many women and children were still on the streets.[92] At the British Council office on Iqbal University campus, "the army shot their way in and massacred the police guard." The British Council representative, had been present but escaped with his life. Such disturbing news from the DHC was being relayed beyond the FCO through situation reports sent to the office of the prime minister himself.[93]

Despite his disquieting communications to London, Sargeant was determined to discourage any public criticism of Islamabad by the British government. On 29 March, he wrote: "Please alert ministers to the probable grave consequences for the British communities here if any official criticism of the conduct of the Pakistani government is voiced at this time." He worried that such actions would "enrage the army, which is in control here, and with which we must maintain best possible relations." He did not address his message as normal to the FCO, where it would have found its way to SAD. Instead, he marked it for the attention of higher powers, namely, Tomlinson.[94]

Archer Blood, the US consul general in Dacca, had already wired Washington accusing Islamabad of "selective genocide," and on 6 April he would dissent from US policy of avoiding public condemnation of the clampdown. Both he and Sargeant worked closely together and shared similar information,[95] yet the British DHC promoted an entirely different approach. Sargeant was deeply immersed in the almost overwhelming day-to-day demands of his pressurized role both as British representative and coordinator of a sizable evacuation. This afforded him little opportunity to step back and consider the bigger picture.[96] In addition, the responsibility for the well-being of so many British, Commonwealth, and foreign nationals weighed heavily on his shoulders, and good relations with the Pakistani army would, no doubt, have helped him carry out his immediate technical responsibilities.[97] It appears that, for these reasons, Sargeant was unable or unwilling to adopt the same moral line as his American counterpart. Throughout the crisis, British diplomats perceived the clashes in East Bengal not as "genocide" but as "civil war."[98]

Developing a Response

Far away, in London, Heath and Douglas-Home were beginning to formulate the British response. As early as 27 March, while addressing a meeting of the Scottish Conservative and Unionist Association in Edinburgh, the prime minister had announced that Britain had no intention of intervening in the affairs of "a completely independent sovereign country."[99] On 29 March, the same day Sargeant was imploring Tomlinson to avoid public condemnation, Douglas-Home made a prepared statement to the House of Commons. Without apportioning blame, the foreign secretary expressed regret for the loss of life in Pakistan, then confirmed the prime minister's line: "This is an internal matter affecting relations between two parts of a sovereign country."[100] In cabinet three days later, having received yet more reports of atrocities through the FCO, Douglas-Home conceded that "the army had acted in a ruthless and punitive fashion."[101] Nevertheless, he maintained the stance that the issue remained "primarily an internal matter for the Government of Pakistan."[102] Britain had no right to intervene. Much to the relief of Sargeant, public neutrality, the first component of the British response had been firmly locked in place. Pickard, who was due to leave for a new posting as British high commissioner to Lagos on 20 April, was told to remain in place.[103]

By the end of March, the nature and scale of the atrocities in East Pakistan had become clearer still. Pickard noted that "political leaders [were] being hunted down and shot." The army was "acting with a callous disregard for life and [was] adopting terror tactics to cow the Bengalis." Although he had no doubt of the army's ability to hold Dacca and Chittagong, he expected increasing resistance elsewhere – a guerilla movement that would "continue indefinitely."[104] Sargeant observed that "a reign of terror" existed in the areas around Dacca, where, with the acquiescence of the army, armed bands of non-Bengali Muhajirs were killing Bengalis and destroying their homes.[105] On 30 March, Pickard wrote to the FCO. Having taken the opportunity to step back and reflect, he remarked that he had "no doubt whatsoever ... that appalling developments [were] taking place," and that the "time will soon come when the horror stories from East Pakistan will be sufficiently authenticated to provide me with a basis for speaking to the [Pakistani] Foreign Secretary." Although aware of the potential threat to bilateral ties from such an approach, the high commissioner believed he had sufficient standing after five years in post, and the appropriate skills, to alert the Pakistani foreign secretary to the "dangers of inaction on his part," and to do so without unduly damaging Anglo-Pakistani relations. He did not suggest he take such a course, however, until as many British nationals as possible had been evacuated from the East.[106]

Whereas Farland and the Canadian high commissioner to Islamabad, John Small, were unwilling to risk bilateral ties with Islamabad, Pickard saw beyond the immediate situation and was reluctant to substitute technical for moral responsibility. Appalled at events, he felt compelled to urge restraint. Thus developed a situation where, in Dacca, the American representative was calling for public condemnation when his British counterpart

Former Great Power 137

was balking at any such prospect and, in Islamabad, the American ambassador was adamant in protecting bilateral relations when his British equivalent was prepared to take a calculated risk.

On the last day of March, Sargeant issued an assessment that contained news of an alarming new direction in the killings: "The Hindus, in particular, [had] apparently been slaughtered in large numbers." The Hindu quarter in Dacca had been "gutted," a member of the DHC's staff had seen a mass grave outside a university hall reserved for Hindus, and the military, it was reported, had burned down a Hindu village just outside Dacca, "killing hundreds."[107] The army appeared to be targeting the ethnically distinct Hindu community. Sargeant continued: "Tales of massacre of Bengalis are legion." Many bodies were said to be floating in the river, and "at least nine truck loads [sic] of bodies, some of the[m] policemen, [had] been buried in the municipal rubbish dump in the last two days." Islamabad's claims that conditions were returning to normal were quite wrong.[108] The same day, in London, the FCO reactivated the Pakistan Emergency Unit, under the charge of Sutherland.[109]

Around the same time Sargeant was refuting Pakistan's claims that Dacca was returning to its customary routines, the Pakistani high commissioner to London was meeting the British prime minister to deliver a letter of explication from Yahya. Justifying the clampdown as a necessary action to preserve the unity of Pakistan, Yahya asserted that "the situation in East Pakistan [was] well under control and normal life [was] being restored." The Pakistani president greatly appreciated that Britain had chosen to uphold the principle of non-interference in the internal affairs of other countries.[110] Much to his visitor's pleasure, Heath reiterated his view that there should be no outside meddling. The prime minister appeared to have some difficulty believing the claims about a return to normality, however. When his guest suggested that published reports of casualties were exaggerated, Heath hinted that press access to the East may provide "a more accurate picture," before reminding the high commissioner that the Pakistani authorities had assured the United Kingdom of its assistance in the event of evacuation.[111]

During the first week of April, British officials in Pakistan set about assessing the likely longer-term outcome of Yahya's intervention. Major Cox recognized that the army faced "a gigantic logistical problem" and had "little control" outside the main towns. He was still unable to assess the potency of Bengali resistance.[112] Pickard, who had already expressed his view that a resistance movement would develop, preventing a return to normal life in the East, confirmed that he had no reason to change this assessment in the light of more recent information.[113] Indeed, on 4 April, the high commissioner stated:

> Eventual end result is likely to be an independent East Pakistan. In terms of investment and raw material sources, our long-term interests may prove to be with a future regime in the East, rather than with the western rump. We must not prejudice our long-term interests, and offend the Indians, in seeking unwisely to defend short-term interests in Pakistan.[114]

Unlike his American and Canadian counterparts in Islamabad, Pickard demonstrated an ability to step back from the immediate situation and consider the larger picture with some detachment, despite the threat to the status of his current role. No doubt his imminent departure for Lagos facilitated this posture.

Douglas-Home made another statement to the House on 5 April, in which he developed a second component of British response policy. Publicly expressing concern for "all sections of the Pakistan community," and underlining once again that the United Kingdom had "no intention of interfering in Pakistan's internal affairs," the foreign secretary stated that the government was "ready to play our part in an international effort to help in mitigating suffering."[115] Thus, London added the provision of humanitarian relief (potential provision only at this stage) to the original policy component of public neutrality.

In Dacca, the stress of arranging the extraction of those for whom he was responsible, and who wished to leave on specially arranged commercial flights, was beginning to take its toll on Sargeant. Believing Dacca "vulnerable to even a moderately competent force of trained, armed men,"[116] he became "doubtful about the wisdom of encouraging a congregation in Dacca, which may become a battlefield."[117] He did not make clear where this force would come from or how it would overcome the thousands of professional troops in and around the city. He continued:

> If a battle for Dacca develops, the airfield could be (a) damaged or (b) denied to the West Pakistanis. This post will then be indefinitely isolated ... There is very little more that I can do to help British subjects in Dacca who have for one reason or another disregarded my repeated advice to leave. And it must be a long time before my office can resume normal functions. I shall, therefore, reduce my staff to a cadre.[118]

Former Great Power 139

A somewhat perplexed Pickard pointed out that the army is "heavily reinforcing its troops in the main centres and we see little reason to doubt that they will hold Dacca firmly for some time to come," but agreed to a "thinning" of the staff.[119]

Twenty minutes after his initial response, the high commissioner, clearly concerned, tried to reassure his colleague with a second reply, reminding the DHC that Douglas-Home, in his statement to the House the previous day, had thanked Sargeant by name for his efforts. In addition, Pickard expressed the hope that "with the evacuation of [the] bulk of UK citizens, [the] strain will be slightly reduced." Moreover, he suggested that Sargeant "ought to consider coming out to West Pakistan for a short rest," with Reginald Burrows possibly taking his place temporarily. Pickard finished his missive by expressing concern for the representative who had escaped the assault on the British Council offices at the university.[120]

Even after reflecting overnight, Sargent was not in the most receptive of moods on 7 April. He snapped back: "Thank you for these thoughts. No repeat no visitors until I am reasonably assured that the army can hold Dacca anyhow over the short term. Naylor is in the same danger as the rest of us, but he may leave Dacca."[121]

The next day, for reasons not entirely clear, Sargeant perceived the situation in Dacca to be more stable and agreed that Burrows should temporarily replace him in order to appreciate the conditions in East Pakistan and "observe in particular the sort of *work we can no longer carry out.*"[122] Sargeant appeared to be reaching his limit. Burrows would temporarily relieve the struggling DHC on 16 April.

Having received a letter from Yahya on 31 March, Heath took a week to consult Douglas-Home and the FCO before sending a considered response in which he introduced the third component of British policy. Douglas-Home agreed with Pickard that, although the Pakistani army was probably capable of holding the main urban centres in the East, it could not suppress over seventy million Bengalis throughout the whole country in the longer term. Under these circumstances, the foreign secretary believed that a political settlement was essential, and the sooner negotiations started, the better. He saw no alternative potential leaders in East Pakistan beyond Mujibur Rahman and the Awami League.[123] Heath concurred, and a reply from the prime minister to Yahya was wired to Pickard on 7 April, with a view to the high commissioner's delivering it personally and seeking to obtain an understanding of Yahya's attitude and mood. The successful pursuit of political accommodation, if it could be achieved, carried with it a convenient subsidiary advantage – stability would help protect British interests in the East, including tea plantation investments and supplies of jute.

Hoping to take advantage of the good rapport between Heath and Yahya during Heath's visit to Pakistan in January, the message adopted a tone that conveyed the British leader's thoughts in a direct manner. While empathizing with Yahya's difficult predicament, Heath called on him to end the "bloodshed and the use of force as soon as possible," before "a resumption of discussions" that, at some point, involve "the political leaders who received such massive support." After suggesting that Yahya publicly assure Mujibur Rahman and other Awami League leaders of their safety, Heath reassured Yahya that London had no intention of intervening and had received "a specific assurance" from New Delhi that it, too, would not interfere. Recalling the warm yet frank exchanges between them in January, Heath encouraged Yahya to confide in him how he saw the situation and how best a political resolution might be achieved.[124] Although the prime minister did not explicitly state that Mujibur Rahman should be part of the discussions, in cabinet the next day Douglas-Home confirmed that this was the government's desire.[125]

It would take another day for Pickard to eventually meet with Yahya. Initially tense, the general slowly relaxed, giving the high commissioner an hour of his time. Yahya said he had not yet reached any firm conclusion as to the exact form political negotiations would take, but some progress along these lines ought to be possible after order was fully restored in the East.[126] Nevertheless, he made it clear that "he had not [sic] intention of negotiating with Mujib [Mujibur Rahman]."[127] The third main component of British policy had now been established: the use of private influence to achieve a political settlement.

From New Delhi, James refrained at this stage from offering advice on how to tackle the East Pakistan problem. Despite, or possibly because of, his five years of experience as British high commissioner to Islamabad between 1961 and 1966, he restricted his attention to discerning the Indian approach to the crisis. His perception, in early April, of India's evolving policy was that New Delhi did not intend to intervene militarily in either East or West Pakistan in the immediate future. Nevertheless, owing to public pressure, among other things, it would grant asylum to East Pakistani political actors, allow East Bengalis to cross into India, and permit non-military supplies to flow the other way. New Delhi would also continue to condemn the policies of Islamabad and encourage private efforts to help East Pakistan. India was in no position to go further, as it did not have sufficient information

Former Great Power   141

concerning either Bengali resistance or Pakistani army progress. Although some arms were being carried across the border on a private basis, the government had not, to James's knowledge, instituted a policy of formal supply.[128] Like Pickard, James was scheduled for a rotation of posts. On 9 May, Terence Garvey took over in New Delhi.[129]

Some two weeks after the clampdown commenced, therefore, Sargeant was suffering under strain and, caught up in the daily grind, was eager that London keep quiet about atrocities and that nothing be done to worsen Anglo-Pakistani relations, especially while British nationals remained in East Pakistan. Pickard recognized the need to extract as many Britons as possible before acting, but felt strongly that the army's actions should not be allowed to pass without private comment to the authorities in Islamabad. James, despite being copied on much of the wire traffic concerning East Pakistan, opted to confine his advice to the consideration of Indian intentions. In London, three main aspects of British policy had already been demonstrated: 1) public neutrality over an internal matter of a sovereign state, 2) willingness to provide humanitarian relief, and 3) the use of private influence to encourage a political settlement.

Challenges Accumulate

On 19 April, the Pakistan Emergency Unit was again stood down.[130] The number of British nationals in East Pakistan had decreased to approximately 230, some of whom could not be contacted while the rest had elected to stay.[131] On the ground in the East wing, the atrocities were continuing and would do so for many weeks to come.[132] As a result, thousands of refugees had begun to flood over the border into India.[133] At the same time, there was confusion over Indian actions, as the Americans had let James know New Delhi was supplying "small arms and communications equipment" to the Bengali resistance. The US source was Archer Blood.[134] A few days after the tipoff, James met the ambassadors to New Delhi of Belgium, France, Germany, Italy, the Netherlands, and the United States at the German ambassador's residence. There "it was generally agreed that the Indian Govt [government] was doing its best, in the face of strong public opinion, to hold a moderate line," and "there was no evidence of organised Indian attempts to supply arms to the East Pakistanis."[135]

Two days before he was temporarily relieved by Burrows, Sargeant found time to write a summary of his thoughts on the crisis. He noted that resistance would soon test the army, but that "it [was] still too early to predict the outcome of the current military campaign." Following the killing of Awami League politicians and student leaders, "the army [was] acting in unrestrained fashion, wantonly killing and destroying, and generally comporting itself like an army of conquest." Consequently, "any [current] talk of a political settlement must be discarded as wilful nonsense." Nevertheless, if Yahya wished to "hand over power to civilians ... then he must reengage in a dialogue with the Awami League." Unfortunately, "all the indications are that he has no such intention."[136] Sargeant's assessment was therefore generally in accord with Douglas-Home's understanding of the situation following Yahya's stated refusal, following delivery of Heath's letter, to negotiate with Mujibur Rahman. Sargeant went on to highlight two practical problems that loomed large on the horizon: first, development aid and technical assistance programs in the East could not readily be restarted, and, second, the likely onset of large-scale famine in the region.[137]

Pickard offered his own lengthy assessments on 22 and 23 April. From a military perspective, the Pakistani army appeared intent on eliminating opposition and then creating conditions of stability in the East. Although guerrilla forces were not yet sufficiently supplied, trained, and organised to provide opposition beyond "extensive harassment," the terrain and monsoon climate worked in their favour. In time, given ready sources of equipment and training, they were likely to grow into a formidable force, though it would take "perhaps three years or more" to develop the capability of mounting "Viet Cong type attacks."[138] From a political standpoint, Yahya would find it impossible to simply release Mujibur Rahman and withdraw the army. On the other hand, an indefinite military campaign would be "contrary to his stated aim." As a result, he appeared to be seeking a political settlement that involved handing power to either a "purged" Awami League or to non–Awami League politicians in the East, perhaps a combination of the two. The problem remained, however, that neither a rump Awami League nor politicians from alternative parties would have any local credibility. At best, such representatives would have to govern with ongoing substantial support from the army. Pickard concluded that this option had little chance of success, and the most likely outcome was that ongoing "guerilla warfare and economic pressures" would force a reluctant West Pakistani withdrawal from the East, leaving chaos in its wake. Nevertheless, the high commissioner believed the search for a political solution must continue, as "it may just be possible that there will be sufficient Bengali acquiescence, albeit sullen, to enable a limping administration to be temporarily restored."[139]

Former Great Power 143

Although Pickard had presented his argument in a more cogent and comprehensive manner, he and Sargeant agreed on the fundamental issues. London stood forewarned that finding a political settlement, while still a worthwhile pursuit, would be a long, uphill struggle. Sutherland agreed with the missives, but Wilford was not convinced. In extensive handwritten notes in response to Sargeant's memorandum, the assistant under-secretary of state wrote: "We should not take it for granted that Mujib's [Mujibur Rahman's] claim that 70,000 [troops] cannot hold down 70,000,000 is necessarily true. It is true only if the 70 million are united and militant. Yahya Khan is doubtless banking on their being neither. He may know his people better than any of us."[140]

His immediate superior was less convinced. Tomlinson jotted below: "Although I agree with much of what Mr. Wilford says, I continue to view the longer-term future in E. Bengal with deep gloom."[141] Wilford remained somewhat more optimistic than those around him, but by late April London was well aware of the difficulties it faced in encouraging a viable political settlement.

Yahya had given his initial reaction to Heath's letter orally in his meeting with Pickard on 9 April. Subsequently, he nominated Mian Arshad Hussain, a former foreign minister, as his special envoy and charged him with visiting Heath in London to explain the East Pakistan situation face to face.[142] Prime minister and envoy met at Downing Street on 27 April. The envoy attempted to reassure Heath that the situation was under control, subject to a "few pockets of resistance" and "some trouble" caused by Indian-trained and supplied insurgents. Heath raised two matters of "special concern": the conduct of the Pakistani army in the East and the very poor economic position of Pakistan as a whole. Hussain accepted that there "might have been some undisciplined action" in the army, but this was only in the "early days" and "under provocation." He confirmed that Yahya was aware of his country's economic plight and taking steps to address the situation.[143]

In a thinly veiled move to tie development aid to political ends, Heath suggested that "the extent to which help could be given was bound to depend to some extent on public feeling and how far the Pakistan Government showed that it was tackling the situation in East Pakistan." He again encouraged external access to the East in order to discourage "wild rumours." In addition, Heath "feared that [the recently proposed] trials of East Pakistan leaders could make a return to normality more difficult."[144] The next day, he wrote to Yahya, again expressing his concern over the "very grave" economic problems Pakistan faced and suggesting that any suffering in the East due to a failure to provide food and other supplies would be "particularly bad." The prime minister was slowly ratcheting up the pressure on the Pakistani president, all the time insisting that the crisis was an internal matter for the government of Pakistan.[145]

At a cabinet meeting on 29 April, Douglas-Home pointed to three recent developments of particular concern, some of which Heath had already taken up with Islamabad: 1) an estimated 200,000 refugees had crossed into India; 2) Pakistan's economic plight was "very serious," its foreign exchange reserves expected to run out in just weeks; and 3) the prospect of famine in the region by July-August was looming.[146] In order to address the humanitarian issues, Douglas-Home had approached William Rogers, the US secretary of state, who was visiting London at the end of April. He persuaded Rogers to join him in making an appeal to U Thant, encouraging the UN secretary-general to "assess the situation and coordinate international relief."[147]

The severity of Pakistan's dire economic situation became increasingly apparent during the first week of May. Islamabad had already issued a communiqué that had amounted to "a six-month moratorium on all service payments due on foreign debt."[148] Following a special meeting of the Pakistan aid consortium in Paris on 30 April, Peter Cargill of the IBRD visited Pakistan to assess the situation. After meeting with Yahya, Cargill believed the president to be "apparently still not fully seized of the implications for West Pakistan of [the] impending economic crisis." A former British civil servant, Cargill had audited Pakistan's accounts and his preliminary estimate was that the assistance required was "far beyond what [the] IBRD or IMF [International Monetary Fund] could provide." Foreign exchange reserves were all but fully depleted.[149] At his meeting with the IBRD representative, Pickard observed that "Cargill was obviously shaken to discover the speed at which time [was] now running out for West Pakistan." The IBRD representative was also "despondent" at Yahya's inability to appreciate the urgency of the situation. In his opinion, without some form of outside intervention, "economic disaster and internal disruption in the West [were] imminent."[150] The Pakistani economy was on the brink of collapse. Pickard considered that the economic plight of the West might force, in time, a withdrawal from the East. He pointed out that, under the circumstances and in the absence of a political settlement for the East, provision of further assistance through the consortium would be a matter of "throwing good money after bad." Moreover, it would be "unacceptable" to British public opinion and provoke a hostile reaction in India.[151]

Former Great Power 145

By the start of May, the pursuit of a political settlement with the encouragement of private British influence appeared to be a considerable challenge. Furthermore, the need to provide humanitarian relief to both East Pakistan and the refugees in India had become increasingly apparent, developmental projects in the East could no longer be pursued, and Pakistan as a whole appeared to be standing on the brink of an economic crash.

6

The Commons Debates and After

In the US diplomatic delegations, Archer Blood, the consul general in Dacca, and Kenneth Keating, the ambassador to New Delhi, had pressed for a forthright public response to the clampdown. James George, the Canadian high commissioner to New Delhi, had tried to make a stand. Of the British representatives abroad, however, no one had adopted a similar line. Instead, it would be Parliament, the press, and ultimately the British public that would pressure the country's leaders. It is to these bodies that our attention will turn in this chapter.

Public Sphere

First Commons Debate
At 11:05 a.m. on 14 May 1971, the House of Commons began a five-hour debate on British policy in response to the East Pakistan crisis. This debate had been a long time in coming. During April and the start of May, Labour MPs had pushed for such a discussion without success; following guidance from the Foreign and Commonwealth Office (FCO), the Leader of the House of Commons, William Whitelaw, had refused to make time in the schedule. The government wished to avoid a public discussion, fearing criticism of either itself or Islamabad. Nevertheless, the pressure had steadily built. Just when the government was considering yielding to Labour demands, backbench MP Bruce Douglas-Mann (Labour, Kensington North)

won a ballot to decide which of the many Early Day Motions submitted would be included on the list of those to be heard by the House. The government would have to engage.[1]

Before discussing the debate, it is useful to examine the nature of the limited exchanges in Parliament up to mid-May. Secretary of State for Foreign and Commonwealth Affairs Alec Douglas-Home had already made two statements in the House, on 29 March and 5 April (Chapter 5), each of which was followed by a few questions from some of those attending. After his first statement, in which he had outlined the British policy of non-interference in what he considered the internal affair of a sovereign state, the response in the House was subdued. The shadow foreign secretary, Denis Healey (Labour, Leeds East), was mainly concerned with the safety of British lives and property.[2] The second response of the day, however, revealed a concern that would be raised in Parliament on several occasions. The Liberal leader, Jeremy Thorpe (Devon North), implored that, "apart from offering our good offices if they should be required, there will be no further involvement." This was "in view of the unhappy experience of this country's involvement in another Commonwealth civil war, namely, Nigeria." Moreover, he insisted that "in particular, there will be no question of supplying arms."[3] The acute discomfort of having recently backed, and indeed armed, the Nigerian federal government while distressing images of the victims of famine in Biafra were hitting the headlines was still sorely felt in parliamentary circles.

Frederic Bennett (Conservative, Torquay) also favoured non-intervention, but for quite different reasons.[4] Bennett's father had been a personal friend of Muhammad Ali Jinnah, the founder of Pakistan, and he had family ties to the country. He would go on to support Islamabad throughout, becoming what Iain Sutherland, the head of the South Asia Department (SAD) of the FCO, would later call an "extreme pro-Pakistan MP."[5] The House soon moved on to other business.

Following Douglas-Home's second statement, on 5 April, the House was more deeply concerned in its response. Decrying the suffering of "all sections of the Pakistan community," the foreign secretary revealed the government's willingness to contribute to humanitarian relief, publicly reaffirmed its neutrality, and restated its policy not to interfere.[6] On this occasion, Healey had more information available to him. "In view of the very convincing reports of indiscriminate bloodshed in East Pakistan," he urged the government to use its influence to bring about an end to the killing and encourage "a peaceful solution of the political problems of East Pakistan in accordance with the wishes of the people of that territory."[7] Douglas-Mann, the member who would win the Early Day Motions ballot for May, demanded ultimately the same but in somewhat more passionate terms, drawing the foreign secretary's attention to an all-party motion that had acquired over one hundred signatures urging the government to do all it could to bring about a cease-fire.[8] These views were very much in accord with those of Douglas-Home and Prime Minister Edward Heath, as would be evidenced in the latter's letter to Pakistani president Yahya Khan of 7 April.

In anticipation of the upcoming debate, the foreign secretary made a third statement to the House on 11 May. He made public the concerns he had recently raised in cabinet and the actions he had taken to address them. He discussed his joint approach, with the Americans, to UN Secretary-General U Thant, made with a view to averting a potential famine in East Pakistan and providing for the large number of refugees fleeing to India. He then described the severe economic strain under which Pakistan was labouring, stating that "consultations" were taking place under the auspices of the Pakistan aid consortium.[9]

As Healey again pressed for progress on a political settlement, Douglas-Home assured him that he agreed such a path was "the only way," and that the government was "in constant touch" with Yahya in an attempt to achieve that goal.[10] Thorpe expressed his concern over ongoing reports of atrocities in the East, suggesting that a team of observers from either the Commonwealth or the United Nations be dispatched to verify the allegations. The foreign secretary responded that he had "no reason to believe that they would be accepted."[11] To Douglas-Mann's contention that the situation should be treated not as an internal affair but, given East Pakistan's democratically approved move to separate, as an "aggressive war between two countries," Douglas-Home suggested that there existed different interpretations of whether the election results gave the Awami League a mandate to secede.[12]

As the major debate approached, therefore, there had been no call in Parliament for public condemnation of Islamabad. Both the Liberals and, more importantly, the leadership of the official opposition were aligned with the government's policies, though perhaps somewhat frustrated that the exertion of private influence was not more rapidly catalyzing progress toward a political settlement. Despite attempts by a few pro-Islamabad MPs, such as Bennett, to persuade otherwise, the number of signatories associated with the all-party motion suggested a certain discomfort and concern around the House. By raising the matter in debate, Douglas-Mann hoped to nourish such sympathies in support of the East.

Douglas-Mann, who had a particular interest in human rights issues and who would soon be condemning Idi Amin's treatment of Ugandan Asians, stated his motion as follows:

> I beg to move that this House, deeply concerned by the killing and destruction which has taken place in East Pakistan, and the possible threat of food shortages later this year, calls upon Her Majesty's Government to use their [sic] influence to secure an end to the strife, the admission of United Nations or other international relief organisations, and the achievement of a political settlement which will respect the democratic rights of the people of Pakistan.[13]

This was a more specific version of a previous motion he had raised that had attracted the signatures of over three hundred members, which Douglas-Mann believed to be a record for the House.[14]

By mid-May, the number of refugees in India had mushroomed to two million. Douglas-Mann and John Stonehouse (Labour, Wednesbury)[15] had visited the camps in West Bengal three weeks earlier, and were appalled by the conditions and the terrible stories of the refugees. Douglas-Mann was convinced that an international relief effort was essential. Although conceding that there had been "atrocities on both sides," he clearly blamed Islamabad for instigating the calamity and, going beyond the bounds of his written motion, called on the government to suspend economic aid "while the war continues."[16] Stonehouse later took the stage to corroborate Douglas-Mann's experiences in Bengal and add strong support for his colleague. During his speech, he became the first MP to use the floor of the House to accuse Islamabad of "genocide."[17]

The government gave the minister for overseas development, Richard Wood, not the foreign secretary, the task of presenting its position. Given that Douglas-Mann's written motion aligned neatly with already adopted policies, Wood had little to add to Douglas-Home's statement made earlier in the week. He took issue, however, with the proposer's verbal appeal for the suspension of development aid. Instead, Wood offered a solution that went a considerable way toward solving the problem. As a matter of principle, he argued, aid should not be used as a political weapon. Nevertheless, the government would suspend aid pending a settlement, without which development funds could not be properly deployed, as Frank Sargeant, the British deputy high commissioner in Dacca (DHC), had pointed out a month earlier.[18] Healey agreed that this solution was a useful way of pressing harder for a political compromise.[19] In due course, the government's stance would be clarified to explain that no development aid at all would be sent to the East before a political settlement, given that it could not be used there, nor any new aid deployed to the West, as the East was now the area clearly in greater need. Aid to the West that was already in the pipeline would continue to flow, however, the government believing that curtailing it would only cause unnecessary harm to its ground-level recipients.[20] The British government might not have been prepared to use development aid as a political weapon but it was content, with a nod to sophistry, to deploy it as a political lever.

Healey raised an important concern relating to London's predicament in determining policy: "Britain, as an ex-Imperial Power, is in a difficult position. We have no right to decide what the Pakistan Government should do. Any advice we give may perhaps often be less welcome than advice which comes from others."[21] The harder the prime minister or his government pressed Yahya, the greater the chances that Britain would stand accused of attempting to reprise its past colonial role. In dealing with Islamabad, there needed to be a fine balance.

It fell to the Northern Irish Protestant cleric Ian Paisley (Protestant Unionist, Antrim North) to reveal another sensitive issue in Britain's predicament that had not passed without comment in West Pakistan. Noting the attempts to draw parallels between East Pakistan and his homeland, Paisley observed: "Members must be aware that the vast majority of people in Northern Ireland want to remain part and parcel of the United Kingdom, whereas the outcome of the election which took place in East Pakistan demonstrated that the vast majority wanted autonomy and the right to govern themselves. The situations are not parallel."[22]

This was certainly true, and the demonstrable difference probably explained why the issue featured neither in higher-level Anglo-Pakistani exchanges nor in Whitehall discussions on the formulation of British policy. Yet the repudiation, voiced by a Protestant firebrand in the face of an increasingly violent backlash against anti-Catholic prejudice, would have sounded better coming from elsewhere.

When put to the House, the motion was passed "by acclamation."[23] Despite some calls from Douglas-Mann and Stonehouse for further action, for the time being the Conservative and Labour leaderships were largely in agreement over the government's approach. Both sides of the House appeared to share deep humanitarian concern over the suffering of East Bengalis, but not even Douglas-Mann's motion recommended public condemnation of Islamabad's actions or a shift in underlying government policy.

Interlude

In terms of its content and MPs' general demeanour, the parliamentary debate was well received in India, and particularly in West Bengal, the region in which most of the refugees had congregated. Stephen Miles, the British deputy high commissioner in Calcutta, noted that respect for the British had declined in recent weeks owing to London's public position of neutrality, which the local community had perceived as a lack of concern. Miles was "somewhat embarrassed" to admit that the visits of Douglas-Mann and Stonehouse in late April and simply the demand for a debate in the House had considerably improved the tenor of Anglo-Indian relations. The downside, as he correctly observed, was that this came at the expense of "no doubt infuriating the Pakistan Government."[24]

Three days after the debate, Apa Pant, the Indian high commissioner to London, called on Heath to discuss the refugee crisis. He complained that the sudden arrival of 2 million displaced people brought not only a severe economic and social burden but also risks of aggravating communal tensions. He requested that Britain make good on its commitment to provide humanitarian relief, apply pressure on Pakistan to achieve a political settlement, and stop all military supplies to Islamabad. Heath agreed that India was acting with restraint and reassured Pant that Britain, too, was anxious about the refugees and was making every effort to ensure that Yahya understood that a political solution was the necessary way forward.[25] A few days after the meeting, Indian prime minister Indira Gandhi wrote to Heath. By 12 May, she explained, the number of refugees had reach over 2.3 million and waves of 50,000 per day were arriving in India. She spelled out more specifically the implications that Pant had already raised: the refugees imposed "an enormous burden" and, as they were arriving in the "over-crowded and politically the most sensitive parts of India," their presence constituted "a grave security risk." Indira Gandhi worried that risks of "link-up between the extremists in the two Bengals [were] real," and implored Heath to use his influence to help secure a political settlement.[26] In the meantime, the FCO had begun to resolve the confusion over whether or not India was abetting the resistance movement. By 12 May, Major Cox, Sargeant's assistant military advisor in Dacca, was "certain that camps had been established in India for the training of guerillas."[27] It would take Heath a little over a week to reply.

Around the time of this exchange between the prime ministers, Cyril Pickard, the British high commissioner to Islamabad, made a visit to the East in advance of his departure on 22 May for his new posting in Lagos. He had delayed his exit for a month. After two days in Dacca and one in Chittagong, his conclusions, barely tempered by diplomatic constraint, were little short of damning:

> General position is clear. The province is dominated by fear. After completion of main military action, *the army, either as deliberate policy or at initiative of local commanders, set out to harass, kill, and drive out all caste Hindus.* They have used massive retaliation in response to all incidents, burning village [sic] and killing unarmed civilians. No man or officer is in any way accountable to the law. The civil law agencies have been replaced by armed Biharis, who terrify the population, and there is a state of complete lawlessness. The situation is, in my view, militarily dangerous: economically suicidal: and politically self-defeating. *I have expressed my general view to the governor. General Tikka Khan is impregnable in his self-deception and stupidity.*[28]

On returning to Islamabad, and immediately before leaving the country, Pickard sought out the Pakistani cabinet secretary, the foreign minister, and the deputy commander-in-chief (under Yahya) of the army. All three appeared to him to be surprised, deeply concerned, and clearly moved at his description of army policy in the East.[29] His freedom of action likely enhanced by the knowledge of his impending departure, Pickard had done his best to promote a change in army policy. The new high commissioner, Laurence Pumphrey, was appointed on 5 June.

Heath replied to Indira Gandhi on 26 May. Empathizing with the Indian predicament and commending her on India's restraint, he reiterated his comments to Pant that Britain was pressing Yahya for a political settlement, then pledged GB£1 million for relief of the refugees. Aware of India's assistance to the guerrillas, he suggested that "to prolong the present situation or to extend the field of operations would inevitably lead to further misery from which only extremists could benefit."[30] His message was veiled but still apparent. The new British high commissioner to New Delhi delivered the missive in person the following day. Indira Gandhi was preoccupied, as Garvey, using a decidedly British turn of phrase, described: "After two or three maiden overs, I bowled a few short balls but she played them back along the carpet."[31]

Pickard's exit was followed swiftly by that of Sargeant. As Douglas-Home rather indelicately announced in the House on 8 June, Sargeant had been "under severe strain and must have a short rest."[32] After his departure on

The Commons Debates and After   153

5 June, it took some weeks before Rae Britten replaced him in July. Shortly before leaving, Sargeant wrote a letter to Reginald Burrows, the deputy high commissioner in Islamabad, and Iain Sutherland, the head of SAD, expounding his thoughts on East Pakistan. He maintained the position, expressed in his memorandum of 14 April, that a political solution would be very hard to find. Before signing off, he reminded Sutherland of the ongoing atrocities being committed, particularly against Hindus, and of the "hatred" of the army felt by so many throughout the East.[33]

Second Commons Debate
Owing to a "serious deterioration" in the situation, Douglas-Home made a fourth statement to the House on 8 June. The total number of refugees in India had exceeded four million, and India had declared a cholera epidemic four days earlier. The British government had announced its intention of paying for vaccine and providing for its swift delivery, and British charities had already dispatched two mass injectors and over a million doses. The foreign secretary recognized that, to stop the hemorrhage of refugees, the underlying cause needed to be addressed. Consequently, Islamabad had to provide a political settlement as a matter of urgency. The government had made clear that, despite Pakistan's economic crisis, no new economic aid would be provided before such an agreement.[34] The foreign secretary explained: "The overriding influence on these people is fear. They fled because they felt that the Pakistan Army was using measures to suppress the population which were intolerable to them ... The only way to get these refugees back is for a political settlement to be contrived which will give them the necessary confidence to return to their homes."[35]

Douglas-Home was also deeply concerned at the prospect of possible widespread famine in East Bengal.[36] Former prime minister Harold Wilson (Labour, Huyton), now the leader of the opposition, remarked that the crisis had developed into "the worst human tragedy that the world has known since the war," and asked that Parliament rearrange its business to allow a debate on the issue.[37] After some discussion, the House agreed to a second debate on East Pakistan, to take place during a specially arranged three-hour session the next day. It is interesting to note that in the preparatory materials for his statement, so as to avoid a potentially incendiary issue, Douglas-Home was advised to adopt the following line: "If pressed. We cannot confirm allegations of army brutality against Hindus in East Pakistan."[38]

Judith Hart (Labour, Lanark), the shadow minister for overseas development, led the opposition in the second debate, largely agreeing with the government's policy but suggesting that a large pledge should be made to the UN relief funds in order express the depth of concern in Britain and to set an example for other donors.[39] Douglas-Home offered to consider her point.[40] Of the more passionate MPs, Stonehouse again accused Islamabad of "genocide," arguing that the United Nations should intervene, directly if necessary, and then raised the possibility of future trials for Pakistani leaders.[41] Bennett, Islamabad's leading advocate in the House, turned up late, then suggested that the references to specific atrocities by some MPs were, in the present situation, doing more harm than good.[42] As a result, the debate became rather heated, with Peter Shore (Labour, Stepney), a senior opposition MP, rounding on Bennett:

> At least we protest, and have a right to protest, against the brutality of an army. Good heavens – a general who wanted to crush a democracy – it is not the first time it has happened – can do it without expelling 5 million people from his country. This is an overkill of brutality and violence of a kind of which we have not seen the like before. So we can protest about that, but what can we do?[43]

Shore had hit the nail on the head. If, as senior Conservative and many senior Labour politicians agreed, the best way to exert influence in Islamabad was through empathetic but genuine and firm private approaches, thereby keeping Yahya on side, what else could they do except continue pressing in the hope that, over time, their efforts would succeed? In the House, only the previous day, Douglas-Home had insisted that a political settlement was necessary.[44] Heath, Douglas-Home, and the FCO were well aware that they faced a severe uphill struggle, but still believed a negotiated settlement possible. Only if it became apparent that Yahya would not urgently and properly pursue such a goal would a fundamental reconsideration of policy be required.

Media and Message

Less than a week later, on 15 June, it became clear that a significant number of less senior Labour MPs did not agree with the line taken by the government and effectively endorsed by their own leadership. Stonehouse put forward a motion calling for the recognition of Bangladesh and the indictment of the Pakistani army for "genocide" in the East. This was signed by more than half the members of the Parliamentary Labour Party, including several former ministers.[45] A significant section of the House did not believe Yahya

The Commons Debates and After   155

would provide a viable solution. Instead of exerting private influence, the dissenters preferred to take a more forthright moral stance publicly. Between the debate and the introduction of Stonehouse's motion, however, the *Sunday Times* had dropped a sizable bombshell that had stirred even deeper concern across the nation.

Before addressing the explosive article of 13 June, it is useful to consider the information provided by and the opinions of the press since the clampdown at the end of March. Simon Dring of the London-based *Daily Telegraph* and Arnold Zeitlin of Associated Press were the only two journalists to escape the roundup in Dacca as the Pakistani army's mission began. Michel Laurent, an Associated Press photographer, also remained at large. Dring successfully extricated himself from the East after witnessing the aftermath of attacks in Dacca on police, Hindus, and students, including the existence of a mass grave at the university. He published his article "How Dacca paid for a 'united' Pakistan" on 30 March, providing a first-hand account for the British public.[46]

The *Times*, a moderate, centre-right newspaper, was first off the mark, however. The previous day, it had already published a front-page, though second-hand, piece based on eyewitness accounts, titled "Tanks smash barricades in Dacca."[47] On the same day that Dring went to press, it followed this with another front-page account, this time by Michel Laurent, under the headline "At Dacca University the burning bodies of students still lay in their dormitory beds ... A mass grave had been hastily covered."[48] Thus, news of the atrocities reached the British public within just a few days. Yet, the initial picture remained somewhat unclear. Retaliatory killings by Bengalis made the *Times* front page on 2 April under the headline "Mass slaughter of Punjabis in East Bengal."[49] Another East Pakistan article made the same front page, titled "Pakistan army said to be wiping out leaders in brutal war." This continued inside, where the banner "War of genocide in East Pakistan" could be found.[50] Despite the weight of reports depicting the suffering of Bengalis, as opposed to non-Bengalis, the *Times*, in an editorial the following day, settled for the noncommittal opinion that "vengeance is everywhere."[51]

By mid-April and into May, the nature of the situation in East Pakistan was becoming clearer, despite pieces recording the atrocious actions of some Bengalis against the Bihari community.[52] In a front-page piece of 13 April titled "Thousands still fleeing frightened Dacca," the *Times* reported that "diplomats in Dacca estimate that up to 6,000 people were killed in a well-prepared assault."[53] During this same period, the vast influx of refugees into India became front-page news.[54] By 1 June, the newspaper had decided who was to blame for the exodus:

> The evidence of the refugees does not confirm the claim made by the army authorities in East Pakistan that order has been restored and that life is returning to normal. The refugees had too many stories to tell of wantonly punitive action in villages by the Pakistan army. Exaggerated many of the stories may have been but in the main the fears of the refugees were plainly started by brutal and indiscriminate action.[55]

At the start of June, stories of the inundation continued as the House sat for its second debate.[56]

Despite many weeks of front-page coverage of the East Pakistan crisis, the British public would still be moved, on 13 June, by a feature in the *Sunday Times*. Anthony Mascarenhas, the former assistant editor of the Karachi *Morning News*, was one of eight journalists invited to East Pakistan for a ten-day tour with the army at the end of April. During the visit, he witnessed the army's "kill and burn" missions around Comilla, which primarily targeted Hindus. The military felt no need to disguise its actions despite the press presence. Seven journalists wrote what they were told; Mascarenhas did not. Instead, he travelled to London, pretending to visit his ailing sister, and took his story to the editor of the *Sunday Times*. Fearing for the welfare of his family in Karachi, he returned to Pakistan to assist in their escape before fleeing himself across the border to Afghanistan, only then giving the signal to publish.[57] Under the front-page, large-font headline "GENOCIDE," an introduction to the extensive feature began: "West Pakistan's Army had been systematically massacring thousands of civilians in East Pakistan since the end of March." A detailed, three-page report was featured in the inside pages.[58] No doubt the Conservative government was relieved that publication occurred only after what could have been, but for providential timing, a particularly highly charged second debate.

South Asians in Britain
In contrast with both Canada and the United States, Britain had sizable communities of South Asian immigrants. In response to events in their former homeland, many people of East Bengali origin joined public protests over the actions of the Pakistani army and demanded an end to the suffering in the East. Their influence was not lost on parliamentarians; Stonehouse,

The Commons Debates and After   157

for example, hailed from the constituency of Wednesbury in the West Midlands, a centre of East Bengali and Indian migrant settlement.

The Pakistani community in Britain comprised about 150,000 people, of which 45 percent, or some 70,000, were of East Bengali descent, the remainder being mainly Urdu-speakers and associated with West Pakistan.[59] The Indian migrant population totalled a little over 300,000, roughly double the number of Pakistanis.[60] Given the alignment of interest groups on the subcontinent, this meant that up to 80,000 would potentiality support the cause of Islamabad, while over 370,000 would perhaps back the stance taken by Mujibur Rahman and New Delhi.

Immigrants from Pakistan came mainly from Sylhet, in East Bengal, and predominantly from Mirpur and Azad Kashmir in the West. The Pakistani community in the United Kingdom had grown from around 5,000 in 1951 to 24,900 in 1961, to 150,000 at the start of the crisis, many having initially migrated to Britain for economic reasons. The East Pakistanis, with their distinctive culture based on the Bengali language, lived apart from those of the West. They had established large communities in several locations but were particularly prominent in the East End of London and parts of the West Midlands. West Pakistanis had likewise formed groupings in various parts of the country, including London and Bradford. The latter city bore the clumsy epithet Bradistan. Most Pakistanis were employed in unskilled and semi-skilled jobs, sending back to Pakistan a significant proportion of their earnings.[61] During the crisis, many in the East Pakistani community withheld these remittances, contributing funds to East Pakistan relief instead.[62]

The Awami League (UK) was established in 1969, after a visit to Britain by Mujibur Rahman. Infighting among the dominant players had already led to the formation of a splinter organization, the London Awami League.[63] Each of these bodies sent a member as part of a group of five representatives of the Bengali community received by Sutherland on 27 March, when they demanded, among other things, British intervention to "stop the slaughter."[64] Both bodies were closely linked to the Bengal Students Action Committee (BSAC), an organization driven by the editor of the Bengali-language London weekly *Janomot*. Though it had only a small following, within a week of the clampdown the committee led a march on several London embassies, then staged a two-day hunger strike near Downing Street. It subsequently published a number of pro-Bengali pamphlets.[65]

Drawing most of its support from Bengali communities in the West Midlands, the Bangla Desh Action Committee for Great Britain (BDAC) had, after March, also published various leaflets and had arranged regular public demonstrations in Trafalgar Square. BSAC and BDAC were coordinated, to the best of its ability, by the London-based Council for the Republic of Bangla Desh, which had organised a five-thousand-strong march to Downing Street on 4 April.[66]

The most significant non-Bengali pressure group was the London-based Action Bangla Desh (ABD), which organized a demonstration at a reception in Mayfair for the touring Pakistan cricket team. Of the three hundred people gathered, two dozen were arrested following scuffles.[67] ABD had also arranged for a sizable advertisement to appear in the *Times* on 13 May, the day before the first House debate. With around two hundred signatures, including those of Douglas-Mann and other MPs, the notice called on the government to halt economic aid and start a huge relief operation.[68] The group placed another advertisement in the *Times* on 30 June, reproducing the text and the names of signatories of a House of Commons motion calling for recognition of Bangladesh, and organized a ten-thousand-strong five-hour rally in Trafalgar Square on 1 August, which Stonehouse would address.[69]

Unexpectedly, a small group calling itself West Pakistanis in Solidarity with Bangla Desh had also come into being.[70] Although the immigrant communities from East and West had previously been united in their fight against racial discrimination, the crisis had caused a rift between them. Despite this, the prospect of intercommunal violence remained remote.[71]

By the end of June, the FCO had received 76 letters from MPs and 184 letters and telegrams from the public addressed to either Douglas-Home or the prime minister. In addition, it had taken delivery of 220 copies of a letter published in *the Guardian,* and fourteen petitions. Excluding the 220 copies, about 60 percent of the communications from the public were from the Bengali community in Britain. None of the messages offered "unqualified support" for the government. Instead, they demanded, through various means, either more action or a stronger line against Islamabad.[72]

Public opinion is difficult to gauge. Nevertheless, measured in terms of well-supported parliamentary motions, the tone of the *Times* and the *Sunday Times* editorials, and the momentum gained by protest movements, it is apparent that, by summer, the British public mood was one of deep concern. In cabinet, four days after Mascarenhas's revelations, Douglas-Home recognized that if the government "indicate[d] quickly that we should be prepared to make further substantial contributions to relieve the impact of the disaster on a once and for all basis, the pressure of public opinion would be reduced."[73] By this time, over five million refugees had reached India.[74]

A British Oxfam doctor with experience of Biafra observed, while visiting the camps, that "there were more refugees now in West Bengal than the whole Ebo [Ibo] population of Nigeria."[75] The balm of relief abroad would, the foreign secretary hoped, have a useful by-product to soothe British consciences at home.

Stumbling toward Recess

Adopting a Forthright Tone

Even before the second debate, Mascarenhas's exposé, and Stonehouse's subsequent motion, the prime minister and the FCO noted the need for greater urgency. A few days before the debate, and recognizing that Britain might otherwise have to act unilaterally, which it wished to avoid, at the prime minister's behest Douglas-Home wrote to U Thant.[76] The foreign secretary sought to impress on the UN secretary-general the need for "the fullest possible public information about the steps you are taking" in arranging the international relief effort. In a rather forceful telegram, Douglas-Home reminded U Thant that the problem was "urgent and growing," and that "public opinion ... [would] not understand if action on both the relief and medical fronts appear[ed] to be delayed or ineffective."[77]

The FCO had also been discussing the possible political options it had available to encourage a political settlement in Pakistan.[78] The day after the debate, a memorandum from the foreign secretary to the prime minister laid out the British strategy. In considering whether the United Kingdom could take "any further initiative," Douglas-Home acknowledged that Yahya's claims that all was under control were "wishful thinking." On 25 May, Yahya had promised to announce a move toward civilian rule in two to three weeks. His statement was imminent and "although his chances of success may [have been] small there seem[ed] no alternative." The foreign secretary believed it "essential," at the very least, that there should be "an appeal for calm, a guarantee of civilian rights and a plea for the people to stay in their villages or to return."[79]

In assessing five possible options to help bring about a viable settlement, Douglas-Home ruled out approaches through the Commonwealth or the permanent members of the UN Security Council, as Yahya considered the issue an internal matter and would therefore "reject intervention from any quarter except from one in a position to exercise direct influence with him (e.g. through aid) or from those whom he regards as friends." The Pakistan aid consortium, the foreign secretary contended, "possessed the greatest influence," but he considered it unwise to cut off all aid, as this would result in the "destruction" of the Pakistani economy and "incalculable results" for India. Having eliminated three options, Douglas-Home was left with bilateral action or an approach through U Thant. Given that the UN secretary-general was already struggling to coordinate an urgent humanitarian response, it was therefore incumbent on the British government to make a further effort through a letter to Yahya, from either the foreign secretary or the prime minister, while at the same time making Indira Gandhi and U Thant aware of the British initiative.[80]

The prime minister wished to send the letters to Yahya and Indira Gandhi in his own name,[81] and the FCO dispatched three missives on 11 June. Heath again addressed Yahya frankly, reminding him that he was "anxiously" awaiting the latter's announcement about a path to political settlement, emphasizing that he and the British government were "convinced that there can be no future for a united Pakistan unless you can resume the process which you started so courageously last year toward civilian-led democratic government." The announcement, Heath recommended, should be "accompanied by a guarantee of civil rights, redress against any illegal acts by the authorities, and a renewed plea to people to stay where they are or return to their homes." Allowing the problems to continue would present the prospect of "unimaginable disaster." The last paragraph contained another veiled threat: "We are anxious to provide, in full measure, such help as we can. The British people have given willingly in the past. Evidence of movement toward a political solution will, more than anything else, ensure continued support for Pakistan."[82] Given the delicate wording normally associated with diplomatic correspondence, the message was forceful, to say the least.

In his letter to Indira Gandhi, Heath reassured the Indian prime minister that he had written to Yahya, appealing to him to address the underlying cause of the refugee problem and pursue a political settlement with urgency. Britain, he told her, would work closely with the United Nations to provide help in addressing the "tragic situation" in northeastern India, with which the Indians were making admirable efforts to cope.[83] Douglas-Home alerted U Thant to the British move.[84] From the prime minister downward, despite general recognition that they faced a very difficult task, the British government appeared to be pursuing vigorously its strategy to encourage privately a political accommodation.

As reports of the ongoing "extermination of Hindus" continued to arrive at the FCO,[85] Indian foreign minister Swaran Singh met Heath at Downing Street during his tour of the major capitals in search of relief aid commitments and further pressure on Islamabad to find a solution. Singh expressed his desire for a united Pakistan, stating that a split was not in India's interests owing to probable resultant instability in the region, and insisted that a viable solution would have to involve the Awami League proper. Heath reiterated the assurances he had recently given Indira Gandhi.[86] Not wishing to be outmanoeuvred, the Pakistani high commissioner to London called on Heath the next day. During the course of their exchange, the high commissioner informed the prime minister that Yahya would be making a public speech about the path to political settlement on 28 June. He did not know the details of the announcement, but "expected it to meet practically all the demands of East Pakistan." Heath said he would await the statement.[87] The high commissioner also delivered a message from Yahya. Its contents were disappointing, the FCO remarking that the communication did "not constitute a reply to the prime minister's message of 11 June and amount[ed] to little more than a series of accusations against the Indian government."[88] It appeared Heath's forthright tone had not gone down well in Islamabad, but only Yahya's proposed announcement on 28 June would reveal whether or not the underlying message had struck its mark.

Back to the Commons

Following the discussions with Singh, Douglas-Home returned to the Commons on 23 June to announce that Britain would make substantial donations to help relieve the refugees. Britain had already covered GB£250,000 of the costs incurred by its charities and, on 20 May, had pledged GB£1 million to the UN appeal that U Thant had launched the previous day. In addition to these sums, the government would now make an additional GB£1 million available to the UN appeal and donate GB£5 million directly to the Indian government, bringing total British humanitarian relief donations from the public purse to over GB£7 million or US$17 million.[89] This was less than a week after the foreign secretary had pointed out, in cabinet, the domestic advantages of such pledges. He also announced that, at a meeting of the Pakistan aid consortium on 21 June, no new pledges of development aid were given.[90] As noted in Chapter 3, the United States was the only party that failed to recommend this suspension. Healey applauded both the relief contributions and the consortium's decision.[91]

As the foreign secretary addressed the House, a delegation of MPs was arriving in Asia on a fact-finding mission. The MPs had left with Douglas-Home's blessing, as he had for some time felt that a balanced delegation (two Conservative and two Labour MPs) visiting both India and Pakistan at the expense of the British, not the Pakistani or Indian, government might provide some insight into the situation on the ground.[92] The group consisted of the following: Toby Jessel (Conservative, Twickenham), James Ramsden (Conservative, Harrogate; former secretary of state for war), Arthur Bottomley (Labour, Middlesbrough East; former minister of overseas development), and Reginald Prentice (Labour, East Ham North; former minister for buildings and public works). The delegates visited East Pakistan from 24 to 28 June and were shocked at what they found. Speaking to the press in Dacca, before leaving, Jessel remarked: "I am sure it is not safe for Hindus, who may be attacked by the Army, or for anyone who was actively connected with the Awami League ... to return," as the military was "continuing to sack villages, and ... there has been a great deal of brutal behavior between Biharis and Bengalis."[93]

During their subsequent tour of West Bengal from 28 to 30 June, the MPs listened to stories from a few of the more than five million refugees then in the camps. After hearing reports of looting, burning of homes, and outright killing, Jessel promised: "We will tell the world about this." Prentice added that the scale of the trauma demonstrated that "the propaganda of the West Pakistan Government is completely false and they are responsible for an enormous amount of human suffering in what must be a lost cause."[94] Such strong condemnation would not be received well in Islamabad.

Decision Time

As Yahya's announcement of 28 June loomed, British diplomats considered the possible outcomes. A not overly optimistic Pumphrey argued that, if the president did not go far enough, then "acceptance of Yahya's programme with all its faults" would be a better option than to "pressure for specific and immediate improvements in it," as the latter course would "do more harm than good" and "set Yahya finally against us."[95] He believed that separation of the two wings was the most likely outcome over time.[96] Although he did not say so, Pumphrey appeared to hold the view that, if Yahya did not make sufficient concessions, then Britain should stand back from the melee, protecting what remained of its influence in Islamabad. The new high commissioner, with his years in Pakistan stretching before him, was more inclined to substitute technical for moral responsibility than his predecessor, Cyril Pickard.

Garvey recognized that if Yahya's statement offered "trivial alleviations only," as he thought would be the case, then the absence of a viable pathway to political settlement would simply strengthen the hand of those in India already pressing Indira Gandhi to take more extreme action. Moreover, if London were to endorse an ineffective offer, then it would receive "nothing but grief" from New Delhi.[97] If the high commissioners were correct, then if Yahya failed to grasp his opportunity Heath and Douglas-Home would have to decide between two main options. First, they could back Yahya and maintain some diplomatic influence in Islamabad, but then see relations with New Delhi deteriorate and find themselves in the uncomfortable position of associating with Yahya as the British public watched the human suffering worsen. The experience of Harold Wilson's government, which had supported the Nigerian federal authorities during the Biafra crisis, highlighted the difficulties with this course. Or, second, they could disavow Yahya and lose diplomatic influence with the military government in Islamabad, but improve relations with the world's largest democracy and be seen by the British populace to be adopting a firm moral stance. Of course, they could attempt to tread a fine line between the two options, trying somehow to keep both Islamabad and New Delhi content and, despite Yahya's inability to deliver, hope that time would provide a solution.

On 28 June, Yahya broadcast to the nation. Members of the Awami League who were still alive could keep their elected positions, but only if they did so in their individual capacities, as their party would be banned. Awami League members considered to have "taken part in anti-state activities, committed criminal acts, or indulged in anti-social activities" would not be permitted to take their seats in the assemblies. Yahya hoped to achieve his goal in around four months.[98] As explained in Chapter 3, even Joseph Sisco of the US State Department, one of the most enthusiastic supporters of Richard Nixon and Henry Kissinger's pro-Islamabad policies, noted that Yahya's statement made political accommodation in Pakistan all but impossible. The *Times* called Yahya's address "well meant, but not well conceived." Its editorial continued: "One can hardly imagine circumstances in which such a political solution could be acceptable to a majority in East Pakistan."[99] Before a cabinet meeting on 8 July, Douglas-Home handwrote a comment on his notes: "Pres. Yahya's speech of 28 June has had virtually no effect."[100] On the same day the cabinet met, Garvey spoke with Indira Gandhi, who insisted that "Yahya's broadcast had held out no prospect of change."[101] The British government had earnestly tried, at times in a most frank and forthright manner, to sway Yahya toward a viable political settlement that included the Awami League. This component of British policy had failed, either because Yahya did not want to achieve accommodation or, owing to pressures on him, was not able to. What would London do next?

Clutching at Straws

Yahya was far from happy with Britain. The day after his broadcast, his reply to Heath reached London. It amounted to little more than a letter of complaint bemoaning Indian exploitation of the crisis and taking Britain to task. He was disappointed with London's policy on economic aid and the treatment of Islamabad in the foreign press. Moreover, he viewed the proceedings of the recent parliamentary debate with "sorrow and anguish."[102] On 3 July, the Pakistani Ministry of Foreign Affairs issued a formal complaint to Pumphrey, condemning the "persistent anti-Pakistani activities that are being conducted in Great Britain" in both Parliament and the press. According to the ministry, the actions had been so grievous as to "leave one wondering whether there [was] any meaning and substance left in Commonwealth association."[103] It appeared that little remained of Anglo-Pakistani diplomatic relations to be worth saving.

Within days, Garvey was pointing out the very same parliamentary exchanges and the recent large sum donated for refugee relief in expressing to Indira Gandhi his hope that the "Indian government no longer believed that H.M.G. [Her Majesty's Government] were hedging their bets."[104] By mid-July, Stonehouse's motion to indict the Pakistani government on charges of genocide and recognize Bangladesh had attracted over two hundred Members' signatures.[105] It appeared that, on reconsideration, London would naturally choose to adopt its second main option, rejecting Yahya's impotent plan with little further risk to its now very poor diplomatic ties with Islamabad, cement closer relations with New Delhi, and revel in the British public's support of a firm moral stance.

Yet, London chose the middle course. Douglas-Home believed that the best way forward was to maintain public neutrality in order to facilitate the process of stabilizing the situation through an increased UN humanitarian presence.[106] Given the ongoing actions of the Pakistani army in the East and Indian support, from West Bengal, of the expanding guerrilla movement, it was very difficult to see how this plan would succeed. Within a week, on 21 July, the foreign secretary was aware that India would almost certainly not accept this.[107] Meanwhile, rumours were circulating in Islamabad that Yahya had commenced proceedings against Mujibur Rahman by means of a military tribunal held in camera.[108] Concerned at the political consequences if Mujibur Rahman were martyred, and in a move reflective of Britain's low prestige in West Pakistan, Douglas-Home had persuaded Abdul Rahman, the former prime minister of Malaysia and a Muslim with close ties to Islamabad, to try to intercede with Yahya on the Awami League leader's behalf.[109]

On 29 July, Heath finally replied to the two letters Yahya had sent in June. In preparing the message for Heath's approval, Douglas-Home observed of Yahya: "He [had] not gone far enough yet to elicit a credible response in East Pakistan and the chances of his doing so have been much reduced by his unqualified commendation of the Army and his branding of Mujib [Mujibur Rahman] as a criminal."[110] Yet, the foreign secretary believed the president's broadcast of 28 June had been "some advance on his previous statements" and Yahya was "genuinely seeking a way out of the present impasse."[111]

By late July, as Douglas-Home clutched desperately for new ideas, British strategy was tinged with an air of poorly justified optimism in the face of frustration and impotence. This unfortunate state of affairs was reflected in Heath's response to Yahya. The forthright quality of previous missives was replaced by a defensive tone. After praising Yahya's June statement as deserving of support, the prime minister addressed the disturbing "gap" that had developed between London and Islamabad, seeking to justify Britain's curtailment of new economic aid on grounds of practicality. New aid should be focused on the East and, in the absence of discernible progress toward a political settlement, the environment there was not conducive to the initiation of further development projects. In expressing his concern that the Indo-Pakistani border in the East would not become "yet another Asian battleground," Heath took the opportunity to introduce a fourth component to British policy.[112] In addition to public neutrality on the internal issue of a sovereign state, the provision of humanitarian relief, and the private encouragement of a political settlement, he appealed for calm and caution as concerns began to grow over Indo-Pakistani tensions.[113] Yahya was unable to find time for the high commissioner; Pumphrey delivered the message to the president's military secretary on 31 July, after a two-day delay.[114]

On 29 July, the day Heath sent his letter to Yahya, the cabinet Defence and Overseas Policy Committee (DOP) convened. This was an influential body, chaired by the prime minister, that brought together an executive of powerful actors to address Britain's international security concerns. Around the table, with the prime minister, sat the secretaries of state for foreign and Commonwealth affairs, defence, trade and industry, and the Home Department, along with the Chancellor of the Exchequer, the cabinet secretary, and armed forces representatives, including the chief of the Defence Staff. This was a committee meant to "get things done." In the event, and while recognizing that India might, in due course, be "provoked into taking military measures," members agreed only to keep the situation in and around East Pakistan under "close review."[115]

Douglas-Home's briefing document, sent to committee members in advance of their discussions, provided a useful summary of the situation at the end of July. The guerrillas were becoming "increasingly effective" with the help of "limited assistance" from India. There had been "little response" in East Pakistan to Yahya's proposals for an accommodation and, although the president was "probably sincere in his wish for an agreed solution," the "prospects for a political settlement were not great." Nevertheless, the foreign secretary still proposed only the pursuit of an increased UN humanitarian presence as the best way forward, even though India, with the backing of the Soviet Union, had already refused. The public line on providing no new aid before the establishment of an appropriate political framework, and "hostile statements" in both Parliament and the British press, meant that London's "stock with the Pakistan Government [was] accordingly low."[116] The only positive note on Anglo-Pakistani relations was that on 12 July Britain had pledged GB£1 million to the UN fund for relief inside East Pakistan.

Pumphrey had assumed his post in early June, but it took him two months to assess in detail the "Pakistan dilemma," which he analyzed in a report of 3 August. The high commissioner conceded that, owing to Yahya's "equal lack of realism in the political and economic fields," nothing less than "a succession of miracles" would be required to avoid descent into chaos and war, which, in Pumphrey's view, was the most probable outcome. The "miracles" required included suspension of Indian aid to the guerrillas and the introduction of a sizable UN presence to guarantee a return to peace in the East; elections under a federal or "confederal" constitution, with the right of either wing to secede after a trial period; and close international cooperation between the United States and the Soviet Union throughout these processes. He believed that, "short of working for something along these lines," there appeared little that Britain could do save "step up" humanitarian relief and continue economic pressure. Alarmingly, Pumphrey noted: "Pinned between humiliation and disaster, The President and his Generals may prefer to go down fighting."[117]

Responses in writing would take some time to materialize. Hugh Byatt, Sutherland's chief assistant at SAD, remarked on 19 August that the chances that London would be able to broker the developments suggested by Pumphrey were "almost negligible." He suggested, possibly before many of his superiors, that: "It may well be that we are approaching a new situation in which we have to evaluate as realistically as we can where our future interests lie. We may conclude that our interest above all is to emerge from the present situation with a workable relationship with India intact."[118]

A month after Pumphrey composed his letter, Garvey suggested that the "miracles" were close to impossibilities. Islamabad would "sooner or later" lose East Pakistan. India would continue to support the guerrillas; "undertakings to the contrary [would] be meaningless and efforts to coerce her not to [back them] fruitless." A UN force would not be able to replace the Pakistani army unless it comprised the well-trained troops of a major power. He concluded with the callous remark: "A withdrawal of the Pak Army without cover or substitute [would] probably lead to substantial massacre, *but this is not our, or the world's, responsibility*."[119]

In maintaining its neutrality, London was attempting to save what remained of its diplomatic prestige in Islamabad and was clutching at straws in the forlorn hope of encouraging some form of political accommodation. It risked incurring the wrath of the British public and severe damage to its ties with New Delhi. Nevertheless, it would continue this approach throughout the fall, attempting to use what little remaining influence it had to discourage moves toward another Indo-Pakistan war. On 5 August, Parliament adjourned for the summer recess. It had never debated Stonehouse's motion on genocide and the recognition of Bangladesh. Mysteriously, the House was unable to find time.[120]

Carrots and Sticks

Military Supply

In the decade following the Second World War, the United Kingdom was, behind the United States, the second-largest global exporter of arms. During this period, its military supply policy was still governed primarily by political and strategic considerations. Britain's relative decline as a global power in later years, however, drove a reassessment of its arms sales rationale, and by 1970 economic considerations had become not the only but the dominant consideration in determining policy decisions. This reflected a range of needs, including supporting the balance of payments, reducing the unit cost of production, protecting the jobs of some 300,000 defence industry contractors, and maintaining the technical skills base required to continue independent production. With this in mind, in 1966, Denis Healey, then secretary of state for defence, had established within his ministry the Defence Sales Organisation. This body was specifically tasked with the challenge of stimulating arms exports. The FCO made the principal recommendation, on a case-by-case basis, as to the suitability of each potential recipient nation. The Ministry of Defence (MOD) normally deferred to the

FCO but, on the few occasions that it wished to persevere with sales despite FCO objections, the matter was referred to the DOP for a final decision. Although it had no formal responsibility for arms supply decisions, Parliament acted as probably the most important constraint on policy. During the 1970s, annual British arms export receipts increased from GB£235 million in 1970–71 to GB£901 million in 1979. This represented approximately 5 percent of the world market.[121]

As discussed in Chapter 5, during the Indo-Pakistan War of 1965, Britain banned supplies of lethal equipment to both sides. In March 1966, however, this policy was adjusted to allow British manufacturers to sell arms on strictly commercial terms to both Pakistan and India. Therefore, although no military aid flowed from London to Islamabad, arms and associated military materiel did. The value of British arms supplies to Pakistan was not normally substantial, but the Pakistani navy had expressed interest in the very large purchase of five Type 21 frigates, worth some GB£60 million. Inconveniently, Islamabad had reached its Export Credits Guarantee Department (ECGD) limit. Although the prime minister was initially keen to facilitate a deal, on reflection the government was unwilling to provide military aid or take the risk of extending further credit. Consequently, by the end of February 1971, London had presented Islamabad with the challenge of finding sufficient funds for the purchase, and there the matter rested.

Responding to an inquiry on arms supply to Pakistan in the House on 26 April, the foreign secretary explained that he had reviewed the situation, and "no contracts have been signed since 1967 with the exception of one for refitting a naval vessel and another for radar equipment. There is none in prospect."[122] Douglas-Home made no comment about smaller commercial purchases. In fact, since the renewal of supplies in early 1966, Britain had exported over GB£5 million worth of equipment, some GB£4 million of which related to radar systems. The remainder comprised a varied mixture of, among other things, gun stores, ammunition, mines, and explosives.[123]

Aware of possible public sensitivity to the supply of arms to a regime involved in a military clampdown, as had been the experience with respect to Nigeria, Sutherland had already contacted the MOD, asking that it take "particular care" in keeping the FCO appraised of all developments concerning arms sales to Pakistan.[124] In an attempt to find a compromise between the perceived demands of the public and those of the arms manufacturers and Islamabad, Sutherland recommended that London continue to permit the export of "non-lethal" military equipment, while blocking the dispatch of "lethal" items. Kenneth Wilford (assistant under-secretary of state, with responsibility for South Asia), noted that mortar cartridges and ammunition fuses, which Sutherland was prepared to let pass, stretched the somewhat elastic boundary between "lethal" and "non-lethal" items. Nevertheless, he, Stanley Tomlinson (the deputy permanent under-secretary of state at the FCO), and Douglas-Home concurred.[125]

Given the unfortunate combination of political pressures and imprecise definitions, a game subsequently ensued in which Pakistan made approaches and the FCO determined which items should be passed and which blocked, providing diplomatic excuses for the latter. Thus, on 18 May, Tomlinson approved Sutherland's recommendation that applications for fuses, mines, and naval gun barrels be approved, but Rapier anti-aircraft missiles and Abbot 105 mm self-propelled guns be refused. The FCO politely informed Islamabad that the Rapiers were beyond Pakistan's economic ability to pay and the Abbots were, regrettably, unavailable.[126] Aware that Islamabad might place unusually large orders for certain "non-lethal" equipment, Whitehall began, toward the end of May, to also monitor for such requests.[127]

In July, the FCO decided that artillery command post vehicles were not available, owing to long delivery times,[128] and called on various excuses to block delivery of percussion primers for shells, detonators for grenades, and an unusually large order for ten million rounds of 7.62 mm tracer ammunition.[129] By the time Parliament had adjourned for its summer recess, Britain had authorized, since the clampdown, GB£323,000 worth of orders, of which only GB£119,000 had been shipped. Of the supplies that had arrived in Pakistan, GB£113,000 were fuses shipped in May. Back orders of the same fuses accounted for GB£170,000 of the GB£204,000 yet to be released.[130]

In June, the US government had been embarrassed by the *New York Times'* disclosure that arms were still being sent to Pakistan despite assurances to the contrary.[131] A few weeks later, on 12 July, Peter Carrington, secretary of state for defence, stood before the House of Lords and stated that "there are no military supplies being sent to Pakistan." This slip placed Sutherland in a quandary: if he were to issue a correction, it would almost certainly lead to a close examination of the government's somewhat gray policy; if he were to ignore the error, then the government could potentially be accused of misleading Parliament. He recommended simply keeping silent and maintaining the current scheme. Tomlinson agreed.[132] Within a month, however, the FCO had come to realize that it was playing a dangerous game and its policy began to slowly change. On 16 August, Tomlinson accepted Byatt's recommendation that, in future, ammunition and components for lethal weapons be considered "lethal" items.[133] In contemplating the GB£170,000 of still unshipped fuses in the fall, Sutherland felt that the risks of possible public disclosure outweighed the rewards of Islamabad's favour. After some discussion, the FCO and MOD concurred.[134] Without cancelling orders, Carrington recommended that the government "hold up all military supplies for the time being." It took, therefore, until the end of November for the supply of arms to completely cease.[135]

In October, the Pakistani navy informally, and quite unexpectedly, renewed its interest in the Type 21 frigates, an interest that had lain dormant since February.[136] Given the crisis in Bengal, to say nothing of the Pakistan's near bankruptcy, a somewhat incredulous FCO suggested to the British High Commission in Islamabad that it maintain a negative stance on economic grounds.[137] During the emergency, Britain supplied minimal quantities of "non-lethal" military equipment to Pakistan in order to help maintain good relations with Islamabad. Nevertheless, in failing to correct Carrington's error, no matter how inadvertent, the government had misled both Parliament and the British public.

Economic Aid

Britain was a member of the Pakistan aid consortium, a body formed in 1960 under the chairmanship of the International Bank for Reconstruction and Development (IBRD) to develop a program of economic aid for the developing country. London had already provided aid loans before the formation of the consortium and had contributed GB£103 million between 1951 and June 1970. At the start of the new decade, Pakistan received more British aid than any other country save India.[138] In July 1970, London pledged a further GB£10 million (US$24 million) for the next year to June 1971, and shortly after the crisis commenced, some GB£8 million had already been committed through the signing of loan agreements.[139] This amount, while only approximately one-fifth of the economic aid in the US pipeline at the time of the clampdown, remained highly significant to Pakistan's tottering economy.

During the crisis, the government was prepared to marshal aid in order to nudge Yahya toward a political settlement, using sophistry to justify its position. Britain's policy on development aid was announced by the minister for overseas development during the first House debate on 14 May and subsequently clarified through a series of meetings and statements. As a matter of principle, Wood argued, aid should not be used as a political weapon. Nevertheless, the government would suspend aid pending a political settlement, without which such funds could not be properly deployed.[140]

The Commons Debates and After

In due course, this would be interpreted to mean no development aid at all to the East before a political settlement, given that it could not be used there, and no new aid to the West, as the East was now the area clearly in greater need. Development aid to the West that was already in the pipeline would continue to flow, however, the government believing that curtailing it would ultimately only cause unnecessary harm to those most in need.[141] On 7 June, Douglas-Home attempted to remove any confusion in an interview on *Panorama*, the BBC's flagship current affairs program:

> We have made it clear to the Pakistan Government that we want the majority of our aid to be applied in East Pakistan and that arrangements for this cannot be put in hand until conditions return to normal. There are political and economic conditions which must govern the granting of further aid to Pakistan. Until these are satisfied, we cannot make any decisions about the provision of new economic assistance.[142]

Meanwhile the bulk of the GB£8 million already agreed continued to flow to Islamabad. Although this was largely unassigned non-project aid, and there was no way of knowing for certain its ultimate destination, the government opted to stand by its formal commitments.[143]

In his statement to the House on 23 June, Douglas-Home revealed that, at a meeting of the Pakistan aid consortium two days earlier, no new pledges of economic aid were given by the consortium as a whole.[144] Britain had promoted its policy at the meeting, with only the United States arguing against.[145] London's position appeared fully justifiable, especially after a damning report on the Pakistani economy and political landscape, originally intended for the gathering of the consortium, was finally released. It had not been completed in time for the meeting, and Robert McNamara, then president of the World Bank, subsequently sought to suppress it. His actions, as the media became aware of them, succeeded only in drawing more attention to the document, and he was pressured into hurriedly distributing the report to the bank's directors. Its contents, indirectly and seemingly inevitably, made their way to the baying press.[146]

On 27 September, Britain committed a further GB£1 million to the Tarbela project on the Indus in West Pakistan, as part of its overall pledge over several years of GB£10 million toward the construction of one of the world's largest earth-filled dams.[147] As the subcontinent moved ever closer to war, the British government continued its policy of refusing new economic aid but keeping the pipeline open with respect to previous commitments to the

West. Although it had not wielded its stick with all its strength, it had given Pakistani knuckles a firm rap, a point of resentment in Islamabad, as demonstrated by its midsummer complaints to London.

Humanitarian Relief

On 28 April, Douglas-Home sent a message to U Thant on behalf of both the United Kingdom and the United States. Secretary of State William Rogers was visiting London and, at Douglas-Home's suggestion, had agreed to make a joint approach to the UN secretary-general to encourage him to organize an international response to the humanitarian emergency developing in Bengal.[148] On 19 May, U Thant launched an appeal to the international community for US$175 million to relieve the suffering of refugees in India, prompting the British government to make an initial pledge of GB£1 million (US$2.4 million) the next day.[149] Some three weeks later, the appeal had raised US$34 million, just over half of which had been provided by the United States.[150] Around this time, the British charities Oxfam, War on Want, Save the Children Fund, Christian Aid, and the Red Cross pooled their resources to launch the India-Pakistan Relief Fund. Following a public appeal, over GB£400,000 worth of donations were received from the British public during the first three days.[151]

Owing to the ongoing flood of refugees into India, however, such sums were insufficient. By the end of June, 6 million people had crossed the border, descending on camps located mainly in West Bengal and Tripura. The former had received 4.5 million displaced people, swelling its population by 10 percent. The latter, a sensitive hill-tribe area, had absorbed 1 million, inflating its population by nearly two-thirds.[152] The British High Commission in New Delhi described West Bengal as the second most populated state in India, characterized by high unemployment and a disturbed political scene that, "despite its political gangsterism, communal riots, [and] daily lists of murders," had "never quite become a complete shambles." It could become so, however, and the refugees could provide the trigger.[153] In addition, West Bengal shared part of its cultural identity with its neighbour to the East, the two having formed one state for extended periods under the Raj. Consequently, Indira Gandhi feared the rise of pan-Bengali nationalism.[154] The imposition, at her behest, of President's Rule on 28 June aimed to provide vital stability but, as Garvey would later observe, "locals, who in monsoon conditions [had] been hardly if at all better off, resent[ed] succouring of refugees, and resultant tensions add[ed] to underlying risk of Hindu-Muslim clashes."[155] India faced not only a severe economic burden but also a socio-political crisis.

As Parliament adjourned for the summer, there were about seven million refugees in some of the most delicate parts of India, and the Indian government's outlays were estimated to be just over GB£1 million per day.[156] On 22 June, Britain's contribution to humanitarian relief stood at only GB£1.25 million. In cabinet on 17 June, however, as previously noted, Douglas-Home recognized that if the British government "indicate[d] quickly that we should be prepared to make further substantial contributions to relieve the impact of the disaster on a once and for all basis, the pressure of public opinion would be reduced."[157] In the House the following week, he announced pledges of an additional GB£1 million to the UN appeal and GB£5 million directly to the Indian government, bringing total British humanitarian relief donations from the public purse to over GB£7 million (US$17 million).[158] Put another way, Britain had promised to pay for the refugees for one week.

On 16 June, U Thant made a separate appeal for humanitarian relief in East Pakistan, and London contributed GB£1 million on 12 July, at a time when Anglo-Pakistani ties were severely strained. It was not until the fall, however, that Britain made its largest contributions. Following renewed appeals from U Thant, London donated a further GB£7.5 million toward the relief of refugees and an extra GB£1 million to help within the borders of East Pakistan, bringing total contributions by the government to GB£16.75 million (US$40 million).[159] Including the latest pledges, British donations to refugee relief at this time, both public and through private charities, represented 18 percent of all international donations promised to India, either directly or through the United Nations.[160] This was clearly a significant amount that helped assuage not only suffering abroad but also, as the foreign secretary had admitted, pangs of conscience at home.

Aftermath

On 9 August, New Delhi and Moscow signed the Indo-Soviet Treaty of Peace, Friendship, and Cooperation. Henry Kissinger, the US national security advisor, would later portray this as an incendiary Cold War deal, but at the time Britain considered it as merely "formalizing an existing situation rather than necessarily marking a new era." Besides increasing Moscow's influence in New Delhi, the Soviet aim, in London's opinion, was to "put themselves in a position to constrain India," and so "reduce the chances of war."[161]

The trial of Mujibur Rahman began in August. At Douglas-Home's behest, former Malaysian prime minister Abdul Rahman appealed to Yahya to "exercise clemency and spare [his] life."[162] It was not possible for London

174   *United Kingdom*

to gauge the impact of its indirect approach, but Mujibur Rahman was not executed and lived to become the first leader of an independent Bangladesh.

By October, tensions between India and Pakistan had risen sufficiently to make war on the subcontinent a very real prospect, and it was toward the prevention of conflict that London turned its attention.[163] Indira Gandhi visited Britain and held talks with Heath on 31 October. From London's standpoint, the main purposes of the meeting were to "elicit from Mrs Gandhi as clear an account as possible of the objectives of Indian policy" and to "stress the importance of continued restraint."[164] During a private conversation with Heath at Chequers, the country residence of the British prime minister, Indira Gandhi confirmed that she was under considerable domestic pressure to act. She also admitted, perhaps evasively, that she "did not know" what result she wanted to see in East Pakistan, as "she feared that whatever was the outcome it would cause trouble for India."[165] On 7 November, Heath wrote to Yahya, imploring him to exercise restraint also.[166]

War erupted a month later, after Pakistan launched an air strike against India on 3 December. On 16 December, after less than two weeks of fighting, West Pakistani troops surrendered in the East. India did not try to press for further success in the West, and East Pakistan subsequently became the independent nation of Bangladesh.

Britain's relative economic decline after the Second World War led to imperial retreat and loss of great power status, its influence on the world stage correspondingly diminished. Nevertheless, at the start of the 1970s, the United Kingdom still had a sizable economy, even by world standards, possessed nuclear weapons, and wielded veto power as a permanent member of the UN Security Council. It had beaten a hasty retreat from the Indian subcontinent in 1947, but had for several years maintained some sway. Beginning in the 1950s, however, American support of Pakistan eroded much of what remained of any authority London still held in Islamabad. In India, misunderstandings over the British stance during the Indo-Pakistan War of 1965 and the rise to power of Indira Gandhi, who did not share her father's affinity for things British, left ties with New Delhi under some strain. As Edward Heath took up the reins of government in 1970, relations with both Islamabad and New Delhi were in need of some repair.

During his trip to South Asia in early 1971, the new prime minister achieved some success. In India, he enjoyed a warm welcome from Indira Gandhi that sparked a new, albeit reserved, optimism in the Foreign and Commonwealth Office. Importantly, in Pakistan, Heath and Yahya Khan established a fine rapport through frank and open exchanges, which the prime minister would call on in their communications during the subsequent crisis.

Domestic strife with the trade unions and particularly in Northern Ireland created unfortunate distractions as the situation in East Pakistan evolved, as did negotiations over Heath's prized foreign policy goal of British entry into the European Community. Moreover, as the clampdown in South Asia commenced, recent lessons from Harold Wilson's taking sides in the domestic conflict of another former colony during the Nigerian civil war still weighed heavily on Westminster and Whitehall.

During the initial weeks of the crisis, no British diplomat like the American Archer Blood or the Canadian James George rose to champion the cause of the East Pakistanis. In Dacca, Frank Sargeant was too distracted and stressed by the call of duty and the organization of evacuations, and the British high commissioner to New Delhi, Morrice James, had little to say before his imminent departure for a new post in Canberra. Like James, Cyril Pickard, the high commissioner to Islamabad, was scheduled to move on. Delaying his exit for a month, until 22 May, he took the opportunity to visit Dacca and, before leaving Pakistan, make known his knowledge of ongoing atrocities to apparently shocked senior officials in West Pakistan. Nevertheless, Pickard still favoured using private influence to encourage Yahya to find a political settlement. Despite being aware of the ongoing slaughter, neither Pickard nor his colleagues in Asia or the FCO sought a firmer public stance. Instead, individual MPs, particularly Bruce Douglas-Mann and John Stonehouse, would lead the charge to condemn and confront.

Alec Douglas-Home developed three components of British policy within two weeks of the clampdown. First, London adopted a stance of public neutrality on an issue it presented as an internal matter of a Commonwealth sovereign state. Second, it expressed a willingness to provide humanitarian relief to mitigate the suffering. Third, as the first two components bought time and alleviated public pressure, it pursued a strategy of privately urging Yahya to seek a timely political accommodation with appropriate Awami League involvement. As tensions between India and Pakistan grew during the summer and particularly in the fall, it added a fourth component – appeals for calm and restraint to avoid an international conflict.

This four-strand policy matched that adopted by Canada, but with an essential difference. For the most part, Ottawa remained aloof, couching its correspondence to Islamabad in restrained, diplomatic terms. By contrast, and despite London's need to consider Pakistan's sensitivity to Britain's imperial past, the missives between Heath and Yahya were characterized from the start by forthright exchange and an apparent urgency to push firmly for the desired results.

Sargeant, Pickard, the FCO, and the government reached a consensus. They recognized, during the spring and early summer, that the pursuit of a political settlement would be an uphill struggle toward the improbable, but still possible, goal of expeditiously achieving stability in the East, thereby bringing an end to the conflict and, conveniently, protecting Britain's commercial interests. Despite the challenging path ahead, they believed that this was the best way forward, and were, arguably, justified in doing so. Even the opposition leadership backed this approach in the House. Taking advantage of what he perceived as their healthy rapport, Heath wrote candid and sincere letters to Yahya on 7 April, 28 April, and 11 June, and on 14 May the government announced publicly its refusal to provide new development aid before significant progress had been made toward political accommodation in the East.

Yahya's statement of 28 June, in which he confirmed the banning of the Awami League and the effective disqualification from office of much of its leadership, was a pivotal event. Even Douglas-Home was forced to admit that Britain's strategy had failed. The following days were marked by a severe deterioration in Anglo-Pakistani relations as Islamabad protested what it perceived to be a hostile British Parliament and press, as well as an unfriendly policy that prohibited new development grants. This was London's opportunity to stand back and reconsider. Oddly, it elected to risk the wrath of British public opinion, already stirred by Anthony Mascarenhas's revelations of 13 June, and to imperil its relations with India, the world's largest democracy, by maintaining its middle course. It appeared unable to discern the changing political landscape on the subcontinent or to recognize any moral imperative. At a time when the new high commissioner to Islamabad, Laurence Pumphrey, was beginning to understand that, given Yahya's chosen line, only "miracles" could provide a political solution that would prevent the eventual secession of the East, London opted to protect what little remained of its ties with the military rulers in Islamabad and stumbled on regardless. Heath's next message to Yahya, on 29 July, was far meeker and more defensive in tone. As the subcontinent moved toward war, Heath preached calm and restraint to both Yahya and Indira Gandhi. Unfortunately, they no longer cared to listen.

PART 4

Cooperation?

7

Interplay between the Three Powers

Whereas previous parts of this book discussed the individual policies of the United States, Canada, and the United Kingdom, this chapter examines the interplay between the three nations in the formulation of their responses to the East Pakistan crisis. It begins by assessing the levels of intimacy in bilateral ties between the three powers at the start of 1971. It then investigates the marked deterioration, over the course of the following twelve months, of Washington's relations with both London and Ottawa, considering the reasons for and the timing and influence of this as it related to the sequence of events in South Asia. It examines the extent to which the three governments cooperated in determining their policies during the key response period, and concludes with an analysis of the unstructured nature of the interplay between the three North Atlantic powers with regard to policy formulation, before considering the implications of this approach in determining each country's respective policy.

The focus of this chapter is, again, the critical period between the beginning of the clampdown, on 25 March 1971, and the end of July, after which attention gradually began to focus less on human rights issues and more on averting the drift toward war on the subcontinent. It is not the intention of this chapter to provide an overly elaborate, and therefore distracting, examination of the complex issues between the three capitals in 1971, which have received much fine scholarly attention elsewhere. Nevertheless, the discussion of bilateral ties provides the vital background context against which cooperation, or otherwise, between London, Ottawa, and Washington must be considered.

Warmth and Accord

London-Ottawa

At the start of the Second World War, Canada was a self-governing dominion of the British Empire, its legislative independence having been effectively established in 1931 under the terms of the Statute of Westminster. Ottawa declared war on Germany in September 1939, only a week after London, and the first Canadian troops arrived in Britain before the year's end. Most Canadians perceived their country as an independent partner of their former ruler, but remained proud of being part of the British Empire. During 1939–45, Canada, in the opinion of Phillip Buckner, "fought for Britain."[1]

A decade later, at the start of 1956, bilateral ties were still "cordial and intimate," and Britain remained Canada's second-largest trading partner and an important source of immigrants. Built particularly on practices developed during the war, close consultation on foreign affairs continued, aided by the good relationship between Secretary of State for External Affairs Lester Pearson and London. In Ottawa, this mutual understanding was "taken for granted."[2] Nevertheless, bilateral ties were dealt a severe blow only months later, as Britain pursued an aggressive policy leading to its invasion of Egypt during the Suez Crisis. Unlike London, Ottawa believed the Egyptian president unlikely to become a future pawn of the Soviet Union. Moreover, Canada had little time for what it considered provocative gunboat diplomacy. In the perception of Ottawa, London had shown neither good sense nor a willingness to consult. Although Pearson worked tirelessly and successfully to arrange the deployment of a UN Emergency Force, which helped facilitate a British retreat, the handling of this crisis had a "lasting impact" on Anglo-Canadian relations.[3] In 1957, John Diefenbaker, a new Canadian prime minister who feared Canada's overdependence on its southern neighbour, sought to switch 15 percent of Canadian imports from the United States to Britain. This idea proved impossible to implement, but it nevertheless indicated that relations between London and Ottawa, although damaged, were not completely broken.[4] Indeed, they recovered well for, as Pierre Trudeau came to power in 1968, diplomatic ties between Britain and Canada were close. There was still a well-established tradition of consultation between ministers, officials, and parliamentarians.[5] As Charles Ritchie, the

Interplay between the Three Powers 181

Canadian high commissioner to London, remarked, though preoccupied with differing interests, London and Ottawa remained "excellent friends."[6]

In the early 1960s, London declared an interest in joining the European common market system, initially causing "deep irritation" in Ottawa. Such a move threatened Canada's beneficial interest in a long-established tariff preference agreement between the two nations that had its origins in the Imperial Economic Conference of 1932.[7] In addition, Canada was concerned about the effects of the common market's protectionist agricultural policy.[8] When Pearson returned to power as prime minister in the mid-1960s, however, he adopted a more philosophical approach to this issue, despite lingering concerns over the likely economic disadvantage to Canada. Pearson recognized that Britain belonged in the European Community, and its entry into the common market, if approved, could reduce Western Europe's "tendency to look inwards," thus offering Canada new potential export opportunities to help compensate for any reduction in trade with the United Kingdom. Britain's induction into the European Community could also offer the strategic Cold War advantage of creating a more united, and therefore stronger, Western Europe.[9] In addition, between 1951 and 1971, imports from the United Kingdom fell from 10 percent to 5 percent of Canada's overall total, and Canadian exports to Britain similarly decreased during the same period from 16 to 8 percent.[10] Canadian economic dependence on Britain had already been significantly reduced.

After the war, and particularly during the 1960s, demographic and domestic political changes resulted in a "gradual unravelling of Britishness in Canada." Neither baby boomers generally nor the growing number of immigrants from locations outside the United Kingdom, had strong nostalgic sentiments for Britain. The French-speaking Canadians in Quebec, whose political sway was on the rise, not only shared this lack of affinity but also, on occasion, nursed considerable resentment.[11] Thus, in the late 1960s, commercial ties and the sense of connectedness with the United Kingdom among the Canadian populace generally were both in decline. As Robert Bothwell has observed, Britain was "fading in Canadian statistics and Canadian consciousness."[12]

As discussed in Chapter 4, shortly after Trudeau came to office, he ordered a comprehensive review of Canadian foreign policy. The review concluded that the reduced intimacy in Anglo-Canadian relations had resulted from a combination of greater Canadian independence, growing Canada-US interdependence, and the relative decline in British power. Specific bilateral irritants included the economic issues discussed above and

182   *Cooperation?*

force reductions in Europe, which saw Canada halve its NATO contingent.[13] Nevertheless, Trudeau's successful handling of the rescue of a British diplomat kidnapped by the Front de liberation du Québec (FLQ) in 1971 earned him considerable respect and much gratitude from London.[14] It was in this context that Trudeau welcomed British prime minister Edward Heath to Ottawa on 16 December 1970, Heath's first stop on a tour of North America. The two prime ministers got along well, and Heath was again grateful one month later when, at the Commonwealth heads of government meeting, in Singapore, Trudeau helped find compromise wording for a declaration on regimes that promoted policies of racial discrimination.[15]

At the start of the East Pakistan crisis, therefore, relations between Canada and the United Kingdom were less intimate than they had once been, but remained close. Nostalgic sentiment had declined, and the level of trade had halved in recent years, although it remained significant. Nevertheless, both countries embraced capitalism and liberal, democratic, parliamentary systems built on the rule of law. They were both founding members of NATO, the Western defensive alliance, and their security services cooperated closely, sharing signals intelligence under the "Five Eyes" alliance. In Canada, Britain enjoyed "soft power in abundance" through English- language-based historical and cultural connections in academia, literature, television programming, and popular music.[16] Importantly, at the government level, the tradition of close cooperation and consultation remained.

Ottawa-Washington

During a speech to the Washington Press Club in 1969, Trudeau famously described Canada's relationship with the United States as being like "sleeping with an elephant," Ottawa being vulnerable to every toss and turn, no matter how carefully performed or generously intended. Consequently, US-Canadian relations were the prime minister's top foreign policy priority.[17] In 1970, 57 percent of Canadian exports went to the US market, while 62 percent of Canadian imports were sourced from the pachyderm to the south.[18] Despite this substantial dependency, Trudeau did not initially consider US influence on Canada to be particularly malignant; he merely accepted it as a "fact of life."[19]

The Canada–United States Automotive Products Agreement (Auto Pact) was of particular importance in trade relations between the two countries. This was a 1965 agreement to abolish tariffs on automobiles and automotive products to effectively create a single market that encompassed both Canada and the United States. Safeguards protected Canadian manufacturers

Interplay between the Three Powers 183

from the Big Three US automobile producers, which were entitled to export automobiles and parts to Canada duty-free, but at the cost of maintaining certain levels of production in Canada and, indeed, raising these proportionately should exports to Canada increase. The lower costs of manufacturing north of the border attracted significant investment in Canada by the Big Three, with eighty-seven new plants and twenty thousand new jobs being created within two years. The Auto Pact "reshaped the economy of central Canada," and most cars manufactured in Canada were sold in the United States.[20]

In the light of this economic dependence, National Security Advisor Henry Kissinger believed that Ottawa was inclined to assert its individuality at times in pursuing foreign policy goals not entirely compatible with those of the Washington, even if the two capitals remained fundamentally aligned in opposition to the Soviet Union and the Eastern Bloc. Neither he nor Nixon was particularly interested in Canadian relations, preferring instead to focus on what they perceived as key global issues. As a result, Secretary of State William Rogers and the State Department managed US-Canadian affairs.[21] The most contentious issue in bilateral ties as 1971 commenced was Vietnam. Trudeau maintained the policy of keeping Canadian troops away from direct involvement in the conflict in Southeast Asia, instead offering Ottawa's services as a facilitator of negotiations, should it be called on. The anti-war movement in Canada grew steadily throughout the 1960s, with Canadian campuses often leading the agitation. Frustration at US policy sometimes morphed into anti-American sentiment, and tensions were fuelled further as US draft dodgers escaped to Canada, where they fell outside the terms of Canadian-US extradition treaties.[22] Although the issue of Vietnam "poisoned public life" in Canada, it did not precipitate an Ottawa-Washington clash at the governmental level, as Trudeau realized that the matter was beyond Canadian influence.[23] Otherwise, Canadian and US policies were generally in accord and, despite the fact that Nixon's and Kissinger's attentions were directed elsewhere, the potential remained for continued harmonious relations.[24]

The Canadian and US economies were closely tied. Like Britain and Canada, the United States embraced capitalism and liberal, democratic systems built on the rule of law. All three were founding members of NATO and, alongside Australia and New Zealand, participated in the Five Eyes intelligence-sharing alliance. In addition, and independently of NATO, US and Canadian forces combined to operate the North American Air Defense Command (NORAD), established in the late 1950s to protect against possible Soviet attack. The United States, like Britain, enjoyed soft power influence in Canada through English-language-based literature, Hollywood movies, television programming, and popular music. At the start of 1971, Canada and the United States were independent, but also cooperative and closely interdependent in a multitude of ways.

Washington-London

Much has been written about the "special relationship" between Britain and the United States, and its discussion in scholarly circles is often the source of much heat and little light. David Reynolds, writing in the mid-1980s, offers a considered and useful examination of Anglo-US ties between the Second World War and 1973, and it is his work that underpins the following analysis.[25]

Although the concept of the "special relationship" may be traced back further, it was Winston Churchill who popularized the term in the immediate aftermath of the Second World War.[26] The notion of a relationship that was imperfect but nevertheless "special" was constructed on the perception of characteristics shared between the two nations: similar interests, first in defeating Germany and then in prosecuting the Cold War; similar ideologies, each country being a capitalist, liberal democracy; and softer linkages, including the use of the same language and, often but not always, warm interpersonal ties. Reynolds considers the effectiveness of the relationship, with the United States as the clearly dominant partner, in terms of its quality and importance in four main areas of cooperation – trade, European security, Cold War diplomacy, and global containment. He identifies two postwar time periods, each with its own distinctive features.[27]

During the first of these periods, 1945–63, the relationship was "not without its frictions, but it was nevertheless uniquely close and uniquely important to both governments and to the shaping of the postwar world."[28] In trade, an area of potentially great importance given the sizes of their two economies, Britain and the United States were the least cooperative, the former adopting protectionist measures in the face of economic decline while the latter promoted the notion of free trade.[29] On the issue of European security, the two powers worked well together on matters of great significance. London assisted with the development of both the Marshall Plan and NATO and, during the 1950s, with substantial economic and military help from Washington, Britain became the principal ally of the United States in sharing the burden of containment in Europe. During much of this period, West Germany was disarmed and France distracted by imperial conflicts in

Interplay between the Three Powers 185

Algeria and Indo-China. British arms production was greater than that of all the other European NATO allies combined, and Britain offered bases for US strategic bombers, a key part of NATO's pre–missile-era nuclear defensive strategy.[30] In the field of Cold War diplomacy, Prime Minister Harold Macmillan played an important role as intermediary with the Soviet Union, helping to bring about talks between Washington and Moscow and, later, to broker the Partial Nuclear Test Ban Treaty of 1963.[31] In terms of global containment, the relationship was less successful. Britain maintained much of its empire as the United States grappled with the dilemma of ideological opposition in the face of a practical need to contain communist expansion. Although the United States shared Britain's concerns about possible Soviet influence in Egypt, Washington, like Ottawa, condemned London's gunboat diplomacy during the Suez Crisis; moreover, it refused to support the stricken pound before Britain withdrew. The incident left the United Kingdom with no illusions as to the limits of US friendship.[32]

From 1963 to 1973, the special relationship decreased in importance owing primarily to Britain's continued relative economic and military decline.[33] Whereas Britain was the third-largest global economic power in 1951, it had been overtaken by Japan, West Germany, and France by 1971, dropping to sixth place. By this time, the Japanese gross national product was roughly twice that of Britain. Rapid economic growth within the European Community had attracted interest in Washington and London, the latter remaining eager to join despite vetoes by Charles de Gaulle in 1963 and 1967. After de Gaulle's resignation from the French presidency in 1969, Heath sensed that the time to reapply for membership was ripe.[34] Nevertheless, bilateral commercial ties remained significant: that same year, 14 percent of all British imports came from the United States and 12 percent of all British exports headed to America.[35] In terms of European defence, Britain was being eclipsed. West Germany rearmed, and joined NATO in 1955. In 1964, its military forces, at least in crude terms of manpower numbers, exceeded those of Britain for the first time. Moreover, while the British military was committed around the globe, West German troops were concentrated in Europe.[36] As negotiations shifted from banning testing to controlling weapons systems, Britain found itself no longer required in superpower negotiations.[37] Finally, in the area of global containment, Britain's economy could no longer support considerable overseas commitments. In 1967, it announced its planned withdrawal from east of Suez by the close of 1971.[38] By the start of the new decade, Britain's value to the United States had eroded.

Although Britain had always been the junior player, the relationship had increasingly become characterized less by partnership and more by dependence.[39] Nevertheless, at the start of 1971, the Anglo-US relationship remained "special," even though it was of more limited importance owing to changes in the international order.[40] There remained vital and distinguishing continuities in the functional areas of intelligence, nuclear, and diplomatic cooperation. In 1946, London and Washington signed the UKUSA Agreement, which governed cooperation between the two powers in the gathering and exchange of signals intelligence. Both countries shared their expertise, the US providing finance to assist in the establishment of the necessary bases. This agreement was adapted over the coming decades to include Australia, Canada, and New Zealand on a more formal basis. London and Washington established liaison offices on both sides of the Atlantic, the National Security Agency established its own bases on British territory, and the two air forces cooperated on European overflights.[41]

After a period of intensive collaboration on the Manhattan Project during the Second World War, the United States passed the Atomic Energy Act of 1946 (the McMahon Act), which prohibited the transfer of nuclear information to all foreign governments, including London. Britain was far from impressed and continued to develop its own nuclear weapons program independently. When the Soviets launched Sputnik in 1957, however, Washington sought a partnership to help overcome the perceived "missile gap." A series of agreements between 1958 and 1960 resulted in an amendment to the McMahon Act. Subsequently, Britain and the United States cooperated closely and, in 1962, America agreed to provide Britain with the Polaris nuclear ballistic missile system. As a result of this cooperation, Britain acquired "uniquely privileged access to US nuclear secrets and weapons."[42]

As well as closely collaborating in the fields of signals intelligence and nuclear weaponry, London and Washington continued the practice of bureaucratic and diplomatic consultation.[43] This was sometimes institutionalized through committees, but often occurred through informal networks of contacts. Suez stood as a clear example of what could happen if such channels were bypassed. Although London and Washington did not always concur, they often cooperated and coordinated and, subject to the occasional shortcoming, were largely able to avoid surprises. Importantly, through both formal and informal contact, each government was normally able to feed its own views into the decision-making process at an early stage, before it became too late to effect changes.[44]

Interplay between the Three Powers

In 1968, the year before President Richard Nixon came to power, the Intelligence and Research Bureau of the State Department prepared a report for Secretary of State Dean Rusk titled "What Now for Britain? Wilson's Visit and Britain's Future." Despite recognizing the United Kingdom's relative decline and a number of minor irritants in bilateral relations, the author insisted that Britain remained "of unparalleled importance as an American ally," observing that Washington and London shared an "unusual intimacy," the two governments collaborating "as each does with no other partner."[45] The Anglo-US relationship was not perfect but, compared with other bilateral ties, it remained unusually close in many important areas.

Summer Discord

Whereas the congenial relationship between London and Ottawa maintained its warm glow during 1971, Washington's connections with these two capitals developed nasty chills as events in South Asia unfolded.

Washington-London

Nixon was delighted when Heath won the British general election of 1970. He had not gotten along well with Harold Wilson and cherished the opportunity to rekindle ties with the United Kingdom by developing a good personal relationship with a fellow conservative leader.[46] The president readily referred publicly to the special relationship between Washington and London and was eager to visit Heath.[47] In October 1970, the two leaders met briefly at Chequers and succeeded in establishing good rapport. Heath's main objective was to nurture "a close personal relationship" and to convey to Nixon how much Britain valued close consultation with its ally.[48] Despite recognizing some irritations, London believed that Anglo-American relations generally were "still good and very close indeed in a wide variety of fields," the prime minister's advisers even admitting that "on balance, we still get more than we give, in some fields a good deal more." Yet, there was already a hint of difficulties ahead, as it had been noted that "sometimes the State Department [did] not know what the White House [was] doing."[49]

Kissinger agreed with the British on the fundamental goal of the trip. He suggested to Nixon that the president's purpose should be to establish personal ties with Heath and "maintain the general momentum and tone of US-UK consultation." On the important matter of Britain's application for entry into the European Community, Kissinger advised Nixon to reconfirm American support for the plan; both considered it a strategically useful way of strengthening Western Europe. Nevertheless, Kissinger felt that

Nixon should underline the need for London to take transatlantic trade into account when agreeing on terms.[50] Shortly after their meeting, Heath made the somewhat controversial announcement, on 26 October, that Britain must pursue her own interests and Commonwealth countries must calculate accordingly. Nixon personally dictated a letter of support, calling the prime minister's actions "bold, gutsy, and right."[51] All appeared well with Anglo-American ties.

In December 1970, Heath headed to Washington for a two-day visit during which he and Nixon expected to build on the success of their earlier meeting. Already, the US government's enthusiasm for Britain's entry into the European Community was beginning to wane, the focus on longer-term strategic benefits shifting to immediate concern over the potential commercial disadvantages at a time when the US economy was faltering. In addition, recent British proposals to raise import duties on grain had not been well received in Washington.[52] Heath intended to emphasize to Nixon that, if its application were successful, Britain would work for an "outward looking community," which would be to America's advantage.[53] Despite such annoyances, the visit was another success. John Freeman, the outgoing British ambassador to Washington, noted the "quite unusual degree of personal cordiality between the leaders of the two nations," Nixon having "set a new precedent" by inviting Heath to Camp David on the second day of discussions.[54] After the visit, the two leaders exchanged warm letters of appreciation, the president admitting that he was "delighted by the degree of sharing" and hoping that Heath would "always feel [himself] at home here in Washington."[55] As 1971 began, not only did Anglo-American ties remain strong but the two leaders had also discovered the good personal rapport they had set out to find three months earlier.

Despite such auspicious beginnings, all was not well with the Washington-London relationship by mid-year. Indeed, by September, Denis Greenhill, permanent under-secretary of state at the Foreign and Commonwealth Office (FCO), had made a handwritten comment on a memorandum describing difficulties between the United States and Britain. These had arisen because of the "realities of power" and "the US Administration's method of work (Kissinger et al.)," the latter being, in his experience, "worse than I ever remember."[56] As the US economy struggled, tensions had continued to grow over Britain's entry to Europe and its introduction of agricultural levies. Such friction would have been more manageable, in London's eyes, if Nixon and Kissinger had followed through on their intention of closely consulting on important issues. Far from doing

Interplay between the Three Powers 189

so, however, they kept London completely in the dark over rapprochement with China and then, on 15 August, announced a comprehensive package of protectionist measures without warning.[57] US economic difficulties had become an important influence on the formulation of foreign policy. By October, Heath was sufficiently concerned that he proposed a meeting with the FCO to "discuss the broad questions of our future relations with the United States."[58]

In November, the new British ambassador to Washington, Lord Cromer,[59] wrote a damning assessment of the process by which US foreign policy was being made: "No disinterested observer could possibly maintain that it is being well made and many of the Washington professionals, inside and outside the Government, think it is a mess." Kissinger dominated the areas in which he was interested, and Secretary of the Treasury John Connally closely controlled economic policy. Nixon appeared "inclined to leave the tactics and even some of the strategy to Kissinger," who had "developed a stranglehold on the Administration's foreign policy in his chosen fields." Because the national security advisor largely kept the State Department in the dark, for Cromer discovering through established channels what was happening with regard to many important issues had become an increasingly difficult task. Nixon remained "very interested indeed in the public reaction to his foreign policy and in particular in its electoral aspects." Consequently, the president had a "penchant for surprise diplomacy" and was content, on trade issues, to listen to Connally and "lend himself to the beating of the nationalist drum."[60] The exasperated Cromer would shortly refer to Kissinger as "a latter day Metternich" in an official dispatch.[61] In December, at a two-day summit meeting in Bermuda, Heath and Nixon would attempt to paper over the cracks.

In his memoirs, Kissinger was eager to blame Heath for the souring of the special relationship. He published early and his account was widely read. Recently, however, scholars have begun to undermine Kissinger's contention that Heath was indifferent toward the United States and enamoured with Europe – a reading of events that conveniently avoided any consideration of the consequences abroad that resulted from Nixon and Kissinger's methods of operation.[62] Heath did prefer the expression "natural" rather than "special" relationship, but this was largely a consequence of the prime minister's need to avoid antagonizing the French during the delicate process of negotiating European entry.[63] Anglo-American ties during 1971 suffered as a consequence of economic incompatibilities, but, more than that, they fell victim to the Nixon-Kissinger system.[64]

Ottawa-Washington

If London was perturbed by the protectionist measures announced by Washington on 15 August, Ottawa was in shock. Canada was the United States' principal trading partner, and Nixon's announcement not only posed an immediate threat to the Canadian economy but also focused attention on just how vulnerable Canada was to the twitches and spasms of the elephant to the south.[65] Bruce Muirhead described Washington's unilateral manoeuvre as "an epochal event in the history of Canada–United States relations."[66]

Without consultation and with Nixon's approval, Connally introduced a comprehensive array of protectionist measures to stimulate US exports and reduce US imports with a view to addressing the American trade deficit. His program included import surcharges, the devaluation of the US dollar (thus making imports more expensive and exports cheaper), and a package of domestic wage and price controls. Connally reserved the right to either reduce or waive altogether the surcharges on goods from countries that did not similarly devalue their own currencies in response. But for the last-minute intervention of Rogers, Connally would also have terminated the Auto Pact with Canada.[67]

Many Canadian exports remained unaffected, as they already entered the United States duty-free, the surcharge being a percentage added to the original duty and any percentage of nothing being nil.[68] Nevertheless, the potential overall impact remained of considerable concern in Ottawa, and Canada dispatched an official delegation to Washington in an attempt to persuade the US government to desist. Connally was in no mood for compromise, but by fall Kissinger had begun to realize that Canada and many other offended allies might be less disposed to cooperate in the pursuit of his strategic initiatives. It took until 6 December, however, for Nixon and Trudeau to meet in Washington, by which time the United States had seen trading improvements with Japan and elsewhere. The president agreed to lift the surcharge without further demands on the Canadian dollar. The unrelenting Connally still tried to threaten Ottawa with cancellation of the Auto Pact if it did not revalue the Canadian dollar upward, but the president accepted the Treasury Secretary's resignation in 1972.[69] As Robert Bothwell remarked, the US-Canadian relationship, "though shaken by Connally, was not dead."[70]

The matter of the Nixon shock could have been laid to rest at this point, but the sense remained in Canada of its exposure to American whim. Ottawa had expected Washington to afford it special consideration in

Interplay between the Three Powers   191

determining policy and, at the very least, the benefit of consultation.[71] A review of the situation during 1972 concluded that, in order to mitigate dependence on the United States, efforts should be made to diversify by enhancing Anglo-Canadian trade relations, particularly as this could lead to future opportunities within the European Community if the United Kingdom's application were accepted.[72]

Limited Exchanges

Although the lack of coordination between the White House and the State Department had been noted by London even before the East Pakistan crisis began, it was only in July, and particularly from 15 August onward, that Washington's relationships with London and Ottawa deteriorated significantly. Throughout the critical first few months between the clampdown and Pakistani president Yahya Khan's disappointing statement of 28 June, relations between all three capitals remained warm. The close bureaucratic and diplomatic ties, both formal and informal, between London and Washington continued to operate, and the well-established tradition of consultation between ministers, officials, and parliamentarians of Britain and Canada functioned as it had before.

During the key response period in South Asia, exchanges between the three North Atlantic powers occurred at four main levels: between diplomatic representatives on the ground in Dacca; between embassies and high commissions in the subcontinental capitals of Islamabad and New Delhi; between diplomats and bureaucrats in the three Western capitals of London, Ottawa, and Washington; and between leaders and senior politicians through high-level exchanges in the form of bilateral meetings and correspondence. Whereas relatively little information flowed between Canada and the United States, British representatives at all levels worked closely with their transatlantic counterparts.

London-Ottawa

Canada had no consulate in Dacca and so relied heavily on information shared by Britain either informally between high commissions on the subcontinent or, more frequently, as relayed through Whitehall to the Canadian High Commission in London. The FCO did not provide the Canadian High Commission with copies of all the communications it received, but instead shared all situation reports, selected telegrams, and some of the UK Joint Intelligence Committee product. In addition, it provided briefings at various levels on an ad hoc basis and accepted responsibility for the evacuation of non–South Asian Commonwealth nationals.[73] By way of reciprocation, Ottawa relayed information to London, including copies of some of John Small's and James George's dispatches home from Islamabad and New Delhi, respectively.[74] Although Canadian reports were forwarded on the understanding that they should be for London's eyes only, the FCO was not averse to sending them on to its high commissions in South Asia on occasion.[75]

Exchanges between senior British and Canadian politicians with regard to the crisis were rare, though the essence of Trudeau's missives to Yahya and Indira Gandhi sometimes made its way to the FCO via the British High Commission in Ottawa.[76] During the three months to the end of June, the only bilateral meeting between senior politicians at which South Asia appeared on the agenda occurred in Lisbon on 2 June. British foreign secretary Alec Douglas-Home and Canadian secretary of state for external affairs Mitchell Sharp were attending a gathering of ministers of the North Atlantic Council, the political decision-making body behind NATO, and had arranged a separate private meeting for brief talks on a number of issues of mutual concern. Douglas-Home hoped to convey to his counterpart the need to provide generous funding for refugee relief. More importantly, in advance of upcoming Pakistan aid consortium talks, he wished to make clear Britain's position that it would not provide new development aid until Islamabad had taken steps toward a political solution. Feeling somewhat exposed in the absence of Ottawa's adoption of a similar public position, Douglas-Home expected to underline the need for "a united front by all the major Western aid donors."[77] Britain had no desire to act in isolation if it could mitigate the consequences of Islamabad's likely unsympathetic response by coordinating its actions with others. In the event, Douglas-Home did not have the time to get his point across to Sharp, the discussion turning to the likelihood of a political settlement in Pakistan before moving on to other issues.[78]

Washington-London

Like Britain, the United States maintained a consulate in Dacca. In the face of adversity, Archer Blood, the consul general, and Frank Sargeant, the deputy high commissioner in Dacca (DHC), cooperated closely on a number of issues. They met frequently to exchange information and coordinate meetings with the Pakistani authorities in the East. Only after lengthy discussions with each other on 29 March did they make their respective decisions to arrange partial evacuations.[79] Although Sargeant left no record of his thoughts on their relationship, Blood considered the DHC his "comrade in arms."[80] After the crisis, the families of the two diplomats holidayed together near Lake Geneva and, on reflection when writing his memoirs, Blood felt "proud and grateful to have had him [Sargeant] as a colleague in those trying days."[81]

The FCO did not relay information to the US embassy in London in the same way it did to the Canadians, and the last round of Anglo-American diplomatic consultations dedicated to South Asian affairs had occurred in London during November 1970, well before the onset of the East Pakistan crisis. It took until the end of September 1971, long after the key response period, for Christopher Van Hollen, the deputy assistant secretary of state in the Bureau of Near Eastern and South Asian Affairs, to approach the FCO with a view to arranging another round of talks in Washington. He did so through Gordon King of the US embassy in London, who acted as the "usual contact" with the FCO's South Asia Department (SAD) on subcontinental concerns.[82] In the absence of prescribed arrangements, consultation continued on a less formal basis between embassies, high commissions, and bureaucracies in both London and Washington and on the subcontinent, but such exchanges remained subject to the providential availability of relevant information and personnel at any given time.[83]

The first meeting between senior American and British representatives occurred in London on 27 April, one month after the clampdown. Rogers was visiting Britain to attend a gathering of the Southeast Asia Treaty Organization (SEATO) and took the opportunity to meet Douglas-Home to discuss a wide range of international issues over a working lunch. During the meeting, the British foreign secretary persuaded his counterpart to write jointly to UN Secretary-General U Thant with a view to establishing an international relief effort. As the rendezvous occurred later on the same day that Heath met with Yahya's special envoy, Douglas-Home was able to confirm that the prime minister had emphasized the need for Yahya to seek an accommodation in the East. Rogers agreed that "there was little more that we could do on the political front."[84]

The two men met again on 3 June at the North Atlantic Council gathering in Lisbon. The day after Douglas-Home talked with Sharp, he again planned to convey the need for generous donations to the UN relief fund and London's wish, at the consortium talks, for a united front against the granting of new aid to Pakistan before progress toward a political settlement in the East.[85] The discussion of Pakistan was brief, meriting only a single paragraph in the minutes, and, although Douglas-Home was able to raise the issue of donations, once again the opportunity to discuss further policy alignment

194   *Cooperation?*

did not present itself.[86] During the three months to the end of June 1971, the issue of the East Pakistan crisis did make its way onto the meeting agendas of Rogers and Douglas-Home. Yet little of substance was decided on or achieved beyond a discussion of similar viewpoints and the sending to the United Nations of a joint communiqué on humanitarian relief, as real power in US foreign affairs resided not in the State Department but in the White House.

Heath was happy to keep Nixon informed of British policy, first writing to the president on the subject of South Asia in February 1971. Having recently returned from his visits to Pakistan and India, the prime minister shared his general impressions of the trip, noting the warmth with which he had been greeted by both Yahya and Indira Gandhi. The latter, he believed, was eager for India to remain non-aligned.[87] Two weeks after writing frankly to Yahya on 7 April, Heath agreed to share the contents of his exchange with "the White House and the State Department, but only at the highest level."[88] Nixon, in contrast, was less forthcoming.

Interestingly, Kissinger visited Britain at the end of June, just before Yahya made his disappointing announcement of the twenty-eighth, and the national security advisor headed to Pakistan and secretly onward to China. The visit was a facade to facilitate another clandestine meeting, this time in Paris with Le Duc Tho, with whom Kissinger was attempting to negotiate an end to the Vietnam conflict. Burke Trend, the British cabinet secretary, arranged the subterfuge under the pretext that his guest was visiting London to advise him about the operation of the US National Security Council (NSC) system. Before secretly taking a British plane to Paris, Kissinger enjoyed lunch with Heath on 24 June and engaged in lengthy discussions with Trend on matters other than the NSC.[89]

Heath's briefing book for the visit described Kissinger as being "prepared to say things to highly-placed British Ministers and officials which he [did] not say to the State Department."[90] The national security advisor did not disappoint, and Trend subsequently sent a lengthy six-page memorandum to the prime minister on what his guest shared with him *privately*. On relations with the Washington bureaucracy, Kissinger several times referred to the State Department and the Pentagon in "very disparaging terms." Indeed, "at the mention of Rogers' name, Kissinger made a gesture of exasperation." When Trend expressed his disappointment at how Rogers was handling Mutual and Balanced Force Reductions talks with the Soviet Union, Kissinger even encouraged him to send a high-level letter of complaint to Washington. It appeared to Trend that Kissinger "had suddenly seen a means by

Interplay between the Three Powers 195

which he could reinforce himself for this particular battle with the detestable 'bureaucrats' in the State Department."[91] The extent of the rift between the White House and State could hardly have been more apparent.

Although discretion evidently did not come naturally to Kissinger, he did not disclose any information concerning the China initiative. Nevertheless, he did touch on Pakistan. Even before his visit to the subcontinent and East Asia, Kissinger gave the following impression:

> He let me [Trend] see that his own sympathies were very much with Pakistan and against India. The Indians, he said, were one of the only two peoples (the other being the Swedes) whom he regarded as totally impossible! He said that the President feels much the same way and has a considerable liking and admiration for Yahya Khan.[92]

Despite Britain's declared position on development aid, Kissinger suggested that Nixon would welcome it "if there were some way in which aid could continue to be made available to Pakistan without endangering the possibility of a political settlement."[93] At a meeting on 21 June, the Pakistan aid consortium had voted against providing new aid, with only the United States dissenting. Just days before Yahya's speech, therefore, Kissinger confirmed the developing differences between Whitehall and White House policies.

Cromer managed to secure some time with Kissinger shortly after the latter's return from South Asia and China, and the national security advisor was again forthcoming. He believed that, despite the views of Kenneth Keating, US ambassador to New Delhi, there was a "grave danger of public opinion and ministers in India talking themselves into war with Pakistan." Dismissively, he insisted that "the US Embassy in Delhi was, if anything, more Indian than the Indians." Kissinger believed Yahya to be "a wholly honourable man" who, unfortunately, lacked the imagination and time to find a political settlement before matters would probably come to a head. The national security advisor again took the opportunity to underline his opinion that the British policy on development aid was "having a harmful rather than helpful effect." On considering Kissinger's stance, Cromer observed: "The fact that Kissinger emphasised three times that the Americans would not be influenced by the helpfulness of the Pakistanis in Kissinger's demarche with China left the impression that the opposite might be the case." Cromer advised London: "It is most important that nothing in this telegram filters back through American official or diplomatic channels as it is highly probable that State Department views are at variance [with Kissinger's]."[94] After the key response period, British and American views would continue to diverge.

During the East Pakistan crisis, no bespoke structure was put in place to facilitate regular meetings to encourage close coordination between Britain and the United States in the formulation of a combined response or, at least, to discourage inertia and drift. This problem was compounded by the lack of cooperation within the US administration, which created considerable challenges in both Washington and London. Although Anglo-American relations remained warm until the late summer of 1971, it had already been noted as early as September 1970 that the State Department did not always know what the White House was doing. Consequently, any properly coordinated UK-US foreign services response would have remained subject to *deus ex machina* interventions from the White House. This was especially so as, unknown to both State and the FCO, Nixon and Kissinger were developing the China initiative during the very period that close Anglo-American cooperation might have better addressed the unfolding human tragedy in East Pakistan.

At the start of 1971, Britain, Canada, and the United States worked closely in a number of different areas, and relations between the capitals, while subject to minor annoyances, were generally warm and certainly far from strained. All three were liberal, democratic, capitalist Cold War allies joined against communism under the umbrella of NATO, a defensive alliance that they had all helped found. Alongside Australia and New Zealand, they participated in the confidential world of signals intelligence–sharing under the Five Eyes alliance. The allies, particularly Canada and the United States, had significant commercial and economic ties, and all three shared strong cultural connections through a common language.

The three North Atlantic powers cooperated in pairs on important projects. Canada and the United States jointly operated the NORAD system, and London and Washington maintained a unique collaboration and exchange in the nuclear field. Although the so-called special relationship between London and Washington had diminished in importance owing to changes in the international order, the tradition of close diplomatic cooperation and consultation continued. Strong bureaucratic ties were similarly maintained between London and Ottawa. Nixon and Trudeau still enjoyed satisfactory rapport, and Heath had developed warm personal connections with his Canadian and American counterparts.

Interplay between the Three Powers 197

Although the agreeable relationship between London and Ottawa continued in 1971, Washington's ties with these two capitals deteriorated significantly. The absence of consultation by the White House on the China initiative and the comprehensive protectionist measures introduced in August rankled in London. The Nixon shock caused even greater displeasure in Ottawa. Yet, it was only after the key response period that Washington's relationships with London and Ottawa significantly deteriorated. Throughout the critical first few months between the clampdown and Yahya's disappointing statement on 28 June, therefore, relations between all three capitals remained warm, and the close bureaucratic and diplomatic ties, both formal and informal, between London and Washington mostly continued to operate as before. The Nixon-Kissinger partnership was an exception to this rule, however, the White House often operating secretively and without consulting the State Department, let alone Ottawa and London. This problem had been noted by Whitehall many months earlier, but only in late June and afterwards were the extent of this new method of operation and its consequences becoming increasingly apparent.

Whereas comparatively little information concerning the South Asian crisis flowed between Canada and the United States, British representatives at all levels worked closely with their transatlantic counterparts. On the ground in East Pakistan, Blood and Sargeant formed a partnership in the face of adversity. In the absence of any Canadian representation in Dacca, the FCO relayed information to Ottawa via the Canadian High Commission in London and received copies of some of Small's and George's dispatches in return. In addition, the embassies, high commissions, and foreign departments on the subcontinent and in the Western capitals exchanged information on a less formal basis.

On occasion, senior representatives in London also discussed the crisis with their counterparts in Ottawa and Washington, either in writing or at meetings arranged for other or broader purposes. Little of substance was decided on or achieved at these high-level exchanges save Douglas-Home and Rogers's sending to the UN of a joint communiqué on humanitarian relief. In the meetings between the American and British secretaries of state, little could have been achieved in any case as real power in US foreign affairs resided in the Nixon-Kissinger White House. Three months after the clampdown, the divergence between Whitehall and White House policies began to show. On 21 June, the United States alone voted against the Pakistan aid consortium's decision not to provide new aid to Islamabad. Within days, Kissinger visited London and revealed more fully his and the president's pro-Pakistan position in *private* and informal conversation with Burke Trend.

During the East Pakistan crisis, even after the extent of the atrocities and the refugee problem was readily apparent, no ad hoc trilateral or bilateral structures to facilitate regular meetings encouraging close coordination between Britain, Canada, and the United States were proposed or established.[95] It is tempting to simply argue that this would not have mattered in any case, as Nixon and Kissinger would have vetoed any US participation in a coordinated effort that did not satisfy their own concerns. This is undoubtedly true, but to end matters there would leave an important point unaddressed for the future. Even if Nixon and Kissinger had wished to act differently, there would still not have existed an apparatus to readily coordinate a combined action between two or more of the three nations. There was no three-power or international equivalent of the FCO's Pakistan Emergency Unit, which had been activated in March, or Canada's India-Pakistan Task Force, which had been established in June. The institutional structure and framework to bring together the right people on a regular basis, enabling them to pool resources, consult, plan, decide, and follow up, did not exist. Any opportunity, therefore, to provide a focused, coordinated response would have been subject to the difficulties of having to work through and around a cumbersome overarching bureaucratic system. In the absence of proper coordination, any individual nation risked isolation and retaliation if it adopted a firmer line. Douglas-Home was acutely aware of Britain's exposure after its early adoption of a tougher policy on new development aid. But for the presence of Nixon and Kissinger in the White House, an appropriate ad hoc coordinating body would likely have improved efficiency and strengthened resolve.

Conclusion

This overall conclusion considers the options available to the administrations in Washington, Ottawa, and London through combination and coordination of their responses to the crisis in East Pakistan. It contrasts the policies adopted in the three capitals before explaining the motives and influences that ultimately precipitated divergence and disagreement. It then analyzes the impact of government institutional culture in determining responses and identifies the techniques employed by the three governments to manage adverse political reactions at home. Specific conclusions for each of the three Western powers may be found at the end of each case study.

On Options

"Intervention" is a word that carries connotations of military invasion and the imposition of will by armed means. Yet, between the highly unlikely choice of going to such extremes and the possibility of doing nothing, the North Atlantic powers had several intermediate options at their disposal to encourage a political solution and an end to the atrocities in East Pakistan.

Public denunciation by the United States, Canada, or the United Kingdom would have risked the wrath of the military dictatorship in Islamabad. Correspondingly, however, it would have encouraged improved relations with more powerful India, the world's largest democracy. Such a posture would have facilitated the adoption of an ethically sound position, in line with the liberal, democratic values promoted by the West during the Cold

War. In addition, it would have helped placate domestic electorates demanding firmer action and conveyed a message of deterrence to any other world leaders considering future clampdowns of their own. If the North Atlantic powers had coordinated their condemnations, then the consequences of any Pakistani rhetorical retaliation would have been dispersed across all three capitals, rather than focused intensely on just one, and the weight of diplomatic pressure on Islamabad would have substantially increased.

Between them, Washington, Ottawa, and London provided Islamabad annually with some US$200 million of development aid.[1] These funds amounted to over one-third of Pakistan's total external assistance. This substantial tranche of aid would have been of great importance to Islamabad at any time, but particularly during the key response period, when the Pakistani economy was floundering and its hard currency reserves close to exhaustion. Economic aid was a powerful lever by which all three donors, especially through combined action, could have brought to bear considerable influence by making its availability or, indeed, the promise of its enhancement,[2] contingent on Islamabad's reaching predetermined milestones along a path toward political accommodation in the East. In June 1971, despite the efforts of President Richard Nixon and Henry Kissinger to persuade otherwise, the Pakistan aid consortium agreed to provide no further development aid, but monies already committed continued to flow from all three capitals into Pakistan's otherwise depleted coffers, the donors deploying neither stick nor carrot effectively. With regard to alternative forms of assistance, Pakistan relied heavily on Canada for training, fuel, materials, and spare parts for the Karachi Nuclear Power Project (KANUPP). Despite the crisis, however, Ottawa chose to continue this joint nuclear venture to provide one-third of the electrical power to the metropolis of Karachi. There is no evidence that, during the key response period, the possibility of implementing targeted sanctions, aimed at those high-level individuals responsible for the atrocities, was ever discussed in Washington, Ottawa, or London.

None of the three powers provided Pakistan with "lethal" military supplies, but all three permitted the flow of "non-lethal" items until at least midsummer, and therefore during the critical first few months of the clampdown. To the military dictatorship, the continued availability of such items provided considerable psychological and practical advantages. The United States permitted US$4 million worth of "non-lethal" end items, ammunition, and spare parts to flow; Canada provided Cdn$2.5 million of communications equipment before turning off the tap at the end of June; and the United Kingdom continued an elaborate charade with the Pakistani

Conclusion   201

authorities until the onset of war, pretending that military supplies were available on commercial terms but scrambling for a variety of excuses to explain why "lethal" items were seemingly no longer obtainable. In the end, London supplied only some GB£150,000 of materiel, the most lethal of which were a large number of fuses.

Under Chapter I of the United Nations Charter, the three North Atlantic powers were forbidden to threaten or employ the use of force to resolve the crisis. Nevertheless, they had at their disposal a variety of other levers with which to help pry political accommodation from Islamabad and better address growing domestic concerns for the protection of human rights. For the most part, and despite the occasional concession to pressure at home, they chose not to bring these to bear on Pakistan and instead pursued softer options. The moral and, in the case of Canada and the United Kingdom, legal duty under Article I of the UN Genocide Convention to prevent a possible genocide amounted to very little. Even if, despite the ongoing chaos, overwhelming evidence could somehow have been gathered contemporaneously to establish an incontrovertible or at least compelling case for genocide, there appeared to be in practice no obligation to act beyond alerting the United Nations.

On Comparison

The three individual case studies have demonstrated the differing positions adopted by the publics, media, congressmen or parliamentarians, diplomats, and even government departments in each country. This section focuses on the variances between the leaderships – the Nixon-Kissinger White House, the Trudeau government, and the Heath government. In terms of its response, the White House leaned most closely toward inaction in support of Islamabad. By contrast, Pierre Trudeau and Edward Heath were more proactive in seeking a political settlement from the safety of neutral ground. Canada and the United Kingdom both adopted policies comprising four main strands: 1) public neutrality in the face of what they perceived as the domestic issue of a sovereign country, 2) use of private influence to promote the pursuit of a political settlement in Pakistan, 3) donation of substantial humanitarian relief, and 4) appeals for restraint as the subcontinent moved toward war. The key difference between Ottawa and London was that the latter, despite complications rooted in its imperial past, proved more prepared to be frank, forthright, frequent, and urgent in its exchanges with Islamabad. In addition, the Heath government publicly adopted a firmer stance by linking the availability of new economic aid to progress toward a political settlement and employing it as a political lever in advance of the Pakistan aid consortium meeting on 21 June. The tactic of using private influence was arguably justifiable until Pakistani president Yahya Khans's announcement of 28 June, which effectively shattered hopes of achieving political accommodation in the East. Yet, in the aftermath of this disappointment, neither government reconsidered and changed this strand of policy, and each drifted down the path of appeasement. In Britain especially, the level of public discontent was significant. On 3 July, Islamabad had issued a formal complaint about what it perceived as the "anti-Pakistani activities" of the British Parliament and press.[3] To Heath, however, the perceived domestic political consequences were still insufficient to merit a change of direction.

Nixon and Kissinger were appeasers from the start. They adopted a policy that was superficially similar to yet quite different in substance from those of their North Atlantic partners. Nixon instructed at the very outset that the United States do nothing, and he maintained this position throughout the key response period. Like Ottawa and London, the White House sustained a position of public neutrality to facilitate its declared aim of privately encouraging political accommodation. Yet, it proved reluctant to bring any private diplomatic pressure to bear on the Pakistani president after the clampdown and especially after 27 April, when the China initiative sprang to life. Instead, Nixon and Kissinger indulged Yahya, attempting to keep fully open the pipelines through which development funding and military supplies flowed. The United States was the only country to vote against the consortium decision to permit no new economic aid to Pakistan. If the White House was reluctant to try to push Yahya toward finding a political solution, it was quite content to lead the way in providing humanitarian relief, and the United States became the most generous international donor by far.

For the first month after the clampdown, the US response was not driven by the China initiative. Elimination of this factor as a principal driving force reveals the importance of other underlying motives. Some of the initial reasons for Nixon and Kissinger's less than strident action were similar to those of Trudeau and Heath – bureaucratic inertia and a reluctance to act precipitately, the preservation of limited national interests in Pakistan as narrowly construed from a realist perspective, and varied levels of deference to the concept of sovereignty under international law. In the case of Nixon and Kissinger, these motives combined with moral apathy and the latter's predilection for focusing on global strategies to the detriment of more regional

Conclusion 203

concerns. Importantly, the president, who with Kissinger had established such close personal control over US foreign policy formulation, had a strong affinity for Yahya and Pakistan. This contrasted profoundly with his aversion to Indira Gandhi and an India that, among other things, insisted on its right to remain non-aligned during the Cold War. Nixon believed strongly that "the Indians are no goddamn good."[4] Trudeau and Heath did not share Nixon's profound preference for Pakistan over India, yet their governments were still reluctant to take firm action; it is not surprising, therefore, that the White House failed to adopt a more robust stance, even before the advent of a far more tangible opportunity with Peking.

After the watershed event of 27 April, rapprochement with China came to dominate Nixon and Kissinger's perception of the situation on the subcontinent and drive their support for Islamabad. In their opinion, the China *démarche* was not only a vital global strategic initiative but also an important domestic opportunity to significantly enhance the president's prestige and improve his chances of re-election the following year. Upsetting Yahya, in their blinkered view, could imperil the whole China venture. From the end of April, the White House course was ever more firmly set.

The Trudeau government did have its own peculiar consideration. It had no wish to adopt a forthright policy that might draw attention to, and possibly even exacerbate, its own separatist problem in Quebec. Despite significant pressure to do more over Biafra, Trudeau had maintained a neutral position owing in part to just such concerns. Heath had also learned from the West African experience. On this issue, his predecessor had suffered acute discomfort as large sections of the British public had denounced London's support of Lagos as the Nigerian federal government blockaded the starving Ibo. Recent involvement in another Commonwealth secessionist issue, therefore, had proved politically most uncomfortable. Especially given Britain's sizable immigrant communities from West Pakistan, India, and East Bengal, this could have been the case once again.

On Government Institutions and Perceived Interests

The hesitancy of leaders was to a considerable extent accommodated by the official environments in which they operated. During 1971, the institutional cultures of the foreign services and government bureaucracies on both sides of the Atlantic had not adjusted to the emerging development of human rights consciousness. Instead, they embraced a certain respect for sovereignty and a preference for making decisions through cost-benefit analysis based on national interests narrowly defined. Human rights considerations did not rank highly on administrative agendas, the slow adjustment to such concerns beginning only in the years after the crisis. Kissinger, for example, established the State Department's Bureau of Human Rights and Humanitarian Affairs in 1975.

On 30 March 1971, Nixon had explained privately to Kissinger: "There's nothing in it for us either way."[5] A month before the China initiative crystallized, the White House perceived no significant consequences to the United States with respect to its limited national interests in Pakistan. Economic links were minimal beyond the donation of aid to Islamabad, and military relations had collapsed after Washington had cut off the supply of materiel during the Indo-Pakistan War of 1965. New satellite technology had reduced the US need for an airbase in Peshawar, the lease for which had not been renewed in 1969. Similarly, as reported by John Small and Cyril Pickard, the Canadian and British high commissioners to Islamabad, Canada and the United Kingdom did not have significant national interests construed in these terms.

The contemporary perception of national interests was primarily based on short- to medium-term economic and strategic concerns, and politicians such as Nixon were only too aware of the need to consider policy within the constraints of a four-year election cycle. The three governments considered themselves responsible for the well-being and, if necessary, evacuation of their expatriate populations in times of trouble. They were also apt to promote stability. Instability discouraged trade and investment, whereas stability encouraged the development of cooperation and alliance, often considered through the lens of Cold War exigency. Broader, longer-term considerations were noticeably absent from cost-benefit calculations. Despite the Western penchant for extolling the virtues of liberal democracy during the Cold War, appreciation of the less tangible benefits of advocating such long-term values was not enmeshed in the cultural fabric of the relevant administrative and political institutions. Indeed, it was the dissenters, the outliers such as Archer Blood, Kenneth Keating, and James George, who seized on and championed these concerns.

The upper echelons of the bureaucracies were populated for the most part by those who fit in with the relevant system and who were imbued with its values. These were the seasoned campaigners who wielded power. When Joseph Sisco moved to quash the nascent rebellion at the State Department, sparked by the Blood telegram that referred to "selective genocide," he called a meeting to make it clear he was not "buying,"[6] and this was sufficient to remind the young staffers of their places. As Blood and George would soon

Conclusion

learn, nonconformity was not conducive to rapid career advancement. Those, like Joseph Farland and John Small, who were willing to substitute technical for moral responsibility by remaining focused on the administrative task at hand, attracted nods of appreciation. In contrast, the dissenters, who drew attention to compelling moral reasons to act, were unable to overcome the normative influences of institutional culture and were labelled "emotional" or otherwise unreliable and portrayed as the voices of unreason.

During the crisis, Washington, Ottawa, and London did not establish the ad hoc apparatus required to facilitate regular, close cooperation in the possible application of joint diplomatic or economic sanction, or the suspension of military supply. The institutional framework to bring together the right people on a regular basis, to focus, to pool resources, to consult, to plan, to decide, and to follow up, did not exist. Thus, any effort to provide a properly coordinated response would have had to work through and around the cumbersome overarching bureaucratic system of normal trilateral exchange. A bespoke coordinating body would likely have strengthened resolve in the three governments by providing assurance that each was not acting alone, and would have improved the efficiency of cooperation between them. Of course, collaboration between the three powers required agreement on policy, and Nixon and Kissinger would never have permitted a coordinated effort that did not satisfy their own agenda. For a future crisis under different circumstances, however, there remained an underlying structural issue to consider.

On Obfuscation and Excuse

Governments deployed an array of techniques to facilitate policies of limited action in the face of public criticism. Despite Islamabad's attempts to isolate East Pakistan by cutting communications and ousting international journalists, Washington and London knew of the atrocities within days of the clampdown. Reports continued to flow throughout the key response period, many revealing the specific targeting of the Hindu community by West Pakistani forces and their supporters. Canada was also quickly made aware of the abuses, as the Foreign and Commonwealth Office (FCO) fed information to Ottawa, primarily through the Canadian High Commission in London.

In the absence of free media access to the East, all three Western governments gained significant control over the flow of information and knowledge. By keeping the contents of their diplomatic reports private and failing to challenge the false propaganda issued by West Pakistan, Washington, Ottawa, and London were able to hide in the fog of war and more readily maintain their public positions of neutrality. The situation on the ground in the East was complex and both sides committed atrocities, but Islamabad led the way. It appeared responsible for the sustained, systematic, and targeted destruction, on a substantial scale, of multiple sections of East Pakistani society, with the Awami League political grouping and the Hindu community suffering particularly severely. Despite the best evidence available confirming the Pakistani state's ongoing campaign to kill swaths of its own populace, the three North Atlantic powers chose only to condemn violence on both sides.

Politicians sometimes added to the confusion by employing evasive rhetorical techniques in response to questions. Mitchell Sharp's statement in the Canadian House of Commons on 7 April that he had "no information *directly* from any representative of the Canadian government" in respect of mass killings was, strictly speaking, true.[7] As Canada had no diplomatic representation in East Pakistan, this was almost inevitable. The secretary of state for external affairs did not tell the whole truth, however, as he had already received evidence via the FCO that confirmed widespread killing by the Pakistani army during the first few days of the clampdown. In early June, British foreign secretary Alec Douglas-Home was advised, if pressed, and despite receipt of diplomatic reports to the contrary, to say only that he could not confirm the targeting of Hindus. In the absence of more specific questions and better-informed inquirers, half-truths could, on occasion, hold sway. This was particularly so in more complex matters, such as arms supply, where even the State Department, which was meant to control exports of materiel, claimed that, owing to an administrative oversight, it had unintentionally allowed some shipments to continue that were already in the system. Labelling techniques were also used to moderate the public discourse. In Ottawa, the government tended to avoid emotive words, such as "genocide" and "slaughter," preferring instead terms such as "cruel war" to describe the unfolding crisis. In London, "civil war" became the government's preferred description as it sought to evade controversy.[8] The best way to prevent divulging potentially provocative information, of course, was to avoid public discussion and debate altogether. In Britain, the FCO issued advice to those in charge of the parliamentary schedule to facilitate this process. The first debate in Westminster came about not because of the government's magnanimity but because Labour MP Bruce Douglas-Mann providentially won an Early Day Motion ballot.

Conclusion 207

The donation of large sums to humanitarian relief was another method employed by the three powers to influence public opinion. This action was clearly justifiable and undoubtedly saved the lives of many displaced people on the subcontinent. Nevertheless, it addressed only the symptoms and not the underlying cause of the strife. As Douglas-Home candidly admitted, it also served a diversionary function in helping to create the impression at home that something was being done, thereby mitigating adverse public opinion to some extent. By midsummer, the United States, Canada, and Britain had donated approximately US$107 million for refugees in India, an amount that had increased to US$143 million by the end of the year.[9]

All three North Atlantic powers readily drew down the veil of sovereignty over what they considered to be Pakistan's internal affair. The concept of sovereignty was enshrined in the very first chapter of the UN Charter, under which the Security Council had no right to intervene in "matters which are essentially within the domestic jurisdiction of any state."[10] The principle of non-interference was widely accepted and ethically justifiable, advocated to prevent bullying and abuse on the international stage, but it also provided a ready excuse for inaction in the face of atrocities. It would take another thirty years before a Canadian-sponsored commission published a report titled *The Responsibility to Protect* (R2P), which promoted the key idea that along with its right to sovereignty came the responsibility of a state to protect its own population. If it failed in this duty, then the international community had a responsibility to act.[11] The basic principles of R2P were adopted by world leaders at the United Nations General Assembly in 2005. This, of course, was too late for the people of East Pakistan, but the very need for subsequent promotion of R2P principles highlighted the dilemma at the heart of non-interference that already existed in 1971: to remain aloof, the Nixon-Kissinger White House and others needed only to wash their hands of the problem in the convenient font of state sovereign rights.

In *"A Problem from Hell,"* Samantha Power studied a selection of US responses to genocide and atrocity crimes from 1945 to the turn of twenty-first century. She concluded: "US policymakers did almost nothing to deter the crime," sometimes even supporting the perpetrators either directly or indirectly.[12] The United States tended to maintain public neutrality, pursue private negotiation, and send relief. Often it did not even try to take diplomatic or economic measures, let alone military action, choosing instead to hide behind the excuse of having insufficient influence. The real reason for staying aloof, however, was that policy makers in Washington, after making their cost-benefit calculations with respect to what they considered to be US national interests, lacked the will to act. Instead, they sought to contain the domestic and international political costs of inaction, the strength of public response normally being insufficient to compel them choose a different course.[13]

Beyond a single paragraph in her monograph, Power did not consider the crisis on the subcontinent. Yet, the tragic events in East Pakistan shed considerable light on the role of developing human rights awareness in the contestation and formulation of US response. The reaction to the crisis of 1971 stands as a remarkably unfortunate instance of White House indifference in the face of mass atrocity and demonstrates the dangers of concentrating so much political power in the hands of just two individuals.

Finally, the conclusions of this analysis as they pertain to the United States largely dovetail with the results of Power's work. More broadly, however, they show that the tendency to maintain public neutrality, pursue private negotiation, and send relief was not limited to Washington. When confronted with large-scale atrocities in 1971, Ottawa and London were also disposed to respond in a markedly similar and ultimately equally inadequate way.

Notes

Introduction

1 Estimates of the number killed by Pakistani forces vary dramatically from 26,000 (West Pakistan estimate) to 3 million (East Pakistan estimate). A recent study by Sarmila Bose questions the reliability of both figures and suggests that at least 50,000 to 100,000 people were killed during the conflict. This number includes all combatants and non-combatants from both sides. Sarmila Bose, *Dead Reckoning: Memories of the 1971 Bangladesh War* (New York: Columbia University Press, 2011), 175–81. The estimate of 10 million refugees is taken from the work of Archer Blood, US consul general in Dacca at the time of the crisis. It is supported by the figures released by the Indian government that estimated 8.3 million refugees to be already in India at the end of August 1971. Indian figures are difficult to verify, but were adopted by the United Nations High Commissioner for Refugees in his reports on the crisis. Archer K. Blood, *The Cruel Birth of Bangladesh: Memoirs of an American Diplomat* (Dhaka: The University Press, 2002), 303. Statistics provided by the Indian Ministry of External Affairs, reproduced in *Bangla Desh Documents* (New Delhi: Ministry of External Affairs, 1971), 446.

2 Samuel Moyn, *The Last Utopia: Human Rights in History* (Cambridge, MA: Belknap Press of Harvard University Press, 2010), 1.

3 Ibid., 2.

4 Ibid., 8, 121.

5 Ibid., 7, 121; Umberto Tulli, "'Whose Rights Are Human Rights?' The Ambiguous Emergence of Human Rights and the Demise of Kissingerism," *Cold War History* 12, 4 (2012): 574–76.

6 Moyn, *Last Utopia*, 4, 129–30.

7 Ibid., 122.

8 Although Kissinger was commonly referred to as the national security advisor, his formal title was "Assistant to the President for National Security Affairs." He served as national security advisor from January 1969 to November 1975 and as Secretary of State from September 1973 to January 1977.

9 Barbara Keys, "Congress, Kissinger, and the Origins of Human Rights Diplomacy," *Diplomatic History* 34, 5 (2010): 823–51. See also Barbara Keys, *Reclaiming American Virtue: The Human Rights Revolution of the 1970s* (Cambridge, MA: Harvard University Press, 2014).

10 Victoria Berry and Allan McChesney, "Human Rights and Foreign Policy-Making," in *Human Rights in Canadian Foreign Policy*, ed. Robert O. Matthews and Cranford Pratt (Montreal and Kingston: McGill-Queen's University Press, 1988), 60, 65.

11 Donald Bloxham and A. Dirk Moses, "Editors' Introduction: Changing Themes in the Study of Genocide," in *The Oxford Handbook of Genocide Studies*, ed. Donald Bloxham and A. Dirk Moses (New York: Oxford University Press, 2010), 3, 5.

12 The Biafran emergency (1967–70) is another potential case worthy of consideration. During the Nigerian civil war, the Ibo minority unsuccessfully sought to secede, but the Nigerian federal government imposed a blockade on rebel-held areas, resulting in widespread starvation.

13 Samantha Power, *"A Problem from Hell": America and the Age of Genocide* (New York: Harper Perennial, 2003), 165.

14 William Schabas, a prominent legal scholar working on the UN Genocide Convention (UNGC), has explained: "The concept of humanitarian intervention with respect to genocide was largely forgotten for several decades, reflecting a general malaise on the subject prevailing during the Cold War." The nature of any obligation to act was, in part, clarified by the International Court of Justice in its ruling in the case of *Bosnia v Serbia*. This judgment was, however, handed down only in 2007, some thirty-six years after the events in East Pakistan. William A. Schabas, *Genocide in International Law: The Crime of Crimes*, 2nd ed. (Cambridge: Cambridge University Press, 2009), 525.

15 Only some twenty-five years after the East Pakistan emergency did academics and statesmen begin to seriously question the principle of sovereignty over domestic issues. In 1996, Francis Deng and others of the Brookings Institution in Washington, DC, introduced the concept of "sovereignty and responsibility." In 2001, this idea was adopted in *The Responsibility to Protect* report published by the International Commission on Intervention and State Sovereignty, which had been formed under Canadian leadership the previous year. This policy document embodied the principle that the right to sovereignty brings the responsibility to protect the domestic population; if a nation-state fails in this duty, then the international community has a responsibility to intervene. The United Nations General Assembly membership adopted these key principles at the world summit of 2005.

16 This contextual examination of the domestic aspects of the crisis is based on the following: Wardatul Akmam, "Atrocities against Humanity during the Liberation War in Bangladesh: A Case of Genocide," *Journal of Genocide Research* 4, 4 (2002): 543–59; Syed Aziz-al Ahsan, "Bengali Nationalism and the Relative Deprivation Hypothesis," *Canadian Review of Studies in Nationalism* 15, 1–2 (1988): 81–90;

Mohammed Abdul Wadud Bhuiyan, *Emergence of Bangladesh and Role of the Awami League* (New Delhi: Vikas, 1982); S.K. Chakrabarti, *The Evolution of Politics in Bangladesh, 1947–1978* (New Delhi: Associated, 1978); Frank Chalk and Kurt Jonassohn, *The History and Sociology of Genocide: Analyses and Case Studies* (New Haven, CT: Yale University Press, 1990), 394–97; G.W. Choudhury, *The Last Days of United Pakistan* (Bloomington: Indiana University Press, 1974); Christophe Jaffrelot, ed., *A History of Pakistan and Its Origins*, trans. Gillian Beaumont (London: Anthem Press, 2002); Rounaq Jahan, *Pakistan: Failure in National Integration* (New York: Columbia University Press, 1972); Rounaq Jahan, "Genocide in Bangladesh," in *Centuries of Genocide: Critical Essays and Eyewitness Accounts*, 4th ed., ed. Samuel Totten and William S. Parsons (New York: Routledge, 2013), 248–76; Ayesha Jalal, *The State of Martial Rule: The Origins of Pakistan's Political Economy of Defence* (New York: Cambridge University Press, 1990); Anthony Mascarenhas, *The Rape of Bangla Desh* (New Delhi: Vikas, 1971); Omar Noman, *Pakistan: A Political and Economic History since 1947* (New York: Kegan Paul International, 1990); and Richard Sisson and Leo E. Rose, *War and Secession: Pakistan, India, and the Creation of Bangladesh* (Berkeley: University of California Press, 1990).

17 Islamabad was declared the official capital of Pakistan in 1967. Previously, the cities of Karachi (1947–58) and Rawalpindi (1958–67) were the seats of government.

18 Some 80 percent of the Pakistani army was of Punjabi origin and, in 1955, only 14 of 908 officers hailed from East Pakistan. Jahan, *Pakistan*, 25.

19 Ibid., 31, 79–81.

20 Ibid., 214.

21 At the time of the East Pakistan crisis, the population of West Pakistan was 55 million and that of East Pakistan 75 million. Leo Kuper, *Genocide: Its Political Use in the Twentieth Century* (New Haven, CT: Yale University Press, 1981), 77.

22 Henry A. Kissinger, *White House Years* (Boston: Little, Brown, 1979), 850. As the US part of this monograph will demonstrate, Kissinger's recollections are far from fully reliable, being largely self-justificatory and highly selective in their use of evidence. They are, at various times, internally contradictory and at odds with the documentary record. Such inconsistencies are statistically remarkable in that the recollections providentially appear always to portray Kissinger in a more positive light. In the core of this study, therefore, Kissinger's memoirs are used to provide only colour, not the substance of argument, which is principally constructed on evidence from archival materials.

23 Press conference, Mujibur Rahman, 26 November 1970, Dacca, quoted in Blood, *Cruel Birth*, 116.

24 The conflict over East Pakistan was a complex affair. After the initial clampdown by Pakistani forces, during which many Bengali civilians were killed, a civil war developed between the Pakistani military and Bengali resisters supported by India. During this war, atrocities by Pakistani forces continued against Bengali Hindus and Muslims. Some non-Bengali civilians in East Pakistan, often with the approval of the Pakistani military, took advantage of the unstable situation to prey on their Bengali counterparts. During the unrest, however, many non-Bengali civilians themselves fell victim to atrocities perpetrated by Bengalis. In addition, some Muslim Bengalis turned on local Hindu communities. The UNGC excludes political and social groups from its

protection. Hence, only the atrocities perpetrated against the Hindu population, in whole or in part, potentially fit within the definition of genocide as contained in this international standard. Nevertheless, several scholars have written extensively on the inadequacies of the UNGC and proffered their own replacement definitions. For those interested in the question of whether the atrocities in East Pakistan amounted to genocide under such rubrics, Wardatul Akmam provides a basic analysis, applying various scholarly definitions of genocide to the case. He concludes that, whereas the actions against the Bengali nation as a whole would only potentially qualify as genocide under the definition of Yehuda Bauer, those perpetrated against the Hindu population would do so under definitions advanced by Frank Chalk and Kurt Jonassohn, Vahakn Dadrian, Helen Fein, and Jack Porter. Akmam, "Atrocities against Humanity," 557.

25 Ramachandra Guha, *India after Gandhi: The History of the World's Largest Democracy* (London: Picador, 2008), 9; Dilip Hiro, *The Longest August: The Unflinching Rivalry between India and Pakistan* (New York: Nation Books, 2015), xiii, 414–15.

26 Hiro, *Longest August*, xiii, 414; Jalal, *State of Martial Rule*, 1.

27 Yasmin Khan, *The Great Partition: The Making of India and Pakistan,* 2nd ed. (New Haven, CT: Yale University Press, 2017), 6.

28 Ibid.

29 Sisson and Rose, *War and Secession,* 43–44; Stanley Wolpert, *A New History of India,* 8th ed. (New York: Oxford University Press, 2009), 368.

30 Yasmin Khan, *Great Partition,* 9.

31 Ibid., 180.

32 Hiro, *Longest August,* xiv.

33 Ibid., 111–33.

34 Throughout this book "China" refers to the mainland People's Republic of China. "Taiwan" is used to refer to the island-based Republic of China.

35 Guha, *India after Gandhi,* 397; Hiro, *Longest August,* 180–89, 420.

36 Guha, *India after Gandhi,* 399.

37 Ibid., 79; Yasmin Khan, *Great Partition,* 10; Sisson and Rose, *War and Secession,* 38–50; Wolpert, *New History of India,* 372–74, 394–97.

38 H.W. Brands, *India and the United States: The Cold Peace* (Boston: Twayne, 1990), 128.

39 For the sake of consistency with quotations from documents of the period and to avoid anachronism, in the main text of this work I have adopted the still-familiar Wade-Giles system for Chinese transliteration, along with the contemporary names and spellings of various places in South Asia. Thus, I use "Peking" rather than "Beijing," and "Dacca" rather than "Dhaka." While I acknowledge that this approach perpetuates the use of older systems of naming and transliteration, often associated with imperialistic attitudes, I believe it avoids confusion and makes this book more readily understandable to the reader.

Chapter 1: Superpower

1 Henry A. Kissinger, *White House Years* (Boston: Little, Brown, 1979), 854.

2 Stephen P. Cohen, "U.S. Weapons and South Asia: A Policy Analysis," *Pacific Affairs* 49, 1 (1976): 49; Shirin Tahir-Kheli, *The United States and Pakistan: The Evolution of an Influence Relationship* (New York: Praeger, 1982), 1–2.

Notes to pages 22–24

3 Robert J. McMahon, *The Cold War on the Periphery: The United States, India, and Pakistan* (New York: Columbia University Press, 1994), 337.

4 Ibid.

5 Ibid., 80, 123, 338.

6 Rashmi Jain, *US-Pak Relations, 1947–1983* (New Delhi: Radiant, 1983), 9.

7 McMahon, *Cold War on the Periphery*, 172–73; Bimal Prasad, "The Super Powers and the Subcontinent," *International Studies* 13, 4 (1974): 720.

8 Syed Rifaat Hussain, "Pakistan and the Superpowers (1947–1988): An Evaluation," *Pakistan Journal of History and Culture* 10, 1 (1989): 21; McMahon, *Cold War on the Periphery*, 338; Tahir-Kheli, *Evolution of an Influence Relationship*, 1–2.

9 Rashmi Jain, *US-Pak Relations*, 2, 14–15; McMahon, *Cold War on the Periphery*, 123.

10 McMahon, *Cold War on the Periphery*, 173. Nixon, as vice president under Eisenhower, enthusiastically supported the provision of military aid to Pakistan following his visit there in 1953.

11 Stephen P. Cohen, "U.S. Weapons and South Asia," 53; Tahir-Kheli, *Evolution of an Influence Relationship*, 24–25. Peshawar was situated in the North-West Frontier Province of Pakistan.

12 McMahon, *Cold War on the Periphery*, 338.

13 Ibid.

14 Ibid., 172–73, 339.

15 Ibid., 339–42.

16 National Security Council meeting, 3 January 1957, quoted in McMahon, *Cold War on the Periphery*, 207.

17 McMahon, *Cold War on the Periphery*, 208, 254–55, 266–67.

18 Tahir-Kheli, *Evolution of an Influence Relationship*, 25.

19 Stephen P. Cohen, "U.S. Weapons and South Asia," 50, 52; Rashmi Jain, *US-Pak Relations*, 15.

20 Stephen P. Cohen, "U.S. Weapons and South Asia," 52n9.

21 Ibid., 50. The United States granted military assistance to India only after the Sino-Indian War of 1962.

22 Rashmi Jain, *US-Pak Relations*, 15.

23 Mehrunnisa H. Iqbal, "Pakistan: Foreign Aid and Foreign Policy," *Pakistan Horizon* 25, 4 (1972): 57–58.

24 Stephen P. Cohen, "U.S. Weapons and South Asia," 54.

25 Ibid., 55.

26 H.W. Brands, *India and the United States: The Cold Peace* (Boston: Twayne, 1990), 103–4; Prasad, "Super Powers and the Subcontinent," 722–23.

27 Brands, *India and the United States*, 99, 108; Dennis Kux, *The United States and Pakistan, 1947–2000: Disenchanted Allies* (Baltimore: Johns Hopkins University Press, 2001), 141.

28 Stephen P. Cohen, "U.S. Weapons and South Asia," 52–53.

29 Brands, *India and the United States*, 108–9; Kux, *United States and Pakistan*, 145, 149; McMahon, *Cold War on the Periphery*, 340.

30 Prasad, "Super Powers and the Subcontinent," 724.

31 Kux, *United States and Pakistan*, 152–54.

32 Brands, *India and the United States*, 112; Kux, *United States and Pakistan*, 160–62.
33 Brands, *India and the United States*, 113; Stephen P. Cohen, "U.S. Weapons and South Asia," 56, 58; Kux, *United States and Pakistan*, 158–68; Prasad, "Super Powers and the Subcontinent," 727–28.
34 Stephen P. Cohen, "U.S. Weapons and South Asia," 62; Rashmi Jain, *US-Pak Relations*, 28.
35 Rashmi Jain, *US-Pak Relations*, 26.
36 US concessions with regard to the arms embargo applied to both Pakistan and India.
37 Rashmi Jain, *US-Pak Relations*, 28–29; Kux, *United States and Pakistan*, 168–79; Prasad, "Super Powers and the Subcontinent," 734–35.
38 Kux, *United States and Pakistan*, 168–79.
39 Nixon's first term was 1969–73.
40 Kissinger, *White House Years*, 848.
41 Pakistan Policy Appraisal Paper, c. 2 February 1971, Roedad Khan, compiler, *The American Papers: Secret and Confidential India-Pakistan-Bangladesh Documents, 1965–1973* (Karachi: Oxford University Press, 1999), 468–80.
42 Kissinger, *White House Years*, 848–49.
43 Ibid., 848.
44 Ibid., 849.
45 Rashmi Jain, *US-Pak Relations*, 31.
46 Kissinger, *White House Years*, 849.
47 Prasad, "Super Powers and the Subcontinent," 720–21.
48 Ibid., 731–32.
49 Ibid., 722–24.
50 Brands, *India and the United States*, 130.
51 Kissinger, *White House Years*, 848.
52 Comprehensive accounts of US-India relations during this period include: Rudra Chaudhuri, *Forged in Crisis: India and the United States since 1947* (New York: Oxford University Press, 2014); Dennis Kux, *India and the United States: Estranged Democracies* (Washington, DC: National Defense University Press, 1992); Paul M. McGarr, *The Cold War in South Asia: Britain, the United States and the Indian Subcontinent, 1945–1965* (Cambridge: Cambridge University Press, 2013); and McMahon, *Cold War on the Periphery*.
53 Richard Sisson and Leo E. Rose, *War and Secession: Pakistan, India, and the Creation of Bangladesh* (Berkeley: University of California Press, 1990), 248.
54 Niloufer Mahdi, "Sino-Pakistan Relations: Historical Background," *Pakistan Horizon* 39, 4 (1986): 63–65.
55 Ibid., 65.
56 Kux, *United States and Pakistan*, 172; Mahdi, "Sino-Pakistan Relations," 66–67; Prasad, "Super Powers and the Subcontinent," 730.
57 Brands, *India and the United States*, 130.
58 Syed Rifaat Hussain, "Sino-Pakistan Ties: Trust, Cooperation and Consolidation," *Journal of South Asian and Middle Eastern Studies* 37, 4 (2014): 16.
59 Mahdi, "Sino-Pakistan Relations," 66.
60 In 1959, Moscow and Washington agreed to suspend atmospheric nuclear testing at a time when Peking sought to further develop its own nuclear arsenal.

Notes to pages 28–29 215

61 Lorenz M. Lüthi, *The Sino-Soviet Split: Cold War in the Communist World* (Princeton, NJ: Princeton University Press, 2008), 345–49; R.K.I. Quested, *Sino-Russian Relations: A Short History* (London: George Allen and Unwin, 1984), 115–29. In addition, see Kissinger, *White House Years,* 166–67.

62 Seymour M. Hersh, *The Price of Power: Kissinger in the Nixon White House* (New York: Summit Books, 1983), 353–55; Quested, *Sino-Russian Relations,* 130–40. In addition, see Kissinger, *White House Years,* 166–67, 171–77.

63 Quested, *Sino-Russian Relations,* 140. In addition, see Kissinger, *White House Years,* 184–86.

64 Odd Arne Westad, *Restless Empire: China and the World since 1750* (London: Bodley Head, 2012), 357–61.

65 Hersh, *Price of Power,* 352–53.

66 Robert G. Sutter, *U.S.-Chinese Relations: Perilous Past, Pragmatic Present* (Lanham, MD: Rowman and Littlefield, 2010), 69.

67 John Robert Greene, *The Limits of Power: The Nixon and Ford Administrations* (Bloomington: Indiana University Press, 1992), 108.

68 Sutter, *U.S.-Chinese Relations,* 71. See also Li Jie, "Changes in China's Domestic Situation in the 1960s and Sino-U.S. Relations," in *Re-examining the Cold War: U.S.-China Diplomacy, 1954–1973,* ed. Robert S. Ross and Jiang Changbin (Cambridge, MA: Harvard University Press, 2001), 313–14.

69 Warren I. Cohen, *America in the Age of Soviet Power, 1945–1991,* vol. 4 of *The Cambridge History of American Foreign Relations,* ed. Warren I. Cohen (New York: Cambridge University Press, 1993), 187; Warren I. Cohen, *America's Response to China: A History of Sino-American Relations,* 5th ed. (New York: Columbia University Press, 2010), 215–18; Hersh, *Price of Power,* 353–55, 363–64; Sutter, *U.S.-Chinese Relations,* 71–72. It should be noted that there is some historiographical debate as to the importance of Lin Piao's role in resisting the move of Chou and Mao toward rapprochement. Yafeng Xia contends that, in Chinese sources, there is little evidence of Lin's being obstructive as Mao sought to mitigate the Soviet threat. Instead, Xia argues that Mao vacillated between the temptation of rapprochement, in the face of the perceived challenge from Moscow, and his urge to pursue the doctrine of class revolution on the global stage, the latter being at odds with US ideology. "When he came to realize that China was in a disadvantageous power position in the international power struggle, Mao would move away from class revolution and make efforts to establish a united front in order to protect China's strength." Yafeng Xia, "China's Elite Politics and Sino-American Rapprochement, January 1969–February 1972," *Journal of Cold War Studies* 8, 4 (2006): 3–28; Yafeng Xia and Kuisong Yang, "Vacillating between Revolution and Détente: Mao's Changing Psyche and Policy toward the United States, 1969–1976," *Diplomatic History* 34, 2 (2010): 423.

70 Greene, *Limits of Power,* 78.

71 Henry A. Kissinger, *Diplomacy* (New York: Simon and Schuster, 1994), 704–5.

72 Robert A. Strong, *Bureaucracy and Statesmanship: Henry Kissinger and the Making of American Foreign Policy* (Lanham, MD: University Press of America, 1986), 57.

73 Kissinger, *White House Years,* 14. In addition, see H.R. Haldeman and Joseph DiMona, *The Ends of Power* (New York: Dell, 1978), 122; Gregory D. Cleva, *Henry*

Kissinger and the American Approach to Foreign Policy (Lewisburg, PA: Bucknell University Press, 1989), 201–2.

74 Strong, *Bureaucracy and Statesmanship*, 60–65.

75 Roger Morris, *Uncertain Greatness: Henry Kissinger and American Foreign Policy* (New York: Harper and Row, 1977), 46. Once a member of Kissinger's National Security Council staff, Morris resigned in 1970 following the US invasion of Cambodia. See also Yukinori Komine, *Secrecy in US Foreign Policy: Nixon, Kissinger and Rapprochement with China* (Burlington, VT: Ashgate, 2008), 2–5.

76 Hersh, *Price of Power*, 29–31; Richard M. Nixon, *RN: The Memoirs of Richard Nixon* (New York: Grosset and Dunlap, 1978), 341.

77 Hersh, *Price of Power*, 25.

78 Ibid., 26; Nixon, *RN*, 341.

79 Joan Hoff, "A Revisionist View of Nixon's Foreign Policy," *Presidential Studies Quarterly* 26, 1 (1996): 110–12; Kissinger, *White House Years*, 42; Strong, *Bureaucracy and Statesmanship*, 58–59; Melvin Small, *The Presidency of Richard Nixon* (Lawrence: University Press of Kansas, 1999), 51–55.

80 Cleva, *Henry Kissinger*, 201–2; Kissinger, *White House Years*, 23, 39; Strong, *Bureaucracy and Statesmanship*, 79–94.

81 Melvin Small, *Presidency of Richard Nixon*, 53. In addition, see Barry M. Rubin, *Secrets of State: The State Department and the Struggle over U.S. Foreign Policy* (New York: Oxford University Press, 1985), 150.

82 Walter Isaacson, *Kissinger: A Biography* (New York: Simon and Schuster, 1992), 189.

83 The first full NSC meeting during the crisis convened on 16 July 1971, over three months after the clampdown had commenced. Christopher Van Hollen, "The Tilt Policy Revisited: Nixon-Kissinger Geopolitics and South Asia," *Asian Survey* 20, 4 (1980): 345n14.

84 Isaacson, *Kissinger*, 203–4; Rubin, *Secrets of State*, 145.

85 Isaacson, *Kissinger*, 204.

86 Joan Hoff, *Nixon Reconsidered* (New York: Basic Books, 1994), 157–66; Peter W. Rodman, *Presidential Command: Power, Leadership and the Making of Foreign Policy from Richard Nixon to George W. Bush* (New York: Alfred A. Knopf, 2009), 38–50.

87 Melvin Small, *Presidency of Richard Nixon*, 37. In addition, see Hoff, *Nixon Reconsidered*, 148, and C.L. Sulzberger, *The World and Richard Nixon* (New York: Prentice Hall Press, 1987), 169–70. Rogers was Nixon's former law practice partner.

88 Haldeman and DiMona, *Ends of Power*, 235.

89 Kissinger, *White House Years*, 28.

90 Hoff, "Revisionist View," 110; Melvin Small, *Presidency of Richard Nixon*, 54.

91 Kissinger, *White House Years*, 47. In addition, see Strong, *Bureaucracy and Statesmanship*, 63–64.

92 Cleva, *Henry Kissinger*, 201–2; Isaacson, *Kissinger*, 205–9; Strong, *Bureaucracy and Statesmanship*, 61–64.

93 Isaacson, *Kissinger*, 207.

94 Kissinger, *White House Years*, 48.

95 Ibid., 163.

Notes to pages 32–35 217

96 Van Hollen, "Tilt Policy Revisited," 357. In addition, see Louis J. Smith and David H. Herschler, "Volume Summary," in *Foreign Relations of the United States, 1969–1976,* ed. Louis J. Smith and David H. Herschler, vol. 1, *Foundations of Foreign Policy, 1969–1972,* http://history.state.gov/historicaldocuments/frus1969-76v01 (hereafter *FRUS Volume 1*).

97 Smith and Herschler, "Volume Summary."

98 Greene, *Limits of Power,* 79, 231–32; Isaacson, *Kissinger,* 143; Kissinger, *Diplomacy,* 703–4, 731; Smith and Herschler, "Volume Summary."

99 Kissinger, *Diplomacy,* 704.

100 Greene, *Limits of Power,* 79.

101 Kissinger, *White House Years,* 224–25; Nixon, *RN,* 394–95.

102 Smith and Herschler, "Volume Summary."

103 First Annual Foreign Policy Report to Congress, Nixon, 18 February 1970, document no. 60 in Smith and Herschler, *FRUS Volume 1.*

104 Stephen E. Ambrose, *The Triumph of a Politician, 1962–1972,* vol. 2 of *Nixon* (New York: Simon and Schuster, 1989), 439–41.

105 Isaacson, *Kissinger,* 766–67. Isaacson's sources: Kissinger's off-the-record talk to Nobel laureates, Paris, 18 January 1988, and *Washington Times,* 22 January 1988.

106 Warren I. Cohen, *America's Response to China,* 198–99; Kissinger, *Diplomacy,* 721.

107 Nixon's interest in rapprochement with the Chinese predated that of Kissinger. Robert Dallek, *Nixon and Kissinger: Partners in Power* (New York: HarperCollins, 2007), 617; Evelyn Goh, "Nixon, Kissinger, and the 'Soviet Card' in the U.S. Opening to China, 1971–1974," *Diplomatic History* 29, 3 (2005): 501; Hersh, *Price of Power,* 352. Hoff, *Nixon Reconsidered,* 197; Isaacson, *Kissinger,* 336.

108 Hoff, "Revisionist View," 116; Nixon, *RN,* 545. Hoff contends that, in the relationship between Nixon and Kissinger, the president took the lead on geopolitical issues, being prepared to make decisions and accept risks. Kissinger "remained the Tonto, not the Lone Ranger, of U.S. foreign policy." Hoff, *Nixon Reconsidered,* 153.

109 Richard M. Nixon, "Asia after Vietnam," *Foreign Affairs* 46, 1 (1967): 113–25, reprinted as document no. 3 in Smith and Herschler, *FRUS Volume 1.*

110 Morris, *Uncertain Greatness,* 202.

111 Stephen E. Ambrose contends that Nixon's anti-communist credentials were crucial in preventing a crippling right-wing backlash after he had publicly announced Kissinger's trip. Indeed, without Nixon to lead it, the Republican right was unable to mount any effective opposition. Ambrose, *Triumph of a Politician,* 654.

112 Greene, *Limits of Power,* 109.

113 Memorandum of Conversation, Nixon and de Gaulle, 1 March 1969, Versailles, extracted as document no. 14 in Smith and Herschler, *FRUS Volume 1.*

114 Kissinger, *White House Years,* 192.

115 Nixon, *RN,* 545.

116 First Annual Foreign Policy Report to Congress, Nixon, 18 February 1970, document no. 60 in Smith and Herschler, *FRUS Volume 1.* The Warsaw talks came to naught, but are briefly discussed in the next section.

117 Kissinger, *White House Years,* 685, 693, 1049. Richard M. Nixon, *The Real War* (New York: Warner Books, 1980), 134. In addition, see Hoff, "Revisionist View," 117, and Isaacson, *Kissinger,* 352.

118 Kissinger, *White House Years*, 763–65.

119 Ibid., 765.

120 Ibid., 194; Morris, *Uncertain Greatness*, 207; Nixon, *RN*, 345. The Soviets supplied much of Hanoi's weaponry overland by rail through China. By restricting these supplies, through cooperation with either Moscow or Peking, Washington would significantly increase the pressure on Hanoi to negotiate an end to the confrontation in Vietnam.

121 Kissinger, *White House Years*, 194. In addition, see Margaret MacMillan, *Nixon and Mao: The Week That Changed the World* (New York: Random House, 2007), 5. As MacMillan explains: "The United States needed some good news." See also Robert D. Schulzinger, *Henry Kissinger: Doctor of Diplomacy* (New York: Columbia University Press, 1989), 86.

122 Hersh, *Price of Power*, 356; Kissinger, *Diplomacy*, 722–23.

123 Nixon, *RN*, 545.

124 Kissinger, *White House Years*, 699.

125 Record of Interview with *Time* Magazine Correspondents, Kissinger, 9 December 1970, Washington, document no. 80 in Smith and Herschler, *FRUS Volume 1*.

126 Chen Jian, *Mao's China and the Cold War* (Chapel Hill: University of North Carolina Press, 2001), 256; Hersh, *Price of Power*, 366–67; Henry A. Kissinger, *On China* (Toronto: Allen Lane, 2011), 226. Nixon, *RN*, 547. Nixon admits: "We learned of Mao's statement within a few days after he made it." Kissinger insists that "no transcript of his [Snow's] interview reached high levels of government, still less the White House," then explains that this was because Snow had been "written off ... as a Beijing [Peking] propagandist."

127 Record of Radio Address Coinciding with the Second Annual Foreign Policy Report to Congress, Nixon, 25 February 1971, document no. 85 in Smith and Herschler, *FRUS Volume 1*.

128 Warren I. Cohen, *America's Response to China*, 204; Kissinger, *White House Years*, 165, 684–85.

129 Hersh, *Price of Power*, 359–60; Kissinger, *White House Years*, 193.

130 Kissinger, *White House Years*, 687–89; Chris Tudda, *A Cold War Turning Point: Nixon and China, 1969–1972* (Baton Rouge: Louisiana State University Press, 2012), 47.

131 Kissinger, *Diplomacy*, 722–23.

132 Kissinger, *White House Years*, 686. See also Evelyn Goh, *Constructing the U.S. Rapprochement with China, 1961–1974: From "Red Menace" to "Tacit Ally"* (New York: Cambridge University Press, 2005), 148.

133 Hersh, *Price of Power*, 360–62; Isaacson, *Kissinger*, 336–37; Kissinger, *White House Years*, 690, 692–93.

134 Hersh, *Price of Power*, 362. Tudda, *Cold War Turning Point*, 52. The incursion into Cambodia occurred on 30 April 1970.

135 Kissinger, *White House Years*, 693.

136 Ibid., 698.

137 Ibid., 187.

138 Ibid., 688.

Notes to pages 38–39   219

139   Hersh, *Price of Power,* 364.
140   Kissinger, *White House Years,* 696; Chi Wang, *The United States and China since World War II: A Brief History* (London: M.E. Sharpe, 2013), 73.
141   Memorandum, Smyser to Kissinger, 7 November 1970, "Letter from Your Friend in Paris, and Other Chinese Miscellania [sic]," document no. 5 in William Burr, ed., *The Beijing-Washington Back-Channel and Henry Kissinger's Secret Trip to China, September 1970–July 1971, National Security Archive Electronic Briefing Book No. 66,* http://www.gwu.edu/~nsarchiv/NSAEBB/NSAEBB66/ (hereafter *NSA Electronic Briefing Book No. 66*); Kissinger, *White House Years,* 52, 698.
142   Memorandum, Smyser to Kissinger, 18 January 1971, "Message from Sainteny," document no. 11 in Burr, ibid.
143   From 1965 onward, Bucharest attempted to forge an independent foreign policy within the Soviet bloc and portrayed itself as a possible bridge between the Cold War camps of East and West. Romania tried to reduce its economic dependency on the Soviet Union and had even publicly supported China during the Sino-Soviet split, developing closer ties with Peking. Mircea Munteanu, "Communication Breakdown? Romania and the Sino-American Rapprochement," *Diplomatic History* 33, 4 (2009): 615–16.
144   Kissinger, *White House Years,* 156–57, 180–81.
145   Ibid., 191.
146   Ibid., 699.
147   Memorandum of Conversation, Kissinger and Ceaușescu, 27 October 1970, Washington, document no. 4 in Burr, *NSA Electronic Briefing Book No. 66.*
148   In the absence of the relevant documents, yet to be declassified, the reason for this delay in delivery is not known. Munteanu speculates that this may have been as a result of one or more of the following factors: Ceaușescu's sense of self-importance, expecting the United States to await his convenience; Bucharest's consideration of possible requests to Washington for preferential treatment; or Ceaușescu's concerns over Moscow's reaction to his being the intermediary that facilitated Sino-US rapprochement. Munteanu, "Communication Breakdown?" 630.
149   Memorandum, Kissinger to Nixon, 12 January 1971, "Conversation with Ambassador Bogdan, Map Room, January 11, 1971," document no. 102 in Steven E. Phillips, ed., *Foreign Relations of the United States, 1969–1976,* vol. 17, *China, 1969–1972,* https://history.state.gov/historicaldocuments/frus1969-76v17 (hereafter *FRUS Volume 17*).
150   Memorandum of Conversation, Kissinger and Bogdan, 29 January 1971, Washington, document no. 10 in Burr, *NSA Electronic Briefing Book No. 66;* Kissinger, *White House Years,* 704.
151   Kissinger, *White House Years,* 181.
152   Memorandum, Lord to Kissinger, 4 June 1971, document no. 71.A.21 in F.S. Aijazuddin, ed., *The White House and Pakistan: Secret Declassified Documents, 1969–1974* (Karachi: Oxford University Press, 2002).
153   Kissinger, *White House Years,* 704.
154   Munteanu argues that there is as yet no evidence from the Romanian archives to suggest that the Chinese were "entirely reticent in dealing through the Romanians,"

220 — Notes to pages 39–44

and that the Romanian channel should not be readily discounted. Munteanu, "Communication Breakdown?" 629.

155 Kissinger, *White House Years,* 180–81; Nixon, *RN,* 546.

156 Kissinger, *White House Years,* 181.

157 This interest manifested itself in the convening of meeting no. 135, on 20 January 1971. Ibid., 191.

158 This meeting took place one day before Nixon met Ceauşescu under similar circumstances.

159 Memorandum of Conversation, Nixon and Yahya, 25 October 1970, Washington, document no. 3 in Burr, *NSA Electronic Briefing Book No. 66.*

160 Kissinger, *White House Years,* 700.

161 Ibid., 701. It is likely that the cyclone that struck East Pakistan on 12 November 1970 distracted Yahya's attention, thus delaying his relaying of the message.

162 Memorandum, Kissinger to Nixon, c. 10 December 1970, "Chinese Communist Initiative," document no. 99 in Phillips, *FRUS Volume 17* (emphasis added).

163 This view was reflected in the lack of urgency and the oral form of Nixon and Kissinger's response via the Romanian channel, over one month later, which signalled a US preference for the Pakistani channel back to the Chinese.

164 Memorandum of Record, 16 December 1970, untitled, document no. 8 in Burr, *NSA Electronic Briefing Book No. 66.*

Chapter 2: Phase One Response

1 Archer K. Blood, *The Cruel Birth of Bangladesh: Memoirs of an American Diplomat* (Dhaka: The University Press, 2002), 195.

2 Ibid., 193–94, 196.

3 Ibid., xvi, 202, 209.

4 Telegram, Blood to Department of State, 28 March 1971, document no. 125 in Louis J. Smith, ed., *Foreign Relations of the United States, 1969–1976,* vol. E-7, *Documents on South Asia, 1969–1972,* http://history.state.gov/historicaldocuments/frus1969 -76ve07 (hereafter *FRUS Volume E-7*).

5 Standard US diplomatic abbreviations at the time: "Pak" – Pakistan/Pakistani, and "Paks" – Pakistanis. No derogatory connotation consciously implied.

6 Telegram, Blood to Department of State, 28 March 1971, document no. 125 in Smith, *FRUS Volume E-7.*

7 Ibid.

8 Ibid.

9 Telegram, Blood to Department of State, 29 March 1971, document no. 126 in Smith, *FRUS Volume E-7.*

10 Telegram, Blood to Department of State, 30 March 1971, document no. 127 in Smith, *FRUS Volume E-7.*

11 Telegram, Blood to Department of State, 31 March 1971, document no. 6 in Sajit Gandhi, ed., *The Tilt: The US and the South Asia Crisis of 1971, National Security Archive Electronic Briefing Book No. 79,* http://www.gwu.edu/~nsarchiv/NSAEBB/ NSAEBB79/ (hereafter *NSA Electronic Briefing Book No. 79*).

12 Telegram, Blood to Department of State, 31 March 1971, document no. 5 in Gandhi, *NSA Electronic Briefing Book No. 79.*

Notes to pages 44–46   221

13 Blood, *Cruel Birth*, 205.

14 Ibid., 209, 213.

15 Benjamin Welles, "Britain May Also Act: Pakistan Airlift to Start Today," *New York Times*, 2 April 1971, 1, 9.

16 Telegram, Blood to Department of State, 6 April 1971, document no. 8 in Gandhi, *NSA Electronic Briefing Book No. 79* (emphasis added). The response to NSSM 118, dated c. 3 March 1971, had recommended strong action in the "very unlikely" event of West Pakistani military intervention in the East. "We [the United States] should be willing to risk irritating the West Pakistanis in the face of such a rash act on their part, and the threat of stopping aid should give us considerable leverage." For, although the United States preferred a united Pakistan, it should be able to adjust to the emergence of two separate states without serious damage to its interests. Response to NSSM 118, c. 3 March 1971, document no. 123 in Smith, *FRUS Volume E-7*. This response is discussed in detail in the next section.

17 Blood, *Cruel Birth*, 248; Roger Morris, *Uncertain Greatness: Henry Kissinger and American Foreign Policy* (New York: Harper and Row, 1977), 218.

18 Morris, *Uncertain Greatness*, 220. Sisco, who chaired the NSC Interdepartmental Group for Near Eastern and South Asian Affairs, was a close friend of Kissinger throughout the crisis and after. In Sisco's obituary in the *Washington Post*, Kissinger explained: "I loved Joe. He was the best type of Foreign Service officer and absolutely indispensable to me." Joe Holley, "Diplomat Joseph J. Sisco Dies at 85: Served as AU President in 1970s," *Washington Post*, 24 November 2004, B07, http://www.washingtonpost. com/wp-dyn/articles/A8945-2004Nov23_2.html.

19 Record of Telephone Conversation, Kissinger and Rogers, 6 April 1971, document no. 20 in Louis J. Smith, ed., *Foreign Relations of the United States, 1969–1976*, vol. 11, *South Asia Crisis, 1971*, http://history.state.gov/historicaldocuments/frus1969 -76v11 (hereafter *FRUS Volume 11*). In addition, see Henry A. Kissinger, *White House Years* (Boston: Little, Brown, 1979), 853.

20 Morris, *Uncertain Greatness*, 220.

21 Blood, *Cruel Birth*, 246–48.

22 Gandhi, *NSA Electronic Briefing Book No. 79*, n6.

23 Telegram, Rogers to Blood, 7 April 1971, document no. 129 in Smith, *FRUS Volume E-7*.

24 Telegram, Blood to Department of State, 10 April 1971, document no. 130 in Smith, *FRUS Volume E-7*. The US government did not formally adopt the UN Genocide Convention until 1986, though Blood appeared to be asserting that a moral duty persisted, possibly because the United States supported the fundamental principles of the convention, if not certain more specific provisions.

25 Blood, *Cruel Birth*, 288.

26 Memorandum of Conversation, Kissinger and Farland, 7 May 1971, Palm Springs, CA, document no. 42 in Smith, *FRUS Volume 11*.

27 Blood, *Cruel Birth*, 258, 289, 323; Kissinger, *White House Years*, 854. After his dismissal, State transferred Blood back to Washington, where he was granted a post in personnel. On 24 June 1971, for his actions over the atrocities, Blood was given the Herter Award, established in 1969 by the American Foreign Service Association, for "extraordinary accomplishment involving initiative, integrity, intellectual courage, and

222   *Notes to pages 46–49*

creative dissent." As others moved on, Blood reached the position of acting director general of the Foreign Service, only to be encouraged to move on himself when Kissinger became secretary of state in 1973. Thereafter, he worked as diplomatic advisor to the Army War College and then deputy chief of mission in New Delhi until his retirement in 1982. Blood, *Cruel Birth*, 324, 344–48. In 2005, the US embassy in Dacca belatedly opened the Archer K. Blood American Center Library; unfortunately, the former consul general had died the previous year. J. Robert Moskin, *American Statecraft: The Story of the U.S. Foreign Service* (New York: St. Martin's Press, 2013), 675.

28 Record of Conversation, Nixon, Kissinger, and Farland, 28 July 1971, Washington, document no. 141 in Smith, *FRUS Volume E-7*.

29 Ibid.

30 Situation Report, Blood to Department of State, 4 April 1971, extracted in Blood, *Cruel Birth*, 205.

31 Blood, *Cruel Birth*, 218.

32 Situation Report, Blood to Department of State, 14 May 1971, extracted in Blood, *Cruel Birth*, 217.

33 Situation Report, Blood to Department of State, 19 May 1971, extracted in Blood, *Cruel Birth*, 219–20.

34 "Bihari" refers specifically to an inhabitant of the neighbouring state of Bihar, but is also used generally to refer to all non-Bengalis.

35 Situation Report, Blood to Department of State, 25 May 1971, extracted in Blood, *Cruel Birth*, 222.

36 "Foggy Bottom" is a metonym for the Department of State in Washington, DC.

37 Keating was a lawyer, a Republican, and a former representative and then senator for New York. He was appointed US ambassador to New Delhi in May 1969 and served there until July 1972, after which he became US ambassador to Tel Aviv.

38 Telegram, Keating to Department of State, 29 March 1971, document no. 3 in Gandhi, *NSA Electronic Briefing Book No. 79* (emphasis added).

39 Telegram, Keating to Department of State, 12 April 1971, reproduced in telegram, John N. Irwin II, Under-Secretary of State, to US UN Mission, 13 April 1971, in Roedad Khan, compiler, *The American Papers: Secret and Confidential India-Pakistan-Bangladesh Documents, 1965–1973* (Karachi: Oxford University Press, 1999), 527–29.

40 Ibid.

41 This report is discussed in detail in the next section.

42 Memorandum, Harold Saunders and Samuel Hoskinson, NSC staff, to Kissinger, 16 April 1971, document no. 28 in Smith, *FRUS Volume 11*.

43 Record of Conversation, Nixon and Kissinger, 4 June 1971, document no. 136 in Smith, *FRUS Volume E-7*.

44 Record of Conversation, Nixon, Kissinger, and Keating, 15 June 1971, document no. 137 in Smith, *FRUS Volume E-7*.

45 Kissinger, *White House Years*, 854.

46 Record of Telephone Conversation, Nixon and Kissinger, 27 July 1971, document no. 108 in Smith, *FRUS Volume 11*. Nixon suggested Keating's immediate removal, but Kissinger suggested that such an action would cause too much political damage for the president at that time and that Nixon should wait until the situation was calmer.

Notes to pages 49–51 223

47 Jussi Hanhimäki, in his study of Kissinger, contends that Kissinger, the realist, often overlooked the domestic and regional ramifications of crises. His priority was the preservation of Cold War stability by establishing and maintaining a balance of power. Kissinger's initiatives were aimed at achieving this goal, and he perceived events as exchanges between players in a global game. Hanhimäki contends that Kissinger saw regional crises through this global strategic lens and thus failed to fully appreciate the local complexities. Jussi Hanhimäki, *The Flawed Architect: Henry Kissinger and American Foreign Policy* (New York: Oxford University Press, 2004), xviii.

48 Dennis Kux, *The United States and Pakistan, 1947–2000: Disenchanted Allies* (Baltimore: Johns Hopkins University Press, 2001), 186.

49 Blood, *Cruel Birth,* 199. In addition, Michel Laurent, an Associated Press photographer, also remained at large.

50 Sydney H. Schanberg, "Heavy Fighting, Raids Reported in East Pakistan," *New York Times,* 28 March 1971, 1. Four years later, Schanberg reported on the Khmer Rouge clampdown in Cambodia, some of his experiences being portrayed in the film *The Killing Fields.*

51 Simon Dring, "How Dacca Paid for a 'United' Pakistan," *Daily Telegraph* (London), republished in the *Washington Post,* 30 March 1971, reproduced in *Bangla Desh Documents* (New Delhi: Ministry of External Affairs, 1971), 345–48. This is a collection of publicly available material, including newspaper articles, government statements, and extracts from the proceedings of the US Congress. Other, similar collections include: K. Arif, *America-Pakistan Relations: Documents* (Lahore: Vanguard Books, 1984), and Rajendra Kumar Jain, *US-South Asian Relations, 1947–1982* (New Delhi: Radiant, 1983).

52 See, for example, Sydney H. Schanberg, "Foreign Evacuees from East Pakistan Tell of Grim Fight," *New York Times,* 7 April 1971, 1.

53 Anthony Mascarenhas, "GENOCIDE," *Sunday Times* (London), 13 June 1971, reproduced in *Bangla Desh Documents,* 358–73 (emphasis added).

54 Editorial, "In the Name of Pakistan," *New York Times,* 31 March 1971, 44.

55 Editorial, "Bloodbath in Bengal," *New York Times,* 7 April 1971, 42.

56 Tad Szulc, "U.S. Military Goods Sent to Pakistan despite Ban," *New York Times,* 22 June 1971, 1. In addition, see Editorial, "Slaughter in East Pakistan," *Washington Daily News,* 15 June 1971, reproduced in *Bangla Desh Documents,* 477–78; Editorial, "Aid for Pakistan?" *New York Times,* 17 June 1971, 40; "Helping to Kill More Bengalis," *Washington Daily News,* 30 June 1971, reproduced in *Bangla Desh Documents,* 407–8; and Editorial, "Pakistan Condemned," *New York Times,* 14 July 1971, 34.

57 A.B.M. Mahmood, "The Bangladesh Liberation War: The Response of U.S. Intellectuals," *Indian Journal of American Studies* 13, 1 (1983): 87–88.

58 A.M.A. Muhith, *American Response to Bangladesh Liberation War* (Dhaka: The University Press, 1996), 12–17.

59 Benjamin Welles, "Britain May Also Act: Pakistan Airlift to Start Today," *New York Times,* 2 April 1971, 1, 9.

60 Statement by Senator Edward Kennedy in the Senate, 1 April 1971, reproduced in *Bangla Desh Documents,* 520–21.

61 Statement by Senator Fred R. Harris in the Senate, 1 April 1971, reproduced in *Bangla Desh Documents*, 521–22.
62 The Pakistan aid consortium was organized by the World Bank to provide economic assistance to Islamabad. It comprised representatives from Belgium, Canada, France, Germany, Italy, Japan, the Netherlands, the United Kingdom, the United States, the International Bank for Reconstruction and Development, and the International Development Association. Document no. 42 in Smith, *FRUS Volume 11*, n5.
63 Letter, Senator Walter Mondale et al. to Rogers, 4 May 1971, untitled, reproduced in *Bangla Desh Documents*, 536.
64 See Statement by Senator Frank Church (Democrat, ID) in the Senate, 18 May 1971, reproduced in *Bangla Desh Documents*, 543–45; Statement by Senator William B. Saxbe (Republican, OH) in the Senate, 22 June 1971, reproduced in *Bangla Desh Documents*, 557–58; Statement by Senator Frank Church in the Senate, 7 July 1971, reproduced in *Bangla Desh Documents*, 562–64; and Statement by Senator William B. Saxbe in the Senate, 12 July 1971, reproduced in *Bangla Desh Documents*, 567–68, in which he wished to add the names of twenty-nine bipartisan co-sponsors to the proposed Saxbe-Church amendment to the Foreign Assistance Act.
65 See Statement by Senator Edward Kennedy in the Senate, 3 May 1971, reproduced in *Bangla Desh Documents*, 533–34; Letter, Senator Edward Kennedy to Rogers, 27 May 1971, untitled, reproduced in *Bangla Desh Documents*, 555–56; and Statement by Senator Edward Kennedy in the Senate, 22 June 1971, reproduced in *Bangla Desh Documents*, 556–57.
66 Statement by Representative Cornelius E. Gallagher in the House of Representatives, 10 June 1971, reproduced in *Bangla Desh Documents*, 547–53.
67 Statement by Representative Cornelius E. Gallagher in the House of Representatives, 1 July 1971, reproduced in *Bangla Desh Documents*, 559–61.
68 NSC Paper, 30 July 1971, "South Asia: Cutting Off Military and Economic Assistance," document no. 19 in Gandhi, *NSA Electronic Briefing Book No. 79*.
69 Kux, *United States and Pakistan*, 183–84.
70 Airgram, Farland to Department of State, 2 February 1971, in Roedad Khan, *American Papers*, 467.
71 Pakistan Policy Appraisal Paper, c. 2 February 1971, in Roedad Khan, *American Papers*, 468–80.
72 Memorandum of Conversation, Kissinger and Farland, 7 May 1971, Palm Springs, CA, document no. 42 in Smith, *FRUS Volume 11*; Blood, *Cruel Birth*, 193–94.
73 Telegram, Farland to Department of State, 31 March 1971, document no. 128 in Smith, *FRUS Volume E-7* (emphasis added).
74 Telegram, Farland to Department of State, 6 April 1971, document no. 21 in Smith, *FRUS Volume 11*.
75 Telegram, Farland to Department of State, 13 April 1971, in Roedad Khan, *American Papers*, 532–36.
76 Telegram, Farland to Kissinger, 21 April 1971, document no. 34 in Smith, *FRUS Volume 11*.
77 Farland's inability to consider the larger picture is highlighted in the previous section of this chapter.

Notes to pages 54–57

78 Zygmunt Bauman, *Modernity and the Holocaust* (Ithaca, NY: Cornell University Press, 2000), 11, 21–27, 98–104.
79 This outlook contrasts markedly with that of Farland's counterpart, Keating, in New Delhi.
80 Memorandum of Conversation, Kissinger and Farland, 7 May 1971, Palm Springs, CA, document no. 42 in Smith, *FRUS Volume 11*.
81 Blood, *Cruel Birth*, 342.
82 Van Hollen was deputy assistant secretary of state in the Bureau of Near Eastern and South Asian Affairs between 1969 and 1972.
83 Christopher Van Hollen, "The Tilt Policy Revisited: Nixon-Kissinger Geopolitics and South Asia," *Asian Survey* 20, 4 (1980): 345.
84 Kissinger, *White House Years*, 854.
85 Ibid., 863–64.
86 Ibid., 854. The Office of Munitions Control fell directly under the purview of the Department of State.
87 Ibid., 856.
88 Van Hollen's Informal Notes of SRG Meeting, Washington, 30 July 1971, quoted in Van Hollen, "Tilt Policy Revisited," 347. Van Hollen wrongly dates the meeting as having taken place on 31 July 1971.
89 Kissinger, *White House Years*, 854. In addition, see Van Hollen, "Tilt Policy Revisited," 343–44.
90 Van Hollen, "Tilt Policy Revisited," 343–44.
91 Kissinger, *White House Years*, 849.
92 Rashid-ul-Ahsan Chowdhury, "United States Foreign Policy in South Asia, 1971," *Journal of the Asiatic Society of Bangladesh* 35, 1 (1990): 60; Morris, *Uncertain Greatness*, 213–14.
93 Memorandum, Kissinger to Rogers, Melvin Laird (Secretary of Defense), and Richard Helms (Director of Central Intelligence), 16 February 1971, document no. 115 in Smith, *FRUS Volume E-7*.
94 Minutes of SRG Meeting, 6 March 1971, Washington, document no. 6 in Smith, *FRUS Volume 11*.
95 Response to NSSM 118, c. 3 March 1971, document no. 123 in Smith, *FRUS Volume E-7* (emphasis added).
96 Kissinger, *White House Years*, 851–52; Minutes of SRG Meeting, 6 March 1971, Washington, document no. 6 in Smith, *FRUS Volume 11*.
97 Memorandum, Kissinger to Nixon, 26 March 1971, document no. 10 in Smith, *FRUS Volume 11*.
98 Minutes of WSAG Meeting, 26 March 1971, Washington, document no. 11 in Smith, *FRUS Volume 11*.
99 Ibid.
100 Ibid.
101 Record of Telephone Conversation, Nixon and Kissinger, 30 March 1971, document no. 15 in Smith, *FRUS Volume 11*.
102 Paper for the SRG, c. 16 April 1971, document no. 132 in Smith, *FRUS Volume E-7*.

103 Minutes of WSAG Meeting, 26 March 1971, Washington, document no. 11 in Smith, *FRUS Volume 11*.
104 Memorandum, Rogers to Nixon, 3 April 1971, document no. 18 in Smith, *FRUS Volume 11*.
105 Paper for the SRG, c. 16 April 1971, document no. 132 in Smith, *FRUS Volume E-7*. See also Van Hollen, "Tilt Policy Revisited," 342.
106 Indira Gandhi, 31 March 1971, quoted in Smith, *FRUS Volume 11*, 30n2. Indira Gandhi was prime minister of India during the crisis. At the start of 1971, she found herself in a strong political position, having won the elections called in December 1970 by a landslide and holding a two-thirds majority in parliament.
107 Kux, *United States and Pakistan*, 189.
108 Record of Telephone Conversation, Nixon and Kissinger, 30 March 1971, document no. 15 in Smith, *FRUS Volume 11*.
109 In April, the one-time exception package had been ordered but not shipped. Indeed, it was not dispatched during the crisis.
110 Paper for the SRG, c. 16 April 1971, document no. 132 in Smith, *FRUS Volume E-7* (emphasis added).
111 Ibid.
112 Minutes of SRG Meeting, 19 April 1971, Washington, document no. 32 in Smith, *FRUS Volume 11*.
113 Kissinger, *White House Years*, 854.
114 Letter, Yahya to Nixon, 17 April 1971, untitled, document no. 29 in Smith, *FRUS Volume 11*.
115 Samantha Power, *"A Problem from Hell": America and the Age of Genocide* (New York: Harper Perennial, 2003), 151.
116 Kissinger, *White House Years*, 855, 914.
117 Conversation between Nixon, Kissinger, and Haldeman, 13 April 1971, Oval Office, United States, Nixon Presidential Materials Project (NPMP), White House Tapes, 478–2.
118 See Chapter 1.
119 Conversation between Nixon, Kissinger, and Haldeman, 12 April 1971, Oval Office, NPMP, White House Tapes, 477–1.
120 Record of Telephone Conversation, Nixon and Kissinger, 29 March 1971, document no. 14 in Smith, *FRUS Volume 11*.
121 Minutes of SRG Meeting, 31 March 1971, San Clemente, CA, document no. 17 in Smith, *FRUS Volume 11*.
122 Record of Conversation, Nixon, Kissinger, and Farland, 28 July 1971, Washington, document no. 141 in Smith, *FRUS Volume E-7*.
123 Joseph E. Thompson, *American Policy and African Famine: The Nigeria-Biafra War, 1966–1970* (New York: Greenwood Press, 1990), 83.
124 Ibid., 30, 97, 104.
125 Melvin Small, *The Presidency of Richard Nixon* (Lawrence: University Press of Kansas, 1999), 107.
126 Kux, *United States and Pakistan*, 179. Kux lists five occasions before Nixon became president. Nixon also made a state visit during a world trip in 1969. See also Bruce

Notes to pages 61–64

O. Riedel, *Avoiding Armageddon: America, India, and Pakistan to the Brink and Back* (Washington, DC: Brookings Institution Press, 2013), 74.

127 Kissinger, *White House Years*, 849. In addition, Kissinger suggests that the "bluff, direct military chiefs of Pakistan were more congenial to ... [Nixon] than the complex and apparently haughty Brahmin leaders of India" (ibid.). Perhaps one further factor in determining Nixon's preference for Pakistan was the historically close alliance between Washington and Islamabad cemented under Nixon's vice presidency during the 1950s.

128 Minutes of SRG Meeting, 9 April 1971, Washington, document no. 23 in Smith, *FRUS Volume 11*. In addition, see Memorandum of Conversation, Kissinger, Saunders, and Keating, 3 June 1971, Washington, document no. 64 in Smith, *FRUS Volume 11*.

129 Kissinger, *White House Years*, 848.

130 Record of Conversation, Nixon and Kissinger, 4 June 1971, document no. 136 in Smith, *FRUS Volume E-7*.

131 Kissinger, *White House Years*, 704.

132 Ibid., 854 (emphasis added). See also ibid., 913. In addition to the Pakistani channel, the Romanian channel flowed both ways. Kissinger therefore contradicts himself. See Chapter 1.

133 Mayumi Itoh, *The Origin of Ping-Pong Diplomacy: The Forgotten Architect of Sino-U.S. Rapprochement* (New York: Palgrave Macmillan, 2011), 139; Kissinger, *White House Years*, 709, 712; Richard M. Nixon, *RN: The Memoirs of Richard Nixon* (New York: Grosset and Dunlap, 1978), 548.

134 "To our surprise – and no little uneasiness – there was no response." Henry A. Kissinger, *On China* (Toronto: Allen Lane, 2011), 231.

135 Letter, Alexander Haig, Deputy Assistant for National Security Affairs, to Vernon Walters, 27 April 1971, untitled, document no. 16 in William Burr, ed., *The Beijing-Washington Back-Channel and Henry Kissinger's Secret Trip to China, September 1970–July 1971*, National Security Archive Electronic Briefing Book No. 66, http://www.gwu.edu/~nsarchiv/NSAEBB/NSAEBB66/ (hereafter *NSA Electronic Briefing Book No. 66*).

136 Yafeng Xia, "China's Elite Politics and Sino-American Rapprochement, January 1969–February 1972," *Journal of Cold War Studies* 8, 4 (2006): 14–15.

137 Memorandum, Kissinger to Nixon, 12 January 1971, "Conversation with Ambassador Bogdan, Map Room, January 11, 1971," document no. 102 in Steven E. Phillips, ed., *Foreign Relations of the United States, 1969–1976*, vol. 17, *China, 1969–1972*, https://history.state.gov/historicaldocuments/frus1969-76v17 (emphasis added) (hereafter *FRUS Volume 17*).

138 Memorandum of Record, 27 April 1971, "Message from Premier Chou En Lai," document no. 17 in Burr, *NSA Electronic Briefing Book No. 66*.

139 Letter, Haig to Walters, 27 April 1971, untitled, document no. 16 in Burr, *NSA Electronic Briefing Book No. 66*. The document bears the handwritten comment, "Never delivered because it crossed with Pak. note."

140 Ironically, 27 April 1971 was also the day Blood received his Meritorious Honor Award, from Farland in Islamabad, for his work in disaster relief following the November cyclone. Blood, *Cruel Birth*, 94.

228   *Notes to pages 64–67*

141 Kissinger, *White House Years,* 717 and 711, respectively.
142 Record of Telephone Conversation, Nixon and Kissinger, 27 April 1971, document no. 120 in Phillips, *FRUS Volume 17.* See Chapter 1 for discussion of the relationship between Sino-American rapprochement and possible US withdrawal from Vietnam.
143 Kissinger, *White House Years,* 718–19.
144 Memorandum, Kissinger to Nixon, 28 April 1971, document no. 9 in Gandhi, *NSA Electronic Briefing Book No. 79* (emphasis conveyed by underlining in original). In addition, see Kissinger, *White House Years,* 856.
145 Memorandum, Haig to Nixon, 28 April 1971, document no. 71.D.8 in F.S. Aijazuddin, ed., *The White House and Pakistan: Secret Declassified Documents, 1969–1974* (Karachi: Oxford University Press, 2002) (emphasis in original).
146 See Record of Telephone Conversation, Nixon and Kissinger, 23 May 1971, document no. 55 in Smith, *FRUS Volume 11;* Record of Conversation, Nixon and Kissinger, 4 June 1971, document no. 136 in Smith, *FRUS Volume E-7;* and Record of Conversation, Nixon, Kissinger, and Keating, 15 June 1971, document no. 137 in Smith, *FRUS Volume E-7.*

Chapter 3: Phase Two Response

1 Archer K. Blood, *The Cruel Birth of Bangladesh: Memoirs of an American Diplomat* (Dhaka: The University Press, 2002), 303.
2 It should be noted that these statistics were provided by the Indian government at the time of the crisis and have not been independently verified. The New Delhi bureaucracy was and remains the only available source, however. At a Paris press conference on 9 July 1971, Prince Sadruddin Aga Khan, the United Nations High Commissioner for Refugees, explained the nature of this difficulty: "The figures present problems. It is the [Indian] government who [sic] gives us the figures. It is impossible for us to verify them. This is also true of the figures given by the Pakistani Government regarding repatriation. The same is true of the proportions stated between the number of Moslems and Hindus: we were given the figures just as you were." At the same press conference, a reporter observed that, on visiting the camps, it became quite apparent that the problem was massive and the majority of people in the camps were clearly Hindu. Record of Press Conference with Prince Sadruddin Aga Khan, 9 July 1971, Paris, reproduced in *Bangla Desh Documents* (New Delhi: Ministry of External Affairs, 1971), 643–49.
3 Record of Conversation, Nixon, Kissinger, and Keating, 15 June 1971, document no. 137 in Louis J. Smith, ed., *Foreign Relations of the United States, 1969–1976,* vol. E-7, *Documents on South Asia, 1969–1972,* http://history.state.gov/historicaldocuments/frus1969-76ve07 (hereafter *FRUS Volume E-7*).
4 Leo Kuper, *Genocide: Its Political Use in the Twentieth Century* (New Haven, CT: Yale University Press, 1981), 77.
5 Record of Conversation, Nixon, Kissinger, and Keating, 15 June 1971, document no. 137 in Smith, *FRUS Volume E-7.*
6 Response to NSSM 133, c. 10 July 1971, document no. 140 in Smith, *FRUS Volume E-7.*

Notes to pages 67–70

7 Record of Conversation, Nixon, Kissinger, and Keating, 15 June 1971, document no. 137 in Smith, *FRUS Volume E-7*.
8 Memorandum of Conversation, Kissinger, Saunders, and Keating, 3 June 1971, Washington, document no. 64 in Louis J. Smith, ed., *Foreign Relations of the United States, 1969–1976*, vol. 11, *South Asia Crisis, 1971*, http://history.state.gov/historic aldocuments/frus1969-76v11 (hereafter *FRUS Volume 11*).
9 Telegram, Farland to Department of State, 14 May 1971, document no. 47 in Smith, *FRUS Volume 11*.
10 Smith, *FRUS Volume 11*, 137n6; Telegram, Farland to Department of State, 5 June 1971, document no. 66 in Smith, *FRUS Volume 11*.
11 Smith, *FRUS Volume 11*, 137n6.
12 Record of Conversation, Nixon, Kissinger, and Keating, 15 June 1971, document no. 137 in Smith, *FRUS Volume E-7* (emphasis added). These extraordinary remarks were made in the Oval Office during a discussion of the problems India faced in having to deal with very large numbers of refugees and how, if possible, to have them return to East Pakistan. Nixon did not explicitly state who should be doing the shooting, but it appears from the context of the full conversation that he was referring to the Indian authorities.
13 Memorandum, Haig to Nixon, 29 April 1971, document no. 38 in Smith, *FRUS Volume 11*.
14 Memorandum, Sisco to Rogers, 18 May 1971, document no. 51 in Smith, *FRUS Volume 11*.
15 Minutes of SRG Meeting, 26 May 1971, Washington, document no. 60 in Smith, *FRUS Volume 11*; Letter, Nixon to Indira Gandhi, 28 May 1971, untitled, document no. 62 in Smith, *FRUS Volume 11*.
16 Memorandum, Kissinger to Nixon, 7 June 1971, document no. 67 in Smith, *FRUS Volume 11*.
17 Memorandum, Saunders and Hoskinson to Kissinger, 14 June 1971, document no. 71 in Smith, *FRUS Volume 11*.
18 Smith, *FRUS Volume 11*, 190n2.
19 Henry A. Kissinger, *White House Years* (Boston: Little, Brown, 1979), 866.
20 Christopher Van Hollen, "The Tilt Policy Revisited: Nixon-Kissinger Geopolitics and South Asia," *Asian Survey* 20, 4 (1980): 346.
21 Nixon adopted a similar policy regarding humanitarian aid for Biafra. Faced with public demands for action, and despite maintaining public neutrality, the United States sent US$72 million in assistance to the Biafrans, making it by far the largest donor during the crisis. Joseph E. Thompson, *American Policy and African Famine: The Nigeria-Biafra War, 1966–1970* (New York: Greenwood Press, 1990), 167.
22 Record of Conversation, Nixon, Kissinger, and Keating, 15 June 1971, document no. 137 in Smith, *FRUS Volume E-7*.
23 H.W. Brands, *India and the United States: The Cold Peace* (Boston: Twayne, 1990), 128.
24 Letter, Indira Gandhi to Nixon, 13 May 1971, untitled, document no. 46 in Smith, *FRUS Volume 11*.
25 Brands, *India and the Unites States*, 128; Kissinger, *White House Years*, 855, 858, 863, 866; Telegram, Galen Stone, Chargé d'Affaires in New Delhi, to Department of State, 4 May 1971, document no. 39 in Smith, *FRUS Volume 11*.

230 Notes to pages 70–73

26 Record of Press Conference with Prince Sadruddin Aga Khan, 9 July 1971, Paris, reproduced in *Bangla Desh Documents*, 643–49. When Pakistan finally granted the United Nations access to the East on 24 July, India refused once again to permit the extension of operations beyond New Delhi. Kissinger, *White House Years*, 863.

27 Memorandum, Rogers to US Embassy in New Delhi, 26 June 1971, document no. 79 in Smith, *FRUS Volume 11*.

28 Kissinger, *White House Years*, 914.

29 Record of Telephone Conversation, Nixon and Kissinger, 23 May 1971, document no. 55 in Smith, *FRUS Volume 11*.

30 Memorandum, Hoskinson and Richard Kennedy, NSC staff, to Kissinger, 25 May 1971, document no. 57 in Smith, *FRUS Volume 11*. The WSAG meeting was held on 26 May 1971.

31 Letter, Nixon to Indira Gandhi, 28 May 1971, untitled, document no. 62 in Smith, *FRUS Volume 11*.

32 Letter, Nixon to Yahya, 28 May 1971, untitled, document no. 63 in Smith, *FRUS Volume 11*. By "danger point," Nixon meant "point of international conflict."

33 Washington's fear of conflict continued throughout the remainder of the key response period and beyond. See, for example, Response to NSSM 133, c. 10 July 1971, document no. 140 in Smith, *FRUS Volume E-7*, which insists that "the danger of war remains real."

34 Letter, Chou to Yahya, c. 13 April 1971, untitled, document no. 71.A.5 in F.S. Aijazuddin, ed., *The White House and Pakistan: Secret Declassified Documents, 1969–1974* (Karachi: Oxford University Press, 2002) (emphasis added).

35 Memorandum, Kissinger to Nixon, 15 May 1971, "Meeting with Ambassador Farland, May 7, 1971," document no. 124 in Steven E. Phillips, ed., *Foreign Relations of the United States, 1969–1976*, vol. 17, *China, 1969–1972*, https://history.state.gov/historicaldocuments/frus1969-76v17 (hereafter *FRUS Volume 17*).

36 Telegram, Farland to Kissinger, 22 May 1971, document no. 25 in William Burr, ed., *The Beijing-Washington Back-Channel and Henry Kissinger's Secret Trip to China, September 1970–July 1971*, National Security Archive Electronic Briefing Book No. 66, http://www.gwu.edu/~nsarchiv/NSAEBB/NSAEBB66/ (hereafter *NSA Electronic Briefing Book No. 66*).

37 Kissinger, *White House Years*, 739.

38 Ibid.

39 Memorandum of Record, 10 May 1971, "Message form the Government of the United States to the Government of the People's Republic of China," document no. 125 in Phillips, *FRUS Volume 17* (emphasis in original).

40 On 19 July 1971, after Kissinger's trip had been announced, the president and his national security advisor briefed White House staff, attempting to explain their original insistence on secrecy and emphasizing the need for this to continue. Nixon: "Without secrecy, there would have been no invitation or acceptance to visit China." Memorandum of Record, 19 July 1971, "Briefing of the White House Staff," document no. 41 in Burr, *NSA Electronic Briefing Book No. 66*.

41 Memorandum of Record, c. 2 June 1971, "Message from Premier of the People's Republic of China Chou En-lai to President Nixon, May 29, 1971," document no. 130 in Phillips, *FRUS Volume 17*.

Notes to pages 73–74   231

42 Seymour M. Hersh, *The Price of Power: Kissinger in the Nixon White House* (New York: Summit Books, 1983), 371; Walter Isaacson, *Kissinger: A Biography* (New York: Simon and Schuster, 1992), 342. In addition, see Kissinger, *White House Years*, 725, and Richard M. Nixon, *RN: The Memoirs of Richard Nixon* (New York: Grosset and Dunlap, 1978), 550. John Robert Greene observes that, after the announcement of Kissinger's trip, Nixon did in fact lose the support of many conservatives whose sympathies lay with Taiwan. John Robert Greene, *The Limits of Power: The Nixon and Ford Administrations* (Bloomington: Indiana University Press, 1992), 112.

43 Memorandum of Record, 19 July 1971, "Briefing of the White House Staff," document no. 41 in Burr, *NSA Electronic Briefing Book No. 66*.

44 Kissinger, *White House Years*, 739. It should be noted that the need for such close secrecy, even among high-level officials, is perhaps also a reflection of the fact that the Nixon administration was prone to leaks. On 13 June 1971, just one month before Kissinger's visit, the *New York Times* began publishing extracts from the Pentagon Papers, classified documents on American involvement in Southeast Asia, leaked by Daniel Ellsberg. Neil Sheehan, "Vietnam Archive: Pentagon Study Traces 3 Decades of Growing U.S. Involvement," *New York Times*, 13 June 1971, 1. In addition, during December, the *New York Times* began publication of the Anderson Papers. These contained some White House documents on the East Pakistan crisis. Charles Radford, a National Security Council staffer, leaked records from WSAG meetings that discussed events in South Asia as the subcontinent moved toward war. These were published by Jack Anderson, in the *New York Times* beginning in December 1971. Introduction to document no. 45 in Sajit Gandhi, ed., *The Tilt: The US and the South Asia Crisis of 1971, National Security Archive Electronic Briefing Book No. 79*, http://www.gwu.edu/~nsarchiv/NSAEBB/NSAEBB79/ (hereafter *NSA Electronic Briefing Book No. 79*); Stephen E. Ambrose, *The Triumph of a Politician, 1962–1972*, vol. 2 of *Nixon* (New York: Simon and Schuster, 1989), 486.

45 Nixon, *RN*, 553.

46 Ibid., 552.

47 Ibid.

48 Memorandum of Record, 4 June 1971, "Message from the Government of the United States to the Government of the People's Republic of China," document no. 132 in Phillips, *FRUS Volume 17*; Letter, Hilaly to Kissinger, 19 June 1971, untitled, document no. 29 in Burr, *NSA Electronic Briefing Book No. 66*.

49 Memorandum, Lord to Kissinger, 4 June 1971, document no. 71.A.21 in Aijazuddin, *White House and Pakistan*.

50 Kissinger, *White House Years*, 732. While others accompanied them on the world tour, Kissinger's companions for the covert mission to China were John Holdridge (NSC China specialist), Winston Lord (NSC staff and Kissinger's "special assistant on the most sensitive matters"), and Dick Smyser (Vietnam specialist). Kissinger, *White House Years*, 730.

51 Hersh, *Price of Power*, 365, 372.

52 Nixon won a landslide victory in the 1972 elections. Although the success of the China initiative undoubtedly assisted his cause, it would be highly speculative to suggest that this was a decisive factor in his re-election to office.

53 See Chapter 2 and, in addition, the previous section of this chapter.

54 Blood, *Cruel Birth*, 292.

55 Ibid., 296–98.

56 Editorial, "Pakistan Condemned," *New York Times*, 14 July 1971, 34.

57 Report of the Pakistan Aid Consortium Mission to East Pakistan, extracted in Blood, *Cruel Birth*, 297–98.

58 Record of Conversation, Nixon, Kissinger, and Keating, 15 June 1971, document no. 137 in Smith, *FRUS Volume E-7*.

59 See Chapter 2.

60 See the previous section of this chapter.

61 Kissinger, *White House Years*, 914.

62 Memorandum of Conversation, Kissinger, Saunders, and Keating, 3 June 1971, Washington, document no. 64 in Smith, *FRUS Volume 11*.

63 Letter, Nixon to Indira Gandhi, 28 May 1971, untitled, document no. 62 in Smith, *FRUS Volume 11*.

64 Letter, Nixon to Yahya, 28 May 1971, untitled, document no. 63 in Smith, *FRUS Volume 11*.

65 Kissinger, *White House Years*, 861.

66 Memorandum, Sisco to Rogers, 30 June 1971, document no. 84 in Smith, *FRUS Volume 11*.

67 Kissinger, *White House Years*, 863.

68 Ibid., 861.

69 Summary of response to NSSM 133, 12 July 1971, document no. 101 in Smith, *FRUS Volume 11*.

70 Response to NSSM 133, c. 10 July 1971, document no. 140 in Smith, *FRUS Volume E-7*. This report discussed the following: US strategy to date; its limitations; possible additional steps open to the administration in terms of urging restraint, providing further humanitarian relief, and encouraging political accommodation; the consequences of curtailing the supply of military or economic development aid; and the prospects of Indo-Pakistani hostilities. It listed the pros and cons associated with the various options, but did not recommend a particular policy. This particular document did not identify the maintenance of public neutrality as a separate, fourth component of US policy.

71 Paper for the SRG, c. 16 April 1971, document no. 132 in Smith, *FRUS Volume E-7*.

72 Statement by Senator Edward Kennedy in the Senate, 1 April 1971, reproduced in *Bangla Desh Documents*, 520–21.

73 Editorial, "Bloodbath in Bengal," *New York Times*, 7 April 1971, 42. Although generally unsympathetic toward White House policy, press opinion was not unanimous. The Washington *Evening Star* of 17 April, for example, urged the US government to use quiet diplomacy to end the bloodshed and take no overt action. Kamal Uddin Ahmed, "Freedom Struggle of Bangladesh and the US Press," *Indian Political Science Review* 17, 1 (1983): 94–95.

74 Blood, *Cruel Birth*, 259.

75 Van Hollen, "Tilt Policy Revisited," 360.

76 Ibid., 343.

77 Geoffrey Warner, "Review Article: Nixon, Kissinger and the Breakup of Pakistan, 1971," *International Affairs* 81, 5 (2005): 1118.

Notes to pages 78–81

78 Melvin Small, *The Presidency of Richard Nixon* (Lawrence: University Press of Kansas, 1999), 32.
79 Greene, *Limits of Power*, 96. In addition, see Ambrose, *Triumph of a Politician*, 417.
80 Ambrose, *Triumph of a Politician*, 417.
81 Ibid., 437; Greene, *Limits of Power*, 98; Nixon, *RN*, 497.
82 Ambrose, *Triumph of a Politician*, 461; Kissinger, *White House Years*, 1012–13.
83 Andrew J. Pierre, *The Global Politics of Arms Sales* (Princeton, NJ: Princeton University Press, 1982), 18.
84 Ibid., 14–15.
85 Ibid., 16. See also Lewis Sorley, *Arms Transfers under Nixon: A Policy Analysis* (Lexington: University Press of Kentucky, 1983), 41, 182–83.
86 Pierre, *Global Politics of Arms Sales*, 46. See also Stephen McGlinchey, "Richard Nixon's Road to Tehran: The Making of the U.S.-Iran Arms Agreement of May 1972," *Diplomatic History* 37, 4 (2013): 841–48; Sorley, *Arms Transfers*, 30–32.
87 Pierre, *Global Politics of Arms Sales*, 48.
88 Ibid.
89 Ibid., 8.
90 Ibid., 48.
91 Ibid., 31.
92 Ibid., 32.
93 Rashmi Jain, *US-Pak Relations, 1947–1983* (New Delhi: Radiant, 1983), 17.
94 Response to NSSM 133, c. 10 July 1971, document no. 140 in Smith, *FRUS Volume E-7*. In addition, see Memorandum, Saunders and Hoskinson to Kissinger, 1 September 1971, document no. 138 in Smith, *FRUS Volume 11*, in which Yahya is quoted as having described the matter of military supply as being of "vital importance."
95 Stephen P. Cohen, "U.S. Weapons and South Asia: A Policy Analysis," *Pacific Affairs* 49, 1 (1976): 52n9.
96 Ibid.; NSC Paper, 13 July 1971, in Enayetur Rahmin and Joyce L. Rahmin, compilers, *Bangladesh Liberation War and the Nixon White House, 1971* (Dhaka: Pustaka, 2000), 149–52. Pakistan had an option to purchase an additional fourteen aircraft on returning others then held. Rashmi Jain, *US-Pak Relations*, 31.
97 Bimal Prasad, "The Super Powers and the Subcontinent," *International Studies* 13, 4 (1974): 727–28.
98 NSC Paper, 13 July 1971, in Rahmin and Rahmin, *Bangladesh Liberation War*, 149–52.
99 Van Hollen, "Tilt Policy Revisited," 344.
100 Memorandum, Kissinger to Nixon, 28 April 1971, document no. 9 in Gandhi, *NSA Electronic Briefing Book No. 79*. In addition, see Kissinger, *White House Years*, 856. Nixon approved Kissinger's recommendation (28 April 1971) a few days later (2 May 1971).
101 The first part of the one-time exception package, the armoured personnel carriers, was in any case due for shipment only in May 1972. Minutes of SRG Meeting, 19 April 1971, Washington, document no. 32 in Smith, *FRUS Volume 11*.
102 Memorandum, Saunders and Hoskinson to Kissinger, 17 May 1971, document no. 50 in Smith, *FRUS Volume 11*.
103 NSC Paper, 13 July 1971, in Rahmin and Rahmin, *Bangladesh Liberation War*, 149–52.

104 Tad Szulc, "U.S. Military Goods Sent to Pakistan Despite Ban," *New York Times*, 22 June 1971, 1.

105 "Helping to Kill More Bengalis," *Washington Daily News*, 30 June 1971, reproduced in *Bangla Desh Documents*, 407–8; Ahmed, "Freedom Struggle," 95; Kissinger, *White House Years*, 859; Smith, *FRUS Volume 11*, 194n3.

106 Memorandum, Haig to Nixon, 25 June 1971, document no. 78 in Smith, *FRUS Volume 11*; Memorandum, Kissinger to Nixon, 30 July 1971, in Rahmin and Rahmin, *Bangladesh Liberation War*, 155–58.

107 Memorandum, Haig to Nixon, 25 June 1971, document no. 78 in Smith, *FRUS Volume 11*.

108 Minutes of SRG Meeting, Washington, 19 April 1971, document no. 32 in Smith, *FRUS Volume 11*.

109 Memorandum, Haig to Nixon, 25 June 1971, document no. 78 in Smith, *FRUS Volume 11*.

110 Editorial, "In the Name of Pakistan," *New York Times*, 31 March 1971, 44; Statement by Senator Fred R. Harris in the Senate, 1 April 1971, reproduced in *Bangla Desh Documents*, 521–22.

111 Rashid-ul-Ahsan Chowdhury, "United States Foreign Policy in South Asia, 1971," *Journal of the Asiatic Society of Bangladesh* 35, 1 (1990): 62.

112 NSC Paper, 30 July 1971, "South Asia: Cutting Off Military and Economic Assistance," document no. 19 in Gandhi, *NSA Electronic Briefing Book No. 79*.

113 Nixon and Kissinger were aided by the fact that "a relatively low point in scheduled military equipment shipments to Pakistan has, by coincidence, meant that military assistance to Pakistan has not become a pressing issue." Memorandum, Kissinger to Nixon, 30 July 1971, in Rahmin and Rahmin, *Bangladesh Liberation War*, 155–58.

114 Imtiaz H. Bokhari, "Playing with a Weak Hand: Kissinger's Management of the 1971 Indo-Pakistan Crisis," *Journal of South Asian and Middle Eastern Studies* 22, 1 (1998): 8; Roger Morris, *Uncertain Greatness: Henry Kissinger and American Foreign Policy* (New York: Harper and Row, 1977), 222.

115 Chowdhury, "United States Foreign Policy in South Asia," 67. China continued military aid to Pakistan after 25 March 1971. Although it honoured previous arms commitments, Peking appeared reluctant to approve new contracts until the crisis was over. Richard Sisson and Leo E. Rose, *War and Secession: Pakistan, India, and the Creation of Bangladesh* (Berkeley: University of California Press, 1990), 251.

116 Rashmi Jain, *US-Pak Relations*, 15.

117 Mehrunnisa H. Iqbal, "Pakistan: Foreign Aid and Foreign Policy," *Pakistan Horizon* 25, 4 (1972): 57–58.

118 Rashmi Jain, *US-Pak Relations*, 26.

119 Pakistan received US$2.7 billion of external economic assistance over the 1965–1970 five-year period. Iqbal, "Pakistan," 59. This averaged US$540 million per year, and the US portion was therefore 28 percent.

120 Paper for the SRG, c. 16 April 1971, document no. 132 in Smith, *FRUS Volume E-7*. In addition, see Telegram, Farland to Department of State, 28 February 1971, document no. 121 in Smith, *FRUS Volume E-7*.

Notes to pages 82–83

121 Record of Conversation, Nixon, Kissinger, and Haldeman, 12 April 1971, Washington, quoted in Smith, *FRUS Volume 11*, 65–66.
122 Paper for the SRG, c. 16 April 1971, document no. 132 in Smith, *FRUS Volume E-7*. "PL-480" refers to primarily food grains supplied under the Agricultural Trade Development and Assistance Act of 1954. Much of this was due for shipment to the East as part of the US response to the cyclone disaster.
123 Editorial, "In the Name of Pakistan," 44. In addition, see Editorial, "Slaughter in East Pakistan," *Washington Daily News*, 15 June 1971, reproduced in *Bangla Desh Documents*, 477–78; Editorial, "Aid for Pakistan?" *New York Times*, 17 June 1971, 40; Editorial, "Pakistan Condemned," *New York Times*, 14 July 1971, 34.
124 Statement by Senator Fred R. Harris in the Senate, 1 April 1971, reproduced in *Bangla Desh Documents*, 521–22.
125 Letter, Senator Walter Mondale et al. to Rogers, 4 May 1971, untitled, reproduced in *Bangla Desh Documents*, 536.
126 Memorandum, Kissinger to Nixon, 28 April 1971, document no. 9 in Gandhi, *NSA Electronic Briefing Book No. 79*. In addition, see Kissinger, *White House Years*, 856.
127 Memorandum, Haig to Irwin, 7 May 1971, document no. 40 in Smith, *FRUS Volume 11*.
128 Memorandum, Kissinger to Nixon, 3 August 1971, document no. 113 in Smith, *FRUS Volume 11*. In addition, see Minutes of SRG Meeting, 19 April 1971, Washington, document no. 32 in Smith, *FRUS Volume 11*.
129 Memorandum, Kissinger to Nixon, 3 August 1971, document no. 113 in Smith, *FRUS Volume 11*.
130 In March 1970, Pakistan's foreign exchange reserves stood at US$353 million, yet only twelve months later they had fallen to just US$164 million. Even this amount included capital assets not normally used to fulfill short-term liability requirements, which stood at US$263 million in March 1971. Disruption to jute exports and other economic activities in East Pakistan after the clampdown compounded Islamabad's "liquidity crisis." Robert McNamara, head of the World Bank, sent Peter Cargill to assess the situation in May 1971. Cargill's initial estimate was that Islamabad required US$500 million of assistance (US$200 million in food aid, US$300 million in cash and commodities) to prevent collapse. Srinath Raghavan, *1971: A Global History of the Creation of Bangladesh* (Cambridge, MA: Harvard University Press, 2013), 94–97.
131 Memorandum of Conversation, Kissinger and Farland, 7 May 1971, Palm Springs, CA, document no. 42 in Smith, *FRUS Volume 11*; Memorandum, Kissinger to Nixon, 15 May 1971, "Meeting with Ambassador Farland, May 7, 1971," document no. 124 in Phillips, *FRUS Volume 17*.
132 Editorial, "Slaughter in East Pakistan," *Washington Daily News*, 15 June 1971, reproduced in *Bangla Desh Documents*, 477–78.
133 Mohammed Abdul Wadud Bhuiyan, "The Bangladesh Liberation Movement and the Big Powers: Some Involvements," *Indian Political Science Review* 17, 1 (1983): 78.
134 Memorandum of Conversation, Kissinger and Farland, 7 May 1971, Palm Springs, CA, document no. 42 in Smith, *FRUS Volume 11*; Memorandum, Kissinger to Nixon, 15 May 1971, "Meeting with Ambassador Farland, May 7, 1971," document no. 124 in Phillips, *FRUS Volume 17*; Memorandum of Conversation, Nixon, M.M. Ahmad

(economic advisor to the president of Pakistan), Hilaly, and Saunders, 10 May 1971, Washington, document no. 44 in Smith, *FRUS Volume 11*.

135 Editorial, "Pakistan Condemned," *New York Times*, 14 July 1971, 34.
136 Kissinger, *White House Years*, 732, 738, 756.
137 Nixon, *RN*, 554.
138 Memorandum, Kissinger to Nixon, 14 July 1971, document no. 9 in Phillips, *FRUS Volume E-13*. It should be noted that Kissinger, despite his best efforts, was not particularly adept at manipulating domestic public opinion. Mario Del Pero, *The Eccentric Realist: Henry Kissinger and the Shaping of American Foreign Policy* (Ithaca, NY: Cornell University Press, 2010), 150–51.
139 Nixon, *RN*, 544.
140 Memorandum of Record, 19 July 1971, "Briefing of the White House Staff," document no. 41 in Burr, *NSA Electronic Briefing Book No. 66*.
141 Memorandum, Kissinger to Nixon, 14 July 1971, document no. 9 in Phillips, *FRUS Volume E-13*.
142 Kissinger, *White House Years*, 765–66.
143 Memorandum of Record, 16 July 1971, "NSC Meeting on the Middle East and South Asia," document no. 103 in Smith, *FRUS Volume 11*.
144 Memorandum, Kissinger to Nixon, 14 July 1971, document no. 9 in Phillips, *FRUS Volume E-13*.
145 Memorandum of Record, 16 July 1971, "NSC Meeting on the Middle East and South Asia," document no. 103 in Smith, *FRUS Volume 11*.
146 Kissinger, *White House Years*, 866.
147 Ibid., 867.
148 Ibid., 866–67.
149 Memorandum, Kissinger to Nixon, 24 August 1971, "Indo-Soviet Friendship Treaty," document no. 132 in Smith, *FRUS Volume 11* (emphasis added).
150 Bhuiyan, "Bangladesh Liberation Movement," 75–77; Chowdhury, "United States Foreign Policy in South Asia," 80; Syed Rifaat Hussain, "Sino-Pakistan Ties: Trust, Cooperation and Consolidation," *Journal of South Asian and Middle Eastern Studies* 37, 4 (2014): 24; Prasad, "Super Powers and the Subcontinent," 737–42. Chowdhury argues that the Chinese military administration was still paralyzed by the repercussions of Lin Piao's attempted coup. Chowdhury, "United States Foreign Policy in South Asia," 80.
151 Kissinger, *White House Years*, 784.
152 Nixon, *RN*, 580.
153 Letter, Nixon to Yahya, 7 August 1971, untitled, document no. 71.B.11 in Aijazuddin, *White House and Pakistan*.
154 Memorandum, Kissinger to Nixon, 28 April 1971, document no. 9 in Gandhi, *NSA Electronic Briefing Book No. 79* (emphasis conveyed by underlining in original).

Chapter 4: Middle Power

1 David Webster, *Fire and the Full Moon: Canada and Indonesia in a Decolonizing World* (Vancouver: UBC Press, 2009), 4.
2 Ibid.

Notes to pages 94–96

3 Ibid., 4–7.

4 Norman Hillmer and J.L. Granatstein, *Empire to Umpire: Canada and the World to the 1990s* (Toronto: Copp Clark Longman, 1994). Steven Holloway has provided a convenient list of some one dozen mediation and peacekeeping operations in which Canada was involved between 1947 and 1971. Steven Kendall Holloway, *Canadian Foreign Policy: Defining the National Interest* (Peterborough, ON: Broadview Press, 2006), 106–7.

5 Hillmer and Granatstein, *Empire to Umpire*, 285–86.

6 Douglas A. Ross, *In the Interests of Peace: Canada and Vietnam, 1954–1973* (Toronto: University of Toronto Press, 1984), 328.

7 Hillmer and Granatstein, *Empire to Umpire*, 289. See also J.L. Granatstein and Robert Bothwell, whose central thesis in their work appropriately titled *Pirouette* is that, having started out to introduce a new approach to Canadian foreign affairs in 1968, Trudeau eventually turned full circle by the time he left office in 1984, by then embracing, among other policies of his immediate predecessors, that of peacemaking. J.L. Granatstein and Robert Bothwell, *Pirouette: Pierre Trudeau and Canadian Foreign Policy* (Toronto: University of Toronto Press, 1990), xi–xiv.

8 Ross, *Interests of Peace*, 325.

9 Robert Bothwell, *Alliance and Illusion: Canada and the World, 1945–1984* (Vancouver: UBC Press, 2007), 307–8.

10 Ibid., 317.

11 Ross, *Interests of Peace*, 324.

12 John Small, "From Pakistan to Bangladesh, 1969–1972: Perspective of a Canadian Envoy," in *"Special Trust and Confidence": Envoy Essays in Canadian Diplomacy*, ed. David Reece (Ottawa: Carleton University Press, 1996), 211. Small was the Canadian high commissioner to Islamabad at the time of the emergency.

13 In 1971, the Canadian dollar stood approximately at par with the US dollar.

14 Memorandum, 19 December 1970, "Briefing Note: Visit of Prime Minister Trudeau to Pakistan – January 1971," Library and Archives Canada (LAC), RG25, vol. 10836, pt. 3, Ext. Pol. Pak., 21/09/70–31/01/72.

15 Munir Ahmad Khan, "Pakistan-Canada Nuclear Relations," in *Fifty Years of Pakistan-Canada Relations: Partnership for the 21st Century*, ed. Muzaffar Ali Qureshi (Islamabad: Area Study Centre for Africa, North and South America, Quaid-i-Azam University, 1998), 58–61.

16 Ibid., 58.

17 Memorandum, 19 December 1970, "Briefing Note: Visit of Trudeau to Pakistan – January 1971," LAC, RG25, vol. 10836, pt. 3; John Small, "Pakistan to Bangladesh," 211–13.

18 Memorandum, 17 December 1970, "Briefing Note: Visit of Trudeau to Pakistan – January 1971," LAC, RG25, vol. 8976, pt. 1, Pak. East, 01/03/71–31/12/73.

19 John Small, "Pakistan to Bangladesh," 210.

20 Robert Bothwell, *Nucleus: The History of Atomic Energy of Canada Limited* (Toronto: University of Toronto Press, 1988), 350–71.

21 James George, former Canadian high commissioner to New Delhi, telephone interview by author, 13 April 2008.

238   *Notes to pages 96–98*

22 Ryan M. Touhey, *Conflicting Visions: Canada and India in the Cold War World, 1946–76* (Vancouver: UBC Press, 2015), 197, 207; Geoffrey Pearson, "Canada, the United Nations and the Independence of Bangladesh," in *Peace, Development and Culture: Comparative Studies of India and Canada,* ed. Harold Coward (Calgary: Shastri Indo-Canadian Institute, 1988), 16. Pearson served as counsellor at the Canadian High Commission in New Delhi during the crisis and was therefore second-in-command to George. Although India received Cdn$1.3 billion of development aid, some four times the Cdn$340 million granted to Pakistan, its population was some four times larger (India, 548 million; Pakistan, 130 million).

23 Touhey, *Conflicting Visions,* 189–202.

24 John Small, "Pakistan to Bangladesh," 213.

25 Memorandum, External Affairs, 19 March 1971, "Notes on Pakistan," LAC, RG25, vol. 10836, pt. 3. These notes summarize Small's initial opinion, relayed to Ottawa some days beforehand.

26 John Small, "Pakistan to Bangladesh," 222; Memorandum, External Affairs, 23 March 1971, "Situation in East Pakistan," LAC, RG25, vol. 8975, pt. 8, Pak., 11/03/71–30/04/72.

27 As the clampdown in Dacca began, the West Pakistani authorities confined all foreign journalists to the Intercontinental Hotel before seizing their notes and film then deporting them the following day. Only Simon Dring of the *Daily Telegraph* (London) and Arnold Zeitlin of Associated Press eluded the initial roundup for several days, but they too were soon expelled. Archer K. Blood, *The Cruel Birth of Bangladesh: Memoirs of an American Diplomat* (Dhaka: The University Press, 2002), 199. In addition, Michel Laurent, an Associated Press photographer, remained at large.

28 Telegram, Small to External Affairs, 26 March 1971, LAC, RG25, vol. 8975, pt. 8.

29 Letter, Yahya to Trudeau, 31 March 1971, LAC, RG25, vol. 10836, pt. 3.

30 Telegram, Small to External Affairs, 30 March 1971, LAC, RG25, vol. 8976, pt. 1.

31 Canada, *House of Commons Debates, 1970–72* (2 April 1971), 4853.

32 Unlike Canada, the United Kingdom maintained a consulate in Dacca. Canadian diplomats regularly exchanged information and analyses with their British counterparts throughout the crisis. In addition, Canada shared information reciprocally with Australia, New Zealand, and the United States.

33 Telegram, Canadian High Commission in London to External Affairs, 2 April 1971, LAC, RG25, vol. 8976, pt. 1.

34 Telegram, Small to External Affairs, 2 April 1971, LAC, RG25, vol. 8976, pt. 1.

35 Over the following weeks, there were several reports of brutality and atrocities from Small in Islamabad and the Canadian High Commission in London, which frequently relayed information shared by the British. On 16 April, Under-Secretary of State for External Affairs Edgar Ritchie prepared a summary of the East Pakistan situation, in which he observed that "the British and American missions in Dacca and foreigners evacuated from East Pakistan [had] largely tended to confirm earlier reports of substantial casualties among the civilian population resulting from random firing by West Pakistan troops and ruthless suppression of those associated with the local nationalist movement." He went on to note that the "killing of Bengalis, both Moslem and Hindu, seems to have been matched in some areas by killings

Notes to pages 98–100

by Bengalis" of the non-Bengali minority that was perceived as having sided with the Pakistani forces. Memorandum, Ritchie to Sharp (technically to the acting minister in Sharp's temporary absence), 16 April 1971, LAC, RG25, vol. 8976, pt. 1. Perhaps more disturbingly, a few days later, a telegram from the Canadian High Commission in London noted: "The Brit [British] deputy highcom [high commissioner] has reported from Dacca that it is evident that the army are continuing to use terror tactics in their clearing operations, and that it may not be easy to persuade them to modify their tactics, which they appear to enjoy, especially where Hindus are involved. As the army advance they are systematically shelling and burning populated places." Telegram, Canadian High Commission in London to External Affairs, 21 April 1971, LAC, RG25, vol. 8976, pt. 2. Despite propaganda from all sides, Ottawa was generally aware, through official channels and reporting in the media, of the atrocities perpetrated by West Pakistani authorities and, to some extent, by other groups.

36 Canada, *House of Commons Debates, 1970–72* (7 April 1971), 4993 (emphasis added).

37 Ibid., (emphasis added).

38 Ibid.

39 Telegram, Small to External Affairs, 26 March 1971, LAC, RG25, vol. 8975, pt. 8.

40 The population of East Pakistan was some 75 million. The Pakistani army in the East totalled some 45,000 to 55,000 troops: Sarmila Bose, *Dead Reckoning: Memories of the 1971 Bangladesh War* (New York: Columbia University Press, 2011), 174. Consequently, the army was outnumbered by over 1,000 to 1.

41 Telegram, Small to External Affairs, 6 April 1971, LAC, RG25, vol. 8976, pt. 1.

42 Telegram, Small to External Affairs, 8 April 1971, LAC, RG25, vol. 10836, pt. 3.

43 Letter, Ritchie to Small, 29 March 1971, LAC, RG25, vol. 10836, pt. 3.

44 Memorandum, Head to Trudeau, 19 April 1971, LAC, RG25, vol. 8975, pt. 8.

45 John Small, "Pakistan to Bangladesh," 225.

46 The population of West Pakistan totalled 55 million.

47 Telegram, George to External Affairs, 10 April 1971, LAC, RG25, vol. 10836, pt. 3.

48 Ibid.

49 It is recognized that the promotion of Canadian human rights and democratic values abroad was not explicit government policy in 1971. Nevertheless, even though the concept may be somewhat anachronistic, the comment concerning the absence of such considerations in the reasoning of Small and others holds true.

50 A number of scholars, including Norman Ingram of Concordia University, have pointed out the possible further, gender-based implications of the label "emotional." Although it is possible that such a marker might have been intended to discredit George by questioning his heterosexuality, or that those learning of such a label might have, in any case, inferred a barely hidden meaning, it is difficult to reach any firm conclusion with regard to such speculation. At the time of the East Pakistan crisis, George was married to his first wife, Carol, and at the time of his interview by this author, in 2008, he was married to his second wife, Barbara.

51 Telegram, Small to External Affairs, 13 April 1971, LAC, RG25, vol. 10836, pt. 3.

240   *Notes to pages 100–4*

52 Memorandum, Head to Trudeau, 19 April 1971, LAC, RG25, vol. 8975, pt. 8. The ˋ
    note "I agree" is handwritten on the memorandum. It is probable that this was Tru-
    deau's response, but the handwriting has yet to be verified by an expert.
53 Ibid.
54 There is speculation that, at the time of the emergency in East Pakistan, Small was
    considered by some in External Affairs to be something of a careerist, while in cer-
    tain quarters George was believed to have "gone native." Touhey, *Conflicting Visions*,
    207. Some forty years later, it is difficult to verify such rumours or assess to what
    extent they influenced the decision-making process in Ottawa. George's US counter-
    part in New Delhi, Ambassador Kenneth Keating, was certainly considered by Presi-
    dent Richard Nixon to be biased in some of his assessments in 1971, as discussed in
    Part 1 of this book. By contrast, in the Canadian archival material considered, there
    is no evidence to substantiate the nature and impact of any speculation with respect
    to George.
55 Telegram, Small to External Affairs, 22 April 1971, LAC, RG25, vol. 8976, pt. 2.
56 Memorandum, Sharp to Trudeau, 4 May 1971, LAC, RG25, vol. 10836, pt. 4.
57 Ibid.
58 Letter, Trudeau to Yahya, 5 May 1971, LAC, RG25, vol. 10836, pt. 4.
59 Telegram, Small to External Affairs, 5 May 1971, LAC, RG25, vol. 8976, pt. 3.
60 Letter, External Affairs to George, 13 May 1971, LAC, RG25, vol. 8914, pt. 10, Ind.
    Pak., 11/02/71–16/09/71.
61 John Small, "Pakistan to Bangladesh," 232.
62 Telegram, George and Small to External Affairs, 29 May 1971, LAC, MG26 O11, vol.
    27, pt. 16 861/I39, Canadian Representation in India, 1971.
63 Letter, George to Trudeau, 1 June 1971, LAC, MG26 O11, vol. 27, pt. 16 861/I39.
64 Memorandum, Head to Trudeau, 28 July 1971, LAC, MG26 O11, vol. 27, pt. 16 861/
    I39.
65 Statistics provided by the Indian Ministry of External Affairs, reproduced in *Bangla
    Desh Documents* (New Delhi: Ministry of External Affairs, 1971), 446. While they
    are difficult to verify precisely, it should be noted that such figures were adopted by
    the UN High Commissioner for Refugees in his reports on the crisis and that West-
    ern visitors to the refugee camps confirmed the existence of a humanitarian crisis on
    a massive scale.
66 Chairman's Introduction to Preliminary Meeting of India-Pakistan Task Force on 30
    June 1971, 30 June 1971, LAC, RG25, vol. 8914, pt. 11; Minutes of Preliminary Meet-
    ing of India-Pakistan Task Force on 30 June 1971, 5 July 1971, LAC, RG25, vol. 8914,
    pt. 12.
67 Minutes of Meeting of India-Pakistan Task Force on 21 July 1971, 29 July 1971, LAC,
    RG25, vol. 8914, pt. 13.
68 Canada, *House of Commons Debates, 1970–72* (2 April 1971), 4852–53.
69 Ibid., (4 May 1971), 5475.
70 One important exception occurred on 17 June, when James McGrath (Progressive
    Conservative, St. John's East) asked if Canada would "send observers into East Pak-
    istan to determine whether or not the charges of genocide, against the Hindus espe-
    cially, have any foundation in fact." In reply, Sharp noted that a complaint had already

Notes to pages 104–7 241

been made to the United Nations that genocide had occurred and that the UN Secretary-General had "not considered it necessary to have inquiries made." Canada, *House of Commons Debates, 1970–72* (17 June 1971), 6813. It may be reasoned from his comments that Sharp considered Canada to have no further obligation to act under the UN Genocide Convention, given that the UN Secretary-General had been informed and had decided not to investigate further.

71 From the early 1960s to 1970, immigration from East and West Pakistan to Canada had built to only some 1,000 people per year. John Small, "Pakistan to Bangladesh," 211. Consequently, the size of the corresponding immigrant communities in Canada was modest compared with the Canadian population as a whole (some 21 million). Moreover, these small communities were embryonic, comprising primarily recent arrivals. During 1971, two lobby groups developed: the Bangla Desh Association of Canada and the Canada-Pakistan Association, supporting East and West Pakistan, respectively. Nevertheless, their size and influence were very much limited. Meanwhile, established religious institutions and charitable organizations focused their activities on raising funds for humanitarian aid (e.g., Combined Appeal for Pakistan Relief). Senior members of various churches and Oxfam of Canada signed the Toronto Declaration of Concern on 22 August 1971. In addition to calling for humanitarian efforts, they requested that Ottawa immediately suspend ongoing economic aid to Pakistan. The latter demand was to no avail. Memorandum, Ritchie to Sharp, 15 September 1971, LAC, RG25, vol. 8914, pt. 14.

72 "Civil War in East Pakistan," *Globe and Mail*, 27 March 1971, 1.

73 "Karachi Forced 2,000,000 Bengali Refugees to Leave East Pakistan, New Delhi Charges," *Globe and Mail*, 17 May 1971, 1.

74 Peter Hazelhurst, "Widespread Terror and Bloodshed in East Pakistan Reported by Bengali Refugees," *Globe and Mail*, 22 May 1971, 1.

75 Robert Duffy, "West Pakistani Charges Army with Genocide," *Globe and Mail*, 14 June 1971, 1.

76 Editorial, "On Pakistan, Honesty," *Globe and Mail*, 7 July 1971, 6.

77 Telegram, George to External Affairs, 8 April 1971, LAC, RG25, vol. 8976, pt. 1. In addition, see Telegram, George to External Affairs, 10 April 1971, LAC, RG25, vol. 10836, pt. 3.

78 George, telephone interview by author, 13 April 2008.

79 Ibid.

80 Canada, *House of Commons Debates, 1970–72* (28 May 1971), 6154.

81 Peter C. Dobell, *Canada in World Affairs*, vol. 17, *1971–1973* (Toronto: Canadian Institute of International Affairs, 1995), 178–79.

82 Memorandum, Ritchie to Sharp, 30 September 1971, LAC, RG25, vol. 10836, pt. 6.

83 Telegram, Small to External Affairs, 19 April 1971, LAC, RG25, vol. 8976, pt. 2.

84 Internal Memorandum, John Harrington, Director of the Pacific and South Asia Division of External Affairs, 19 May 1971, LAC, RG25, vol. 10836, pt. 4.

85 John Small, "Pakistan to Bangladesh," 232.

86 Arnold Smith, *Stitches in Time: The Commonwealth in World Politics* (Don Mills, ON: General, 1981), 136.

87 Internal Memorandum, Harrington, 19 May 1971, LAC, RG25, vol. 10836, pt. 4.

242   *Notes to pages 107–10*

88 Canada, *House of Commons Debates, 1970–72* (30 June 1971), 7518.

89 John Small, "Pakistan to Bangladesh," 228.

90 Tad Szulc, "U.S. Military Goods Sent to Pakistan Despite Ban," *New York Times*, 22 June 1971, 1.

91 Canada, *House of Commons Debates, 1970–72* (16 June 1971), 6775.

92 "Sharp Supports Separatist Rule to Halt East Pakistan Conflict," *Globe and Mail*, 17 June 1971, 1.

93 Canada, *House of Commons Debates, 1970–72* (17 June 1971), 6813 (emphasis added).

94 It is probable that Canada's standing was not significantly affected as even the United States, one of Islamabad's staunchest supporters, was forced to reconsider all military supply shipments about this time.

95 The three MPs were Andrew Brewin (New Democrat, Greenwood), Georges-C. Lachance (Liberal, Lafontaine), and Heath MacQuarrie (Progressive Conservative, Hillsborough). Telegram, External Affairs to Small, 21 July 1971, LAC, RG25, vol. 8914, pt. 13; Telegram, External Affairs to Small, 22 July 1971, LAC, RG25, vol. 10836, pt. 5; Memorandum, External Affairs to Sharp, 5 August 1971, LAC, RG25, vol. 10836, pt. 6.

96 As John English has observed, Trudeau disliked Indira Gandhi. This genuine distaste, however, was not readily apparent either in Trudeau's correspondence with the Indian prime minister or in Canadian foreign policy formulation on East Pakistan in 1971. John English, *Just Watch Me: The Life of Pierre Elliott Trudeau*, vol. 2, *1968–2000* (Toronto: Alfred A. Knopf Canada, 2009), 376.

97 Letter, Trudeau to Indira Gandhi, 13 August 1971, LAC, MG26 O7, vol. 473, pt. 840/I39, Ind., 1968–1975 (emphasis added).

98 Letter, Trudeau to Yahya, 13 August 1971, LAC, MG26 O7, vol. 480, pt. 840/P152, Pak. (Samples only of letters of concern), 1970–1972 (emphasis added).

99 Telegram, Trudeau to Yahya, 11 August 1971, LAC, RG25, vol. 10836, pt. 6. Mujibur Rahman was found guilty and sentenced to death, but the sentence was never carried out. He survived to lead Bangladesh immediately after independence.

100 Canada was involved in another forlorn effort to privately promote political accommodation. In June and November, Canadian Arnold Smith, Secretary-General of the Commonwealth, attempted to encourage a political solution with the aid of George and Small. Ottawa supported this Commonwealth initiative, despite some concern about being drawn into any subsequent peacekeeping operation should the project be successful. Memorandum, Ritchie to Sharp, 9 July 1971, LAC, RG25, vol. 8914, pt. 12. Unfortunately, this effort came to naught as India and Pakistan failed to respond to Smith's approaches. Arnold Smith, *Stitches in Time*, 136–38, 140.

101 Telegram, Small to External Affairs, 7 September 1971, LAC, RG25, vol. 10836, pt. 6.

102 John Small, "Pakistan to Bangladesh," 231.

103 Memorandum, Ritchie to Sharp, 2 April 1971, LAC, RG25, vol. 8976, pt. 1.

104 On 25 October 1971, the People's Republic of China gained both UN membership and a permanent seat on the Security Council, replacing the Republic of China.

105 Memorandum, Andrew, 27 August 1971, LAC, RG25, vol. 10836, pt. 6. Supporting memoranda explaining detailed reasoning not attached. In a later document

Notes to pages 110–14 243

discussing the possibility of establishing a UN observer force, Colonel R.S. Christie, Director Operations, Department of National Defence, explained that difficulties included the absence of approval by New Delhi, the presence of the "uncontrollable" guerrilla forces in East Pakistan, and the enormous cost of an operation sufficient to patrol the inhospitable terrain of the 1,500-mile (2,400-kilometre) border between India and East Pakistan. Consequently, a significant Canadian contribution to such an effort would require either a substantial increase to the military budget or a realignment of existing priorities. Letter, Christie to India-Pakistan Task Force, 27 October 1971, LAC, RG25, vol. 8915, pt. 15, Ind. Pak., 17/09/71–31/12/72.

106 Dobell, *Canada in World Affairs,* 179.
107 India's refusal is often attributed to its reluctance to impede cross-border guerrilla operations.
108 Memorandum, Ritchie to Sharp, 30 September 1971, LAC, RG25, vol. 10836, pt. 6.
109 Ibid.
110 Dobell, *Canada in World Affairs,* 178–79.
111 George, telephone interview by author, 13 April 2008.
112 Telegram, Small to External Affairs, 18 November 1971, LAC, RG25, vol. 8976, pt. 8.
113 Memorandum, External Affairs to Sharp, 30 November 1971, "Meeting with Secretary of State Rogers, Washington, December 3, 1971," LAC, RG25, vol. 8915, pt. 18.
114 Telegram, George to External Affairs, 13 December 1971, LAC, RG25, vol. 8915, pt. 18. At the Department of External Affairs in Ottawa, many remained concerned throughout the crisis that India might choose to exploit events for political gain. See, for example, Andrew's comments at the preliminary meeting of the India-Pakistan Task Force, observing, with respect to the possibility of war on the subcontinent, that "India would 'never get as good a chance again.'" Minutes of Preliminary Meeting of India-Pakistan Task Force on 30 June 1971, 5 July 1971, LAC, RG25, vol. 8914, pt. 12.
115 George, telephone interview by author, 13 April 2008.
116 Dobell, *Canada in World Affairs,* 180–81. Although Nixon and Kissinger initiated a round of high-pressure diplomatic activity and sent a carrier task force into the Bay of Bengal in order to deter India from destroying West Pakistan, George and others (including Van Hollen) believe that this did not determine India's decision to desist from further prosecution of the war.
117 George, telephone interview by author, 13 April 2008; Pearson, "Canada, the United Nations," 21.
118 Editorial, "On Pakistan, Honesty," *Globe and Mail,* 7 July 1971, 6.
119 Mitchell Sharp, letter to the editor, *Globe and Mail,* 10 July 1971, 6.
120 Memorandum, Harrington, 30 August 1971, LAC, RG25, vol. 10836, pt. 6.
121 It is interesting to note that similarities between the Quebec and East Pakistan situations did not escape the attention of concerned parties in Pakistan itself in 1971. Writing in *Pakistan Horizon,* the journal of the Pakistan Institute of International Affairs, Mehrunnisa Ali observed: "The gradual progress toward the settlement of the problem in Canada has a lesson to offer, that much can be achieved without endangering national integrity, through tolerance and by peaceful democratic processes." Mehrunnisa Ali, "The Problem of Quebec," *Pakistan Horizon* 24, 3 (1971): 31.
122 John Small, "Pakistan to Bangladesh," 231.

Chapter 5: Former Great Power

1 Paul M. Kennedy, *The Realities behind Diplomacy: Background Influences on British External Policy, 1865–1980* (London: Allen and Unwin, 1981), 315.
2 Ibid., 319.
3 Ibid., 341.
4 Ibid., 342.
5 Ibid., 376.
6 Ibid., 329–31.
7 David Reynolds, *Britannia Overruled: British Policy and World Power in the Twentieth Century*, 2nd ed. (Harlow, Essex: Pearson Education, 2000), 208.
8 Kennedy, *Realities behind Diplomacy*, 373–74.
9 Ibid., 331; Reynolds, *Britannia Overruled*, 209.
10 Reynolds, *Britannia Overruled*, 208.
11 Ibid., 212.
12 Ibid., 211–12.
13 Whitehall is the main location, in London, of the offices of the British government.
14 Kennedy, *Realities behind Diplomacy*, 376.
15 Reynolds, *Britannia Overruled*, 215–17.
16 Technically, Britain was applying for membership in the European Communities. These comprised the following: the European Economic Community (EEC), the European Coal and Steel Community, and the European Atomic Energy Community. It was common contemporary practice, however, to refer to all three simply as the European Community. In addition, the EEC was often referred to as the Common Market. Complicating matters further, when the EEC subsequently became part of the European Union under the Treaty of Maastricht (effective 1993), it was renamed the European Community.
17 Kennedy, *Realities behind Diplomacy*, 379.
18 Reynolds, *Britannia Overruled*, 209.
19 Ibid., 224.
20 Kennedy, *Realities behind Diplomacy*, 377–78.
21 Ibid., 380.
22 Paul M. McGarr, *The Cold War in South Asia: Britain, the United States and the Indian Subcontinent, 1945–1965* (Cambridge: Cambridge University Press, 2013), 2.
23 Ibid., 1–2.
24 Ibid., 348.
25 Ibid., 351.
26 Ibid., 320–22, 338, 353.
27 The contemporary exchange rate was GB£1.00 = US$2.40, with the US and Canadian dollars resting approximately at par.
28 McGarr, *Cold War in South Asia*, 324–25.
29 Ibid., 334.
30 After the ceasefire of September 1965, a peace settlement between India and Pakistan was signed at Tashkent, in the Soviet Union, in January 1966.
31 McGarr, *Cold War in South Asia*, 337.
32 Ibid., 343.

Notes to pages 124–28

33 Ibid., 342–44.

34 Ibid., 2.

35 Andrew Marr, *A History of Modern Britain* (London: Macmillan, 2007), 319–20.

36 Ibid., 321.

37 Ibid., 319. Heath would achieve his ambition in 1973.

38 Commonly abbreviated as foreign secretary.

39 According to Heath's biographer, Philip Ziegler, "Home had indicated he wanted to go to the foreign office ... Heath had total confidence in Home's ability and, anyway, thought it only proper that the former Prime Minister should have whatever post he wanted." Philip Ziegler, *Edward Heath: The Authorised Biography* (London: Harper Press, 2010), 238.

40 For a detailed discussion of events in Northern Ireland between 1969 and the end of 1971, see David McKittrick and David McVea, *Making Sense of the Troubles: A History of the Northern Ireland Conflict* (London: Viking, 2012), 61–87.

41 Marr, *History of Modern Britain*, 316.

42 Ibid., 317.

43 Ibid., 318.

44 Chibuike Uche, "Oil, British Interests and the Nigerian Civil War," *Journal of African History* 49, 1 (2008): 111–13.

45 Prime Minister's Briefing Book, Section 11, Cyclone Disaster Assistance, 16 December 1970, The National Archives of the United Kingdom: Public Record Office (NAUK), Cabinet Office Files, CAB 133/423, Visit of the Prime Minister to Pakistan, 8–9 January 1971.

46 Prime Minister's Briefing Book, Section 1, Steering Brief, 1 January 1971, NAUK, CAB 133/423.

47 Membership included Britain, Belgium, Canada, France, Germany, Italy, Japan, the Netherlands, and the United States.

48 Prime Minister's Briefing Book, Section 12c, British Economic Relations with Pakistan: Aid, 16 December 1970, NAUK, CAB 133/423; Report, Cyril Pickard, British high commissioner to Islamabad, to the Foreign and Commonwealth Office (FCO), 30 December 1970, "Review of 1970," NAUK, Foreign and Commonwealth Office Files, FCO 37/869, Pakistan: Annual Review 1970.

49 Prime Minister's Briefing Book, Section 1, Steering Brief, 1 January 1971, NAUK, CAB 133/423.

50 Prime Minister's Briefing Book, Section 12a, Trade and Investment, 17 December 1970, NAUK, CAB 133/423.

51 Prime Minister's Briefing Book, Section 9, Arms Supplies, 21 December 1970, NAUK, CAB 133/423.

52 Ibid.

53 Prime Minister's Briefing Book, Section 8, Indo-Pakistan Relations and Kashmir, 16 December 1970, NAUK, CAB 133/423.

54 Report, Pickard to FCO, 30 December 1970, "Review of 1970," NAUK, FCO 37/869.

55 Prime Minister's Briefing Book, Personality Notes, Yahya Khan, 18 December 1970, NAUK, CAB 133/423.

56 Report, Pickard to FCO, 18 January 1971, "The Prime Minister's Visit to Pakistan," NAUK, FCO 37/752, Visit of British Prime Minister, Edward Heath, to Pakistan and India, 8–11 January 1971; Memorandum, Hugh Byatt, South Asia Department at the FCO, to Stanley Tomlinson, Deputy Under-Secretary of State at the FCO, 28 January 1971, NAUK, FCO 37/752 (quotations from Byatt).

57 Report, Pickard to FCO, 18 January 1971, "The Prime Minister's Visit to Pakistan," NAUK, FCO 37/752.

58 Prime Minister's Briefing Book, Section 1, Steering Brief, 30 December 1970, NAUK, CAB 133/419, Visit of the Prime Minister to India, 9–12 January 1971.

59 Report, Morrice James, British high commissioner to New Delhi, to FCO, 31 December 1970, "India 1970," NAUK, FCO 37/813, India: Annual Review 1970.

60 Populations in 1971: India, 548 million; Pakistan, 130 million.

61 Memorandum, O. G. Forster to Peter Moon, private secretary (foreign affairs), to the Prime Minister, 10 January 1971, NAUK, Prime Minister's Office Files, PREM 15/449, Prime Minister's Office: Correspondence and Papers, 1970–1974, Subseries: India, Visit of Prime Minister to India, Jan 1971.

62 Report, James to FCO, 31 December 1970, "India 1970," NAUK, FCO 37/813.

63 Prime Minister's Briefing Book, Personality Notes, Indira Gandhi, 16 December 1970, NAUK, CAB 133/423.

64 Report, James to FCO, 22 January 1971, "Visit to India by the Prime Minister of Great Britain," NAUK, FCO 37/752. This was the first "substantive" visit to India of a British prime minister since 1958. During lengthy tête-à-têtes, Heath and Indira Gandhi discussed a wide variety of issues, including UK immigration policy, Britain's ongoing negotiations to enter the European Community, the potential supply of British arms to South Africa, and London's concerns over Indian Ocean security in the face of perceived Soviet intentions to expand its influence. Exchanges on Indo-Pakistan relations were limited, but Indira Gandhi expressed a desire to resume trade and solve more tractable issues between the two countries before addressing the major issue of the Kashmir dispute. Heath relayed Yahya's hope that trade would be reopened after Pakistan's successful return to democratic government. Report, James to FCO, 22 January 1971, "Visit to India by the Prime Minister of Great Britain," NAUK, FCO 37/752.

65 Ibid.

66 Handwritten comment on memorandum, Byatt to Tomlinson, 29 January 1971, NAUK, FCO 37/829, Political Relations between India and UK.

67 Memorandum, Douglas-Home to Heath, 24 February 1971, NAUK, PREM 15/566, Prime Minister's Office: Correspondence and Papers, 1970–1974, Subseries: Pakistan, Visit of Prime Minister to Pakistan.

68 Memorandum, Sutherland to Douglas-Home, 3 March 1971, NAUK, FCO 37/876, Political Crisis in East Pakistan.

69 Telegram, Sargeant to FCO, 4 March 1971, NAUK, PREM 15/567, Prime Minister's Office: Correspondence and Papers, 1970–1974, Subseries: Pakistan, Internal Situation; Memorandum, Byatt to Sutherland, 4 March 1971, NAUK, FCO 37/876 (quotations, Sargeant).

70 Memorandum, Byatt to Sutherland, 4 March 1971, NAUK, FCO 37/876; Memorandum, Denis Greenhill, Permanent Under-Secretary of State at the FCO, 16 March

Notes to pages 131–35 247

1971, NAUK, FCO 37/877, Political Crisis in East Pakistan; Telegram, FCO to Sargeant, 5 March 1971, NAUK, PREM 15/567.

71 Telegram, Sargeant to FCO, 5 March 1971, NAUK, PREM 15/567.

72 Telegram, Douglas-Home to Sargeant, 5 March 1971, NAUK, FCO 37/876.

73 Telegram (and handwritten comment on telegram), Sargeant to Douglas-Home, 6 March 1971, NAUK, FCO 37/877.

74 Telegram, Sargeant to FCO, 11 March 1971, NAUK, FCO 37/877.

75 Memorandum, Greenhill, 16 March 1971, NAUK, FCO 37/877; Note for the Secretary of State's Use in Cabinet, 17 March 1971, NAUK, FCO 37/878, Political Crisis in East Pakistan.

76 Note for the Secretary of State's Use in Cabinet, 17 March 1971, NAUK, FCO 37/878.

77 Telegram, Tomlinson to Sargeant, 19 March 1971, NAUK, FCO 37/878. Sargeant and his wife, Joan, arrived in Dacca in October 1970. He had previously served as British consul general in Lubumbashi, Democratic Republic of the Congo.

78 Telegram, Sargeant to FCO, 21 March 1971, NAUK, FCO 37/878.

79 Memorandum, Sutherland to Douglas-Home, 22 March 1971, NAUK, FCO 37/878.

80 Telegram, Sargeant to FCO, 24 March 1971, NAUK, FCO 37/878.

81 Wood was the son of the former foreign secretary, Lord Halifax. D. Richard Thorpe, *Alec Douglas-Home* (London: Sinclair-Stevenson, 1996), 406.

82 Greenhill was held in high regard by Douglas-Home. Thorpe, *Alec Douglas-Home*, 406.

83 Telegram, Sargeant to FCO, 26 March 1971, NAUK, FCO 37/879, Political Crisis in East Pakistan.

84 Telegram, Pickard to FCO, 26 March 1971, NAUK, FCO 37/878.

85 Telegram, Pickard to FCO, 26 March 1971, NAUK, FCO 37/879.

86 Memorandum, T.D. O'Leary to Burke Trend, 26 March 1971, NAUK, PREM 15/567; Memorandum, SAD to Prime Minister's Office, 28 March 1971, "Pakistan Situation Report," NAUK, PREM 15/567.

87 Memorandum, T.D. O'Leary to Burke Trend, 26 March 1971, NAUK, PREM 15/567; Telegram, Sargeant to FCO, 28 March 1971, NAUK, FCO 37/879.

88 Telegram, Cox to FCO, 27 March 1971, NAUK, FCO 37/879.

89 Telegram, Pickard to FCO, 27 March 1971, NAUK, FCO 37/879.

90 Telegram, Alan Brown, British deputy high commissioner in Karachi, to FCO, 27 March 1971, NAUK, FCO 37/879.

91 Telegram, Sargeant to FCO, 28 March 1971, NAUK, FCO 37/879.

92 Telegram, Sargeant to FCO, 28 March 1971, NAUK, FCO 37/879.

93 Telegram, Sargeant to FCO, 27 March 1971, NAUK, FCO 37/879; Memorandum, SAD to Prime Minister's Office, 28 March 1971, "Pakistan Situation Report," NAUK, PREM 15/567 (quotation, SAD).

94 Telegram, Sargeant to Tomlinson, 29 March 1971, NAUK, FCO 37/879.

95 Archer K. Blood, *The Cruel Birth of Bangladesh: Memoirs of an American Diplomat* (Dhaka: The University Press, 2002), 232–33, 323.

96 Sargeant had already complained of being "hopelessly overloaded" during the taxing but still less stressful experience of coordinating the evacuations of mid-March, before the clampdown began. Telegram, Sargeant to FCO, 11 March 1971, NAUK, FCO 37/877.

97 Sargeant did not call for a general evacuation. The decision to begin extracting those wishing to leave, however, was made on 29 March 1971. Blood, *Cruel Birth*, 233. Blood mistakenly wrote "May 29." Nevertheless, it is clear from the context that he meant March 29. Special flights were arranged using commercial airlines.

98 A. Dirk Moses, "Civil War or Genocide? Britain and the Secession of East Pakistan in 1971," in *Civil Wars in South Asia: State, Sovereignty, Development*, ed. Aparna Sundar and Nandini Sundar (New Delhi: Sage, 2014), 146–51.

99 Telegram, FCO to Pickard, 27 March 1971, NAUK, FCO 37/879.

100 Memorandum to Douglas-Home, c. 28 March 1971, "Statement and Notes for Supplementaries for 29 March 1971," NAUK, FCO 37/879.

101 Cabinet Conclusions, 1 April 1971, NAUK, CAB 128/49, Cabinet Conclusions.

102 Memorandum, Sutherland to Douglas-Home, 31 March 1971, "Cabinet Brief for 1 April 1971," NAUK, FCO 37/880, Political Crisis in East Pakistan.

103 Memorandum to Douglas-Home, c. 28 March 1971, "Statement and Notes for Supplementaries for 29 March 1971," NAUK, FCO 37/879.

104 Telegram, Pickard to FCO, 29 March 1971, NAUK, PREM 15/567.

105 Telegram, Sargeant to FCO, 30 March 1971, NAUK, FCO 37/879.

106 Telegram, Pickard to FCO, 30 March 1971, NAUK, FCO 37/880.

107 Telegram, Sargeant to FCO, 31 March 1971, NAUK, FCO 37/880.

108 Ibid.

109 Memorandum, Greenhill, 31 March 1971, NAUK, FCO 37/880.

110 Letter, Yahya to Heath, 31 March 1971, NAUK, FCO 37/880.

111 Memorandum, Moon to FCO, 31 March 1971, NAUK, PREM 15/568, Prime Minister's Office: Correspondence and Papers, 1970–1974, Subseries: Pakistan, Internal Situation.

112 Telegram, Cox to Pickard, 2 April 1971, NAUK, FCO 37/880.

113 Telegram, Pickard to FCO, 4 April 1971, NAUK, FCO 37/881, Political Crisis in East Pakistan.

114 Ibid.

115 United Kingdom, *House of Commons Debates*, vol. 815 (5 April 1971), 36–37.

116 Telegram, Sargeant to FCO, 5 April 1971, NAUK, FCO 37/881.

117 Telegram, Sargeant to FCO, 6 April 1971, NAUK, FCO 37/881.

118 Ibid.

119 Telegram, Pickard to Sargeant, 6 April 1971, NAUK, FCO 37/881. See also Telegram, Pickard to FCO, 8 April 1971, NAUK, FCO 37/882, Political Crisis in East Pakistan.

120 Telegram, Pickard to Sargeant, 6 April 1971, NAUK, FCO 37/881. At this point, the number of UK nationals in East Pakistan had declined to around two hundred, just less than half of whom remained in Dacca.

121 Telegram, Sargeant to Pickard, 7 April 1971, NAUK, FCO 37/881.

122 Telegram, Sargeant to Pickard, 8 April 1971, NAUK, FCO 37/882 (emphasis added).

123 Telegram, Douglas-Home to Moon, 6 April 1971, NAUK, FCO 37/928, Political Relations with UK: Visit of Prime Minister Edward Heath to Pakistan, 8–9 January.

124 Telegram, FCO to Pickard, 7 April 1971, NAUK, FCO 37/928.

Notes to pages 140–44

125 Cabinet Conclusions, 8 April 1971, NAUK, CAB 128/49.
126 Telegram, Pickard to FCO, 9 April 1971, NAUK, FCO 37/928.
127 Ibid.
128 Telegram, James to FCO, 8 April 1971, NAUK, FCO 37/882.
129 On 10 May, James was appointed British high commissioner to Canberra.
130 Memorandum, Sutherland to Greenhill, 19 April 1971, NAUK, FCO 37/884, Political Crisis in East Pakistan.
131 Of the 230 registered, just over 70 were of Pakistani origin. Initial estimates of UK citizens in the East had not included many people in this subcategory, as visitors of Pakistani extraction did not normally formally register their presence. British nationals of non-Pakistani origin had, therefore, declined from just under 1,000 at the beginning of March to some 160 by mid-April. SAD recognized that there were likely more UK citizens of Pakistani origin who had still not registered. Memorandum and Attachment, Sutherland to Tomlinson, 16 April 1971, NAUK, FCO 37/883, Political Crisis in East Pakistan.
132 See, for example: Telegram, Burrows to Pickard, 18 April 1971, NAUK, FCO 37/883, and Telegram, Cox to FCO, 31 [sic] April 1971, NAUK, FCO 37/885, Political Crisis in East Pakistan.
133 Record of Conversation, Greenhill and Apa Pant, Indian high commissioner to London, 19 April 1971, NAUK, FCO 37/884.
134 Telegram, James to FCO, 15 April 1971, NAUK, FCO 37/883.
135 Telegram, James to FCO, 21 April 1971, NAUK, FCO 37/884.
136 Memorandum, Sargeant to Sutherland, 14 April 1971, NAUK, FCO 37/883.
137 Ibid.
138 Memorandum, Pickard to FCO, 22 April 1971, NAUK, FCO 83/884.
139 Telegram, Pickard to FCO, 23 April 1971, NAUK, FCO 37/885.
140 Handwritten comment (23 April 1971) on memorandum, Sutherland to Tomlinson and Wilford, 23 April 1971, NAUK, FCO 83/884.
141 Handwritten comment (24 April 1971) on memorandum, Sutherland to Tomlinson and Wilford, 23 April 1971, NAUK, FCO 83/884.
142 Letter, Yahya to Heath, 18 April 1971, NAUK, FCO 37/894, Political Crisis in East Pakistan.
143 Record of the Prime Minister's Meeting with Mr. Mian Arshad Hussain, 27 April 1971, NAUK, PREM 15/568.
144 Ibid.
145 Letter, Heath to Yahya, 28 April 1971, NAUK, PREM 15/568.
146 Cabinet Conclusions, 29 April 1971, NAUK, CAB 128/49.
147 Douglas-Home's handwritten comment on memorandum, undated [c. end of April 1971], "Brief for Secretary of State's Use in Cabinet," NAUK, FCO 37/887, Political Crisis in East Pakistan. For more on UN-related matters, see Chapter 6.
148 Memorandum, Sutherland to Douglas-Home, 25 April 1971, NAUK, FCO 37/885.
149 Telegram, Pickard to FCO, 4 May 1971, NAUK, FCO 37/886, Political Crisis in East Pakistan.
150 Telegram, Pickard to FCO, 6 May 1971, NAUK, FCO 37/886.
151 Ibid.

250   *Notes to pages 147–50*

Chapter 6: The Commons Debates and After

1 The Leader of the House of Commons was the government minister responsible for scheduling parliamentary business. Toward the end of April, the Labour Party proposed the following motion: "That this House is gravely concerned at the profound suffering of the people in East Pakistan and calls on the Government of Pakistan to accept the aid offered by the International Red Cross and other bodies for those in need and hopes for an early political settlement which takes account of the views of the people of the regions as expressed through the democratic processes." Whitelaw was advised that any ensuing discussion was "bound to be considered unwelcome interference [by Islamabad]." Moreover, as Douglas-Mann had won first place in the ballot on Early Day Motions for 14 May, "it is likely that he will choose Pakistan as his subject. The FCO would not wish to have two debates on Pakistan and would prefer the subject to be debated as a Private Member's Motion if it has to be debated at all. It would be helpful if the position could be held until Mr Douglas-Mann has named his subject." It was suggested that Whitelaw take the following line: "I will certainly discuss this matter [of finding time for Labour's proposed motion] through the usual channels to see what, if anything, can be done." Memorandum, 29 April 1971, "Opposition Motion on Pakistan – Brief for Leader of House," The National Archives of the United Kingdom: Public Record Office (NAUK), Foreign and Commonwealth Office Files, FCO 37/885, Political Crisis in East Pakistan. See also Draft Letter, Graham to P.L.P. Davies, Lord President's Office, undated [c. 3 May 1971], NAUK, FCO 37/885.
2 United Kingdom, *House of Commons Debates*, vol. 814 (29 March 1971), 1148.
3 Ibid., 1149.
4 Ibid.
5 Memorandum, Sutherland to Graham, 13 October 1971, NAUK, FCO 37/933, Visits of UK Ministers and MPs to Pakistan. Bennett would serve as chair of the Pakistan Society, 1981–89.
6 United Kingdom, *House of Commons Debates*, vol. 815 (5 April 1971), 36.
7 Ibid., 38.
8 Ibid., 40.
9 United Kingdom, *House of Commons Debates*, vol. 817 (11 May 1971), 207.
10 Ibid., 209.
11 Ibid., 210.
12 Ibid., 211.
13 United Kingdom, *House of Commons Debates*, vol. 817 (14 May 1971), 753.
14 Ibid.
15 Stonehouse's constituency, Wednesbury, incorporated large populations of East Pakistani and Indian immigrants. He was closely associated with the charity War on Want.
16 United Kingdom, *House of Commons Debates*, vol. 817 (14 May 1971), 756 and 760, respectively.
17 Ibid., 810.
18 Ibid., 761–67.
19 Ibid., 786.

Notes to pages 150–54   251

20 United Kingdom, *House of Commons Debates,* vol. 818 (8 June 1971), 864. Douglas-Home made it clear to M.M. Ahmad, Yahya's economic advisor, during talks in London on 18–19 May, that any new British aid would be dependent on a political settlement for the East. Memorandum, Sutherland to Douglas-Home, 27 May 1971, NAUK, FCO 37/887, Political Crisis in East Pakistan.

21 United Kingdom, *House of Commons Debates,* vol. 817 (14 May 1971), 783.

22 Ibid., 815.

23 Telegram, FCO to Pickard, 17 May 1971, NAUK, FCO 37/886, Political Crisis in East Pakistan.

24 Memorandum, Miles to Male, 13 May 1971, NAUK, FCO 37/829, Political Relations between India and UK.

25 Memorandum, Moon to FCO, 14 May 1971, NAUK, Prime Minister's Office Files, PREM 15/568, Prime Minister's Office: Correspondence and Papers, 1970–1974, Subseries: Pakistan, Internal Situation.

26 Letter, Indira Gandhi to Heath, delivered 18 May 1971, written 13 May 1971, NAUK, PREM 15/568.

27 Telegram, Cox to FCO, 12 May 1971, NAUK, FCO 37/886.

28 Telegram, Pickard to FCO, 19 May 1971, NAUK, FCO 37/886 (emphasis added).

29 Telegram, Pickard to FCO, 21 May 1971, NAUK, FCO 37/887.

30 Telegram, FCO to Garvey, 26 May 1971, NAUK, PREM 15/568. The GB£1 million contribution to refugee relief had been announced publicly on 20 May 1971.

31 Telegram, Garvey to FCO, 27 May 1971, NAUK, FCO 37/829.

32 United Kingdom, *House of Commons Debates,* vol. 818 (8 June 1971), 868. Sargeant and Blood departed Dacca on the same day, 5 June 1971. The fifty-three-year-old DHC had made his career in the diplomatic corps following the Second World War. After three months of rest, he commenced a course for senior officers in September 1971, before receiving a comfortable posting as British consul general in Lyon. He and Blood met one more time shortly afterwards, and in somewhat less trying circumstances, when their families holidayed together on the shores of Lake Geneva. Archer K. Blood, *The Cruel Birth of Bangladesh: Memoirs of an American Diplomat* (Dhaka: The University Press, 2002), 323, 343.

33 Letter, Sargeant to Burrows and Sutherland, 5 June 1971, NAUK, FCO 37/888, Political Crisis in East Pakistan.

34 United Kingdom, *House of Commons Debates,* vol. 818 (8 June 1971), 862.

35 Ibid., 867.

36 Ibid., 864.

37 Ibid., 865.

38 Memorandum, undated [c. 8 June 1971], "Statement and Notes for Douglas-Home," NAUK, FCO 37/887.

39 United Kingdom, *House of Commons Debates,* vol. 818 (9 June 1971), 1070–77.

40 Ibid., 1077.

41 Ibid., 1097.

42 Ibid., 1110–11.

43 Ibid., 1119.

44 United Kingdom, *House of Commons Debates,* vol. 818 (8 June 1971), 864.

45 John Groser, "Labour MPs Indict Army Atrocities in Pakistan," *Times* (London), 16 June 1971, 1.

46 Simon Dring, "How Dacca Paid for a 'United' Pakistan," *Daily Telegraph* (London), 30 March 1971.

47 Brian May, "Tanks Smash Barricades in Dacca," *Times* (London), 29 March 1971, 1.

48 Michel Laurent, "At Dacca University the Burning Bodies of Students Still Lay in Their Dormitory Beds ... a Mass Grave Had Been Hastily Covered," *Times* (London), 30 March 1971, 1.

49 Nicholas Tomalin, "Mass Slaughter of Punjabis in East Bengal," *Times* (London), 2 April 1971, 1.

50 Louis Heren, "Pakistan Army Said to Be Wiping Out Leaders in Brutal War," *Times* (London), 2 April 1971, 1, 6.

51 Editorial, "The Slaughter in East Pakistan," *Times* (London), 3 April 1971, 15.

52 See, for example, Peter Hazelhurst, "Officer Admits That Bengalis Are Murdering Biharis," *Times* (London), 17 May 1971, 1

53 Dennis Neeld, "Thousands Still Fleeing Frightened Dacca," *Times* (London), 13 April 1971, 1.

54 See, for example, Peter Hazelhurst, "Call for Aid to Pakistan Refugees," *Times* (London), 6 May 1971, 1.

55 Editorial, "Bengal's Suffering Millions," *Times* (London), 1 June 1971, 11. See also Editorial, "The Terror That Perpetuates Terror," *Times* (London), 14 July 1971, 13.

56 Peter Hazelhurst, "Half Hindu Population Flees from East Bengal Fearing Persecution by Muslim Troops," *Times* (London), 5 June 1971, 4.

57 Mark Dummett, "Bangladesh War: The Article That Changed History," *BBC Magazine*, 16 December 2011, https://www.bbc.com/news/world-asia-16207201.

58 Anthony Mascarenhas, "GENOCIDE," *Sunday Times* (London), 13 June 1971, 1, 12–14. The Pakistani journalist's work was syndicated around the world. Mascarenhas settled in London and later published *The Rape of Bangla Desh* (New Delhi: Vikas, 1971).

59 Memorandum, K. Katzer to Sutherland, 3 June 1971, NAUK, FCO 37/970, Pakistan Community in UK.

60 Michael Rendall and John Salt, "The Foreign-Born Population," in *Focus on People and Migration,* ed. Roma Chappell (Basingstoke, Hampshire: Palgrave Macmillan, 2005), 134.

61 Memorandum, K. Katzer to Sutherland, 3 June 1971, NAUK, FCO 37/970.

62 Srinath Raghavan, *1971: A Global History of the Creation of Bangladesh* (Cambridge, MA: Harvard University Press, 2013), 138–39.

63 Memorandum, K. Katzer to Sutherland, 3 June 1971, NAUK, FCO 37/970.

64 Memorandum, Sutherland to Tomlinson, 27 March 1971, NAUK, FCO 37/970.

65 Memorandum, K. Katzer to Sutherland, 3 June 1971, NAUK, FCO 37/970.

66 Ibid.

67 Peter Scott, "Mob Attacks Pakistan Cricket Team," *Times* (London), 29 April 1971, 1.

68 Memorandum, K. Katzer to Sutherland, 3 June 1971, NAUK, FCO 37/970.

69 Memorandum, Sutherland to Tomlinson, 23 July 1971, NAUK, FCO 37/970; Telegram, FCO to Pumphrey, 2 August 1971, NAUK, FCO 37/970.

Notes to pages 158–63   253

70 Memorandum, K. Katzer to Sutherland, 3 June 1971, NAUK, FCO 37/970.
71 Clifford Longley, "Bitterness Divides Pakistani Community," *Times* (London), 1 May 1971, 2.
72 Memorandum, P.F. Walker of SAD to Ian McCluney, 25 June 1971, NAUK, FCO 37/888.
73 Cabinet Conclusions, 17 June 1971, NAUK, Cabinet Office Files, CAB 128/49, Cabinet Conclusions.
74 Memorandum, Byatt to Douglas-Home, 16 June 1971, NAUK, FCO 37/887.
75 Memorandum, Eleanor Lane to the British deputy high commissioner in Calcutta, 11 June 1971, NAUK, FCO 37/887.
76 Memorandum, Moon to McCluney, FCO, 2 June 1971, NAUK, PREM 15/569, Prime Minister's Office: Correspondence and Papers, 1970–1974, Subseries: Pakistan, Internal Situation. See also Telegram, Sutherland to Moon, 2 June 1971, NAUK, FCO 37/950, Famine Relief for Pakistani Refugees in India.
77 Memorandum Attachment, Moon to Heath, 3 June 1971, NAUK, PREM 15/569. See also Telegram, Sutherland to Moon, 2 June 1971, NAUK, FCO 37/950.
78 Memorandum, Wilford to Royle, 8 June 1971, NAUK, FCO 37/887.
79 Memorandum, Graham to Moon, 10 June 1971, NAUK, FCO 37/887.
80 Ibid.
81 Memorandum, Moon to Graham, 11 June 1971, NAUK, FCO 37/887.
82 Telegram, FCO to Pumphrey, 11 June 1971, NAUK, FCO 37/887.
83 Telegram, FCO to Garvey, 11 June 1971, NAUK, FCO 37/887.
84 Telegram, FCO to UK Mission, UN New York, 11 June 1971, NAUK, FCO 37/887.
85 Telegram, Arthur Collins, First Secretary, Dacca, to FCO, 14 June 1971, NAUK, FCO 37/887. See also Michael Hornsby, "Villagers Still Pay with Their Lives for Being Hindus in Pakistan," *Times* (London), 1 July 1971, 1.
86 Memorandum, 21 June 1971, "Note of the Prime Minister's Meeting with Mr. Swaran Singh," NAUK, PREM 15/569.
87 Memorandum, Moon to McCluney, 22 June 1971, NAUK, PREM 15/569.
88 Telegram, FCO to Pumphrey, 23 June 1971, NAUK, FCO 37/888.
89 United Kingdom, *House of Commons Debates,* vol. 819 (23 June 1971), 1436–37.
90 Ibid.
91 Ibid., 1437–38. China would provide Pakistan with a US$100 million rescue package (Chapter 3).
92 Telegram, Douglas-Home to Pumphrey, 8 June 1971, NAUK, FCO 37/929, Political Relations between Pakistan and UK.
93 Michael Hornsby, "MP Says Refugees Would Be Unwise to Return," *Times* (London), 29 June 1971, 6.
94 "British MPs Shaken by Bengal Misery," *Times* (London), 30 June 1971, 7.
95 Telegram, Pumphrey to FCO, 25 June 1971, NAUK, PREM 15/569.
96 Telegram, Pumphrey to FCO, 8 July 1971, NAUK, PREM 15/569.
97 Telegram, Garvey to FCO, 28 June 1971, NAUK, PREM 15/569.
98 Telegram, Pumphrey to FCO, 28 June 1971, NAUK, PREM 15/569.
99 Editorial, "Well Meant, but Not Well Conceived," *Times* (London), 29 June 1971, 15.

100 Handwritten comment on memorandum, Sutherland to Douglas-Home, 7 July 1971, NAUK, FCO 37/889, Political Crisis in East Pakistan.

101 Telegram, Garvey to FCO, 8 July 1971, NAUK, PREM 15/569.

102 Letter, Yahya to Heath, delivered 29 June 1971, NAUK, PREM 15/569.

103 Telegram, Pumphrey to FCO, 3 July 1971, NAUK, FCO 37/929.

104 Telegram, Garvey to FCO, 8 July 1971, NAUK, PREM 15/569.

105 United Kingdom, *House of Commons Debates,* vol. 821 (15 July 1971), 723–24.

106 Memorandum, Sutherland to Douglas-Home, 14 July 1971, "Note for Secretary of State's Use in Cabinet," NAUK, FCO 37/889.

107 Memorandum, Sutherland to Douglas-Home, 21 July 1971, "Note for Secretary of State's Use in Cabinet," NAUK, FCO 37/890, Political Crisis in East Pakistan.

108 Telegram, Pumphrey to FCO, 15 July 1971, NAUK, FCO 37/889. The rumours were incorrect; the trial actually began in mid-August 1971.

109 Memorandum, Sutherland to Douglas-Home, 21 July 1971, "Note for Secretary of State's Use in Cabinet," NAUK, FCO 37/890.

110 Memorandum, Graham to Alan Simcock, Prime Minister's Private Office, 21 July 1971, NAUK, PREM 15/569.

111 Memorandum, Graham to Simcock, 21 July 1971, NAUK, PREM 15/569.

112 Telegram, FCO to Pumphrey, 29 July 1971, NAUK, PREM 15/569.

113 Concerns over Indo-Pakistani tensions and the future course of events in Bengal were already being aired at the end of June. Speaking Note for the Secretary of State's Use in Western European Union Ministerial Meeting of 1 July 1971, c. 30 June 1971, NAUK, FCO 37/889.

114 Telegram, Burrows to FCO, 31 July 1971, NAUK, FCO 37/929.

115 Minutes of DOP Meeting, 29 July 1971, NAUK, CAB 148/115, Cabinet Office: Defence and Oversea Policy Committees and Sub-Committees: Minutes and Papers. The DOP agreed that the execution of Mujibur Rahman was an example of the kind of Pakistani action that might provoke an Indian armed response. The committee also discussed at length the adverse reaction in Islamabad to Britain's policy on new economic aid, and Douglas-Home resolved to publicly explain, once more, the British position. The foreign secretary noted the dilemma that the more he emphasized British friendship for Pakistan, "the greater the risk of incurring Indian displeasure."

116 Memorandum for the DOP by the Secretary of State for Foreign and Commonwealth Affairs, 27 July 1971, NAUK, CAB 148/116, Cabinet Office: Defence and Oversea Policy Committees and Sub-Committees: Minutes and Papers.

117 Letter, Pumphrey to Douglas-Home, 3 August 1971, NAUK, FCO 37/892, Political Crisis in East Pakistan.

118 Memorandum, Byatt to Tomlinson, 19 August 1971, NAUK, FCO 37/892.

119 Handwritten memorandum, Garvey to SAD, 3 September 1971, NAUK, FCO 37/892 (emphasis added).

120 See, for example, United Kingdom, *House of Commons Debates,* vol. 821 (15 July 1971), 723–24.

121 Andrew J. Pierre, *The Global Politics of Arms Sales* (Princeton, NJ: Princeton University Press, 1982), 8, 100–7. Its 5 percent market share made the United Kingdom

Notes to pages 168–72

joint fourth supplier in the world arms export rankings, equal with West Germany and behind, in descending order of share, the United States, the Soviet Union, and France.

122 United Kingdom, *House of Commons Debates*, vol. 816 (26 April 1971), 29.
123 Memorandum, Sutherland to Tomlinson and Wilford, 7 April 1971, NAUK, FCO 37/937. Telegram, FCO to Pickard, 17 April 1971, NAUK, FCO 37/937, Export of Military Equipment from UK to Pakistan.
124 Memorandum, Sutherland to MOD, 2 April 1971, NAUK, FCO 37/937.
125 Memorandum, Sutherland to Tomlinson and Wilford, 7 April 1971, NAUK, FCO 37/937; Telegram, FCO to Pickard, 17 April 1971, NAUK, FCO 37/937.
126 Memorandum, Sutherland to Tomlinson, 18 May 1971, NAUK, FCO 37/937.
127 Memorandum, Byatt to British High Commission in Islamabad, 27 May 1971, NAUK, FCO 37/937.
128 Memorandum, Sutherland to Tomlinson, 9 July 1971, NAUK, FCO 37/938, Export of Military Equipment from UK to Pakistan.
129 Memorandum, Sutherland to Tomlinson, 23 July 1971, NAUK, FCO 37/938; Telegram, FCO to Garvey, 30 July 1971, NAUK, FCO 37/938.
130 Memorandum, MOD to SAD, 27 July 1971, NAUK, FCO 37/938.
131 See Chapter 3.
132 Memorandum, Sutherland to Tomlinson, 21 July 1971, NAUK, FCO 37/938.
133 Memorandum, Byatt to Tomlinson, 16 August 1971, NAUK, FCO 37/939, Export of Military Equipment from UK to Pakistan.
134 Memorandum, Sutherland to Tomlinson, 20 October 1971, NAUK, FCO 37/940, Export of Military Equipment from UK to Pakistan.
135 Memorandum, Carrington to Douglas-Home, 25 November 1971, NAUK, FCO 37/940.
136 Letter, Burrows to Sutherland, 12 October 1971, NAUK, FCO 37/936, Sale of Royal Navy Frigates to Pakistan.
137 Telegram, FCO to Burrows, 9 November 1971, NAUK, FCO 37/936.
138 See Chapter 5.
139 United Kingdom, *House of Commons Debates*, vol. 815 (21 April 1971), 405–6.
140 United Kingdom, *House of Commons Debates*, vol. 817 (14 May 1971), 766–67.
141 United Kingdom, *House of Commons Debates*, vol. 818 (8 June 1971), 864.
142 Memorandum, c. 7 June 1971, "Secretary of State's Interview on *Panorama* on 7 June," NAUK, PREM 15/569.
143 United Kingdom, *House of Commons Debates*, vol. 822 (2 August 1971), 208.
144 United Kingdom, *House of Commons Debates*, vol. 819 (23 June 1971), 1436–37.
145 See Chapter 3.
146 "World Bank Condemns Pakistan Government," *Times* (London), 12 July 1971, 1.
147 Memorandum, Sutherland to Douglas-Home, 23 September 1971, NAUK, FCO 37/930, Political Relations between Pakistan and UK.
148 Telegram, Douglas-Home to UK Mission, UN Geneva, 28 April 1971, NAUK, FCO 37/945, Famine Relief to East Pakistan.
149 Telegram, Douglas-Home to UK Mission, UN Geneva, 4 June 1971, NAUK, FCO 37/951, Famine Relief for Pakistani Refugees in India.

150 Telegram, UK Mission, UN New York, to FCO, 11 June 1971, NAUK, FCO 37/952, Famine Relief for Pakistani Refugees in India.
151 Robert Fisk, "Nearly £500,000 Raised in Britain in Three Days," *Times* (London), 12 June 1971, 1.
152 Research Study of 2 July 1971, Bureau of Intelligence and Research of the US Department of State, released to UK 16 August 1971, NAUK, FCO 37/958, Famine Relief for Pakistani Refugees in India.
153 Letter, Male to Douglas-Home, 26 July 1971, NAUK, FCO 37/958.
154 Letter, Indira Gandhi to Heath, delivered 18 May 1971, written 13 May 1971, NAUK, PREM 15/568.
155 Telegram, Garvey to FCO, 28 September 1971, NAUK, FCO 37/959, Famine Relief for Pakistani Refugees in India.
156 Letter, Male to Douglas-Home, 26 July 1971, NAUK, FCO 37/958.
157 Cabinet Conclusions, 17 June 1971, NAUK, CAB 128/49.
158 United Kingdom, *House of Commons Debates,* vol. 819 (23 June 1971), 1436–37.
159 Memorandum, Sutherland to Wilford, 15 October 1971, NAUK, FCO 37/960, Famine Relief for Pakistani Refugees in India.
160 Telegram, Douglas-Home to "Certain Missions," 21 October 1971, NAUK, FCO 37/960.
161 Memorandum, FCO to Moon, 12 August 1971, NAUK, PREM 15/445, Prime Minister's Office: Correspondence and Papers, 1970–1974, Subseries: India, Treaty between India and Soviet Union.
162 Telegram, British High Commission in Kuala Lumpur to FCO, 21 August 1971, NAUK, FCO 37/892.
163 Memorandum, Moon to FCO, 12 October 1971, NAUK, FCO 37/893, Political Crisis in East Pakistan.
164 Prime Minister's Briefing Book, Section 1, Steering Brief, 21 October 1971, NAUK, CAB 133/405, Visit of the Indian Prime Minister to the United Kingdom.
165 Memorandum, 31 October 1971, "Record of Meeting between the Prime Minister and Mrs. Indira Gandhi," NAUK, PREM 15/569.
166 Telegram, Douglas-Home to Pumphrey, 7 November 1971, NAUK, PREM 15/569.

Chapter 7: Interplay between the Three Powers

1 Phillip Buckner, "Canada and the End of Empire, 1939–1982," in *Canada and the British Empire,* ed. Phillip Buckner (New York: Oxford University Press, 2008), 107.
2 John Hilliker and Greg Donaghy, "Canadian Relations with the United Kingdom at the End of Empire, 1956–1973," in Buckner, *Canada and the End of Empire,* 25.
3 Ibid., 30.
4 Ibid., 31–32.
5 Ibid., 41.
6 Ibid., 40.
7 Ibid., 33.
8 Robert Bothwell, *Alliance and Illusion: Canada and the World, 1945–1984* (Vancouver: UBC Press, 2007), 345.
9 Hilliker and Donaghy, "Canadian Relations with the United Kingdom," 35.

Notes to pages 181–86

10 Douglas McCalla, "Economy and Empire: Britain and Canadian Development, 1783–1971," in Buckner, *Canada and the British Empire,* 253.
11 Buckner, "Canada and the End of Empire," 122.
12 Bothwell, *Alliance and Illusion,* 344.
13 Hilliker and Donaghy, "Canadian Relations with the United Kingdom," 40–41.
14 Prime Minister's Briefing Book, Section 1, Steering Brief, 9 December 1970, The National Archives of the United Kingdom: Public Record Office (NAUK), Cabinet Office Files, CAB 133/397, Visit of the Prime Minister to Ottawa, December 1970.
15 Hilliker and Donaghy, "Canadian Relations with the United Kingdom," 42.
16 Robert Bothwell, *Your Country, My Country: A Unified History of the United States and Canada* (New York: Oxford University Press, 2015), 341.
17 Robert Bothwell, "Canada–United States Relations: Options for the 1970s," *International Journal* 58, 1 (2002–03): 65.
18 Calculated from tables G401–407 and G408–414 in Statistics Canada, *Historical Statistics of Canada,* "Section G: The Balance of International Payments, International Investment Position, and Foreign Trade," http://www.statcan.gc.ca/pub/11-516-x/sectiong/4147439-eng.htm#4.
19 Bothwell, "Canada–United States Relations," 66.
20 Bothwell, *Alliance and Illusion,* 189.
21 Bothwell, "Canada–United States Relations," 67–68.
22 Ibid., 71–74.
23 Ibid., 88.
24 Ibid., 69.
25 David Reynolds, "A 'Special Relationship'? America, Britain and the International Order since the Second World War," *International Affairs* 62, 1 (1985–86): 1–20.
26 Ibid., 1–2.
27 Ibid., 5–7.
28 Ibid., 10.
29 Ibid., 7.
30 Ibid., 8.
31 Ibid., 9, 14.
32 Ibid., 9–10.
33 Ibid., 13.
34 Ibid., 13–14.
35 Department of State, United Kingdom Facts Book, December 1970, United States, Nixon Presidential Materials Project (NPMP), Box Files, Box 942, VIP Visits, United Kingdom, Prime Minister Heath, Dec 1970.
36 Reynolds, "A 'Special Relationship'?" 13.
37 Ibid., 14.
38 Ibid., 14–15.
39 Ibid., 17.
40 Ibid., 16.
41 Ibid., 11. See also R. Gerald Hughes and Thomas Robb, "Kissinger and the Diplomacy of Coercive Linkage in the 'Special Relationship' between the United States and Great Britain, 1969–1977," *Diplomatic History* 37, 4 (2013): 867–68.

42 Reynolds, "A 'Special Relationship'?" 13. See also Hughes and Robb, "Coercive Linkage," 868–72.
43 Reynolds, "A 'Special Relationship'?" 10.
44 Ibid., 10–11.
45 Jonathan Colman, "Communication: 'What Now for Britain?' The State Department's Intelligence Assessment of the 'Special Relationship,' 7 February 1968," *Diplomacy and Statecraft* 19, 2 (2008): 351.
46 Alex Spelling, "Edward Heath and Anglo-American Relations, 1970–1974: A Reappraisal," *Diplomacy and Statecraft* 20, 4 (2009): 638–40.
47 Reynolds, "A 'Special Relationship'?" 1.
48 Prime Minister's Briefing Book, Section 1, Steering Brief, 3 October 1970, NAUK, CAB 133/392, Visit of the President of the United States, October 1970.
49 Prime Minister's Briefing Book, Section C1, Anglo–United States Relations, 23 September 1970, NAUK, CAB 133/392.
50 Memorandum, Kissinger to Nixon, undated, "Your Visit to England, Saturday, October 3, 1970," NPMP, Box 470, Visit of Richard Nixon, President of the United States, Briefing Book, United Kingdom, Oct 1970.
51 Letter, Nixon to Heath, 18 November 1970, NPMP, Box 764, Presidential Correspondence, United Kingdom, Prime Minister Heath, 1970.
52 Memorandum, Kissinger to Nixon, undated, "The Visit of Prime Minister Heath, December 17–18," NPMP, Box 942.
53 Prime Minister's Briefing Book, Section 1, Steering Brief, 11 December 1970, NAUK, CAB 133/398, Visit of the Prime Minister to Washington, December 1970.
54 Letter, Freeman to FCO, 8 January 1971, NAUK, Foreign and Commonwealth Office Files, FCO 82/58, Visit of Mr. Edward Heath, Prime Minister, to USA, December 1970.
55 Letter, Nixon to Heath, 22 January 1971, NPMP, Box 764.
56 Handwritten comment on memorandum, Graham to Greenhill, 9 September 1971, NAUK, FCO 82/61, Meetings between Mr. William Rogers, Secretary of State for USA, and Secretary of State for Foreign and Commonwealth Affairs, Sir Alec Douglas-Home.
57 Memorandum, Graham to Greenhill, 9 September 1971, NAUK, FCO 82/61.
58 Memorandum, FCO to Moon, 5 November 1971, NAUK, FCO 82/64, Political Relations between UK and USA.
59 Rowland Baring, 3rd Earl of Cromer.
60 Letter, Cromer to Greenhill, 12 November 1971, NAUK, FCO 82/66, Briefs for Meeting between Mr. Richard Nixon, President of USA, and Prime Minister of UK, Mr. Edward Heath, Bermuda, December 1971.
61 Letter, Cromer to Douglas-Home, 17 December 1971, NAUK, FCO 37/754, Consultations on South Asian Affairs between UK and USA.
62 Andrew Scott, *Allies Apart: Heath, Nixon and the Anglo-American Relationship* (New York: Palgrave Macmillan, 2011), 198–200.
63 Spelling, "Heath and Anglo-American Relations," 641–42.
64 Ibid., 655. In addition, see Scott, *Allies Apart,* 200.
65 In 1970, US exports to Canada totalled US$9.1 billion and imports from Canada amounted to US$11.0 billion. Memorandum, Peter Peterson, Assistant to the

Notes to pages 190–93

President for International Economic Affairs, to Nixon, 4 December 1971, NPMP, Box 912, VIP Visits, Canada, Prime Minister Trudeau, 12/06/71.

66 Bruce Muirhead, "From Special Relationship to Third Option: Canada, the U.S., and the Nixon Shock," *American Review of Canadian Studies* 34, 3 (2004): 439.

67 Bothwell, "Canada–United States Relations," 76–78.

68 Ibid., 80.

69 Ibid., 79–82.

70 Bothwell, *Alliance and Illusion*, 343.

71 Muirhead, "Special Relationship to Third Option," 439.

72 Hilliker and Donaghy, "Canadian Relations with the United Kingdom," 42.

73 Handwritten comment on memorandum, British High Commission in Wellington to Byatt, 15 April 1971, NAUK, FCO 37/884, Political Crisis in East Pakistan. The FCO also provided the Australian and New Zealand high commissions in London with similar information. Covering Memorandum, J. Birch, SAD, to British High Commission in New Delhi, 25 June 1971, NAUK, FCO 37/955, Famine Relief for Pakistani Refugees in India. Some examples of relevant telegrams between London and Ottawa may be found in Chapter 4.

74 See, for example: Covering Memorandum, Canadian High Commission in London to Sutherland, 10 May 1971, NAUK, FCO 37/886, Political Crisis in East Pakistan; and Covering Memorandum, Canadian High Commission in London to Byatt, 19 July 1971, NAUK, FCO 37/898, Attitudes of Other Countries to Political Situation in East Pakistan.

75 Covering Memorandum, J. Birch, SAD, to British High Commission in New Delhi, 25 June 1971, NAUK, FCO 37/955.

76 See, for example, Letter, D. Wyatt, British High Commission in Ottawa, to SAD, 31 August 1971, NAUK, FCO 37/899, Attitudes of Other Countries to Political Situation in East Pakistan.

77 Steering Brief for the Secretary of State's Meeting with Mr. Mitchell Sharp, undated, NAUK, FCO 82/24, Meetings between Sir Alec Douglas-Home, Secretary of State for Foreign and Commonwealth Affairs, and Mr. Mitchell Sharp, Minister of External Affairs of Canada.

78 Record of a Conversation between the Foreign and Commonwealth Secretary and the Canadian Minister of External Affairs, 2 June 1971, NAUK, FCO 82/24. Sharp stated that Canadian representatives believed that the secession of the East was inevitable. Douglas-Home accepted that "most people were beginning to think this now." Before discussing Pakistan, the two ministers first spoke of Trudeau's recent visit to Moscow, Mutual and Balanced Force Reductions, and Britain's attempt to join the European Community. After the brief exchange on Pakistan, the conversation moved on to the matters of the Canadian Constitution and the Queen's recent visit to Canada.

79 Archer K. Blood, *The Cruel Birth of Bangladesh: Memoirs of an American Diplomat* (Dhaka: The University Press, 2002), 233. Blood mistakenly wrote "May 29." Nevertheless, it is clear from the context that he meant March 29.

80 Ibid., 232, 323.

81 Ibid., 323, 343.

82 Memorandum, Sutherland to British Embassy in Washington, 1 October 1971, NAUK, FCO 37/754.

83 For example, when normal diplomatic communications between East and West Pakistan were cut, Joseph Farland, the US ambassador to Islamabad, drew the attention of Cyril Pickard, the British high commissioner to Islamabad, to the clampdown on 26 March (Chapter 5).

84 Record of a Meeting between the Foreign and Commonwealth Secretary and the United States Secretary of State, 27 April 1971, NAUK, FCO 82/59, Visit of Mr. William Rogers, Secretary of State of USA to UK, April 1971. Note: there are two sets of minutes on file, one being a continuation of the other.

85 Steering Brief for Secretary of State's Meeting with Mr. William Rogers, undated, NAUK, FCO 82/60, Meetings between Mr. William Rogers, Secretary of State for USA, and Secretary of State for Foreign and Commonwealth Affairs, Sir Alec Douglas-Home.

86 Record of a Conversation between the Foreign and Commonwealth Secretary and the United States Secretary of State, 3 June 1971, NAUK, FCO 82/60.

87 Telegram, Douglas-Home to British Embassy in Washington, 1 February 1971, NAUK, Prime Minister's Office Files, PREM 15/715, Exchanges between Prime Minister and US President.

88 Telegram, Douglas-Home to British Embassy in Washington, 21 April 1971, NAUK, FCO 37/928, Political Relations with UK: Visit of Prime Minister Edward Heath to Pakistan, 8–9 January. The United States was also informed about Heath's forthright third letter to Yahya of 11 June. Briefing Book for the Visit of Dr. Henry Kissinger, Section 17, Pakistan and India, 21 June 1971, NAUK, CAB 133/408, Visit of Dr. Henry Kissinger to London, 24–26 June 1971.

89 Henry A. Kissinger, *White House Years* (Boston: Little, Brown, 1979), 1021.

90 Briefing Book for the Visit of Dr. Henry Kissinger, Section 20, Dr. Henry A. Kissinger: Biographical Note, 22 June 1971, NAUK, CAB 133/408.

91 Memorandum, Trend to Heath, 28 June 1971, NAUK, PREM 15/1272, Visits of Doctor Kissinger to UK.

92 Ibid.

93 Ibid.

94 Telegram, Cromer to FCO, 21 July 1971, NAUK, PREM 15/445, Prime Minister's Office: Correspondence and Papers, 1970–1974, Subseries: India, Treaty between India and Soviet Union.

95 Given the number of issues that could have emerged on the complex global stage, it is not suggested that such structures between small groups of governments could have been maintained on a permanent basis with a view to addressing all possible crises.

Conclusion

1 Washington, US$150 million; Ottawa, Cdn$25 million; and London, GB£10 million. The Canadian and US dollars were roughly at par at this time, while a British pound bought some $2.40 of either.

2 In the mid-1960s, the United States provided Pakistan with some US$400 million of economic development aid each year, US$250 million more than when the clampdown commenced.

Notes to pages 202–8

3 Telegram, Pumphrey to FCO, 3 July 1971, The National Archives of the United Kingdom: Public Record Office (NAUK), Foreign and Commonwealth Office Files, FCO 37/929, Political Relations between Pakistan and UK.

4 Record of Conversation, Nixon and Kissinger, 4 June 1971, document no. 136, Louis J. Smith, ed., *Foreign Relations of the United States, 1969–1976*, vol. E-7, *Documents on South Asia, 1969–72*, http://history.state.gov/historicaldocuments/frus1969-76ve07.

5 Record of Telephone Conversation, Nixon and Kissinger, 30 March 1971, document no. 15, Louis J. Smith, ed., *Foreign Relations of the United States, 1969–1976*, vol. 11, *South Asia Crisis, 1971*, http://history.state.gov/historicaldocuments/frus1969-76v11.

6 Roger Morris, *Uncertain Greatness: Henry Kissinger and American Foreign Policy* (New York: Harper and Row, 1977), 220.

7 Canada, *House of Commons Debates, 1970–72* (7 April 1971), 4993 (emphasis added).

8 A. Dirk Moses, "Civil War or Genocide? Britain and the Secession of East Pakistan in 1971," in *Civil Wars in South Asia: State, Sovereignty, Development*, ed. Aparna Sundar and Nandini Sundar (New Delhi: Sage Publications, 2014), 150–55.

9 Midsummer: United States, US$88 million; Canada, US$2 million (Cdn$2 million); and United Kingdom, US$17 million (GB£7 million). End of year: United States, US$88 million; Canada, US$20 million (Cdn$20 million); and United Kingdom, US$35 million (GB£14.5 million).

10 UN Charter, c. I, art. 2, para. 7.

11 International Commission on Intervention and State Sovereignty, *The Responsibility to Protect* (Ottawa: International Development Research Centre, 2001), xi.

12 Samantha Power, *"A Problem from Hell": America and the Age of Genocide* (New York: Harper Perennial, 2003), 504.

13 Ibid., 504–9.

Bibliography

Archival Sources

Canada
Library and Archives Canada
Department of External Affairs
Mitchell Sharp Fonds
  Prime Minister's Office, Pierre Trudeau – Priority Correspondence
  Prime Minister's Office, Pierre Trudeau – Secret
  Privy Council Office

United Kingdom
The National Archives of the United Kingdom: Public Record Office
  Cabinet Office Files
  Foreign and Commonwealth Office Files
  Prime Minister's Office Files

United States
National Archives
  State Subject Numeric Files
Nixon Presidential Materials Project
  Box Files
  Institutional Files
  Kissinger Office Files
  White House Tapes

Books and Articles

Ahmed, Kamal Uddin. "Freedom Struggle of Bangladesh and the US Press." *Indian Political Science Review* 17, 1 (1983): 92–97.

Aijazuddin, F.S. *From a Head, through a Head, to a Head: The Secret Channel between the US and China through Pakistan.* Karachi: Oxford University Press, 2000.

–, ed. *The White House and Pakistan: Secret Declassified Documents, 1969–1974.* Karachi: Oxford University Press, 2002.

Akmam, Wardatul. "Atrocities against Humanity during the Liberation War in Bangladesh: A Case of Genocide." *Journal of Genocide Research* 4, 4 (2002): 543–59.

Ali, Mehrunnisa. "The Problem of Quebec." *Pakistan Horizon* 24, 3 (1971): 20–31.

Ambrose, Stephen E. *The Triumph of a Politician, 1962–1972.* Vol. 2 of *Nixon.* New York: Simon and Schuster, 1989.

Arif, K. *America-Pakistan Relations: Documents.* Lahore: Vanguard Books, 1984.

Aziz-al Ahsan, Syed. "Bengali Nationalism and the Relative Deprivation Hypothesis." *Canadian Review of Studies in Nationalism* 15, 1–2 (1988): 81–90.

Bangla Desh Documents. New Delhi: Ministry of External Affairs, 1971.

Bass, Gary J. *The Blood Telegram: Nixon, Kissinger, and a Forgotten Genocide.* New York: Alfred A. Knopf, 2013.

Bauman, Zygmunt. *Modernity and the Holocaust.* Ithaca, NY: Cornell University Press, 2000.

Berry, Victoria, and Allan McChesney. "Human Rights and Foreign Policy-Making." In *Human Rights in Canadian Foreign Policy,* edited by Robert O. Matthews and Cranford Pratt, 59–76. Montreal and Kingston: McGill-Queen's University Press, 1988.

Bhuiyan, Mohammed Abdul Wadud. "The Bangladesh Liberation Movement and the Big Powers: Some Involvements." *Indian Political Science Review* 17, 1 (1983): 65–79.

–. *Emergence of Bangladesh and Role of the Awami League.* New Delhi: Vikas, 1982.

Blood, Archer K. *The Cruel Birth of Bangladesh: Memoirs of an American Diplomat.* Dhaka: The University Press, 2002.

Bloxham, Donald, and A. Dirk Moses. "Editors' Introduction: Changing Themes in the Study of Genocide." In *The Oxford Handbook of Genocide Studies,* edited by Donald Bloxham and A. Dirk Moses, 1–15. New York: Oxford University Press, 2010.

Bokhari, Imtiaz H. "Playing with a Weak Hand: Kissinger's Management of the 1971 Indo-Pakistan Crisis." *Journal of South Asian and Middle Eastern Studies* 22, 1 (1998): 1–23.

Bose, Sarmila. *Dead Reckoning: Memories of the 1971 Bangladesh War.* New York: Columbia University Press, 2011.

Bothwell, Robert. *Alliance and Illusion: Canada and the World, 1945–1984.* Vancouver: UBC Press, 2007.

–. "Canada–United States Relations: Options for the 1970s." *International Journal* 58, 1 (2002–03): 65–88.

–. *Nucleus: The History of Atomic Energy of Canada Limited.* Toronto: University of Toronto Press, 1988.

–. *Your Country, My Country: A Unified History of the United States and Canada.* New York: Oxford University Press, 2015.

Bibliography

Brands, H.W. *India and the United States: The Cold Peace*. Boston: Twayne, 1990.

Buckner, Phillip. "Canada and the End of Empire, 1939–1982." In *Canada and the British Empire*, edited by Phillip Buckner, 107–26. New York: Oxford University Press, 2008.

Burr, William, ed. *The Beijing-Washington Back-Channel and Henry Kissinger's Secret Trip to China, September 1970–July 1971. National Security Archive Electronic Briefing Book No. 66*. http://www.gwu.edu/~nsarchiv/NSAEBB/NSAEBB66/.

Canada. House of Commons. *Minutes of the Standing Committee on External Affairs and National Defence: "Foreign Policy for Canadians" (Pakistan), October 5, 1971.* 28th Parl., 3rd Sess., 1970–1971. Issue 32: 1–39.

–. *House of Commons Debates, 1970–72.*

Chakrabarti, S.K. *The Evolution of Politics in Bangladesh, 1947–1978*. New Delhi: Associated, 1978.

Chalk, Frank, and Kurt Jonassohn. *The History and Sociology of Genocide: Analyses and Case Studies*. New Haven, CT: Yale University Press, 1990.

Chaudhuri, Rudra. *Forged in Crisis: India and the United States since 1947*. New York: Oxford University Press, 2014.

Chen Jian. *Mao's China and the Cold War*. Chapel Hill: University of North Carolina Press, 2001.

Choudhury, G.W. *The Last Days of United Pakistan*. Bloomington: Indiana University Press, 1974.

Chowdhury, Rashid-ul-Ahsan. "United States Foreign Policy in South Asia, 1971." *Journal of the Asiatic Society of Bangladesh* 35, 1 (1990): 55–87.

Cleva, Gregory D. *Henry Kissinger and the American Approach to Foreign Policy*. Lewisburg, PA: Bucknell University Press, 1989.

Cohen, Stephen P. "U.S. Weapons and South Asia: A Policy Analysis." *Pacific Affairs* 49, 1 (1976): 49–69.

Cohen, Warren I. *America in the Age of Soviet Power, 1945–1991*. Vol. 4 of *The Cambridge History of American Foreign Relations*, edited by Warren I. Cohen. New York: Cambridge University Press, 1993.

–. *America's Response to China: A History of Sino-American Relations*. 5th ed. New York: Columbia University Press, 2010.

Colman, Jonathan. "Communication: 'What Now for Britain?' The State Department's Intelligence Assessment of the 'Special Relationship,' 7 February 1968." *Diplomacy and Statecraft* 19, 2 (2008): 350–60.

Dallek, Robert. *Nixon and Kissinger: Partners in Power*. New York: HarperCollins, 2007.

Debnath, Angela. "British Perceptions of the East Pakistan Crisis 1971: 'Hideous Atrocities on Both Sides.'" *Journal of Genocide Research* 13, 4 (2011): 421–50.

Del Pero, Mario. *The Eccentric Realist: Henry Kissinger and the Shaping of American Foreign Policy*. Ithaca, NY: Cornell University Press, 2010.

Dobell, Peter C. *Canada in World Affairs*. Vol. 17, *1971–1973*. Toronto: Canadian Institute of International Affairs, 1995.

Douglas-Home, Alec. *The Way the Wind Blows: An Autobiography*. London: Collins, 1976.

English, John. *Citizen of the World: The Life of Pierre Elliott Trudeau*. Vol. 1, *1919–1968*. Toronto: Alfred A. Knopf Canada, 2006.

–. *Just Watch Me: The Life of Pierre Elliott Trudeau.* Vol. 2, *1968–2000.* Toronto: Alfred A. Knopf Canada, 2009.

Farrell, John A. *Richard Nixon: The Life.* London: Scribe, 2017.

Ferguson, Niall. *The Idealist, 1923–1968.* Vol. 1 of *Kissinger.* New York: Penguin, 2015.

Gandhi, Sajit, ed. *The Tilt: The U.S. and the South Asian Crisis of 1971. National Security Archive Electronic Briefing Book No. 79.* http://www.gwu.edu/~nsarchiv/NSAEBB/NSAEBB79/.

Ganguly, Shivaji. *U.S. Policy toward South Asia.* Boulder, CO: Westview, 1990.

Goh, Evelyn. *Constructing the U.S. Rapprochement with China, 1961–1974: From "Red Menace" to "Tacit Ally."* New York: Cambridge University Press, 2005.

–. "Nixon, Kissinger, and the 'Soviet Card' in the U.S. Opening to China, 1971–1974." *Diplomatic History* 29, 3 (2005): 475–502.

Granatstein, J.L., and Robert Bothwell. *Pirouette: Pierre Trudeau and Canadian Foreign Policy.* Toronto: University of Toronto Press, 1990.

Greene, John Robert. *The Limits of Power: The Nixon and Ford Administrations.* Bloomington: Indiana University Press, 1992.

Guha, Ramachandra. *India after Gandhi: The History of the World's Largest Democracy.* London: Picador, 2008.

Haldeman, H.R., and Joseph DiMona. *The Ends of Power.* New York: Dell, 1978.

Hanhimäki, Jussi. *The Flawed Architect: Henry Kissinger and American Foreign Policy.* New York: Oxford University Press, 2004.

Head, Ivan L., and Pierre Elliott Trudeau. *The Canadian Way: Shaping Canada's Foreign Policy, 1968–1984.* Toronto: McClelland and Stewart, 1995.

Healey, Denis. *The Time of My Life.* London: Michael Joseph, 1989.

Heath, Edward. *The Course of My Life: My Autobiography.* London: Hodder and Stoughton, 1998.

Hersh, Seymour M. *The Price of Power: Kissinger in the Nixon White House.* New York: Summit Books, 1983.

Hilliker, John, and Greg Donaghy. "Canadian Relations with the United Kingdom at the End of Empire, 1956–1973." In *Canada and the End of Empire,* edited by Phillip Buckner, 25–46. Vancouver: UBC Press, 2005.

Hillmer, Norman, and J.L. Granatstein. *Empire to Umpire: Canada and the World to the 1990s.* Toronto: Copp Clark Longman, 1994.

Hiro, Dilip. *The Longest August: The Unflinching Rivalry between India and Pakistan.* New York: Nation Books, 2015.

Hoff, Joan. *Nixon Reconsidered.* New York: Basic Books, 1994.

–. "A Revisionist View of Nixon's Foreign Policy." *Presidential Studies Quarterly* 26, 1 (1996): 107–29.

Holloway, Steven Kendall. *Canadian Foreign Policy: Defining the National Interest.* Peterborough, ON: Broadview Press, 2006.

Hughes, R. Gerald, and Thomas Robb. "Kissinger and the Diplomacy of Coercive Linkage in the 'Special Relationship' between the United States and Great Britain, 1969–1977." *Diplomatic History* 37, 4 (2013): 861–905.

Hussain, Syed Rifaat. "Pakistan and the Superpowers (1947–1988): An Evaluation." *Pakistan Journal of History and Culture* 10, 1 (1989): 19–32, 63–64.

–. "Sino-Pakistan Ties: Trust, Cooperation and Consolidation." *Journal of South Asian and Middle Eastern Studies* 37, 4 (2014): 1–31.

Bibliography 267

International Commission on Intervention and State Sovereignty. *The Responsibility to Protect*. Ottawa: International Development Research Centre, 2001.

Iqbal, Mehrunnisa H. "Pakistan: Foreign Aid and Foreign Policy." *Pakistan Horizon* 25, 4 (1972): 54–71.

Isaacson, Walter. *Kissinger: A Biography*. New York: Simon and Schuster, 1992.

Itoh, Mayumi. *The Origin of Ping-Pong Diplomacy: The Forgotten Architect of Sino-U.S. Rapprochement*. New York: Palgrave Macmillan, 2011.

Jaffrelot, Christophe, ed. *A History of Pakistan and Its Origins*. Translated by Gillian Beaumont. London: Anthem Press, 2002.

Jahan, Rounaq. "Genocide in Bangladesh." In *Centuries of Genocide: Essays and Eyewitness Accounts*, 4th ed., edited by Samuel Totten and William S. Parsons, 248–76. New York: Routledge, 2013.

–. *Pakistan: Failure in National Integration*. New York: Columbia University Press, 1972.

Jain, Rajendra Kumar. *US-South Asian Relations, 1947–1982*. New Delhi: Radiant, 1983.

Jain, Rashmi. *US-Pak Relations, 1947–1983*. New Delhi: Radiant, 1983.

Jalal, Ayesha. *The State of Martial Rule: The Origins of Pakistan's Political Economy of Defence*. New York: Cambridge University Press, 1990.

James, Morrice. *Pakistan Chronicle*. New York: St. Martin's Press, 1993.

Kennedy, Paul M. *The Realities behind Diplomacy: Background Influences on British External Policy, 1865–1980*. London: Allen and Unwin, 1981.

Keys, Barbara. "Congress, Kissinger, and the Origins of Human Rights Diplomacy." *Diplomatic History* 34, 5 (2010): 823–51.

–. *Reclaiming American Virtue: The Human Rights Revolution of the 1970s*. Cambridge, MA: Harvard University Press, 2014.

Khan, Munir Ahmad. "Pakistan-Canada Nuclear Relations." In *Fifty Years of Pakistan-Canada Relations: Partnership for the 21st Century*, edited by Muzaffar Ali Qureshi, 51–67. Islamabad: Area Study Centre for Africa, North and South America, Quaid-i-Azam University, 1998.

Khan, Roedad, compiler. *The American Papers: Secret and Confidential India-Pakistan-Bangladesh Documents, 1965–1973*. Karachi: Oxford University Press, 1999.

–, compiler. *The British Papers: Secret and Confidential India-Pakistan-Bangladesh Documents, 1958–1969*. Karachi: Oxford University Press, 2002.

Khan, Yasmin. *The Great Partition: The Making of India and Pakistan*. 2nd ed. New Haven, CT: Yale University Press, 2017.

Kissinger, Henry A. *Diplomacy*. New York: Simon and Schuster, 1994.

–. *On China*. Toronto: Allen Lane, 2011.

–. *White House Years*. Boston: Little, Brown, 1979.

The Kissinger Conversations, Supplement: A Verbatim Record of U.S. Diplomacy, 1969–1977. http://search.proquest.com/dnsa_kc.

The Kissinger Conversations, Supplement II: A Verbatim Record of U.S. Diplomacy, 1969–1977. http://search.proquest.com/dnsa_47.

The Kissinger Telephone Conversations: A Verbatim Record of U.S. Diplomacy, 1969–1977. http://search.proquest.com/dnsa_ka.

Komine, Yukinori. *Secrecy in US Foreign Policy: Nixon, Kissinger and Rapprochement with China*. Burlington, VT: Ashgate, 2008.

Kuper, Leo. *Genocide: Its Political Use in the Twentieth Century.* New Haven, CT: Yale University Press, 1981.

Kux, Dennis. *India and the United States: Estranged Democracies.* Washington, DC: National Defense University Press, 1992.

–. *The United States and Pakistan, 1947–2000: Disenchanted Allies.* Baltimore: Johns Hopkins University Press, 2001.

Li Jie. "Changes in China's Domestic Situation in the 1960s and Sino-U.S. Relations." In *Re-examining the Cold War: U.S.-China Diplomacy, 1954–1973*, edited by Robert S. Ross and Jiang Changbin, 288–320. Cambridge, MA: Harvard University Press, 2001.

Lüthi, Lorenz M. *The Sino-Soviet Split: Cold War in the Communist World.* Princeton, NJ: Princeton University Press, 2008.

MacMillan, Margaret. *Nixon and Mao: The Week That Changed the World.* New York: Random House, 2007.

Mahdi, Niloufer. "Sino-Pakistan Relations: Historical Background." *Pakistan Horizon* 39, 4 (1986): 60–68.

Mahmood, A.B.M. "The Bangladesh Liberation War: The Response of U.S. Intellectuals." *Indian Journal of American Studies* 13, 1 (1983): 85–95.

Marr, Andrew. *A History of Modern Britain.* London: Macmillan, 2007.

Mascarenhas, Anthony. *The Rape of Bangla Desh.* New Delhi: Vikas, 1971.

McCalla, Douglas. "Economy and Empire: Britain and Canadian Development, 1783–1971." In *Canada and the British Empire*, edited by Phillip Buckner, 240–58. New York: Oxford University Press, 2008.

McGarr, Paul M. *The Cold War in South Asia: Britain, the United States and the Indian Subcontinent, 1945–1965.* Cambridge: Cambridge University Press, 2013.

McGlinchey, Stephen. "Richard Nixon's Road to Tehran: The Making of the U.S.-Iran Arms Agreement of May 1972." *Diplomatic History* 37, 4 (2013): 841–60.

McKittrick, David, and David McVea. *Making Sense of the Troubles: A History of the Northern Ireland Conflict.* London: Viking, 2012.

McMahon, Robert J. *The Cold War on the Periphery: The United States, India, and Pakistan.* New York: Columbia University Press, 1994.

–. "The Danger of Geopolitical Fantasies: Nixon, Kissinger, and the South Asia Crisis of 1971." In *Nixon in the World: American Foreign Relations, 1969–1977*, edited by Fredrik Logevall and Andrew Preston, 249–68. New York: Oxford University Press, 2008.

Morris, Roger. *Uncertain Greatness: Henry Kissinger and American Foreign Policy.* New York: Harper and Row, 1977.

Moses, A. Dirk. "Civil War or Genocide? Britain and the Secession of East Pakistan in 1971." In *Civil Wars in South Asia: State, Sovereignty, Development*, edited by Aparna Sundar and Nandini Sundar, 142–64. New Delhi: Sage, 2014.

Moskin, J. Robert. *American Statecraft: The Story of the U.S. Foreign Service.* New York: St. Martin's Press, 2013.

Moyn, Samuel. *The Last Utopia: Human Rights in History.* Cambridge, MA: Belknap Press of Harvard University Press, 2010.

Muhith, A.M.A. *American Response to Bangladesh Liberation War.* Dhaka: The University Press, 1996.

Muirhead, Bruce. "From Special Relationship to Third Option: Canada, the U.S., and the Nixon Shock." *American Review of Canadian Studies* 34, 3 (2004): 439–62.

Munteanu, Mircea. "Communication Breakdown? Romania and the Sino-American Rapprochement." *Diplomatic History* 33, 4 (2009): 615–31.

Nixon, Richard M. *The Real War*. New York: Warner Books, 1980.

–. *RN: The Memoirs of Richard Nixon*. New York: Grosset and Dunlap, 1978.

Noman, Omar. *Pakistan: A Political and Economic History since 1947*. New York: Kegan Paul International, 1990.

Pearce, Edward. *Denis Healey: A Life in Our Times*. London: Little, Brown, 2002.

Pearson, Geoffrey. "Canada, the United Nations and the Independence of Bangladesh." In *Peace, Development and Culture: Comparative Studies of India and Canada*, edited by Harold Coward, 15–23. Calgary: Shastri Indo-Canadian Institute, 1988.

Phillips, Steven E., ed. *Foreign Relations of the United States, 1969–1976*. Vol. E-13, *Documents on China, 1969–1972*. https://history.state.gov/historicaldocuments/frus1969-76ve13.

–, ed. *Foreign Relations of the United States, 1969–1976*. Vol. 17, *China, 1969–1972*. https://history.state.gov/historicaldocuments/frus1969-76v17.

Pierre, Andrew J. *The Global Politics of Arms Sales*. Princeton, NJ: Princeton University Press, 1982.

Power, Samantha. *"A Problem from Hell": America and the Age of Genocide*. New York: Harper Perennial, 2003.

Prasad, Bimal. "The Super Powers and the Subcontinent." *International Studies* 13, 4 (1974): 719–49.

Quested, R.K.I. *Sino-Russian Relations: A Short History*. London: George Allen and Unwin, 1984.

Raghavan, Srinath. *1971: A Global History of the Creation of Bangladesh*. Cambridge, MA: Harvard University Press, 2013.

Rahmin, Enayetur, and Joyce L. Rahmin, compilers. *Bangladesh Liberation War and the Nixon White House, 1971*. Dhaka: Pustaka, 2000.

Rendall, Michael, and John Salt. "The Foreign-Born Population." In *Focus on People and Migration*, edited by Roma Chappell, 131–52. Basingstoke, Hampshire: Palgrave Macmillan, 2005.

Reynolds, David. *Britannia Overruled: British Policy and World Power in the Twentieth Century*. 2nd ed. Harlow, Essex: Pearson Education, 2000.

–. "A 'Special Relationship'? America, Britain and the International Order since the Second World War." *International Affairs* 62, 1 (1985–86): 1–20.

Riedel, Bruce O. *Avoiding Armageddon: America, India, and Pakistan to the Brink and Back*. Washington, DC: Brookings Institution Press, 2013.

Rodman, Peter W. *Presidential Command: Power, Leadership and the Making of Foreign Policy from Richard Nixon to George W. Bush*. New York: Alfred A. Knopf, 2009.

Ross, Douglas A. *In the Interests of Peace: Canada and Vietnam, 1954–1973*. Toronto: University of Toronto Press, 1984.

Rubin, Barry M. *Secrets of State: The State Department and the Struggle over U.S. Foreign Policy*. New York: Oxford University Press, 1985.

Schabas, William A. *Genocide in International Law: The Crime of Crimes*. 2nd ed. Cambridge: Cambridge University Press, 2009.

Schulzinger, Robert D. *Henry Kissinger: Doctor of Diplomacy*. New York: Columbia University Press, 1989.

Scott, Andrew. *Allies Apart: Heath, Nixon and the Anglo-American Relationship*. New York: Palgrave Macmillan, 2011.

Sharp, Mitchell. *Which Reminds Me ... A Memoir*. Toronto: University of Toronto Press, 1994.

Sisson, Richard, and Leo E. Rose. *War and Secession: Pakistan, India, and the Creation of Bangladesh*. Berkeley: University of California Press, 1990.

Small, John. "From Pakistan to Bangladesh, 1969–1972: Perspective of a Canadian Envoy." In *"Special Trust and Confidence": Envoy Essays in Canadian Diplomacy*, edited by David Reece, 209–38. Ottawa: Carleton University Press, 1996.

Small, Melvin. *The Presidency of Richard Nixon*. Lawrence: University Press of Kansas, 1999.

Smith, Arnold. *Stitches in Time: The Commonwealth in World Politics*. Don Mills, ON: General, 1981.

Smith, Louis J., ed. *Foreign Relations of the United States, 1969–1976*. Vol. E-7, *Documents on South Asia, 1969–1972*. http://history.state.gov/historicaldocuments/frus1969-76ve07.

–, ed. *Foreign Relations of the United States, 1969–1976*. Vol. 11, *South Asia Crisis, 1971*. http://history.state.gov/historicaldocuments/frus1969-76v11.

Smith, Louis J., and David H. Herschler, eds. *Foreign Relations of the United States, 1969–1976*. Vol. 1, *Foundations of Foreign Policy, 1969–1972*. http://history.state.gov/historicaldocuments/frus1969-76v01.

Smith, Simon C. "Coming Down on the Winning Side: Britain and the South Asian Crisis of 1971." *Contemporary British History* 24, 4 (2010): 451–70.

Sorley, Lewis. *Arms Transfers under Nixon: A Policy Analysis*. Lexington: University Press of Kentucky, 1983.

Spelling, Alex. "Edward Heath and Anglo-American Relations, 1970–1974: A Reappraisal." *Diplomacy and Statecraft* 20, 4 (2009): 638–58.

Statistics Canada. *Historical Statistics of Canada*. "Section G: The Balance of International Payments, International Investment Position, and Foreign Trade." http://www.statcan.gc.ca/pub/11-516-x/sectiong/4147439-eng.htm#4.

Strong, Robert A. *Bureaucracy and Statesmanship: Henry Kissinger and the Making of American Foreign Policy*. Lanham, MD: University Press of America, 1986.

Sulzberger, C.L. *The World and Richard Nixon*. New York: Prentice Hall Press, 1987.

Sutter, Robert G. *U.S.-Chinese Relations: Perilous Past, Pragmatic Present*. Lanham, MD: Rowman and Littlefield, 2010.

Tahir-Kheli, Shirin. *The United States and Pakistan: The Evolution of an Influence Relationship*. New York: Praeger, 1982.

Thompson, Joseph E. *American Policy and African Famine: The Nigeria-Biafra War, 1966–1970*. New York: Greenwood Press, 1990.

Thorpe, D. Richard. *Alec Douglas-Home*. London: Sinclair-Stevenson, 1996.

Touhey, Ryan M. *Conflicting Visions: Canada and India in the Cold War World, 1946–76*. Vancouver: UBC Press, 2015.

Trudeau, Pierre Elliott. *Memoirs*. Toronto: McClelland and Stewart, 1993.

Tudda, Chris. *A Cold War Turning Point: Nixon and China, 1969–1972*. Baton Rouge: Louisiana State University Press, 2012.

Tulli, Umberto. "'Whose Rights Are Human Rights?' The Ambiguous Emergence of Human Rights and the Demise of Kissingerism." *Cold War History* 12, 4 (2012): 573–93.

Bibliography

Uche, Chibuike. "Oil, British Interests and the Nigerian Civil War." *Journal of African History* 49, 1 (2008): 111–35.

United Kingdom. *House of Commons Debates,* 1970–71.

Van Hollen, Christopher. "The Tilt Policy Revisited: Nixon-Kissinger Geopolitics and South Asia." *Asian Survey* 20, 4 (1980): 339–61.

Wang, Chi. *The United States and China since World War II: A Brief History.* London: M.E. Sharpe, 2013.

Warner, Geoffrey. "Review Article: Nixon, Kissinger and the Breakup of Pakistan, 1971." *International Affairs* 81, 5 (2005): 1097–118.

–. "Review Article: Nixon, Kissinger and the Rapprochement with China, 1969–1972." *International Affairs* 83, 4 (2007): 763–81.

Webster, David. *Fire and the Full Moon: Canada and Indonesia in a Decolonizing World.* Vancouver: UBC Press, 2009.

Westad, Odd Arne. *Restless Empire: China and the World since 1750.* London: Bodley Head, 2012.

Wolpert, Stanley. *A New History of India.* 8th ed. New York: Oxford University Press, 2009.

Xia, Yafeng. "China's Elite Politics and Sino-American Rapprochement, January 1969–February 1972." *Journal of Cold War Studies* 8, 4 (2006): 3–28.

Xia, Yafeng, and Kuisong Yang. "Vacillating between Revolution and Détente: Mao's Changing Psyche and Policy toward the United States, 1969–1976." *Diplomatic History* 34, 2 (2010): 395–423.

Ziegler, Philip. *Edward Heath: The Authorised Biography.* London: Harper Press, 2010.

Index

Acheson, Dean, 121

Action Bangla Desh (ABD), 158

aid to Pakistan consortium, 51, 64, 74, 82–83, 89, 106–7, 115, 127, 144, 148, 159–61, 170–71, 192–93, 195, 197, 200, 202, 224n62. *See also* Cargill, Peter; International Bank for Reconstruction and Development (IBRD)

Amin, Idi, 124, 149

Amnesty International, 5

Andrew, Arthur, 103–4, 110

Arms Control and Disarmament Agency, 79

Associated Press, 50, 155

Association for Asian Studies, 51

Atomic Energy Act (McMahon Act), 186

Awami League, 9–11, 44, 53, 97–98, 100, 108–9, 130, 139–40, 142, 148, 161–64, 175–76, 206; Six-Point Program, 9–11; suppression of, 43, 50, 76, 110, 114. *See also* Kahn, Yahya; Rahman, Mujibur

Awami League (UK), 157

Bané, Pierre de, 104

Bangla Desh Action Committee for Great Britain (BDAC), 157–58

Bangla Desh Association of Canada, 107

Bangladesh Information Center, 51

Bangladesh League of US Scholars, 51

Bauman, Zygmunt, 54, 136–37, 162, 205

BBC, 132; *Panorama*, 171

Bengal Students Action Committee (BSAC), 157–58

Bennett, Frederic, 147–48, 154, 250n5

Bhutto, Zulfikar Ali, 11, 56

Biafra, 210n12; Canadian policy, 95, 113, 203; UK policy, 126, 147, 159, 163, 168, 175, 203; US policy, 61, 229n21

Blood, Archer, 58, 141, 204–5, 221n27; atrocity reports, 43–48, 51, 53, 59, 61, 68, 74, 87, 135; background and character, 42–43, 46, 57; dissent from US policy in South Asia, 21, 43–49, 52, 55, 77, 87–88, 135–37, 146, 175, 204; Sargeant, Frank, 135, 192–93, 197

Bogdan, Corneliu, 39, 74

Bottomley, Arthur, 162
Bourassa, Robert, 94, 112
British Council, Dacca, 134–35, 139
Britten, Rae, 153
Bureau of Asian and Pacific Affairs. *See* Department of External Affairs, Bureau of Asian and Pacific Affairs
Bureau of Human Rights and Humanitarian Affairs. *See* Department of State, Bureau of Human Rights and Humanitarian Affairs
Bureau of Intelligence and Research. *See* Department of State, Bureau of Intelligence and Research
Bureau of Near Eastern and South Asian Affairs. *See* Department of State, Bureau of Near Eastern and South Asian Affairs
Burrows, Reginald, 133, 139, 141, 153
Byatt, Hugh, 133, 166, 169

Cambodia, 37–38, 55, 60, 63
Canada, foreign relations: India, 93–94, 96–97; Pakistan, 93–96. *See also* Canada-UK relations; Canada-US relations; Trudeau, Pierre
Canada Deuterium Uranium (CANDU) nuclear reactor, 95
Canada-UK relations, 4, 15, 179–82, 186; interplay during crisis, 98, 187, 190–92, 196–98, 205–6. *See also* Heath, Edward; Trudeau, Pierre
Canada–United States Automotive Products Agreement (Auto Pact), 182–83, 190
Canada-US relations, 4, 15, 95, 179–84, 186; interplay during crisis, 4, 187, 190–91, 196–98, 205. *See also* Nixon, Richard; Trudeau, Pierre
Canadian International Development Agency (CIDA), 104, 110
Cargill, Peter, 74, 144. *See also* aid to Pakistan consortium; International Bank for Reconstruction and Development (IBRD)

Carrington, Peter, 169–70
Carter, Jimmy, 5
Case, Clifford, 51, 81
Ceauşescu, Nicolae, 38–40, 74. *See also* China-US rapprochement, back channel, Romania
China, 212*n*34, 242*n*104; and India, 71–72; Indo-Pakistan hostilities of 1971, 86; secessionist issues, 72, 90. *See also* Chou En-lai; Cold War containment; Mao Tse-tung; Sino-Indian War; Sino-Soviet split
China, foreign relations: India, 29, 96; Pakistan, 14, 19, 21–22, 24–27, 29, 56, 71, 83–84, 90, 102, 114–15, 127. *See also* China-US rapprochement
China-US rapprochement: back channel, Pakistan, 19–21, 27, 38–41, 62–64, 66, 71–74, 84, 86–87, 90, 220*n*161; back channel, Romania, 38–41, 62–63, 65, 74, 87, 219*n*143, 219*n*148, 219*n*154; back channels, various, 31, 37–38, 63–64, 72, 84, 86–87, 90; Chinese signals, 28–29, 36–41, 215*n*69; US signals, 28–29, 33–41; Warsaw talks, 28–29, 35, 37–40, 63; watershed event, 62–65, 86–87, 202–3. *See also* Chou En-lai, US rapprochement; Kissinger, Henry; Mao Tse-tung; Nixon, Richard
Chou En-lai, 28–29, 84; and Pakistan, 27; US rapprochement, 28–29, 37–40, 62–65, 66, 72–73, 84, 86–87, 215*n*69; and Yahya Khan, 71–72, 84
Church, Frank, 52
Churchill, Winston, 184
CIA, 29–30
clampdown in East Pakistan, 74–75, 86, 132–35, 151–52; atrocities, 3, 11, 141, 153, 160, 162, 205; casualty statistics, 209*n*1; complexity, 211*n*24; motivation, 11. *See also* Blood, Archer; Cox, Major; guerrilla resistance in East Pakistan;

Pickard, Cyril; Sargeant, Frank; Trudeau, Pierre, atrocity reports

Cold War containment, 4–6, 14, 20–25, 29, 33, 77–78, 86, 94, 121–24, 127–28, 130, 166, 173, 181, 183–85, 196, 199–200, 203–4. *See also* China-India relations; China-Pakistan relations; India non-alignment; Indo-Soviet Treaty of Peace, Friendship, and Cooperation; Sino-Indian War; Sino-Soviet split; US-India relations; US-Pakistan relations

Commonwealth, 93, 122, 126–27, 129, 134–35, 147–48, 159, 164, 175, 182, 188, 192, 203. *See also* Smith, Arnold

Connally, John, 189–90

Council for the Republic of Bangla Desh, 158

Cox, Major, 134, 137, 151

Cromer, Lord, 189, 195–96, 258n59

Cuban Missile Crisis, 24

Cultural Revolution, 28

Daily Telegraph (London), 50, 134, 155

de Gaulle, Charles, 34, 185

de-escalation: Canada (*see* Trudeau, Pierre, de-escalation); UK (*see* Heath, Edward, de-escalation); US (*see* Nixon, Richard, de-escalation)

Defence and Overseas Policy Committee (DOP), 165–68

Defence Sales Organisation. *See* Ministry of Defence (MOD), Defence Sales Organisation

Department of Defense, 80

Department of External Affairs, 102–4, 111, 115; Bureau of Asian and Pacific Affairs, 103; Division of Pacific and South Asian Affairs, 102, 107; human rights, 5–6; military supply, 107. *See also* Sharp, Mitchell

Department of National Defence, 104

Department of State, 29, 37–38, 43, 57, 73, 183, 187, 189, 191, 194–97; Bureau of Human Rights and Humanitarian Affairs, 5, 204; Bureau of Intelligence and Research, 56, 187; Bureau of Near Eastern and South Asian Affairs, 77, 193; dissent channel, 44; influence reduced, 29–32; military supply, 50, 55, 80–82, 89, 206; Office of Munitions Control (OMC), 80; preferred policy in South Asia, 21, 55; suppression of dissent, 45–48, 88, 204. *See also* Rogers, William

Devoir, 113

Diefenbaker, John, 180

Division of Pacific and South Asian Affairs. *See* Department of External Affairs, Division of Pacific and South Asian Affairs

Dorfman, Robert, 51

Douglas-Home, Alec, 131, 133, 139, 148–49, 152–54, 159, 165, 206; background and character, 125, 245n39; economic aid, 153, 161, 166, 171, 192–93, 198, 251n20; humanitarian relief, 138, 147–48, 153, 158–61, 172–73, 175, 193, 197, 207; military supply, 130, 168–69; and Mitchell Sharp, 192–93; public stance of UK, 135–36, 147, 164, 175; South Asia policy, 22, 132, 135–45, 154, 159–67, 173–76, 201–4; and William Rogers, 144, 172, 193–94, 197. *See also* Foreign and Commonwealth Office (FCO)

Douglas-Mann, Bruce, 146–51, 158, 175, 206

Dring, Simon, 50, 134, 155

Duffy, Robert, 105

East Pakistan, 3; Bengali nationalism, 8–12; cyclone, 10, 42, 46, 127, 134. *See also* Awami League; clampdown in East Pakistan; Khan, Yahya; Rahman, Mujibur

East Pakistan Rifles, 43–44, 98, 134

economic aid: Canada (*see* Trudeau, Pierre, economic aid); UK (see Heath, Edward, economic aid); US (see Nixon, Richard, economic aid)

Eisenhower, Dwight, 22–23

European Community, 122, 125, 175, 181, 185, 187–89, 191, 244n16

excuses for inaction. See obfuscation and excuse

Export Credits Guarantee Department (ECGD), 128, 130, 168

Farland, Joseph, 58, 68, 83, 133, 205; background and character, 53, 57; China initiative, 52, 54, 72; support of US policy in South Asia, 21, 46, 49, 52–55, 136–38; suppression of dissent, 45–46, 88

Foreign Assistance Act, 52

Foreign and Commonwealth Office (FCO), 130–33, 135–36, 139, 146, 151, 154, 158–61, 167–70, 174–76, 189, 191–93, 196–97, 205–6, 250n1; Pakistan Emergency Unit, 131–32, 137, 141, 198; South Asia Department (SAD), 131–32, 135, 193. See also Byatt, Hugh; Douglas-Home, Alec; Greenhill, Denis; Sutherland, Iain; Tomlinson, Stanley; Wilford, Kenneth

Foreign Military Sales (FMS), 80–81

Foreign Policy for Canadians, 94, 181

Freeman, John, 188

Friends of East Bengal, 51

Front de liberation du Québec (FLQ), 94, 182

Gallagher, Cornelius E., 52

Gallup polls, 78

Gandhi, Indira, 103, 163–64, 172, 226n106; background and character, 124, 129–30, 174; clampdown assessment, 58, 99; and Edward Heath, 126, 129–30, 151–52, 160–61, 174, 176, 194; Indo-Soviet Treaty, 85, 109; Nixon, 61, 69, 71, 88–89, 203; and Pierre Trudeau, 106, 108–9, 115, 192, 242n96; strategic aims, 70–71, 111–12, 163, 174

Garvey, Terence, 141, 152, 162–64, 167, 172

General Accounting Office, 82

George, James, 96, 104, 192, 197, 204–5; background and character, 100; dissent from Canadian policy in South Asia, 93, 98–100, 102–3, 106, 115, 146, 175, 204, 239n50; and Pierre Trudeau, 103–4; Quebec separatism, 112–13; strategic aims of India, 102, 105–6, 111–12

Globe and Mail, 104–5, 107, 112–13

Graham, John, 131

Greenhill, Denis, 133, 188

Griffel, Eric, 46

Guardian, 158

guerrilla resistance in East Pakistan, 3, 11–13, 70, 74, 76, 85, 100, 102, 105–6, 109, 111–12, 136–38, 141–43, 151–52, 164, 166–67, 242n105. See also clampdown in East Pakistan; India, guerrilla support

Haig, Alexander, 64, 74

Haldeman, H.R., 60

Halperin, Morton, 30

Harrington, John, 107, 113

Harris, Fred R., 51, 82

Hart, Judith, 153–54

Head, Ivan, 99–100, 103

Healey, Denis, 147–50, 161, 167

Heath, Edward, 133, 135, 165, 188; background and character, 124; and Biafra, 126, 147, 159, 163, 168, 175, 203; de-escalation, 165, 167, 174–76, 201; economic aid, 4, 127, 129, 142–45, 149–50, 153, 159–61, 164–66, 170–72, 176, 192–93, 195, 198, 200–2, 251n20; and Henry Kissinger, 194; humanitarian relief, 127, 138, 143–45, 147–48, 151–53, 158–61, 164–66, 172–73, 175, 193, 197, 201, 207; and India, 144, 151, 160–61; and Indira Gandhi, 126, 129–30, 151–52, 160–61, 174, 176, 194; Indo-Pakistan hostilities of

1971, 174; military supply, 4, 123, 127–30, 151, 167–70, 200–1; and Pakistan, 161; public stance of UK, 135–37, 144, 147, 151, 164–65, 167, 175, 199–201; and Pierre Trudeau, 182, 196; US, 189, 193, 196; and Richard Nixon, 187–88, 194, 196; South Asia policy, 22, 132, 135–45, 154, 159–67, 173–76, 201–4; South Asia visit, 119, 126–30, 174–75, 194; world view, 119–22, 124–26, 174–75, 185; and Yahya Khan, 126–30, 137, 139–40, 142–44, 148, 160–61, 164–65, 174–76, 194

Hilaly, Agha, 39–40, 63–64, 72, 76

Huang Chen, 84

human rights, development of Western awareness of, 3, 5–7, 15, 33, 58, 61, 69, 79, 95, 113, 115, 149, 199–201, 203–5, 239*n*49. *See also* institutional culture

humanitarian relief: Canada (*see* Trudeau, Pierre, humanitarian relief); UK (*see* Heath, Edward, humanitarian relief); US (*see* Nixon, Richard, humanitarian relief)

Hussain, Mian Arshad, 143, 193

Imperial Economic Conference, 181

India: and China, 71–72; guerrilla support, 3, 11–12, 70, 76, 105–6, 109, 111, 141–43, 151–52, 164, 166–67, 242*n*105; outbreak of war, 85–86; partition violence, 12–13, 122–23; policy of non-alignment, 14, 22–24, 26–27, 29, 58, 124, 129, 166, 194, 203; refugee statistics, 209*n*1, 228*n*2; refugees, 3, 11–12, 14, 21, 47, 50, 52, 66–71, 74–77, 85–86, 88–90, 102–6, 108, 110–11, 141, 144–45, 148–49, 151–56, 158–62, 164, 172–73, 192, 198, 207; regional tension, 12–14, 22–23, 25, 69, 86, 89–90, 103, 108; strategic aims, 3, 11, 69–71, 85–86, 105–6, 111–12, 140–41, 161. *See also* Cold War

containment; Gandhi, Indira; Heath, Edward; Indo-Pakistan war of 1965; Kashmir dispute; Nixon, Richard; Sino-Indian War; Trudeau, Pierre

India-Pakistan Relief Fund, 172

India-Pakistan Task Force, 103–4, 198

Indian National Congress, 12, 120–21

Indo-Pakistan war of 1965, 9, 13–14, 24, 27, 79–80, 82, 96, 107, 123–24, 128–29, 168, 174, 204

Indo-Soviet Treaty of Peace, Friendship, and Cooperation, 85, 109, 173

institutional culture, 5–6, 15, 199, 203–5. *See also* Blood, Archer; Department of State, dissent channel; Department of State, suppression of dissent; Farland, Joseph, suppression of dissent; George, James; human rights, development of Western awareness; Keating, Kenneth; Kissinger, Henry, suppression of dissent; Nixon, Richard, suppression of dissent; Sisco, Joseph, suppression of dissent

International Bank for Reconstruction and Development (IBRD), 58, 74, 83 106–7, 127, 144, 170–71, 224*n*62. *See also* aid to Pakistan consortium; Cargill, Peter

International Monetary Fund, 58, 144

International Security Assistance and Arms Exports Control Act, 79

Irish Republican Army (IRA), 125

James, Morrice, 124, 129–30, 133, 140–41, 175

Janomot (London), 157

Jessel, Toby, 162

Jinnah, Muhammed Ali, 99, 147

Johnson, Lyndon, 24, 30, 61

Joint Intelligence Committee, 191

Karachi Nuclear Power Project (KANUPP), 4, 93, 95–96, 100, 114, 200

Kashmir dispute, 12–13, 27, 96, 123, 127–28, 157
Keating, Kenneth, 69, 75, 141; background and character, 222n37; dissent from US policy in South Asia, 21, 48–49, 52, 55, 59–60, 88, 146, 195, 204; humanitarian relief, 67–69
Kennedy, Edward, 44, 51–52, 77
Kennedy, John F., 24–25, 30
Kennedy, Richard, 76
key response period, 65, 86–88; phase one, 20–21; phase two, 21
Khan, Ayub, 9–10, 24, 123
Khan, Munir Ahmad, 96
Khan, Sultan, 75
Khan, Tikka, 152
Khan, Yahya, 11, 38–40, 55–56, 59–60, 79, 80–81, 83–85, 90, 99, 107, 109, 111–12, 142–44, 148, 150–52, 154–55, 164, 166, 170, 175, 191; background and character, 10; and Chou En-lai, 71–72, 84; clampdown, 3, 42, 44, 50, 57–58, 68, 133; and Edward Heath, 126–30, 137, 139–40, 142–44, 148, 160–61, 164–65, 174–76, 194; and Henry Kissinger, 195, 202; and Mujibur Rahman, 97, 130–32, 173–74; new constitution, 10; and Pierre Trudeau, 97, 101, 106, 108–9, 115, 192; political accommodation, 76, 110, 114, 120, 159, 161–66, 176, 193–94, 197, 202; and Richard Nixon, 22, 26, 29, 49, 53, 59, 61–62, 66, 71–75, 77–78, 86, 88–90, 195, 202–3. *See also* China-US rapprochement, back channel, Pakistan
King, Gordon, 193
Kissinger, Henry, 52, 55, 75, 188, 194, 204, 207, 210n8, 211n22; back channels, general, 31–32; callous observations, 61, 84; and Canada, 183, 190; China, rapprochement, 14–16, 19–21, 34–41, 57, 59–60, 62–66, 71–75, 77–78, 83–84, 86–87, 89–90, 195–96, 202–3, 217nn107–8,

231n44; China, second visit, 86; China, secret first visit, 20, 52, 54, 66, 71–74, 76, 83–84, 90, 194; de-escalation, 84–85, 195; dissent within bureaucracy, 15; economic aid, 82–83, 195, 200, 202; and Edward Heath, 194; human rights, 5; humanitarian relief, 68–69; and India, 26, 84, 195; and Indira Gandhi, 70; Indo-Pakistan hostilities of 1971, 85–86; Indo-Soviet treaty, 85, 173; military supply, 78–81, 202; motivation during crisis, 59–62, 84, 87–89, 202–3; National Security Council, 30–31; and Pakistan, 195; personalization of foreign policy, 15, 20, 29–32, 37, 73–74, 189, 197–98, 203; public stance of US, 19, 77–78, 89; South Asia policy, 15, 21–22, 55–60, 65–66, 69, 71–72, 74–76, 84–90, 114–15, 163, 195, 198, 201–5; suppression of dissent, 45–49, 59, 88; UK, 187–90, 194–98; world view, 20, 32–33, 223n47; Washington Special Actions Group, 31; and William Rogers, 31, 194–95; and Yahya Khan, 195, 202. *See also* National Security Council (NSC); Nixon, Richard
Korean War, 22, 33
Kosygin, Aleksei, 28

Laos, 60, 63
Laurent, Michel, 155
Le Duc Tho, 194
Lin Piao, 28–29, 40, 86, 215n69
London Awami League, 157
London Declaration, 122

Macmillan, Harold, 185
MacQuarrie, Heath, 104
Male, Peter, 133
Manhattan Project, 186
Mao Tse-tung, 28–29, 36, 40, 83, 86, 215n69

Index 279

Marglin, Stephen, 51
Marshall Plan, 184
Martial Law Administration, 43
Mascarenhas, Anthony, 50, 105, 156, 158–59, 176
Mason, Edward S., 51
Mathias, Charles, Jr., 81
McNamara, Robert, 171
Miles, Stephen, 151
military supply: Canada (*see* Trudeau, Pierre, military supply); UK (*see* Heath, Edward, military supply); US (*see* Nixon, Richard, military supply)
Ministry of Defence (MOD), 170; Defence Sales Organisation, 167–68. *See also* Carrington, Peter
Ministry of Foreign Affairs, Pakistan, 164
Mondale, Walter, 51, 81–82
Morning News (Karachi), 156
Moss, John E., 52, 81
Muskie, Edmund, 52
Muslim League, 8–9, 12
Mutual and Balanced Force Reductions, 194

National Assembly, 10–11, 43, 108–9, 130
National Security Agency, 186
National Security Council (NSC), 34, 49, 52, 56–58, 60, 67, 71, 76, 79–81, 84–85, 194, 216n83; new system, 30–32, 194; Senior Review Group (SRG), 30–31, 55–59, 61, 81. *See also* Kissinger, Henry
NATO, 4, 122, 181–85, 196; North Atlantic Council, 192–93
Nehru, Jawaharlal, 123–24
New York Times, 44, 50, 73–74, 77, 81–82, 169
Nixon, Richard, 52, 56, 187, 189, 207; back channels, general, 31–32; and Biafra, 61, 229n21; callous observations, 49, 68, 86; and Canada, 183; China, rapprochement, 15–16, 19–21, 28, 33–41, 57, 59–60, 62–66, 71–75,

77–78, 83–84, 86–87, 89–90, 189, 196–97, 202–3, 217nn107–8, 217n111, 231n44; China, visit of 1972, 20, 86; de-escalation, 66, 69–71, 74–76, 84–86, 88–89, 195; dissent within bureaucracy, 15; economic aid, 4, 14, 23–25, 27, 29, 51, 58–59, 64, 75, 82–83, 85, 89–90, 107, 170, 195, 200, 202; and Edward Heath, 187–88, 194, 196; humanitarian relief, 59, 64, 66–69, 75–76, 88–89, 202, 207; and India, 26, 49, 62, 84, 88–89, 195, 197, 203; and Indira Gandhi, 61, 69, 71, 88–89, 203; Indo-Pakistan hostilities of 1971, 85–86; military intervention, 78; military supply, 4, 14, 22–26, 50, 55, 57–59, 61, 64, 75, 78–82, 89–90, 107, 200–2, 204, 206, 213n10, 214n36, 233n94; motivation during crisis, 59–62, 84, 87–89, 202–3; National Security Council, 30–31; and Pakistan, 26, 29, 61, 88, 195, 203, 213n10, 227n127; personalization of foreign policy, 15, 20, 29–32, 37, 73–74, 189, 197–98, 203; and Pierre Trudeau, 190, 196; public stance of US, 19, 57, 59, 75, 77–78, 87–89, 199–200, 202; South Asia policy, 15, 21–22, 55–60, 65–66, 69, 71–72, 74–76, 84–90, 114–15, 163, 195, 198, 201–5; suppression of dissent, 45–49, 59, 88; and United Kingdom, 188–89; Washington Special Actions Group, 31; and William Rogers, 31; world view, 20, 32–33; and Yahya Khan, 22, 26, 29, 49, 53, 59, 61–62, 66, 71–75, 77–78, 86, 88–90, 195, 202–3. *See also* Kissinger, Henry
Nixon Doctrine, 32, 79
North American Air Defense Command (NORAD), 4, 183–84, 196
North Atlantic Council. *See* NATO, North Atlantic Council
Northern Ireland, 125–26, 150, 175

obfuscation and excuse, 15, 80–82, 88,
  98–99, 104, 107, 113–14, 135–36,
  153, 158, 167–70, 205–7, 250n1
October Crisis of 1970. *See* Quebec
  separatism
Office of Munitions Control (OMC).
  See Department of State, Office of
  Munitions Control (OMC)
Operation Demetrius, 125

Padma, 107
Paisley, Ian, 150
Pakistan, 3, 68; domestic fission, 8–12,
  130–32; financial difficulties, 58, 74,
  82–83, 90, 106–7, 130, 143–45, 148,
  153, 170–71, 200, 235n130;
  outbreak of war, 85–86; partition
  violence, 12–13, 122–23; regional
  tension, 12–14, 22–23, 25, 69, 86,
  89–90, 103, 108. *See also* Cold War
  containment; East Pakistan; Heath,
  Edward; Indo-Pakistan war of 1965;
  Kashmir dispute; Khan, Yahya;
  Nixon, Richard; Trudeau, Pierre
Pakistan Atomic Energy Commission, 96
Pakistan Emergency Unit. *See* Foreign
  and Commonwealth Office (FCO),
  Pakistan Emergency Unit
Pakistan Peoples Party, 11
Panorama. See BBC, *Panorama*
Pant, Apa, 151–52
parliamentary debates, UK, 120; first
  debate, 146–51; second debate,
  153–54, 156, 159
Partial Nuclear Test Ban Treaty, 28, 185
Pearson, Lester, 180–81
Pickard, Cyril, 98, 133, 136, 139–41, 152;
  atrocities, 133, 136, 152; UK policy
  in South Asia, 134, 136–39, 141–44,
  151–52, 162, 175–76, 204
PL-480 relief, 82, 235n122
Pompidou, Georges, 125
Prentice, Reginald, 162
Press Trust of India, 104–5
public opinion, Canada, 101, 104–5,

207; parliament, 98, 104–10, 180,
  182, 191, 201, 206; press, 97, 104–5,
  107, 112–13, 205–6. *See also* South
  Asian community, Canada;
  Standing Committee on External
  Affairs and Defence, House of
  Commons, Canada
public opinion, UK, 15–16, 144, 146,
  158–59, 163–64, 167, 170, 173,
  175–76, 202, 207; parliament, 105,
  119–20, 135–36, 138, 146–59, 161–62,
  164, 166–71, 173, 175–76, 180, 182,
  191, 201–2, 206, 250n1; press, 120,
  127–28, 134, 137, 146, 154–56, 158,
  162–64, 166, 176, 202, 205–6. *See
  also* parliamentary debates, UK;
  South Asian community, UK
public opinion, US, 55, 77, 207; Congress,
  5, 21, 44, 51–52, 55, 57, 64, 69, 73,
  77–82, 88–90, 201; intellectuals, 21,
  51–52, 88; press, 21, 34, 44, 49–52,
  57, 69, 73–74, 77, 81–83, 88, 171,
  205–6; pro-Bangladesh associations,
  21, 51–52, 88
public stance: Canada (*see* Trudeau,
  Pierre, public stance of Canada);
  UK (*see* Heath, Edward, public
  stance of UK); US (*see* Nixon,
  Richard, public stance of US). *See
  also* public opinion, Canada; public
  opinion, UK; public opinion, US
Pumphrey, Laurence, 152, 164–65;
  UK policy in South Asia, 162,
  166–67, 176

Quebec separatism, 15–16, 93–95,
  112–14, 181–82, 203, 243n121

Rădulescu, Gheorghe, 39
Rahman, Abdul, 164, 173–74
Rahman, Mujibur, 10–11, 56, 109–11,
  134, 139–40, 142–43, 157; trial, 109,
  164–65, 173–74, 242n99; and
  Yahya Khan, 97, 130–32, 173–74.
  See also Awami League

Ramsden, James, 162
Responsibility to Protect, The (R2P), 207, 210n15
Ritchie, Charles, 180–81
Ritchie, Edgar, 99, 106, 110, 115
Rogers, William, 31–32, 37, 44–45, 51, 73, 76, 81–82, 183, 190, 194–95; and Douglas-Home, Alec, 144, 172, 193–94, 197. *See also* Department of State
Royal National Lifeboat Institution, 127
Rusk, Dean, 187

Sainteny, Jean, 38, 63, 72
Sargeant, Frank, 133–34, 175; anxiety, 131–32, 134–36, 138–39, 141, 152–53; and Archer Blood, 135, 192–93, 197; atrocity reports, 134–37, 141–42, 153; background and character, 247n77, 251n32; evacuation plan, 131–34; UK policy in South Asia, 132, 135–37, 141–43, 149, 152–53, 176
Saunders, Harold, 76
Saxbe, William B., 52
Schanberg, Sydney, 50, 223n50
Senior Interdepartmental Group, 30
Senior Review Group (SRG). *See* National Security Council (NSC), Senior Review Group (SRG)
Shakespeare, Frank, 46
Sharp, Mitchell, 103, 105–11; and Douglas-Home, Alec, 192–93; obfuscation, 98–99, 104, 206; Quebec separatism, 112–13; South Asia policy, 98, 100–1, 104, 114. *See also* Department of External Affairs
Shore, Peter, 154
Singh, Hari, 13
Singh, Swaran, 160–61
Sino-Indian War, 13–14, 24, 26–27
Sino-Soviet split, 20, 22, 27–29, 35, 214n60. *See also* Cold War containment

Sisco, Joseph, 56, 76, 163, 221n18; suppression of dissent, 45, 204
Six-Day War, 126
Small, John, 97, 102–3, 109, 111, 192, 197, 205; background and character, 99–100; support of Canadian policy in South Asia, 93, 98–103, 106, 136–38, 204
Smith, Arnold, 242n100
Snow, Edgar, 36, 218n126
South Asia Department (SAD). *See* Foreign and Commonwealth Office (FCO), South Asia Department (SAD)
South Asian community: Canada, 241n71; UK, 120, 156–59, 203
Southeast Asia Treaty Organization (SEATO), 193
Soviet Union, 26, 31–36, 38–40, 58, 69, 85–86, 99, 111, 115, 120–22, 124, 127–30, 166, 173, 180, 183–85, 194. *See also* Cold War containment; Indo-Soviet Treaty of Peace, Friendship, and Cooperation; Sino-Soviet split
Standing Committee on External Affairs and Defence, House of Commons, Canada, 110
Statute of Westminster, 180
Stoessel, Walter, Jr., 37
Stonehouse, John, 149–51, 154–59, 164, 167, 175
Suez Crisis, 94, 121, 123, 180, 185–86
Sunday Times (London), 50, 105, 155–56, 158
Sutherland, Iain, 137, 147, 153, 157; military supply, 168–70; UK policy in South Asia, 131–33, 143

Taiwan, 36, 40, 63, 72–73, 77, 87, 90, 212n34, 242n104
Tashkent Declaration, 124, 244n30
Thant, U, 109, 144, 148, 159–61, 172–73, 193. *See also* UN
Thatcher, Margaret, 124

Thorpe, Jeremy, 147–48
Tibet, 72, 90
Times (London), 155–56, 158, 163
Tomlinson, Stanley, 130, 132–33, 135, 143, 169
Trend, Burke, 133, 194–95, 197–98
Trudeau, Pierre, 180; atrocity reports, 97–98, 100–2, 114, 238*n*35; background and character, 94; and Biafra, 95, 113, 203; de-escalation, 93, 104, 106, 108–11, 113, 115, 201; economic aid, 4, 93–97, 99–101, 106–7, 114–15, 200–2; and Edward Heath, 182, 196; humanitarian relief, 99, 101–4, 106, 108, 110–11, 113, 115, 201, 207; and Indira Gandhi, 106, 108–9, 115, 192, 242*n*96; Indo-Pakistan hostilities of 1971, 104, 111–12; and Ivan Head, 99–100, 103; military supply, 4, 97, 106–8, 115, 200–1; James George, 103–4; and John Small, 99, 103; and Mitchell Sharp, 100–1, 104; public stance of Canada, 101, 107–8, 113–15, 199–201; and Richard Nixon, 190, 196; South Asia policy, 93, 95–102, 104, 106–10, 113–15, 175, 201–4; South Asia visit, 95, 103; UK, 182, 192; US, 14, 182–83; world view, 93–95, 181; and Yahya Khan, 97, 101, 106, 108–9, 115, 192

UK, foreign relations: Canada (*see* Canada-UK relations); India, 119–24, 126, 129–30, 151, 174 (*see also* Heath, Edward); Pakistan, 119–24, 126–30, 151, 174 (*see also* Heath, Edward)
UK-US relations, 4, 15, 179–80, 184–87; interplay during crisis, 4, 120–21, 133, 135, 141, 144, 148, 172, 187–89, 191–98, 205. *See also* Heath, Edward; Nixon, Richard
UKUSA Agreement, 186

UN, 13, 38, 40, 70, 88, 108–10, 115, 148, 154, 160, 164, 166–67, 194; Canada peacekeeping, 94; Charter, 7, 59, 201, 207; General Assembly, 110, 207, 210*n*15. *See also* Thant, U
UN Emergency Force, 180
United Nations Genocide Convention (UNGC), 6–7, 45, 201, 210*n*14, 211*n*24, 221*n*24, 240*n*70
United Nations High Commissioner for Refugees (UNHCR), 70, 75–76, 108, 110, 209*n*1, 228*n*2, 240*n*65
United Nations Security Council (UNSC), 7, 57, 85, 109, 122–23, 159, 174, 207, 242*n*104
US, foreign relations: Canada (*see* Canada-US relations); India, 23–27, 29, 123, 129 (*see also* Nixon, Richard); Pakistan, 22–26, 29, 123, 127, 174 (*see also* Nixon, Richard); UK (*see* UK-US relations)
USS *Enterprise*, 86

Van Hollen, Christopher, 55, 69, 77, 80, 90, 193
Victoria Constitutional Conference, 112
Vietnam War, 5, 24, 28, 32, 35–36, 60, 63–64, 77–78, 83, 95, 183, 194, 218*n*120
Vietnamization, 32, 78

Walters, Vernon, 38, 84
War Measures Act. *See* Quebec separatism
Washington Daily News, 83
Washington Post, 50
Washington Press Club, 182
Washington Special Actions Group (WSAG), 31, 57–58, 71
Weber, Max, 54
West Pakistanis in Solidarity with Bangla Desh, 158
Whitelaw, William, 146, 250*n*1

Index

Wilford, Kenneth, 133, 143, 168–69
Wilson, Harold, 121–22, 124–26, 153,
163, 175, 187
Woldman, Joel, 56
Wood, Richard, 133, 149, 170

World Bank. *See* International Bank
for Reconstruction and
Development (IBRD)

Zeitlin, Arnold, 50, 155